SOCIOPATHIC SOCIETY

OTHER BOOKS BY CHARLES DERBER

Marx's Ghost (2011)
"By using a time capsule technique to bring back Karl Marx to the 21st century, Charles Derber engages him in an illuminating taboo-shredding conversation about economies, workers, corporations, and governments. Derber opens minds, challenges facile assumptions, and liberates conventional inhibitions."

—RALPH NADER

Greed to Green (2010)
"There's no way to solve climate change without also shifting, in profound ways, our idea of what constitutes success and growth and progress. This is the right book at the right—and crucial—moment."

—BILL MCKIBBEN, author of *The End of Nature* and creator of the student-based "Step It Up" campaign to cut carbon emissions and of 350.org, today's leading climate change movement

The Wilding of America, 4th ed. (2006)
"*The Wilding of America* holds the glass up to our time, and one winces at the likeness."
—JACK BEATTY, *Atlantic Monthly* and *On Point* political analyst at NPR

Hidden Power (2005)
"*Hidden Power* is the must-read book of the year. Buy three copies, at least, because you'll want to share a few with friends, and will never want to part with your own well-marked-up copy."

—THOM HARTMANN, best-selling author and host of *Air America*

Hidden Power was selected as one of the top three current events books by the Independent Book Publishers Association.

Regime Change Begins at Home (2004)
"Derber provides a penetrating and compelling analysis of why this particular regime's days are numbered."

—JULIET SCHOR, author of *The Overworked American* and *Born to Buy*

People before Profit (2003)
"Professor Derber's impressive analysis is an important contribution to the ongoing worldwide debate about globalization."

—SENATOR EDWARD KENNEDY

The Pursuit of Attention (2000)
"Competition and individualism in America are fresh topics in his hands, and he works out a theory of great interest."

—RICHARD SENNETT, author of *Hidden Injuries of Class* and *The Corrosion of Character*

Corporation Nation (2000)
"A work of generous imagination … and a sober plan of action for Americans committed to a truly just and equitable social order."

—JONATHAN KOZOL, author of *Amazing Grace* and *Savage Inequalities*

Power in the Highest Degree (1990) coauthored with William Schwartz and Yale R. Magrass
"An excellent guide to understanding the system of Mandarin capitalism … and its wide-ranging human consequences."

—NOAM CHOMSKY, author of *Perilous Power* (2006)

SOCIOPATHIC SOCIETY

A People's Sociology of the United States

CHARLES DERBER

Paradigm Publishers
Boulder • London

Copyright © 2013 by Paradigm Publishers

Published in the United States by Paradigm Publishers, 5589 Arapahoe Avenue, Boulder, CO 80303 USA.

Paradigm Publishers is the trade name of Birkenkamp & Company, LLC, Dean Birkenkamp, President and Publisher.

Library of Congress Cataloging-in-Publication Data

Derber, Charles.
    Sociopathic society : a people's sociology of the United States / Charles Derber.
        pages cm
    Includes bibliographical references.
    ISBN 978-1-61205-438-4 (pbk. : alk. paper)
    1. Avarice—United States.   2. Acquisitiveness—United States.   3. Violence—United States.   4. Capitalism—United States.   5. Values—United States.   6. United States—Social conditions.   I. Title.
    BJ1535.A8D47 2013
    306.0973—dc23

                                                                        2013021151

Printed and bound in the United States of America on acid-free paper that meets the standards of the American National Standard for Permanence of Paper for Printed Library Materials.

Designed and Typeset by Straight Creek Bookmakers.

17   16   15   14   13   1   2   3   4   5

Contents

Foreword

Noam Chomsky

A prominent theme in current policy discourse is "America's decline" as power allegedly shifts to the rising giants China and India. The range of opinion, and the common concerns, are revealed very well in the year-end editions of the most prestigious of the US establishment journals, *Foreign Affairs*, the journal of the Council of Foreign Relations. In December 2012, in bold face and oversize letters, the front cover read, "Is America Over?" The lead article called for "retrenchment" in the "humanitarian missions" abroad that are consuming the country's wealth. Less than a year later in the same journal, the lead article questioned whether retrenchment is the right policy or whether the US should continue to reign worldwide in the interests of global peace and justice.

True, the world is not exactly pleading for Washington to carry forward its campaign of disinterested benevolence, particularly the Global South, its main target since the US replaced Britain as global hegemon after World War II. But there is a simple response to such objections, the one given by the British Foreign Office at the war's end, when it recognized that "the economic imperialism of US business interests is quite active under the cloak of a benevolent and avuncular nationalism, which is attempting to elbow us out." As officials ruefully observed, US elites believe that "the United States stands for something in the world—something of which the world has need, something which the world is going to like, something, in the final analysis, which the world is going to take, whether it likes it or not." And they had the power to try to compel the world to "take it."

Among US elites, little has changed, as the debate between the two extremes illustrates. Nevertheless, by now the decline in US power that began a few years after the war has become a matter of serious concern as global power has become diversified—though despite the relative decline, the United States faces no competitor for global domination in the foreseeable future.

Ignored in the debate over "America's decline" is the fact that it is to a large extent self-administered, beginning in the 1970s and escalating sharply under Reagan and his successors. In the 1970s the economy was substantially redesigned, shifted to financialization, with radical changes in the nature of banks along with no less radical growth in their scale. By 2007, on the eve of the latest crash, for which they were largely responsible, the financial institutions earned about 40 percent of corporate profits. They were quickly bailed out under the government's too-big-to-fail insurance policy—the TARP bailout that received so much attention was the least of it—and by now the major banks are bigger and more powerful than ever, while bonuses are munificent and the perpetrators are immune.

Production did not cease as finance moved to a dominant role. It was sent offshore, to places where labor could be more harshly exploited and environmental concerns of the kind introduced under Richard Nixon—the last liberal president—could be ignored. By now corporate profits across the board are enormous.

The term "redesigned" is appropriate. The reshaping of the economy was a choice by those whom Adam Smith called "the masters of mankind," who are "the principal architects of [government] policy" and pursue their "vile maxim: All for ourselves and nothing for anyone else." Other choices were possible, and still are. What the masters selected was a version of the neoliberal policies that have been harmful if not disastrous to the general population almost wherever applied. The same was true, not surprisingly, in the United States. Through this period economic growth continued (though more slowly than before), but the profits went overwhelmingly to a tiny sector of super-rich while for the majority, real incomes stagnated and declined. Concentration of wealth has reached historic peaks and is far greater than in comparable societies. The more general consequences are found in a recent study of the OECD—the organization of the rich countries—which found that the United States ranks twenty-seventh out of thirty-one countries in social justice, despite the fact that it is the richest and most powerful major country in history, with incomparable advantages.

Concentration of wealth yields concentration of political power, hence legislation and administrative decisions that accelerate the vicious cycle in the financial sector that creates what a director of the British Bank called a "doom loop," with recurring financial crises, each more severe than the last. We are now advancing toward the next one. There were none before the redesign of the economy, when New Deal regulations still were observed. Among many other deleterious effects is the shredding of democracy. By now control of government is narrowly concentrated at the peak of the income scale, while the large majority "down below" are virtually disenfranchised. The current political-economic system is a form of plutocracy, diverging sharply from democracy, if by that concept we mean political arrangements in which policy is significantly influenced by the public will.

Even without reading the conclusions extensively documented in the literature of professional political science, the public is of course not unaware of these developments. To mention just one illustration, a recent poll finds that "just 11% of adults believe Congress is a good reflection of the views of the

American people." The poll didn't ask, but most people probably understand that Congress is very sensitively attuned to the concerns of the tiny fraction of super-rich and the corporate sector.

The results of the neoliberal era are reviewed in a recent publication of the Economic Policy Institute, which has been the major source of reputable data on these developments for years. It is entitled *Failure by Design*. The study points out that the failure, while real, is class-based. For the designers it is a spectacular success. And as the study also points out, the term "design" is entirely appropriate.

What has been in progress is a kind of sociocide, to borrow a term that is normally used for the destruction of societies under military occupation or imperial rule. In this case the sociocide is self-administered, but as the global economy is taking new forms, that does not matter for the masters as much as it did in earlier years.

The real shift of global power is not from the United States to China but from the servants to the masters, worldwide. The developing picture is aptly described in a brochure for investors produced by Citigroup, the huge bank that is once again feeding at the public trough, as it has done regularly for over thirty years in a cycle of risky loans, huge profits, crash, bailout. The bank's analysts describe a world that is dividing into two blocs: the plutonomy and the rest, in a global society in which growth is powered by the wealthy few and largely consumed by them. Then there are the "non-rich," the vast majority, now sometimes called the global precariat, the workforce living a precarious existence. In the United States, they are subject to "growing worker insecurity," the basis for a healthy economy, as Federal Reserve chair Alan Greenspan explained to Congress while lauding his performance in economic management.

The masters labor to undermine those parts of government that benefit the population, but concealed in their antigovernment rhetoric is the demand for a very powerful state, one that caters to their interests. These are basic contours of current political life—such as it is.

In this lucid and informed study, Charles Derber breaks through the necessary illusions and shows how the United States is being turned into a "sociopathic society," with control concentrated among intertwined economic, political, and military elites and reflections of its sociopathy rippling through every social stratum. But he also shows that there remains real hope that mass mobilization by currently fragmented social movements can reverse the sociopathic impetus. As he documents, a majority of the US population embraces progressive values. This is a force that can be mobilized to stem the sociopathic tide, if it develops a clear understanding of alternatives at home and abroad and works with existing movements while building new ones such as Occupy Wall Street.

Derber's judicious book is an important step toward fulfilment of that urgent agenda.

Preface

This book argues that the idea of a "sociopathic society" is necessary to understand today's world. Remarkably, no such concept exists in US political vocabulary, except as shorthand for discussing the prevalence of a large number of psychopathic or sociopathic people in the United States. Any discussion in the United States of sociopathy typically turns into a conversation about people with mental illness.

The real derangement is in the failures of our ideas and the success of our sociopathic society in undermining the very language for critiquing it. In this book, I develop a concept of sociopathic society that is structural, rooted in the political and economic system rather than in psychiatry. It shows that sociopathic individuals in the United States are often successful and well-adjusted, most of them sane and socially integrated. They are more likely to be conforming to the values and rules of conduct in our society than violating them. It is the rules and values that are at least metaphorically "sick."

The absence of the vocabulary and critique we need reflects the power of established elites to control discourse and mask the sociopathic DNA of our corporate society. Fortunately, a history of global and Western social thought offers the tools for analyzing and changing sociopathic systems, despite the waning of those traditions in the US academy.

In Chapter 1, I try to revive these traditions—on the political economy and culture of capitalism—to introduce a theory of sociopathic society and what we can do about it, a subject that has absorbed me over many years. Since the Reagan era, I have been observing and writing about the frightening evolution of American sociopathy. In this book, in addition to presenting my new theory of sociopathic society, I have included selective material I wrote during the 1990s up to the present moment to show how and why we got to the current crisis. After Chapter 1, I flesh out my theory with essays on several different areas of our society and politics, discussed in six parts or sections. Each section includes historical and contemporary snapshots and analyses.

I introduce each part with a brief overview, linking a particular sociopathic arena to the general theory and the sociopathy discussed in other sections. Part II discusses sociopathy and culture, showing how the American Dream has become a master sociopathic script corrupting everyday life and social interaction. Part III is in turn an institutional analysis of corporate capitalism and the sociopathy of its profit-maximizing, self-destructive tendencies.

Part IV examines the sociopathy of a US foreign policy aiming for global hegemony. Part V analyzes our environmental practices that helped create climate change and now threaten to destroy civilization. Part VI looks at the ultimate sociopathic system, fascism, which could return in new forms.

In an extended conclusion (Part VII), I look at the prospects for creation of a more democratic and humane society. Contrary to prevailing wisdom, I show that there is hope for such an alternative order. I discuss new values among the majority of Americans and animating US social movements that could save us from looming sociopathic disaster. Whether they will succeed remains an open question, but they must prevail to ensure democracy and the very survival of civil society.

PART I
Sociopathic Society

1

An Anatomy of Sociopathic Society

After a New England Nor'easter, a friend, a celebrated intellectual, told me about the aftermath of the storm in his community. He lives in an affluent suburb north of Boston and the power had gone out in the whole town, a frequent event. He told me that there had been a proposal to lay the electric lines underground to prevent these inconveniences. But the community majority rejected the small tax hike involved, indicating that they preferred to get their own generators or go without power rather than pay for their neighbor's power. What a "sociopathic society," he exclaimed.

A bolt of electricity shot through me. "Sociopathic society." The words seem a contradiction in terms, but they go to the heart of my thinking and writing over recent decades.

Only a few weeks after my conversation with my friend, the December 12, 2012, massacre at Sandy Hook Elementary School in Newtown, Connecticut, shocked the nation. A young killer murdered six adults and twenty children between the ages of five and ten, with a semi-automatic Bushmaster rifle, using high-capacity magazines designed for war. It was just the latest of a series of horrific mass killings in schools (the nightmares of Virginia Tech and Columbine High School), movie theaters (the shooter who killed twelve and injured fifty-eight in a midnight screening of *The Dark Knight Rises* in Aurora, Colorado), shopping malls (two gunned down in a mall in Clackamas, Oregon, in the same week as Newtown), and places of worship (the bigoted gun assault on the Sikh temple in suburban Milwaukee, Wisconsin). In the three weeks following Newtown, two thousand more gun deaths were reported and the US gun manufacturers sold thousands of new semi-automatic weapons and high-capacity clips, as guns flew off Walmart shelves and frenzied buyers emptied out gun stores. The US Congress did nothing.

Americans might not recognize the term "sociopathic society," but they were staring it in the face. They were afraid, rightly, for their children and themselves.

Our current crisis involves far more than military-style gun massacres and an armed, angry population. It reflects an economy, politics, and culture that are a fertile foundation for a sociopathic society.

My argument in this book is that the United States, with a long history of socio-pathic institutions and practices, is now evolving toward a full-blown sociopathic society. We still have a chance to change course. But our society is increasingly structured to turn people and institutions toward sociopathic behavior that harms other individuals and entire societies, including our own. The United States is beginning to socially unravel, haunted now by the specter of war with weapons of mass destruction, economic meltdowns, and uncontrolled climate change.

Is the United States—the world's most powerful nation—already a so-ciopathic society?

Many think so. A 2009 report from the public interest group the Public Record argued bluntly, "The economic elite have launched an attack on the US public and society is unraveling at an increased rate."[1] The first section of the report, buttressed by statistics on inequality, poverty, joblessness, hunger, homelessness, crime, uninsured health care, low quality schools, high student debt, crumbling infrastructure, and the like, is called "Societal Breakdown." The theme crops up everywhere. Conservatives such as David Brooks and liberals such as Robert Reich write about the unraveling of the US social fabric. Brooks writes that

> In the half-century between 1962 and the present ... the social fabric has deteriorated. Social trust has plummeted. Society has segmented.... The American social fabric is now so depleted that even if manufacturing jobs miraculously came back we still would not be producing enough stable, skilled workers to fill them. It's not enough just to have economic growth policies. The country also needs to rebuild orderly communities.[2]

Reich's book *Beyond Outrage* argues that offshoring and outsourcing are the real big business in America, leaving Americans without jobs or wages that keep society alive.[3] Arianna Huffington in *Third World America*[4] writes that the United States is degrading into the misery and chaos of the world's impoverished failed states. Nobel economist Paul Krugman simply proclaims, "Banana Republic, here we come."

All of this suggests that the United States is crossing a threshold toward a sociopathic society.

***

A sociopathic society breeds routinized, institutionalized pervasive and fierce sociopathy that chips away at its own foundations.

Sociopathy is antisocial behavior by an individual or institution that typi-cally advances self-interest, such as making money, while harming others and attacking the fabric of society. In a sociopathic society, sociopathic behavior, both by individuals and institutions, is the outcome of dominant social values and power arrangements. *A sociopathic society, paradoxically, creates dominant social norms that are antisocial—that is, norms that assault the well-being and survival of much of the population and undermine the social bonds and sustainable environmental conditions essential to any form of social order. This reign of antisocial social norms is crucial to my definition of sociopathic society.* Like an autoimmune disease, such antisocial societal programming leads to behavior that weakens and can, in the most extreme scenario, kill the society itself.

You might ask whether "antisocial social norms" are possible, and whether a sociopathic society can actually exist. A good and crucial question.

One might want to argue on relativistic grounds that whatever a society prescribes is "social" and thus social norms cannot be antisocial within a particular society. By that argument genocide in Nazi Germany is "social" because it is defined as good by that society. My argument against that is twofold. First, while what is "social" has inherent subjective qualities defined by a society, there is an objective limit having to do with harm, death, and sustainability, as well as with universal human rights. Social norms or practices that undermine the society or environment of the society endorsing them—or wiping out their population—are, in my argument, antisocial, because they harm and kill not only many people but, in many cases, even the society endorsing the practice. I would add that genocide violates one of a core set of universal human rights that are embraced in UN covenants signed by almost all societies today, and that social relativism of the "social" reaches its limits when it violates these universal rights.

Second, prevailing social norms are largely constructed by elites and do not necessarily represent either the values or interests of the larger population. The Jews and gypsies and Slavs killed by the Nazis in Germany did not see this socially prescribed practice as "social" or in the social interest—and they rejected the genocidal norms. Elites are in the business of constructing definitions of what is "social" that reflect their own interests, not those of the general population. When I talk about antisocial social norms, I am taking the view that elites' definition of the "social" may be enforced by the law and the elite itself but should be called antisocial if it hurts the general populace. What is "social" for the elites is often "antisocial" for the general population. If one accepts that elites tend to shape and enforce social norms and that the general public—especially when hurt by those norms—has a different idea or interest in what is defined as "social," then the idea of antisocial social norms becomes easier to understand.

Sociopathic behavior is not always self-interested in the strict sense of the term. A suicide bomber who kills innocents is engaging in sociopathy even though he is killing himself for what he regards as a higher purpose.

Soldiers in unjust wars who kill thousands on the battlefield also practice such "altruistic" sociopathy, even though the soldier may perceive himself as making the ultimate sacrifice.

Sociopathic behavior, whether practiced by individuals or institutions, can be physically violent, but more often it is not. An example from the corporate world is when the CEOs of Goldman Sachs, Bank of America, AIG, and other bailed-out Wall Street giants in the Great Recession increased their own compensation after driving their banks and much of America into a ditch. One defining mark of a sociopathic society is that most sociopathic behavior is perfectly legal and conforms to social norms and expectations. As a codification of antisocial norms, the law itself becomes sociopathic in the most full blown sociopathic societies.

Sociopathic people often have narcissistic, competitive, and antisocial personalities, but, in contrast to what psychological theories tell us, this can be the outcome of the hardwiring of sociopathic society. Sociopathic personalities may be embracing the reigning societal values rather than rejecting them. In a sociopathic society, narcissists and antisocial individuals—one might think of O. J. Simpson, Donald Trump, Lance Armstrong, or Bernie Madoff—can appear entirely normal, since they often are pillars of the community and know how to succeed under existing rules of the game. Many of them are political leaders, CEOs of major corporations, high military officers, or high-ranking church clergy.

Sociopathic institutions rule the landscape of sociopathic society. These can be economic (corporations such as Enron), political (a self-serving Congress of millionaires), or military (a detention center such as Guantanamo), but they all advance institutional self-interest by harming others and undermining society. Sociopathic institutions do this because the design of the institutions is destructive and unsustainable; they essentially dig their own graves and can kill off the larger host society.

The witty documentary film and best-selling book *The Corporation*, written by law professor Joel Bakan, makes the point tellingly by imagining the corporation as a patient on the couch being diagnosed by a psychiatrist.[5] The psychiatrist goes through a checklist of symptoms evidenced by his patient—insatiable greed, self-preoccupation, power lust, willingness to harm others without remorse, pursuit of profit at the expense of communities and the whole society. The behavior is sociopathic, but it is embedded in the corporate law and power arrangements that make up the "corporate patient" on the couch. The patient is programmed such that it cannot act differently. Bakan writes that the corporation is "pathological"; it is

singularly self-interested and unable to feel genuine concern for others in any context ... deliberately programmed, indeed legally compelled, to externalize costs without regard for the harm it may cause to people, communities, and the natural environment. Every cost it can unload onto someone else is a benefit to itself, a direct route to profit.[6]

The problem here is not a rotten apple—such as Enron or its corporate accountant, Arthur Anderson—but a rotten barrel. The media portrayed Enron as a rotten apple spoiled by bad leaders. Bakan's point, though, is that Enron was acting as the corporate system requires, much like the other leading financial firms, as became evident in the Wall Street meltdown of 2008. Bank of America, Goldman Sachs, J. P. Morgan Chase, Countrywide, Washington Mutual, and AIG—all programmed to maximize short-term profit—carried out unethical, destructive behavior, whether predatory loans or issuing toxic financial instruments that they secretly bet would fail. The problem is not a few bad leaders but a corporate DNA placing profits over people and chartered by a larger sociopathic economic system (the barrel).

***

The idea of sociopathic society requires some distinctions and nuances. First, we need to distinguish the *types* of sociopathic behavior. Physical violence, such as murder or rape, is one terrible form that individuals commit (and institutions such as sweatshops or the military often sanction), particularly prevalent in the United States, with violent crime rates, especially with guns, far higher here than in other advanced societies. But there are more prevalent nonviolent sociopathic personal acts, part of the fabric of daily life in the United States, almost all perfectly legal, such as cheating on tests or on your spouse or lying to friends or, as we shall see, simply monopolizing the conversation and never listening.

In a sociopathic society, sociopathic individual behavior is so pervasive and socially accepted that perpetrators don't think of themselves as doing anything wrong. When cyclist champion Lance Armstrong first acknowledged in a 2013 interview with Oprah Winfrey that he had been doping—using performance-enhancing drugs—and lying about it for years, she asked him if he believed he was cheating.

> *Oprah:* Did you feel you were cheating?
>
> *Armstrong:* No. At the time, no. I viewed it as a level playing field. I looked up the definition of "cheat." The definition of cheat is to gain an advantage over a rival or foe. I didn't do that. I viewed it as a level playing field.[7]

Armstrong is rationalizing but not entirely wrong, arguing that it was the rules of the game and the larger culture that drove his behavior:

> *Armstrong:* I did not invent the culture [of cheating] but I did not try to stop it.[8]

What was that sociopathic culture all about in his view?

Armstrong: It was this ruthless desire to win. Win at all costs, truly.[9]

Armstrong is describing accurately the sociopathic world of sports that has taken over in all the major athletic fields, as sports became big business. "Win at all costs" is a mantra beyond sports, of the entire corporate world. But Armstrong's self-justifying goes too far. In fact, he implied he was doing an honorable thing by sustaining his charitable foundations and sponsors despite his competitive disadvantage caused by his cancer. He called himself "humanitarian."

In a sociopathic society such as the United States, the most important sociopaths are powerful institutions such as giant corporations and the military. Economic sociopathic acts by large corporations are a crucially important form, illustrated not just by the Wall Street banks that crashed the economy but by Walmart, Disney, and other huge retail enterprises that source caps, T-shirts, skirts, and pants from super-exploitative and dangerous sweatshops around the world, including Bangladeshi factories that spectacularly collapsed in May 2013 and killed instantly over 1,300 workers. Or consider that virtually all Fortune 500 firms use accounting tricks that transfer most of their taxable income or cash holdings to foreign subsidiaries, the current favored corporate tax strategy, or offshore havens such as the Cayman Islands, to avoid taxes. There is political sociopathic behavior by governments and political parties, such as suppressing the vote or buying elections, and passing tax laws or subsidies that unfairly benefit politically connected corporations. And there is military sociopathy by the Pentagon and CIA, such as fighting Mid-East wars for oil in the name of democracy, or detaining suspects without habeas corpus or other legal rights, and torturing captured prisoners. In all these cases, the sociopathic behavior is typically legal and normatively valued, reflecting the objectives of profit maximization or military control that elites have programmed and much of the population has come to accept as legitimate.[10]

We now see sociopathy on a grand scale, both legal and illegal, by other major institutions, including spectacular examples in religion, such as the cover-up of sexual crimes by leading Catholic Church officials to protect their power and privilege. Consider also the entertainment establishment, happy to make big profits off of horrific violence against women in video games (such as *Grand Theft Auto 4* and *Vice City Stories*), or by marketing Hollywood "slasher" films specializing in male killers raping and murdering women. Or, as illustrated in the case of Lance Armstrong above, the huge doping scandals in baseball, football, and cycling, often covered up or tolerated by the corporate sponsors or multibillion-dollar sports franchises.[11]

The most widespread and corrosive US sociopathy—much of it legal—is perpetrated by the biggest corporations not just on Wall Street but in every major economic sector. Huge global pharmaceutical companies such as Merck and giant for-profit hospital chains, such as Humana, profit by using patents and lobbying to restrict access to essential generic medicines for epidemics that could save thousands of lives. The largest gun manufacturers, such as Freedom Group, and huge tobacco companies, such as Philip Morris, hook young people globally on their lethal high-profit products and block regulation vital to saving hundreds of thousands of lives. For-profit universities recruit students they know won't graduate but will be strapped for life with special high-interest loans that must be paid back in full, even if you are a dropout after one semester.

The range and types of corporate sociopathy are large and varied but not surprising since they reflect the sociopathic programming of capitalist corporate charters, mandating profits at the expense of harm to workers or the environment, defined as "externalites," costs on society that the companies don't have to pay.[12] Corporations that do not pursue profit in this way can be sued for violation of their fiduciary obligation. In that spirit, giant retailers such as Walmart pay miserably low minimum wage salaries and no benefits to part-time workers—often desperate women, minorities, or older people at the edge of hunger or homelessness. The biggest food and beverage companies, such as McDonald's and Coca-Cola, sell unhealthy products dished out by low-paid workers or school vending machines, targeting low-income and young consumers. The biggest agricultural companies, such as ADL, take huge government subsidies as they produce monoculture industrialized crops that destroy the soil and spread fossil fuel toxins into the water and air. The giant oil companies, such as Exxon and Shell, engage in sociopathic climate denial and greenwashing while fighting climate control treaties and law to protect their profits. Most of this sociopathic behavior conforms to the expectations of investors who seek and are legally entitled to profit maximization despite the high social costs just enumerated.

Second, we can ask about the *degree or extent* of sociopathy across various societal sectors. In the ultimate sociopathic society—German Nazism or Italian Fascism come to mind—the entire society is structured around sociopathic values and institutions. These are societies of unabated destruction, hatred, and death, leading to genocide and total self-destruction, as when Hitler's regime collapsed under the weight of its own evil ambitions. In other societies, including the United States, the extent and depth of sociopathy varies by institutional sector, region, and economic status, with strong sociopathic tendencies in parts of the system—such as the financial, prison, or military sectors—but more benign and democratic possibilities in other parts, from low-income, urban community development organizations to the local or community agricultural sector to numerous altruistic nonprofits and grassroots social movements for justice and environmental sustainability. In contrast to prevailing wisdom in the United States, we shall see that sociopathy is most prevalent and dangerous at the top, in the corporate suites, rather than on the streets below. As the Sicilian adage goes, "The fish rots from the head first." But all US strata—from top to bottom—have long been plagued by sociopathic invasion, which constitutes the real "trickle down" from the top. Thus, the sociopathic behavior of gangs and drug-dealers on the street often mirrors the business strategies of the more respected sociopaths in the suites.[13]

Third, we need to distinguish the *targets* of sociopathic destruction. These can be vulnerable individuals—disproportionately African American or other minorities in the United States—who are dispatched to unemployment, prison, or death (there are more young African Americans in the prison system than in higher education). Other major targets are foreign countries the United States claims it can rightfully attack (which can be any country in the world, according to a May 2013 Obama administration interpretation of the 2001 Authorization to Use Force Act,[14] since young men anywhere can be called terrorist combatants in a war against the United States) or the core infrastructure of one's own society. In the United States, all three targets are under severe assault, reflected in mass surplus triaged populations, endless wars around the world waged in the name of a highly moralistic militarism, and a particularly devastating new assault on the social and environmental infrastructure of the United States itself.

In his best-seller, *Collapse,* Jared Diamond has examined factors leading earlier societies to collapse, concluding that environmental variables often play a leading role, along with adverse military, trade and economic forces, and overpopulation.[15] Americans in a fossil-fuel-driven capitalist system committed to unlimited growth and consumption need to look closely at the history of such extinct societies. Environmental government and corporate practices, along with mass consumerism by the general population, now threaten the long-term survival of civil society and are undoubtedly the most dangerous sociopathy in the United States today.

Fourth, we need to look at the *extent to which the sociopathy can be healed.* Some sociopathic societies cannot self-correct, because of the depth and scale of the problem. In the United States, the prognosis is less gloomy; we can lead ourselves out of our structural crisis if we—the mass of ordinary citizens—open our eyes and imagination, think clearly about our collective survival, and mobilize to change course. Yet some elements of the sociopathic crisis, such as climate change, are already so severe that even in the most positive scenario, great damage will be done and mitigation rather than total solution is our best hope.

***

One of the great obstacles to change in the United States is the tendency to see the problem in individual or psychological terms rather than social and structural ones. Americans see people rather than systems, and they have been taught to believe that all behavior reflects free personal choice, supported by the moral teachings of an exceptionalist American society. If an American engages in violence or other forms of sociopathic behavior, this psychological paradigm suggests there can be only one of three explanations: (1) the individual is mentally ill, (2) the individual is evil and has freely chosen to be antisocial, or (3) the individual has failed to receive or accept the social morals that a good society imparts.

The problem of sociopathy in the United States has been taken over by the psychiatric profession and is treated as a psychological disorder. The concept of sociopathy refers to an individual and not to a social institution or society itself. The idea of sociopathic society is not even part of the vocabulary.

This is made explicit in the Bible of psychiatry, the *Diagnostic and Statistical Manual of Mental Disorders* (known as the DSM).[16] The official list and explanation of the profiles of psychological disorder, it defines an "Antisocial Personality Disorder (APD)," a psychiatric classification of what we typically describe as sociopathy or antisocial behavior in the United States. The DSM defines it as an individual person's "pervasive pattern of disregard for and violation of the rights of others," as "indicated by three or more of the following":

1. *failure to conform to social norms with respect to lawful behaviors as indicated by repeatedly performing acts that are grounds for arrest;*
2. *deception, as indicated by repeatedly lying, use of aliases, or conning others for personal profit or pleasure;*
3. *impulsiveness or failure to plan ahead;*
4. *irritability and aggressiveness dictated by repeated physical fights or assaults;*
5. *reckless disregard for safety of self or others;*
6. *consistent irresponsibility, as indicated by repeated failure to sustain consistent work behavior or honor financial obligations;*
7. *lack of remorse, as indicated by being indifferent to or rationalizing having hurt, mistreated, or stolen from another.*[17]

The DSM explains that the antisocial disposition is rooted in genetic, biological, and neurological pathologies, including problems in healthy levels of hormones and neurotransmitters such as serotonin. Psychiatrists also discuss "Limbic Neural Maldevelopment," identifying brain pathologies that lead to higher levels of antisocial behavior. The idea that APD or sociopathy may also be socially or culturally conditioned is considered possible by some psychiatrists but is seen as secondary or derivative.

In fact, the psychiatric paradigm makes it impossible to see sociopathy as a problem caused by society itself. At root, psychiatrists and their paradigm see sociopathy as *"the failure to conform to social norms."* Those abiding by societal rules are by definition prosocial or antisociopathic. It is the very inability to follow society's rules that marks the sociopath, and a society in which everyone embraced and followed social values and rules would be blissfully free of sociopathy.

But this shows why the psychological perspective is incapable of conceiving a sociopathic society, a social order in which the reigning values and rules encourage antisocial behavior. The sociopath in such a society—whether a person, corporation, or government—is acting true to the dominant culture and economic system, performing an antisocial script programmed by the society itself.

This seems paradoxical, and it leads us again to the confounding question discussed earlier: how can a society embrace values that are antisocial?

Conceptualizing this paradox in depth is central to defining and analyzing sociopathic society. It turns our attention away from speculative biological and psychological pathologies and toward hard-edged socioeconomic realities. One example is our corporate capitalism's culture and economic imperative of unfettered consumption, defined as essential both to economic growth in the current order and to personal happiness. American consumerism exemplifies antisocial social programming, since society is prescribing behavior that is unsustainable and both socially and environmentally destructive.

At the heart of sociopathic society are cultural values such as unsustainable mass consumerism and deep-seated economic and political institutional arrangements and laws prioritizing profits over people leading toward societal self-cannibalization. In the case of the United States, it leads to questions about our short-term, consumerist, and quarterly-profit-driven corporate economy, about our militarized foreign policy, and about the American Dream itself that mainstream thinkers and media consider too subversive to discuss—and that the psychiatric or psychological perspectives cannot easily conceive because they define sociopathy as *the failure to conform to a society designed from the beginning as "free" and destined to thrive.*

The prevailing psychological perspective in the United States accepts the existing socioeconomic order, as well as its culture, as largely rational and benign. More generally, it tends to presume the goodness of economic, political, and cultural arrangements. It can be helpful to describe sociopathic personalities—as suggested by the popularity of psychological books such as *The Sociopath Next Door*[18] and *Without Conscience*.[19] But the psychiatric perspective is dangerous itself because by focusing on biology and clinical psychology, it cannot allow us to understand sociopathy as a social system that creates personal pathology among people conforming to society's norms. This psychological paradigm is itself sociopathic, in the sense that it distracts us from the social and institutional realities that give rise to the sociopathic problem in the first place.

***

In the go-go 1980s, in the film *Wall Street,* Michael Douglas played the swashbuckling financier Gordon Gekko. Gekko's motto was "Greed Is

Good." It became iconic not because of Gekko's flamboyant embodiment of this philosophy but because Gekko summed up the Reagan revolution, the latest political regime change shaping our current sociopathic society.

We have to shift from psychological to social theory to drill down to the bedrock of sociopathic society. It is super-capitalism, plutocratic politics, and hyperindividualistic culture—a transformation in our political economy—brewing our current sociopathic society. The prophets of this sociopathic transformation lived 150 years ago in Europe. They were the founders of modern sociology: Max Weber, Karl Marx, and Emile Durkheim.

These writers sought to understand the modern industrial capitalist order that was exploding into being in their own lifetimes. Sociology emerged to make sense of the convulsive birth of the new modern order, much as Charles Darwin tried to understand the birth and evolution of species, and Albert Einstein later searched for the explosive foundation of the universe itself.

Marx, Weber, and Durkheim had to think big and think critically. The rise of modern capitalist societies was turning traditional societies upside down. The founding sociologists marveled at the technological and financial revolutions that were creating wealth at a scale never before seen, while recoiling at the horrendous poverty and industrial misery that novelists such as Charles Dickens—sickened by the malnourished children, brutal work houses, eighteen-hour factory workdays, and beggars dying on the street—were immortalizing in their literary works, such as *A Christmas Carol*,[20] about the sociopathy of the new capitalist Scrooges.

Marx, Weber, and Durkheim saw the progress that industrial capitalism was bringing, but they also were haunted by the sociopathy of modernity. Their work is a brilliant first effort to analyze contemporary sociopathic society. They pinned down its roots as meticulously as the butterfly species pinned into Darwin's notebooks.

Marx, Weber, and Durkheim did not explicitly name or conceptualize sociopathic society, nor is their work a full or adequate analytical blueprint of its crisis. But they laid the foundation for dissecting the sociopathy now scarring America and other highly developed societies.

The Marxist tradition—while largely buried in the United States after the horrors of communist regimes such as Stalinism and Maoism as well as the unrelenting American propaganda against anything smacking of socialism—remains a foundation stone for understanding the sociopathy of capitalist societies. Marx got a great deal wrong about capitalist developments, predicting wildly premature death scenarios of capitalist societies. Yet despite his many mistakes, he proved correct about the sociopathic strains at the heart of the system.[21]

Marx recognized the contradictions, never ceasing to praise capitalism for liberating humanity from the brutality and poverty of medieval feudalism, and marveling at the revolutions of technology, productivity, and prosperity that capitalism unleashed. But he showed that this miraculous revolution in production was built on exploitation inconsistent with the survival of capitalism and the society itself. Marx saw a system dehumanizing labor—and reducing human relations to "cash payment" and to "the icy water of egotistical calculation."[22] His view now seems prophetic that the relentless drive for profit creates a class of sociopathic corporate employers stripping freedom and meaning from work and turning global workers into beasts of burden. Marx saw that this sociopathic dynamic would prove efficient and economically profitable in the short run but would ultimately threaten capitalist society's own infrastructure and humanity. In the *Communist Manifesto*, Marx writes that capitalism is becoming "no longer compatible with society":

> Hitherto, every form of society has been based, as we have already seen, on the antagonism of oppressing and oppressed classes.... And here it becomes evident that the bourgeoisie is unfit any longer to be the ruling class in society, and to impose its conditions of existence upon society as an overriding law. It is unfit to rule because it is incompetent to assure an existence to its slave within his slavery, because it cannot help letting him sink to such a state, that it has to feed him, instead of being fed by him. Society cannot live under this bourgeoisie; in other words, its existence is no longer compatible with society.[23]

This is Marx's explicit indictment of capitalism as sociopathic. Weber also saw serious sociopathic crises in the rising modern order. Marx had focused mainly on sociopathy in the corporation and the economy, but Weber saw that the entire society—the government, military, churches, schools, and other institutions—were embracing a corporate, bureaucratic structure. Bureaucracy—a generic corporate structure enforcing hierarchy and stifling autonomy in the name of rationality and order—became the universal sociopathic structure ruling modern society.[24]

Weber famously called bureaucracy an "iron cage." It turned its employees into dehumanized functionaries who saw their control as socially virtuous. Bureaucrats are sociopathic "specialists without spirit, sensualists without heart; this nullity imagines that it has attained a level of civilization never before achieved."[25]

Weber captures the sociopathic threat of bureaucratic repression masked as civilizational uplift. He would have none of it. He saw that in the name of efficiency and rationality, the iron cage stripped control from workers and citizens alike, squeezing out the soft emotion and creative self-expression that is the lifeblood of society. Weber's analysis was in some ways more gloomy than Marx's. Marx was optimistic that capitalist crises driven by its own sociopathy ensured the collapse of capitalism itself and midwifed a revolutionary transition to a post-sociopathic socialist order. Weber saw no alternative to a society increasingly dominated by bureaucracy and bureaucratic elites—and, while he favored socialism, did not see it as an antidote to the sociopathy of the iron cage.

Emile Durkheim also saw a sociopathic meltdown, although of somewhat different causes and one that could be avoided. Durkheim is famous for his analysis of suicide.[26] But this involved not just individuals but ultimately the possibility of societal suicide, society killing itself through an egoistic and individualistic breakdown in the social bonds that form society itself. Durkheim was influenced by his peer and fellow countryman Alexis de Tocqueville, who wrote that individualism is "a deliberate and peaceful sentiment which disposes each citizen to isolate himself from the mass of his fellows ... which at first saps only the virtue of public life, but in the long run ... attacks and destroys all others and is eventually absorbed into pure egoism."[27]

Durkheim thought a more positive form of individualism could help create a new social solidarity, but his work was shaped by concern with "the causes of imminent social disintegration and the practical measures needed to avoid it."[28] This led him to a lifelong concern with a socially corrosive egoism, brought on by society itself, where "society is not sufficiently integrated at all points to keep all its members dependent upon it ... [and where] society, disordered and weakened, lets too many people escape from its influence too completely."[29]

Durkheim feared a sociopathy of egoistic individualism bred in part by industrial capitalist society. It was creating a weakened social solidarity and breeding more atomized and egoistic people who could not connect with each other or the society, bringing to mind a recent Pew survey of the United States in which 25 percent of Americans said they had nobody to talk to about personal matters and another 25 percent said they had just one person to share with.[30]

***

Marx, Weber, and Durkheim offer basic ideas for understanding contemporary sociopathic society, giving rise to more recent thinkers in their respective tradition who move us closer to a theory of sociopathic society and the prospects of saving ourselves from it. A brief look shows that a subterranean fear of sociopathy haunts successive generations of the most insightful social analysts.

We need to tease out this specter through a few of the most brilliant spooked by it.

In Marx's case, the "descendant" list is long. We look quickly at two from the Frankfurt School, a European-rooted community of thinkers about the psychology and culture of capitalism. One is Erich Fromm. In best-selling books such as *Escape from Freedom,* Fromm highlighted the psychological and cultural sociopathy that arose from the personal anxieties bred by capitalist societies.[31] Western capitalism trumpeted freedom, but it was, Fromm argued, the negative or anxious freedom of individuals struggling to survive in a society that had broken down community and forced "free" individuals to sink or swim on their own. Fromm argued that socially unsupported or disaffiliated individuals become hyperindividualistic and self-centered, turning against all others in a desperate struggle for survival that breeds mass sociopathy.

Herbert Marcuse, a second famous Frankfurt School thinker, emigrated from Europe to the United States and became a philosophical inspiration to the US New Left in the 1960s. Marcuse developed a blazing critique of the repressiveness of modern technocratic consumer capitalism in two of his most famous works, *One-Dimensional Man* and *Eros and Civilization.*[32] Melding Marx's analysis of exploitation with Sigmund Freud's ideas about psychodynamic repression and Weber's focus on sterile hyperbureaucratic rationality, Marcuse argued that ruthless but sophisticated elites and corporate institutions created a condition of "surplus repression," that destroys society by creating an atomized mass of robotic "one-dimensional" people who cannot love or bond. Swimming in sociopathy, they cannot create either the individuality or solidarity on which society is based.

Americans are sucked into a life defined by mass consumption and identification of happiness with big houses, cars, and other commodities. One-dimensional man is produced by the "commodity fetishism"[33] of capitalism, a one-dimensional society glorifying shallow sexual hedonism, consumer-based private pleasures, and grinding, conformist work. Marcuse writes,

> The so-called consumer society and the politics of corporate capitalism have created a second nature of man which ties him libidinally and aggressively to the commodity form. The need for possessing, consuming, handling and constantly renewing the gadgets, devices, instruments, engines, offered to and imposed upon the people, for using these wares even at the danger of one's own destruction, has become a "biological" need.[34]

One-dimensional capitalist society is sociopathic in the sense that it strips creative, dissenting, and true erotic sensibility from its citizens and undermines the loving spirit and public engagement on which society depends if it is to thrive and ultimately survive. Yet Marcuse remained hopeful that intellectuals, students, and those not locked into the corporate machine could rediscover the life force and solidarity to transform the sociopathic system.

Moving from the Frankfurt School toward neo-Marxist American thinkers of the mid-twentieth century, two very different figures come to mind: a Harvard professor and a factory worker. Both brought Marxism up to date for a global audience, and both helped clarify the sociopathic core of the US model.

The Harvard professor was Paul Sweezy. In his 1966 book coauthored with Paul Baran, *Monopoly Capital,*[35] one of the most important Marxist works by American authors after World War II, Sweezy argued that capitalism had moved from its competitive form toward monopolization. Monopoly capitalism is run by gigantic, oligopolistic global companies in league with corporate politicians, and it is doomed by multiple forms of sociopathy inherent in the monopoly system.

Sweezy argued that monopoly capital's great problem was overproduction and excess capacity: too many production lines without enough people demanding or able to afford what they produced. Demand crises could be partially alleviated by sociopathic strategies, all evident today, including huge military spending, saturation advertising, and encouragement of unsustainable debt. These could slow but not halt tendencies toward stagnation, which led to sociopathic financial strategies based on speculation and deception—on display in the 2008 Wall Street meltdown—to keep giant banks profitable and credit in circulation. Sweezy predicted deepening economic and financial crises that could ultimately bring down the entire system itself. Beyond the economic contradictions, Sweezy had a grim view of monopoly capitalist society, all aspects of social and personal life deformed by the overwhelming dominance of the giant corporation and its impulse to do nothing but "accumulate, accumulate, accumulate":

> Disorientation, apathy, and often despair, haunting Americans in all walks of life, have assumed in our times the dimensions of a profound crisis. This crisis affects every aspect of national life and ravages both its socio-political and its individual spheres—everyman's everyday existence.... The malaise deprives work of meaning and purpose; turns leisure into joyless, debilitating laziness; fatally impairs the educational system and the conditions for healthy growth in the young; transforms religion and church into commercialized vehicles of "togetherness" and destroys ... the family.[36]

Harry Braverman was the factory worker. He became a labor organizer and leading socialist scholar. His most important book, *Labor and Monopoly Capital*,[37] remains a riveting and foundational analysis of the capitalist degradation of work and sociopathic forms of twentieth-century modern management. Based partly on his own factory experience, Braverman showed that Taylorism—the early-twentieth-century "scientific management" theory based on time-and-motion studies and developed by the obsessive-compulsive industrial engineer Frederick Taylor—remained the dominant model for managing not just blue-collar but also white-collar and increasingly professional employees.

Taylor was laser-focused on stripping away creative thought from the worker and turning her into a robot. Using a stopwatch, Taylor programmed each physical motion down to nanoseconds and dictated a rigid, unwavering protocol of mechanistic steps for each job. Braverman cites Taylor's own words of how to instruct a factory worker named Schmidt:

> You will do exactly as this man [the manager] tells you tomorrow, from morning to night. When he tells you to pick up a pig [iron] and work, you

pick it up and you walk, and when he tells you to sit down and rest you sit down. You do that right through the day. And what's more, no back talk.... Schmidt started to work, and all day long, was told by the man who stood over him with a watch, "Now pick up a pig and walk. Now sit down and rest."[38]

Braverman shows that Taylor also "believed that the forms of control he advocated could be applied not only to simple labor, but to labor in its most complex form."[39] In other words, the new "knowledge" economy is, in reality, a recipe for a huge mass of "deskilled" and mercilessly controlled workers whose labor has been cheapened and dehumanized. It is sociopathy reminiscent of Charlie Chaplin's imagery of workers helplessly sucked into a sadistic roller coaster assembly line in that wonderful cinematic depiction of sociopathic work: *Modern Times.*

In the late twentieth century, American neo-Marxism took a new turn by focusing on globalization, a shift partly spurred and reinforced by the rise of mass movements—symbolized by the flamboyant 1999 Battle of Seattle, where tanks battled protesters as downtown Seattle burned—against neoliberal capitalist globalization. The new focus on the economy as a global rather than national system is the center of "world-systems theory," pioneered by the economic historian and social theorist Immanuel Wallerstein.[40] World-system analysts helped globalize the idea of sociopathy, suggesting that we cannot think of it as simply a destructive and suicidal national society but as a global social order with the same horrifying attributes.

Wallerstein argues that the economy is a global system and that it makes no sense to look at nation-states as the unit of analysis. The class divisions traditionally conceived at the heart of capitalist nation-states are now divisions between the global "core" and "periphery," the former being the developed Western capitalist states of the United States and Europe and the latter their formerly legally colonized subject nations in Latin America, Africa, and Asia. The global core owns the means of production and controls power in the global system, redistributing wealth from the periphery to the core itself. The periphery is forcibly subjugated both by economic and military violence to its designated role of providing cheap labor and resources to the core, a relation which is sociopathic to the extreme. Eventually, the core and periphery are "deterritorialized," with the core being the rich in all countries and the periphery being the workers in all countries, including the most developed. All the national sociopathic contradictions of capitalism are thereby globalized within and across nations.[41]

* * *

Many other important thinkers, not identified with Marxism, saw the rise of a terrifying sociopathic society. Three from the mid-twentieth century stand out, one a bold sociologist on a motorcycle who helped inspire the New Left revolt of the 1960s. The second is a literary icon famous for his dystopian novels. The third was a liberal economist who saw in the coming of affluence the perpetuation of poverty and a deepening sociopathic division between the haves and the have-nots.

The sociologist is C. Wright Mills, who died too young, at age forty-six, after writing three major books in the conformist 1950s that blew apart the comforting and legitimating myths of a postwar free America. America in the 1950s defined itself as a paradise of blissful white-picket, white-collar life—and most sociologists of the era tended to agree. Mills argued this paradise was sociopathic hell.

In this most famous work, *The Power Elite,*[42] Mills argued that democracy had become an illusion as three overlapping hierarchies of sociopathic power—the corporations, politicians, and the Pentagon—took command. Mills drew on Weber here, highlighting the rise of bureaucratic systems throughout society, managed from the top by an intertwined economic, political, and military elite who seek to dominate both America and much of the rest of the world. The sociopathic dominance strategies inside the country are legal and rationalized as in all bureaucratic systems. Domination of the rest of the world is more transparently sociopathic, since it involves near-genocidal military violence, soon to explode, during Mills's life, in the Vietnam War.

Mills described America as a system of "organized irresponsibility," governed at the top by a power elite with "an expedient, amoral attitude." He wrote,

> A society that is in its higher circles and on its middle levels widely believed to be a network of smart rackets does not produce men with an inner moral sense; a society that is merely expedient does not produce men of conscience. A society that narrows the meaning of "success" to the big money and in its terms condemns failure as the chief vice, raising money to the plane of absolute value, will produce the sharp operator and the shady deal. Blessed are the cynical, for only they have what it takes to succeed.[43]

It is hard to imagine a better description of sociopathic society!

In his great 1957 work, *The Sociological Imagination,*[44] Mills called for his discipline to abandon its role as legitimator of this sociopathic order. Mills thought intellectuals had moral responsibility to analyze power and denounce it when it became sociopathic and eroded democracy. To justify such power in the rising American corporate society was itself an act of intellectual sociopathy. *The Sociological Imagination* was a call for a public, critical sociology that spoke truth to power and helped inspire popular movements to challenge the sociopathic power elites destroying democracy in the name of democracy.

Consider next the iconic novelist George Orwell. Nobody ever wrote more powerfully about sociopathic society.

Orwell evokes vividly the specter of high-tech sociopathic society haunting millions of us in the twentieth and twenty-first centuries. The wildly successful novelistic and film series *Hunger Games* has strong Orwellian undertones that testify to the sociopath fears of our collective imagination. Orwell's are militarist dystopias, described in *1984*,[45] Orwell's greatest work, and *Animal Farm*,[46] that rule by electronic propaganda, surveillance, and repression. There can be no trusting social bonds, loving solidarity, or true society because all are taught to see others as dangerous: informers, spies, terrorists, or enemies of the state. These Orwellian nightmares project through a glass darkly the post-9/11 America waging a war on terrorism that has become a war against much of the world as well as the American population itself, subjecting us to warrantless surveillance by the FBI on our phone calls and e-mails, blanketing us with endless war propaganda about the threat of terrorists, and executing repressive police tactics such as electronic fencing off, teargasing, and beating of peaceful protestors in US cities, which I have witnessed personally in antiglobalization, labor, peace, and Occupy protests.

Big Brother ruled by transforming ideology and language itself into a sociopathic weapon against his own people. Slogans such as "War Is Peace" were perfect examples of doublethink, creating a vocabulary that melded contradictory ideas in ways that made it impossible to dissent from the regime. Big Brother became a substitute for society itself. People loved Big Brother but hated "the enemy"—who were all other societies and, in all likelihood, your neighbor in the next apartment.[47]

Orwell showed that social life disintegrates in the face of mistrust and terror, as when his hero, Winston, in *1984*, encounters the girl who will become his lover:

> The girl at the next table had turned partly around and was looking at him. It was the girl with dark hair.... The instant that she caught his eye she looked away again. The sweat started out on Winston's backbone. A horrible pang of terror went through him.... Why was she watching him? ... His earlier thought returned to him; probably she was not actually a member of the Thought Police, but then it was precisely the amateur spy who was the greatest danger of all.[48]

Orwell captures society degrading into a mass of strangers fearing or hating each other, in our society perhaps expressed in road rage against other drivers or fear in a park at dusk that the person walking behind you might have a gun and attack you.

Orwell also paints the larger trend toward authoritarian control and unconstitutional executive power in formally democratic societies such as the

United States today. There are strong Weberian themes here, but *1984* was a hot rather than cold bureaucratic dictatorship. Three-minute hate sessions, featuring videos on tele-screens several times a day, showed "our" noble military fighting the evil empires threatening the nation. The screaming video sessions—that rallied people behind Big Brother in a hysterical and irresistible collective orgy of hatred—brilliantly anticipated contemporary sociopathic society's use of militarism and patriotism to maintain the support of a chained population. Yet as Big Brother thrived, society died, a casualty of terror, torture, and brilliant ideological manipulation.[49]

John Kenneth Galbraith was a very different prophet of sociopathic society, an elegant 6'7" Harvard professor and advisor to presidents who towered over the intellectual landscape as much as he did physically over his colleagues. Galbraith, the leading American economist and public intellectual of the mid- to late twentieth century, offered a less flamboyant picture than Orwell, but it was no less important as a contribution to the anatomy of sociopathic society. Galbraith's great achievement was to show that the "affluent society," the title of one of his major works,[50] was not a democratic paradise for all but increasingly a sociopathic corporate plutocracy that locked millions into poverty.

Galbraith rejected the view of most of his academic economist colleagues, at Harvard and elsewhere, who saw US capitalism as a competitive free market system based on universal natural laws. He did not see capitalism as an inherently sociopathic system, but he moved beyond the abstract equations of his fellow economists to look at the history and politics of the real-life institutions, such as the big corporations and the government, that partnered to run the "free" market. This partnership undermined what Galbraith called "countervailing power"[51] essential to limit corporate greed and ensure vital public goals of jobs and justice. In his most influential book, *The New Industrial State*,[52] he showed that government was abdicating the countervailing role, and, in its role as handmaiden to the big companies, abandoning its role as protector of society and collaborating in a corporate sociopathic regime that undermined the public good for corporate profits.

In *The Affluent Society,* Galbraith brilliantly dissects the sociopathy of an America that invests in private comforts and luxuries while abandoning the public goods, such as housing, health care, and public transit, essential for the well-being of the majority and society itself:

> Capitalism has never anywhere provided good houses at moderate cost. Housing, it seems unnecessary to stress, is an important adjunct of a successful urban life. Nor does capitalism provide good health services, and when people live close together with attendant health risks, these too are important. Nor does capitalism provide efficient transportation for people—another essential of the life of the Metropolis. In Western Europe and Japan the failure of

capitalism in the fields of housing, health and transportation is largely, though not completely, accepted. There industries have been intensively socialized. In the United States there remains the conviction that, however contrary the experience, private enterprise will eventually serve.[53]

Put simply, Galbraith says America feeds the elites and starves the people, bloating private fortunes and bankrupting the public services that permit society itself to exist.

***

Galbraith brings us to the final set of theorists, most still living at this writing, who have brought into focus a clearer view of twenty-first-century sociopathic society. The economist who has stepped into Galbraith's big shoes is Paul Krugman, a Nobel Prize winner and *New York Times* columnist, with the acerbic wit and economically informed biting critique that mercilessly exposes the sociopathy of the Wall Street and Washington elites who created the 2008 new Great Depression. Krugman also reveals the sociopathy of his own profession of academic economics that has provided cover for the policies that drove America into a ditch and may keep it there. As Krugman puts it, "What the 1% wants becomes what economic science says we must do."[54]

Like Galbraith, Krugman is a Keynesian who does not see capitalism as intrinsically sociopathic, but as vulnerable to irrationality and susceptible to takeover by sociopathic forces. The most dangerous are wealthy Wall Street banks and other giant corporations, who turn capitalist finance into a speculative frenzy leading to bubbles that pop and destroy much of the confidence, credit, and spending that keep the capitalist engine purring. This caused the housing and financial 2008 meltdown, which Krugman views as a predictable sociopathic disaster, easily prevented or corrected had national leaders acted in the public interest.[55]

But Washington elites were themselves sociopathic actors, in Krugman's views, wedded to and often hailing from the Wall Street they were supposed to police. National leaders from both parties shoveled massive money to the sociopathic financiers who caused the crisis, while failing to bail out foreclosed homeowners and provide the major stimulus needed to turn the economy around. Jobs disappeared, infrastructure rotted and President Obama, despite his progressive image, failed to mobilize countervailing power and stop the bleeding, deferring to Wall Street and the wealthy's obsession with deficit-reduction rather than job creation, in what might be described as passive sociopathy. Krugman is not the least surprised by any of this:

Thus, the average American is somewhat worried about budget deficits, which is no surprise given the constant barrage of deficit scare stories in the news media, but the wealthy, by a large majority, regards deficits as the biggest problem we face. And how should the budget deficit be brought down? The wealthy favor cutting federal spending on health care and Social Security—that is, "entitlements"—while the public at large actually wants to see spending on these programs rise. You get the idea: The austerity agenda looks a bit like simple expression of upper-class preferences, wrapped in a façade of academic rigor.[56]

Krugman not only sees a government of, by, and for the 1 percent but a newly sociopathic Republican Party so conservative that, like fascism, it threatened capitalism itself from the Far Right. Krugman sees sociopathic evil in the antiscientific, fundamentalist political culture and abysmal economic ignorance dished up by the Tea Party and the Christian Right. These groups have taken over much of the Republican Party. They deny climate change, beat the drums for more aggressive military intervention, and seek to shrink and drown the social welfare government in the bathtub, as antitax activist Grover Norquist puts it. Krugman has been a crucial voice naming the sociopathic Far Right US agenda for what it is: a grave danger to civil society.

In his Keynesian embrace of capitalism, even Krugman has not offered an expansive enough view of the forces creating mad sociopathy in the United States. Three more radical voices have helped fill that vacuum. One is Ralph Nader, who has been advancing our understanding of corporate sociopathy since the 1960s and 1970s, when in his path-breaking book *Unsafe at Any Speed*[57] he documented how the Detroit car corporations knowingly took the lives of their consumers to make a buck, fully aware that their cars' defects would cause mass death. The fact that the companies coldly calculated the dollar value of each life, seeing that their possible payouts to families would only marginally dent their profits, was a visceral demonstration of corporate sociopathy that echoed through American culture and helped create a new consumer movement.

Since that era, Nader has expanded his vision of corporate sociopathy, focusing on the political role of large corporations in taking over government and bending it to its will at the expense of the public interest.[58] The critical insight is that the free market is a myth, as public and private sectors meld in an unholy marriage to run the country. He has said, accurately,

> Every single agency and department in Washington is overwhelmingly controlled by corporations. They have 10,000 Political Action Committees. They put their high executives in high government positions. They have 35,000 full-time lobbyists. Just imagine that—even the Labor Department is not controlled by trade unions—it's controlled by corporations.
>
> It isn't just the government under the CONTROL of corporations—the government IS the corporation now! The corporation IS the government![59]

Nader has been a leader in exposing "corporate welfare," the enormous subsidization of companies by governments who dish out tax breaks, depreciation, export subsidies, foreign investment tax havens, and other multibillion-dollar giveaways that bleed the public treasury.[60] At the same time, he has been a leading voice showing that both Democrats and Republicans have become servants of the corporation, creating a political duopoly ensuring that the corporate agenda triumphs, whoever wins elections.

As Nader became the leading analyst of modern corporate sociopathy, Noam Chomsky emerged as the leading critic of the sociopathic foreign policy of the United States, as it has tried to exercise unbridled global hegemony or dominance since World War II. Chomsky, a professor for many years at MIT, is one of the founders of modern linguistics as well as the great decoder of US foreign policy. He is a polymath Renaissance thinker, making contributions to linguistics, political theory, philosophy, psychology, political economy, and the sociology of the mass media, all while playing a major role in building popular resistance and grassroots movements against sociopathic regimes around the world, most notably the United States itself. Chomsky first gained attention in the 1960s when he critiqued the Vietnam conflict as an American war against the legitimate nationalist impulses of the Vietnamese people. He highlighted the complicity of the intelligentsia and media in legitimating a lethal, antidemocratic, and unjust war.[61] Then, in an unprecedented outpouring of critical and brilliant scholarship on US wars, Chomsky demonstrated with searing factual power the endless sociopathic violence the United States has unleashed on the world to maintain its own hegemonic power and corporate profits.[62]

Chomsky's work has gained a large worldwide audience. He is viewed by many as the most influential public intellectual on the globe, a standing arising from the rigor of his arguments and the "shock and awe" that his analysis evokes—not sugarcoated by any of the official moral arguments for US interventionism. He inverts the mythology of American exceptionalism embraced by virtually the entire American political and social elite, including especially the mass media, of which Chomsky has written influential indictments as sociopathic apologists for American power.[63] Chomsky argues that the United States has been engaging in a form of state terrorism for decades, undermining democratic regimes and installing and propping up dictators—whether the Somozas in Nicaragua, the Shah in Iran, the Duvaliers in Haiti, Sukarno in Indonesia, or the House of Saud in Saudi Arabia—who all became clients or puppets under US control. The death squads that kill hundreds of thousands in these regimes, Chomsky argues, are ultimately blood on the hands of the US state.[64]

Chomsky doesn't ever mince words, especially about such matters as US state terrorism:

The phrase "war on terrorism" should always be used in quotes, because there can't possibly be a war on terrorism, it's impossible. The reason is it's led by one of the worst terrorist states in the world, in fact it's led by the only state in the world which has been condemned by the highest international authorities for international terrorism, namely the World Court and Security Council, except that the US vetoed the resolution.[65]

Because such hegemonic and enduring state terrorism is the most frightful form of sociopathic policy—and because Chomsky links it to core economic and political interests of the US corporate regime—Chomsky is arguably the most powerful living writer on American sociopathy. While he does not single out the United States as historically unique, he shows that permanent war is as integral to US society and as self-serving as the imperial violence carried out by virtually all prior global empires, such as the British Empire that morally justified and disguised its own sociopathic wars in the name of the "white man's burden." The Americans simply renamed it "Manifest Destiny" in the guise of "spreading liberty."

One of Chomsky's close friends was his fellow Bostonian, Howard Zinn, a third major radical analyst of systemic American sociopathy. Zinn was a fighter pilot in World War II; became a major mentor to civil rights activists during the uprisings of the 1960s, when he taught at Atlanta's African American Spellman College; and then began a long, brave career at Boston University, where he linked scholarship to a leading activist role in the antiwar, civil rights, and labor movements.[66] He was a leading historian of the United States from "below," looking less at the elites than the ordinary Americans who were subject to slavery, sexism, and class exploitation, as well as cannon fodder for America's endless wars.

Zinn's great work was *A People's History of the United States*, which has sold over two million copies.[67] I recommend it for every American student. It not only graphically captures the sociopathic ruthlessness of capitalism and militarism throughout US history but also shows that Americans never allowed themselves to become passive victims. Zinn's history of the United States is a history of popular social movements—the abolitionists, suffragettes, prairie populists, labor organizers, and peace activists—who never stopped organizing to overcome and reverse the sociopathic forces crushing their lives and undermining the great rhetorical ideals of American democracy. Zinn made clear why we need brave movements, prepared to engage in protest and civil disobedience, to end our sociopathic system: "Civil disobedience is not our problem. Our problem is civil obedience. Our problem is that millions have been killed because of this obedience.... Our problem is that people are obedient while the jails are full of petty thieves ... [and] the grand thieves are running the country. That's our problem."[68]

Zinn was much mourned when he died in 2010 at age eighty-seven. He was an irrepressible life-affirming personality whose entire life and enormously influential work demonstrated that the best and most important intellectual work arises from immersion in the struggles of ordinary people for dignity and justice. Zinn moved generations of students toward an understanding of sociopathic society and into a life of activism, with some of his most fervent admirers being Matt Damon and Ben Affleck, who bring up *The People's History* in their Oscar-winning debut film, *Good Will Hunting,* and later worked with Zinn to transform his work into powerful films, including documentaries of *The People's History,* with a mass audience.

***

Howard Zinn's work leads naturally to the final great questions about the future of sociopathic society. What are the prospects of creating a more humane and democratic social order? What would that society look like? What are the main obstacles to change? How can people organize to challenge dominant elites and the most powerful global institutions? Zinn's work offers inspiration to those who retain hope that the power of people to transform even the most powerful and destructive systems cannot be denied.

The trajectory of sociopathic society is toward destruction. It promotes destruction of other nations, of its own citizens, of the natural environment, and, ultimately, societal self-destruction. These destructive tendencies are part of the defining core of sociopathic societies and they cannot be denied. This, however, does not mean that they cannot be stopped and reversed.

Even Karl Marx, the classic theorist of the sociopathic self-destructiveness of capitalist societies, saw this very reality as the basis of hope. Marx argued that capitalism was doomed by its own sociopathic contradictions and would give birth as it died to a new liberating socialist society. Marx's optimism, though, has now been tempered by the new great existential crises caused by today's sociopathic societies. These threats, particularly climate change, put time limits on the prospects for change and survival, adding a new dimension to the gravity of the sociopathic crisis.

Nonetheless, there are realistic grounds for hope. The United States is not monolithically sociopathic and the Far Right is a vocal but small minority, with only about 10 percent of the population, at this writing, identifying with the Tea Party. There are large sectors of the population who are not sociopathic, and evidence is growing that, even as the American Dream has become a more frenzied recipe for greed and "me, me, me," there are new values rising among the US majority. As I show later, a Pew polls says that only about 50 percent of young Americans say they have a positive reaction to capitalism, and a conservative Rasmussen poll shows, remarkably, a fairly divided population between support of capitalism or socialism. And there are many dedicated and creative social movements animated by these new values that could lead to a more just, tolerant, peaceful, and sustainable society.

But can they catch fire and win mass support? This is a tall order and could easily fail. The movements have not yet crystallized a concrete alternative of postcapitalist new economies and societies, although theorists of a new green and participatory political economy are beginning to analyze and help inspire many new global experiments. In the United States, one sees models of worker-owned companies and consumer co-ops, local participatory budgeting experiments from Portland, Oregon, to neighborhoods in Boston, and farmer markets, local food sourcing, and urban farming. But even should these models prove viable, the larger problem is the mobilization of national large-scale political will, especially in the United States, to achieve radical and widespread whole-system change. Even the youthful millennial generation are not drawn, in the main, to system-changing social movements that galvanized young people in the 1960s.

Nonetheless, the most important lesson of Howard Zinn's work is that the United States has bred mass popular social movements for societal change throughout its history. While these movements ebb and flow, they never disappear, and they remain today a fragmented but important part of the social landscape. In a period when the Far Right seemed dominant and the Left seemed invisible or extinct, the emergence of the Occupy Wall Street movement showed the possibility of unexpected popular uprisings that challenge the sociopathic society.

***

The Occupy movement taught us hopeful lessons. Going up against the most powerful banks in the world, people living in makeshift tents on the streets can make a dramatic statement and change the terms of political discourse. Concepts of the "1 percent" and the "99 percent" have become part of the mainstream conversation and now focus national attention on the sociopathic crisis of extreme inequality. This is central to solving sociopathy and saving society, since the chasm of 1 versus 99 is so big and divisive that it tears apart and destroys society itself.

What was Occupy all about? Here is what some Occupiers have said:

> Going forward, our intent is to ... act as seeds of the insurgent imagination, encouraging us to dream and act for a better world. As Zinn wrote, "Where progress has been made, wherever any kind of injustice has been overturned, it's been because people acted as citizens, and not as politicians. They didn't just moan. They worked, they acted, they organized, they rioted if necessary to bring their situation to the attention of people in power. And that's what we have to do today. Some people might say, 'Well, what do you expect?'
> "And the answer is that we expect a lot.
> "People say, 'What, are you a dreamer?'
> "And the answer is yes, we're dreamers.
> "We want it all."[69]

Occupy connected with—and was inspired by—a global revolutionary spirit for justice and democracy that surfaced in the Arab Spring and in many of the Orange, Velvet, and other popular movements occupying the streets of some of the most sociopathic societies around the world. Just as we must now analyze institutions within a global rather than national context, so social movements are arising in concert with a globalized youth and political culture. The disinclination to get out on the streets and join movements among many young Americans may change as they witness students on the streets fighting higher fees and student debt in Canada and England, Arab students in North Africa pouring into the squares of their capital cities and bravely opposing dictators in Tunisia and Egypt, and indigenous peasants fighting global corporations to retain their land and way of life from Bolivia to Canada to Australia.

The 1 versus the 99. This was the heart of Occupy.

The Occupiers were tireless and creative activists:

> We are blocking bridges, shutting down ports, disrupting foreclosures. We are marching in the streets, forming affinity groups, creating our own media, making connections to other struggles. Protest and civil disobedience are now just the ever-changing surface of something deeper and more powerful: an evolving public insurgency with openness, democracy and non-violent direct action as its primary weapons. That's what's been happening since September 2011, and that's what is happening right now.[70]

To bring the long era of sociopathic society to an end, US activists—and their colleagues in other nations—do not have to get the majority of the population to join them on the streets. Rather, they need to show that they speak for their values and offer concrete systemic remedies for their personal problems and the nation's socioeconomic crises. The movements will have to connect with the vast majority who sympathize with many of their goals but are not street activists themselves.

For that majority not out on the streets, there is a crucial role of changing from the inside the sociopathic corporations and neighborhoods where they work and live. I am hopeful about these "insider" change agents because I see large numbers of them in my own classrooms, as well as on many other campuses and in communities where I speak. They are potential allies, many with a reformist spirit who may sympathize with or come to support the more visionary challenges organized by the popular movements. At the same time, both the movements and their reformist allies must join to build a progressive political party—which could be a reconstructed Democratic Party or a new Green party—that breaks out of the grip of the corporations and seeks to replace "corpocracy" with real democracy.

There is no way of predicting the outcome of the coming contest between the reigning sociopathy and the population suffering under its grip. What we know is that hope is realistic and systemic change both necessary and possible. The need for transformation has never been more urgent, since the sociopathic society unchecked will doom life and society itself. Those who love life and believe in justice have only this one last chance to act. Their actions can succeed if they are unwaveringly committed and understand that they are fighting—in the context of global corporate power, nuclear war, and climate change—for the most important life-sustaining revolution of all time. Howard Zinn deserves the last word here:

> To be hopeful in bad times is not just foolishly romantic. It is based on the fact that human history is a history not only of cruelty, but also of compassion, sacrifice, courage, kindness.
>
> What we choose to emphasize in this complex history will determine our lives. If we see only the worst, it destroys our capacity to do something. If we remember those times and places—and there are so many—where people have behaved magnificently, this gives us the energy to act, and at least the possibility of sending this spinning top of a world in a different direction.
>
> And if we do act, in however small a way, we don't have to wait for some grand utopian future. The future is an infinite succession of presents, and to live now as we think human beings should live, in defiance of all that is bad around us, is itself a marvelous victory.[71]

Sociopathy and the New American Dream

Introduction to Part II

Sociopathic Individualism and Everyday Life

Most Americans learn to see the world through a psychological or individual lens. They view sociopathy as essentially psychopathology—and they view a sociopathic society as another name for a mental health crisis. This became apparent in the reaction to the 2012 Sandy Hook school massacre, and other rampant military-style gun shootings, in which much of the media and millions of Americans saw the problem mainly as a mental illness epidemic to be resolved by identifying and more carefully tracking or confining "crazy" people.

While it is a societal problem requiring change in our ruling economic and political institutions and elites, sociopathy has a very personal expression and translates into agonizing problems of social interaction and everyday life, often involving verbal, emotional, or physical violence. I start the book discussing this personal side of the crisis, since most Americans struggle with it in their daily lives, in their marriages, and in their broader psychological and social worlds.

In the first chapter of this section, I offer an analysis of the "wilding of America." Wilding is self-interested behavior that harms others and weakens the social fabric, a defining mark of sociopathy. In the essay on wilding, I show, first, that wilding is pervasive across the American landscape, shaping both individuals and institutions, such as corporations and governments. It affects almost all Americans, a besieged population struggling with survival, competitiveness, cheating, and lying in schools, sports, workplaces, and families. Second, I argue that wilding represents a form of extreme cultural individualism that has become the basis of a new and sociopathic American Dream, emphasizing personal and monetary success at the expense of others.

Third, I show that the culture of hyperindividualism, and the American Dream itself, is the master script of our twenty-first-century capitalist economic system.

In the second chapter of the section, I zoom in on the personal "micro" level and focus on everyday conversation. Conversation is at the heart of social life, and it requires authentic reciprocity and attention to the other. I identify a crisis of "conversational narcissism," when people are unable to listen. Despite ritual displays of civility or politeness, they seek to monopolize the conversation. It is a subtle but dehumanizing form of sociopathy in everyday life. When conversation is degraded in this way, people lose the capacity for deep and sustainable connection and intimacy, threatening the solidarity and very existence of society.

A third short chapter in this section looks at the gun violence epidemic as a frightening expression of sociopathy in everyday life. It shows that economic, political, and cultural forces all contribute to the crisis and help define for everyone the terrifying reality of sociopathic society, one where it is hard to feel safe.

2

The Good Man Fills His Own Stomach
All-American Crimes and Misdemeanors

The readings of history and anthropology ... give us no reason to believe that societies have built-in self-preservative systems.

—*Margaret Mead*

Wilding in Black and White

On April 19, 1989, a group of six teenagers, ages fourteen to sixteen, went into Central Park. According to police at the time, the youths came upon a young woman jogging alone past a grove of sycamore trees. Allegedly using rocks, knives, and a metal pipe, they attacked her. Some pinned her down while others beat and raped her. Police reported that one defendant, seventeen-year-old Kharey Wise, held the jogger's legs while a friend repeatedly cut her with a knife. They then smashed her with a rock and punched her face.

What most captured public attention about the story were the spirits of the assaulters during and after their crime. According to fifteen-year-old Kevin Richardson, one of the boys arrested, "Everyone laughed and was leaping around." One youth was quoted by police as saying, "It was fun ... something to do." Asked if they felt pretty good about what they had done, Richardson said, "Yes." Police reported a sense of "smugness" and "no remorse" among the youths.

From this event, a new word was born: *wilding*. According to press reports, it was the term the youths themselves used to describe their behavior—and it seemed appropriate. The savagery of the crime, which left the victim brain-damaged and in a coma for weeks, evoked the image of a predatory lion in the bush mangling its helpless prey. Equally shocking was the blasé attitude of the attackers. It had been no big deal, a source of temporary gratification and amusement. They were "mindless marauders seeking a thrill," said Judge Thomas B. Galligan of Manhattan, who sentenced three of the teenagers to a maximum term of five to ten years, charging them with turning Central Park into a "torture chamber." These were youths who seemed stripped of the emotional veneer of civilized humans, creatures of a wilderness where anything goes.

The story of wilding quickly became tied to the race and class of the predators and their prey. The convicted youths were black and from the inner city, although from stable working families. The victim was white, with degrees from Wellesley and Yale, and a wealthy twenty-eight-year-old investment banker at Salomon Brothers, one of the great houses of Wall Street.

To white, middle-class Americans, wilding symbolized something real and terrifying about life in the United States. Things were falling apart, at least in the hearts of America's major cities. Most suburbanites did not feel their own neighborhoods had become wild, but they could not imagine walking into Central Park at night.

The fear of wilding became fear of the Other: those locked outside of the American Dream. They had not yet invaded the world most Americans felt part of, but they menaced it. The Central Park attack made the threat real, and it unleashed fear among the general population and a backlash of rage among politicians and other public figures. Mayor Ed Koch called for the death penalty. Donald Trump took out ads in four newspapers, writing, "I want to hate these murderers.... I want them to be afraid." Trump told *Newsweek* that he "had gotten hundreds and hundreds of letters of support."

On December 19, 2002, in a sensational turn of events, Justice Charles J. Tejada of Manhattan's State Supreme Court took only 5 minutes to reverse the convictions of the five "wilders," who had already served their multiyear sentences. The judge acted after another man, Matias Reyes, in jail for murder and rape, confessed to committing the Central Park rape himself, and DNA evidence conclusively linked Reyes to the crime. It appears that the earlier confessions may have been forced in a circus trial potentially involving police misconduct and racism. Patricia Williams, a law professor who attended the 1991 trial, remembers a hysterical atmosphere in the courtroom, with tourists and celebrities "lined up around the block for admission, as though it were a Broadway show." Williams noted that the confessions were full of inconsistencies elicited by "unorthodox" police tactics. These included eighteen to thirty hours "of nonstop questioning," sometimes taking place "in the back of a police car" and "in the middle of the night." Using hindsight twelve years later, it seemed as if the public and the police had needed to confirm their views of African American and Latino youth—and all the "Others" in America at the time as wilders.

But while the term *wilding* may have come into the media based on a false conviction and racism, it is a surprisingly useful way to characterize an evolving and deeply disturbing feature not of African Americans or the Other but of American society as a whole. Instead of focusing mainly on the "black wilding" that did not occur in the park, suppose we think of "white wilding" as a way to characterize morally unsettling and often violent behavior that is rampant throughout our culture. As an extreme example, consider a second remarkably vicious crime that grabbed people's attention all over the country just a few months after the Central Park rape. On October 23, 1989, Charles and Carol Stuart left a birthing class at Boston's Brigham and Women's Hospital, walked to their car parked in the adjoining Mission Hill neighborhood, and got in. Within minutes, Carol Stuart—eight months pregnant—was dead, shot point-blank in the head. Her husband, a stunned nation would learn from police accounts two months later, had been her assassin. He had allegedly killed her to collect hundreds of thousands of dollars in life insurance money in order to open a restaurant. Opening a restaurant, Americans everywhere learned, had long been Charles Stuart's American Dream.

Many white, middle-class Americans seemed to believe Stuart's story when he told police that a black gunman had shot him and his wife, leaving Carol Stuart dead and Charles Stuart himself with a severe bullet wound in the abdomen. When Stuart's brother, Matthew, went to the police to tell them of Charles's involvement, and when Charles Stuart subsequently apparently committed suicide by jumping off the Tobin Bridge into the Mystic River, some of the threads connecting his crime to the horrible rape in Central Park began to emerge. Stuart had duped a whole nation by playing on the fear of the wild Other. Aware of the vivid images of gangs of black youths rampaging through dark city streets, Stuart brilliantly had concocted a story that would resonate with white Americans' deepest anxieties. Dr. Alvin Poussaint, Harvard professor and adviser to Bill Cosby, said, "Stuart had all the ingredients.... [H]e gave blacks a killer image and put himself in the role of a model, an ideal Camelot type that white people could identify with."

Charles Stuart's crime became a national obsession. A twenty-one-year-old Oklahoman visiting Boston told a *Boston Globe* reporter, "You wouldn't believe the attention this is getting back home. It's all anyone can talk about. I've taken more pictures of this fur shop and Stuart's house than any of the stuff you're supposed to take pictures of in Boston." The quiet block the Stuarts lived on in Reading, a Boston suburb, became what the *Globe* called a "macabre mecca," with hundreds of cars, full of the curious and the perplexed, parked or passing by. One reason may have been that white, middle-class Americans everywhere had an uncomfortable sense that, as the 1990s emerged, the Stuart case was telling them something about themselves. Stuart, after all, was living the American Dream and reaping its benefits—he was a tan, athletic man with working-class roots, making more than $100,000 a year selling fur coats, and married to a lovely, adoring wife, living the good life in suburban Reading, complete with a swimming pool. Had the American Dream itself become the progenitor of a kind of wilding? Was it possible that not only the inner cities of America but also its comfortable suburbs were becoming wild places? Could "white wilding" be a more serious problem than the "black wilding" publicized in the mass media and so readily embraced by the public at large? Was America at the turn of the decade becoming a wilding society?

To answer these questions, we have to look far beyond such exceptional events as the Central Park rape and the Stuart murder. We shall see that there are many less extreme forms of wilding, including a wide range of antisocial acts that are neither criminal nor physically violent. Wilding includes the ordinary as well as the extraordinary, may be profit oriented or pleasure seeking, and can infect corporations and governments as well as individuals of each race, class, and gender.

The Mountain People: A Wilding Culture

Between 1964 and 1967, anthropologist Colin Turnbull lived among the people of Uganda known as the Ik, who were unfortunately expelled by an uncaring government from their traditional hunting lands to extremely barren mountainous areas. In 1972, Turnbull published a haunting book about his experiences that left no doubt that a whole society can embrace wilding as a way of life.

When Turnbull first came to the Ik, he met Atum, a sprightly, barefoot old man with a sweet smile, who helped guide Turnbull to remote Ik villages. Atum warned Turnbull right away that everyone would ask for food. Although many would indeed be hungry, he said, most could fend for themselves, and their pleas should not be trusted. Turnbull, Atum stressed, should on no account give them anything. But before he left that day, Atum mentioned that his own wife was severely ill and desperately needed food and medicine. On reaching his village, Atum told Turnbull his wife was too sick to come out. Later, Turnbull heard exchanges between Atum and his sick wife, and her moans of suffering. The moans were wrenching, and when Atum pleaded for help, Turnbull gave him food and some aspirin.

Some weeks later, Atum had stepped up his requests for food and medicine, saying his wife was getting sicker. Turnbull was now seriously concerned, urging Atum to get her to a hospital. Atum refused, saying that "she wasn't that sick." Shortly thereafter, Atum's brother-in-law came to Turnbull and told him that Atum was selling the medicine that Turnbull had been giving him for his wife. Turnbull, not terribly surprised, said that "that was too bad for his wife." The brother-in-law, enjoying the joke enormously, finally explained that Atum's wife "had been dead for weeks" and that Atum had "buried her inside the compound so you wouldn't know." No wonder Atum had not wanted his wife to go to the hospital. Turnbull thought, "She was worth far more to him dead than alive."

Startling to Turnbull was not only the immense glee the brother-in-law seemed to take in the "joke" that had been inflicted upon his dying sister, but the utter lack of embarrassment that Atum showed when confronted with his lie. Atum shrugged it off, showing no remorse whatsoever, saying he had simply forgotten to tell Turnbull. This was one of the first of many events that made Turnbull wonder whether there was any limit to what an Ik would do to get food and money.

Some time later, Turnbull came across Lomeja, an Ik man he had met much earlier. Lomeja had been shot during an attack by neighboring tribesmen and was lying in a pool of his own blood, apparently dying from two bullet wounds in the stomach. Still alive and conscious, Lomeja looked up at Turnbull and asked for some tea. Shaken, Turnbull returned to his Land Rover and filled a big, new, yellow enamel mug. When he returned, Lomeja's wife was bending over her husband. She was trying to "fold him up" in the dead position although he was not yet dead, and she started shrieking at Turnbull to leave Lomeja alone, saying Lomeja was already dead. Lomeja found the strength to resist his wife's premature efforts to bury him and tried to push her aside. Turnbull managed to get the cup of tea to Lomeja, who was still strong enough to reach out for it and sip it. Suddenly, Turnbull heard a loud giggle and saw Lomeja's sister, Kimat. Attracted by all the yelling, she had "seen that lovely new, bright yellow enamel mug of hot, sweet tea, had snatched it from her brother's face and made off with it, proud and joyful. She not only had the tea, she also had the mug. She drank as she ran, laughing and delighted at herself."

Turnbull came to describe the Ik as "the loveless people." Each Ik valued only his or her own survival and regarded everyone else as a competitor for food. Ik life had become a grim process of trying to find enough food to stay alive each day. The hunt consumed all of their resources, leaving virtually no reserve for feelings of any kind or for any moral scruples that might interfere with filling their stomachs. As Margaret Mead wrote, they were "a people who have become monstrous beyond belief." Scientist Ashley Montagu wrote that the Ik are "a people who are dying because they have abandoned their own humanity."

Ik families elevated wilding to a high art. Turnbull met Adupa, a young girl of perhaps six, who was so malnourished that her stomach was grossly distended and her legs and arms spindly. Her parents had decided she had become a liability and threw her out of their hut. Because she was too weak now to go out on long scavenging ventures, as did the other children, she would wander as far as her strength would allow, pick up scraps of bone or half-eaten berries, and then come back to her parents' place, waiting to be brought back in. Days later, her parents, tiring of her crying, finally brought her in and promised to feed her. Adupa was happy and stopped crying. The parents went out and "closed the asak behind them, so tight that weak little Adupa could never have moved it if she had tried." Adupa waited for them to come back with the food they had promised, but they did not return until a whole week had passed, when they knew Adupa would be dead. Adupa's parents took her rotting remains, Turnbull writes, and threw them out "as one does the riper garbage, a good distance away." There was no burial—and no tears.

Both morality and personality among the Ik were dedicated to the single all-consuming passion for self-preservation. There was simply "not room in the life of these people," Turnbull observes dryly, "for such luxuries as family and sentiment and love." Nor for any morality beyond "marangik," the concept of goodness, which means filling one's own stomach.

The Ik in Us

Long before the rape in Central Park or the Stuart murder, Ashley Montagu, commenting on Turnbull's work, wrote that "the parallel with our own society is deadly." In 1972, when Turnbull published his book, wilding had not yet become part of the American vocabulary, nor did most Americans face declining living standards, let alone the kind of starvation experienced by the Iks. Americans were obviously not killing their parents or children for money, but they dedicated themselves to self-interested pursuits with a passion not unlike that of the Ik.

In America, a land of plenty, there was the luxury of a rhetoric of morality and feelings of empathy and love. But was not the American Dream a paean to individualistic enterprise, and could not such an enterprise be conceived in some of the same unsentimental metaphors used by Turnbull about the Ik? The Ik community, he writes, "reveals itself for what it is, a conglomeration of individuals of all ages, each going his own way in search of food and water, like a plague of locusts spread over the land."

America now faces a wilding epidemic that is eating at the country's social foundation and could rot it. The American case is much less advanced than that of the Ik's, but the disease is deeply rooted and is spreading through the political leadership, the business community, and the general population. Strong medicine can turn the situation around, but if we fail to act now, the epidemic could prove irreversible.

Only a handful of Americans are "ultimate wilders" like Charles Stuart. Such killers are noteworthy mainly because they may help wake us up to the wilding plague spreading among thousands of less extreme wilders who are not killers. Wilding includes a vast spectrum of self-centered and self-aggrandizing behavior that harms others. A wilding epidemic tears at the social fabric and threatens to unravel society itself, ultimately reflecting the erosion of the moral order and the withdrawal of feelings and commitments from others to "number one."

The wilding virus comes in radically different strains. There is *expressive wilding*: wilding for the sheer satisfaction of indulging one's own destructive impulses, the kind found among the American youth who heave rocks off highway bridges in the hope of smashing the windshields of unknown drivers passing innocently below. The hockey and soccer parents who attack coaches and other parents are expressive wilders, as are drivers engaging in road rage. Road rage has reached such epidemic proportions—as has workplace rage, school rage, and air rage—that leading pundits now talk of "dies irae," or America's day of rage. The country's most famous perpetrators in recent years include O. J. Simpson, who acted out the domestic violence that is one of the most common and Ik-like forms of expressive wilding. His alleged repeated abuse of his wife to sate his jealousy, maintain his control, or simply gratify his emotions of the moment evokes serious questions about the nightmarish spread of family violence among rich and poor alike. The national obsession with Simpson during his trial reflects the fear that when a country's icon beats his wife black and blue, smashes her windshield with a baseball bat, stalks her, and is finally charged with her murder and acquitted in a controversial verdict, we all participate in the crime, for heroes act out the passions and values of the cultures that create them.

Although mainly an example of expressive wilding (in 2001 he was arrested for road rage violence), Simpson also modeled *instrumental wilding*. Not simply for fun or purely emotional gratification, instrumental wilding is wilding for money, career advancement, or other calculable personal gain. Simpson began as a youngster, running with gangs and stealing food. Fantastically ambitious and opportunistic, he later naturally took to a life of single-minded corporate salesmanship, obsessively remaking his voice, wardrobe, and demeanor according to the image lessons of the Hertz ad executives who greased his career. He wheeled and dealed to sign movie deals and buy companies, such as a Pioneer Chicken franchise (destroyed in the Los Angeles riots of 1992), and eventually succumbing to the greed soaked financial dealings that led him, along with other entrepreneurial high rollers of his era, to bad loans and collapsed business deals.

Most instrumental wilding involves garden varieties of ambition, competitiveness, careerism, and greed that advance the self at the cost of others. Expressive and instrumental wilding have in common an antisocial self-centeredness made possible by a stunning collapse of moral restraint and a chilling lack of empathy. I am mainly concerned with instrumental wilding because it is the form most intimately connected with the American Dream and least understood in its poisonous effects on society.

Although much wilding is criminal, there is a vast spectrum of perfectly legal wilding, exemplified by the careerist who indifferently betrays or steps on colleagues to advance up the ladder. Some forms of wilding, such as lying and cheating, are officially discouraged, but others, like the frantic and single-minded pursuit of wealth, are cultivated by some of the country's leading corporations and financial institutions. Likewise, there are important differences in the severity of wilding behaviors; killing a spouse for money is obviously far more brutal than stealing a wallet or cheating on an exam. But there are distinct types and degrees of infection in any affliction, ranging from terminal cases such as that of Stuart, to intermediate cases such as the savings and loan crooks of the 1980s, to those who either are petty wilders or who rarely exhibit symptoms at all. The latter categories include large numbers of Americans who may struggle internally with their wilding impulses but remain healthy enough to restrain them. The variation is similar to that in heart disease: Those with only partial clogging of their arteries and no symptoms are different from those with full-blown, advanced arteriosclerosis, and those least afflicted may never develop the terminal stage of the illness. But these differences are normally of degree rather than of kind; the same underlying pathology is at work among people with both mild and severe cases.

There are, nonetheless, real differences between white lies or misdemeanors (forms of petty wilding) and serious wilding of the Central Park or Charles Stuart variety. Petty wilding occurs in all cultures, will persist as long as most people are not saints, and, in limited doses, does not necessarily threaten civil order. When wilding is so limited that it does not constitute a grave social danger, it might better be described as "incipient wilding" and is not of concern here.

However, certain types of petty wilding are growing at an alarming rate in America. Such transgressions on an epidemic scale can reach a critical mass and become as serious a threat to society as violent crime or huge investment scams on Wall Street. Lying is an important example of petty wilding that now not only infects many friendships and marriages but also has become a pervasive problem in our political system, with leaders charged with lying to the nation about their reasons for going to war, about authorizing torture, and about misrepresenting scientific findings, such as whether such problems as global climate change are caused by human activity. It is not the degree of brutality or violence, but the consequences for society that ultimately matter, and I thus consider the full spectrum of wilding acts—from petty to outrageous—that together constitute a clear and present danger to America's social fabric.

Economic, Political, and Social Wilding

Wilding, in sociological terms, extends far beyond random violence by youth gangs (the current definition in *Webster's Dictionary*) to include three types of assault on society. *Economic wilding* is the morally uninhibited pursuit of money by individuals or businesses at the expense of others. *Political wilding* is the abuse of political office to benefit oneself or one's own social clans, or the wielding of political authority to inflict morally unacceptable suffering on citizens at home or abroad. *Social wilding* ranges from personal or family acts of violence, such as child or spousal abuse, to collective forms of selfishness that weaken society, such as affluent suburbs turning their backs on bleeding inner cities.

Economic wilders include Bernie Madoff, the Wall Street financier who confessed to running a $60 billion Ponzi scheme, part of the 2008 Wall Street meltdown. Madoff is joined by a host of executives at AIG, Merrill Lynch, Lehman Brothers, and other Wall Street firms, whose economic wilding nearly brought down the entire system. Economic wilders are a different species from the kids in Central Park, since they wild for money rather than fun or sex. Partly because of differing opportunities and incentives, people wild in different ways and for exceedingly varied reasons and motives, ranging from greed and lust to the gaining of attention or respect. The different forms of wilding, however, are all manifestations of degraded American individualism.

Wilding is individualism run amok, and the wilding epidemic is the face of America's individualistic culture in an advanced state of disrepair. An individualistic culture promotes the freedom of the individual and in its healthy form nurtures human development and individual rights. In its degraded form, it encourages unrestrained and sociopathic self-interest.

Wilding and Not Wilding: Varieties of Individualism

Wilding—a degenerate form of individualism—encompasses a huge variety of antisocial behavior. It includes so many seemingly unrelated acts that it might appear to stand for everything—or nothing. But wilding includes only a small subset of the entire range of behaviors that sociologists describe as *individualistic*, a term that arguably can be applied to any self-interested behavior. In a society such as that of the United States, which is dominated by individualistic values and a market system that rewards self-interest, some might argue that virtually any socially prescribed behavior has an individualistic dimension.

I propose a far more restrictive definition of *wilding*. Not all individualistic behavior is wilding, nor is *wilding* an umbrella term for any form of self-interested or "bad" behavior. As noted earlier, *wilding* refers to self-oriented behavior that hurts others and damages the social fabric, which excludes many types of individualistic action. The Jewish sage Hillel wrote, "If I am not for others, what am I?" Yet he also said, "If I am not for myself, who will be for me?" His maxims suggest that many forms of self-interest are necessary and contribute to the well-being of others.

A doctor who works hard to perfect her medical skills may advance her own career, but she also saves lives. A superbly conditioned professional athlete may enrich himself by his competitiveness or ambition, but he also entertains and gives pleasure to his fans. If I strive to be the best writer I can be—an individualistic aspiration—I am educating others while fulfilling myself. In none of these cases is individualistic behavior itself necessarily wilding. Actions that advance one's own interests and either help or do not harm others are not forms of wilding, even when motivated by competitiveness or acquisitiveness.

Wilding includes only individualistic behavior that advances or indulges the self by hurting others. If the doctor advances her skills and career by cheating on tests, trampling on her colleagues, or using her patients as guinea pigs, her self-interest has degraded into wilding. The athlete who illicitly uses steroids to win competitions is wilding by cheating against his rivals and deceiving his fans.

Whereas all wilding behavior hurts others, not all hurtful behavior is wilding. If I get angry at a friend, I may hurt him, but that reaction does not necessarily make it wilding. Such anger may be justified because it was motivated by a wrong done to me, and it may ultimately serve to repair the relationship. Interpersonal relations inevitably involve misunderstanding, aggression, and hurt, which degrade into expressive wilding only when the hurt is intentional and purely self-indulgent, and when the perpetrator is indifferent to the pain inflicted on the other. Motivation, empathy, and the level of harm inflicted are key criteria in deciding whether wilding has occurred. Deliberate physical or emotional abuse is clearly wilding, whereas impulsive acts that cause less harm and lead to remorse and remediation are more ambiguous cases and may not constitute wilding at all.

Similarly complex considerations apply to institutional wilding enacted by corporations or governments. Instrumental wilding takes place whenever institutions pursue goals and strategies that inflict serious harm on individuals, communities, or entire societies. Some of the most important forms of economic wilding, both legal and criminal, involve routine profiteering by rapacious businesses exploiting employees, consumers, and communities. The line between corporate self-interest and economic wilding is blurred in today's global economy, but not all profits arise out of exploitation, and many profitable businesses are not engaged in economic wilding. Socially responsible or employee-owned businesses that add to social well-being by creating jobs, raising the standard of living of employees, improving the environment, and enhancing the quality of life of their customers may be highly profitable but are hardly examples of wilding. Systemic connections exist between American capitalism and wilding, but not all forms of capitalism breed wilding.

Finally, not all crime, violence, or evil behavior is individualistic wilding. The horrific ethnic cleansing in Bosnia and the genocidal warfare in Rwanda and the Sudan constitute wilding by almost any definition, but such wilding is rooted in fierce and pathological tribal or communal loyalties and is hardly an expression of rampant individualism. Individualism and communitarianism can each generate their own forms of wilding; the individualistic variant is the type endemic in the United States. My indictment of individualistic wilding should not be viewed as a preference for the communitarian form, because wilding in many of the world's cruelest societies has its roots in the excesses of community. Wilding can be avoided only by respecting the rights of individuals and the needs for community, a balancing act too many societies have failed dismally to achieve.

Varieties of Wilding

Wilding: Self-interested or self-indulgent behavior that hurts others and weakens the social fabric

Motives for Wilding	*Instrumental Wilding*	Wilding for money or other calculable gain, such as robbery
	Expressive Wilding	Wilding for emotional gratification, such as rape
Domains of Wilding	*Economic Wilding*	Wilding in the economy for money, career advancement, or other material gain
	Political Wilding	Wilding in politics for political power or advancement
	Social Wilding	Wilding in civil society for status, respect, or other social ends
	Environmental Wilding	Wilding in the natural environment, such as reckless polluting that causes global warming
Degrees of Wilding	*Petty Wilding*	Minor wilding, involving small gain or harm, such as cheating on a test
	Full-Blown Wilding	Major wilding, involving significant gain or serious harm, such as large-scale financial fraud
	Ultimate Wilding	Extreme wilding, such as the murder of a spouse or child for money
Perpetrators of Wilding	*Individual Wilding*	Wilding by individuals
	Institutional Wilding	Wilding by corporations, governments, churches, or other institutions
	Systemic Wilding	Wilding perpetrated by economic systems such as capitalism or cultural systems such as individualism
Legality of Wilding	*Criminal Wilding*	Wilding that involves breaking the law, such as armed robbery
	Legal Wilding	Wilding that is within the law, such as lying to a friend
Physicality of Wilding	*Violent Wilding*	Wilding that involves physical violence, such as murder
	Nonviolent Wilding	Wilding that is not physically violent, such as white-collar fraud

The Two Americas: Are We All Wilders?

Although the wilding epidemic now infects almost every major American institution, cooperative behavior survives, and in every community one finds idealists, altruists, and a majority of citizens seeking to live lives guided by moral principles. About two-thirds of Americans give money to charity, and about half roll up their sleeves and do volunteer work or become social activists; these are among the many hopeful indications that America can still purge itself of this epidemic.

For an analyst of wilding, there are two Americas: the America already seriously infected and the America that has not yet succumbed and remains a civil society. The majority of ordinary Americans, it should be stressed, are part of the second America, and they retain a moral compass and emotional sensibilities that inhibit severe wilding behavior. But as the epidemic continues to spread, individual interests will increasingly override common purposes, and the self—rather than family or community—increasingly will grab center stage in both Americas. Not everyone will become a wilder, but nobody will be untouched by wilding culture.

Wilders who catch the fever profoundly infect their own vulnerable communities, families, and workplaces. One dangerous criminal on a block can make a community wild, inducing aggression, violence, and a fortress mentality among normally peaceable neighbors. A particularly competitive salesperson or account executive can transform an entire office into a jungle, because those who do not follow suit may be left behind. The new ethos rewards the wilder and penalizes those who cling to civil behavior. One defense against wilding in modern America is to embrace it, spreading wilding behavior among people less disposed to be wilders who are still struggling against wilding as a way of life.

Many Americans misread the epidemic of AIDS as a problem of deviant and disadvantaged groups. They are at risk of making the same miscalculation about the wilding epidemic, to which no sector of the society has any immunity. Its ravages may be most noticeable among the poor and downtrodden, but the virus afflicts the respected and the comfortable just as much; it exists in the genteel suburbs as well as in the inner cities. Indeed, American wilding is, to a surprising degree, an affliction of the successful, in that the rich and powerful have written the wilding rules. It is ever more difficult to climb the ladder without internalizing those rules.

The progress of the wilding epidemic is shaped less by the percentage of sociopaths than by the sociopathy of society's elites and the rules of the success game they have helped define. A wilding society is one in which wilding is a route to the top, and in which legitimate success becomes difficult to distinguish from the art of wilding within—or even outside—the law.

The wilding epidemic is now seeping into America, mainly from the top. Although the majority of business and political leaders remain honest, a large and influential minority—concentrated on Wall Street—not only are serving as egregious role models but also are rewriting the rules of the American success game in their own interests.

Our current wilding crisis is rooted politically in the "free market" revolution that began with President Ronald Reagan. The "Reagan Revolution" advanced the most ambitious class agenda of the rich in over a century, creating an innovative brew of market deregulation and individualistic ideology that helped fan the flames of wilding across the land. Former president George W. Bush, despite his rhetoric of compassionate conservatism, tried to complete the revolution of greed that Reagan began, while also taking the country to war on false pretenses, one of the worst forms of political wilding. Whether President Barack Obama will decisively take America in a new direction remains to be seen.

Wilding and the New American Dream: Individualism Today and Yesterday

Many signs point to a corruption of the American Dream in our time. Most Americans do not become killers to make it up the ladder or to hold on to what they have, but the traditional restraints on naked self-aggrandizement seem weaker—and the insatiability greater.

The fantasy mushroomed in the late 1990s with young dot-com entrepreneurs dreaming of becoming millionaires before turning thirty. The "new economy" brought the age of "me.com" in which everyone looked for a fast fortune, whether by creating a new tech start-up or scoring big in day trading. Jonathan Lebed, a fifteen-year-old New Jersey suburban high school kid, made over $800,000 day trading and recommending stocks on the Internet. In 2000, the Securities and Exchange Commission accused him of violating laws regulating stock promotions and made him return over $200,000. This didn't stop many of his fellow students and even many of his teachers from rushing to join him on a new Internet venture that might make them all rich.

In 2001, journalist David Callahan bemoaned the new ethos of greed: "The economy of the late 1990s offered the promise of such extraordinary wealth that it brought out the worst in people.... The ideal of working hard over many years to achieve wealth lost traction. The pressure to pursue wealth instead of other goals grew enormously as the media focused on those winning big in the new economy. It became easy to feel that missing the gold rush was plain stupid." A young person himself, Callahan continues, "I've seen the resulting distortion of values everywhere in Generation X—my generation and in those coming after it. It's hard to stick to a goal related to something other than money.... Who wants to be a school teacher when you can be a millionaire?"

A new version of the American Dream has now emerged, more individualistic, expansive, and morally perverted than most of its predecessors. Journalist Laurence Shames suggests that the name of the American game has become simply "more." Unrestrained greed has certainly been the name of the game for America's richest people, including the "masters of the universe"—the elite money managers on Wall Street. In 2008, managers in the nine big banks receiving government bailouts took for themselves an astonishing $32.6 billion in bonuses, even as their banks lost money. About 5,000 top managers received $5 billion in bonuses, with 200 in Goldman Sachs sharing $1 billion and 101 in Morgan Stanley sharing $577 million.

In 2005, presenting its annual list of America's 400 wealthiest individuals, Forbes reported that, for the first time, virtually all 400—374, to be precise—were billionaires. In 2008, all 400 were worth at least $1.3 billion and the total wealth of the top 400 was an astonishing $1.57 trillion, more than the combined wealth of 40 percent of the American population. Bill Gates was the richest man, worth $57 billion, a sum equal to the wealth of almost all 650 million people in Africa.

For less privileged and especially poor Americans, the new gilded Dream became a recipe for wilding based on collapsed possibilities. A dream of having more had been sustainable when real income for ordinary Americans kept growing, as it had through most of American history. But when real income begins to stagnate and decline for millions in the bottom half of America, an unprecedented development in the last decades of the twentieth century, an outsized Dream becomes an illusion, inconsistent with the reality of most Americans' lives. In an analysis of wage trends since 2000, economist Jared Bernstein, now an advisor to President Obama and Vice President Biden, wrote in 2007 that real wages, especially among middle and lower income workers, stagnated throughout the 2000s, even before the Great Recession of 2008 hit. He is unequivocal that wage growth since 2000 was minuscule, and disappeared entirely after 2003: "The wages of all of these workers—the median worker and those with either high school or college degrees—have been flat or falling since 2003." He predicted that "more downward pressure on wage growth is likely. The recent slowing of productivity growth and rising unemployment are likely to place further pressure on most workers' real wages in the near to medium terms." A year later, the Great Recession hit, unemployment skyrocketed to about 10 percent, and wages and household income plunged further among middle and lower income workers, while the top tier of managers took home their million dollar bonuses. The ratio between the average CEO's pay and the average worker's wage went from 41 to 1 in 1975 to 344 to 1 in 2008. As wages declined, millions more Americans went into debt in order to try to achieve an American Dream receding out of their reach helping catalyze the economic collapse of 2008. Outsized Dream, downsized lives. To weave grandiose materialist dreams in an era of restricted opportunities is the ultimate recipe for social wilding.

A new age of limits and polarization in the early twenty-first century sets the stage for an advanced wilding crisis. In an America deeply divided by class, the American Dream, and especially the new Gilded Dream, cannot be a common enterprise and is transformed into multiple wilding agendas, unleashing wilding among people at every station, but in different ways. Among those at the bottom, the Dream becomes pure illusion; wilding, whether dealing drugs or robbing banks, beckons as a fast track out of the ghetto and into the high life. Among the insecure and slipping great American middle class, wilding becomes a growth area for those who are endowed with classic American initiative and ingenuity and are unwilling to go down with their closing factories and downsized offices. For the professional and business classes at the top, wilding passes as professional ambition and proliferates as one or another variant of dedicated and untrammeled careerism. Ensconced inside heavily fortified suburban or gentrified enclaves, these elites also pioneer new forms of social wilding in what former labor secretary Robert Reich calls "a politics of secession," abandoning society itself as part of a panicky defense against the threat from the huge, covetous majority left behind. The wilding crisis, as we see later, arises partly out of a virulent new class politics.

The seeds of America's wilding plague were planted long before the current era. A century ago, Alexis de Tocqueville observed that conditions in America led every "member of the community to be wrapped up in himself" and worried that "personal interest will become more than ever the principal, if not the sole spring" of American behavior. Selfish and mean-spirited people can be found in every culture and every phase of history, and wilding is certainly not a new phenomenon in American life. As one of the world's most individualistic societies, America has long struggled to cope with high levels of violence, greed, political corruption, and other outcroppings of wilding.

Over the last 100 years, American history can be read as a succession of wilding periods alternating with eras of civility. The robber baron era of the 1880s and 1890s, an age of spectacular economic and political wilding, was followed by the Progressive Era of the early twentieth century, in which moral forces reasserted themselves. The individualistic license of the 1920s, another era of economic and political wilding, this time epitomized by the Teapot Dome scandal, yielded to the New Deal era of the 1930s and 1940s, when America responded to the Great Depression with remarkable moral and community spirit. The moral idealism of a new generation of youth in the 1960s was followed by the explosion of political, economic, and social wilding in the current era.

American wilding is a timeless and enduring threat, linked to our national heritage and most basic values and institutions. The wilding problem riddles our history, for it is embedded in the origins of free market capitalism and the individualistic culture that has helped shape the American Dream and our own national character. What distinguishes the current epidemic is the subtle legitimation of wilding as it breeds a new culture of corruption in Washington; the severity of the wilding crisis in US militarist foreign policy that endangers our most precious civil liberties; the wilding epidemic, symbolized by Bernie Madoff and top executives, in banking and commerce; the spread of wilding into universities, films, TV, popular music, and other vital cultural centers; and the subsequent penetration of wilding culture so deeply into the lives of the general population that society itself is now at risk.

Roots of Wilding: Durkheim, Marx, and the Sociological Eye

More than a century ago, the founders of sociology had their own intimations of a wilding crisis that could consume society. The great French thinker, Emile Durkheim, recognized that individualism was the rising culture of the modern age. While Durkheim believed that individualism could ultimately be a healing force, he also feared that it could poison the bonds that make social life possible. Karl Marx, who gave birth to a different school of sociology, believed that the economic individualism of capitalism might erode all forms of community and reduce human relations to a new lowest common denominator: the "cash nexus."

Sociology arose as an inquiry into the dangers of modern individualism, which could potentially destroy society itself. The prospect of the death of society gave birth to the question epitomized by the Ik: What makes society possible and prevents it from disintegrating into a mass of sociopathic and self-interested isolates? This core question of sociology has become the vital issue of our times.

Although sociology does not provide all the answers, it does offer a compelling framework for understanding and potentially solving the wilding epidemic. Durkheim never heard of wilding or the Ik, but he focused like a laser on the coming crisis of community. He saw that the great transformation of the modern age was the breakdown of traditional social solidarity and the rise of an individual less enmeshed in community. In Durkheim's view, egoism posed a grave danger, arising where "the individual is isolated because the bonds uniting him to other beings are slackened or broken" and the "bond which attaches him to society is itself slack." Such an individual, who finds no "meaning in genuinely collective activity," is primed for wilding, the pursuit of gain or pleasure at the expense of others with whom there is no sense of shared destiny.

The other great danger is *anomie,* which Durkheim defined as a condition of societal normlessness that breeds crime and suicide. Anomie arises when social rules are absent or confusing and individuals are insufficiently integrated into families, neighborhoods, or churches to be regulated by their moral codes. Durkheim believed that modern individualistic societies were especially vulnerable to this kind of failure of socialization. As community declines, it leaves the individual without a moral compass, buffeted by disturbing and increasingly limitless "passions, without a curb to regulate them." Anomie fuels instrumental wilding, making the individual more vulnerable to fantasies of limitless money and power. It also feeds expressive wilding of the O. J. Simpson variety, weakening the personal and community controls that sustain civilized values.

Although Durkheim captured the kind of breakdown of community that is currently contributing to the American wilding epidemic, he lacked the economic and political analysis that would help explain why wilding is startlingly pervasive among America's ruling elites and trickling down to the population at large. American wilding is a form of socially prescribed, antisocial behavior, modeled by leaders and reinforced by the rules of our "free market" game. As such, it reflects less the insufficient presence of society in individuals than overconformity to a society whose norms and values are socially dangerous.

Marx wrote that the market system "drowns the most heavenly ecstasies of religious fervor, of chivalrous enthusiasm, of philistine sentimentalism, in the icy water of egotistical calculation." In capitalism, from a Marxist perspective, wilding is less a failure of socialization than an expression of society's central norms. To turn a profit, even the most humane capitalist employer commodifies and exploits employees, playing by the market rules of competition and profit maximization to buy and sell their labor power as cheaply as possible.

From a Marxist perspective, the American Dream is capitalism's master script. It dictates that each of us look out for "number one." If we fail to play our egoistic, competitive role in this capitalist script, profits are threatened and capitalism itself would unravel. For Marx, values themselves are the most carefully crafted "products" of the economic system. The capitalist elites script the individualistic American Dream because their wealth and power depend on the population believing fervently in the script's economic rationality and moral legitimacy.

While this script might seem pure greed or selfishness, it comes wrapped in high morality. One of the founders of classical economics, the eighteenth-century political philosopher, Adam Smith, developed the principle of the "invisible hand," which says that the best way to ensure the common good is for each individual to pursue his or her own self-interest. The invisible hand of the market transforms this self-oriented behavior by millions of producers and consumers into a miraculous common good. Self-interest, paradoxically, protects the "commons," the shared resources and prosperity that ensure the well-being of society as a whole.

In 1981, Ronald Reagan became president of the United States, and proclaimed in his inaugural speech that his goal was for every American to become rich. The Reagan Revolution helped turn the American Dream into one of fevered and extreme individualism that became a form of socially approved wilding. By dismantling regulations that had helped to rein in financial speculation, debt, and monopolies, this economic wilding, based in greed, helped make the wealthy even wealthier. The new motto: Get rich fast!

Americans looked up to the business leaders and politicians who got rich the fastest, symbolized by Gordon Gekko, the movie character played by Michael Douglas in the film *Wall Street.* Gekko's memorable line, "Greed is good," is a philosophy that permeated the greedy AIG and Bear Stearns executives in Wall Street and trickled down to millions of workers and consumers out to make a fast buck and spend it even faster. If we didn't have enough, and nothing seemed enough, Wall Street made available easy credit and debt, leading most of us to live beyond our means.

Marx would see extreme deregulation as one reason for the evolution of the American Dream into a wilding script. But, more important, Marx would explain the new extreme individualism as a reflection of growing systemic capitalist crises. As capitalism matures or "ages," it tends toward stagnation. One reason is the "wage paradox": Each corporation tries to force down wages to make more money. But when all corporations do this, they create a crisis of aggregate consumer demand, because the low wages mean workers can't buy what the companies produce. In the age of globalization, this becomes an extreme crisis in the United States, since corporations have access to billions of impoverished global workers and can force wages of US workers way down, leaving them with little income to spend at the mall.

American capitalists tried to solve this dilemma by making available super-easy credit and debt to the beleaguered US worker, so he or she could keep buying. "Use that plastic card in your wallet to keep shopping. If you couldn't afford a house, we'll give you a subprime mortgage and let you worry about the debt later." This logic, of course, led to the great economic meltdown of 2008. The actions of both the lenders and the borrowers, but especially the lenders, were one of the great forms of economic wilding in modern history, a sign of how capitalism can script a wilding culture that undermines capitalism itself.

The champions of Western capitalism—from Adam Smith to Milton Friedman—agree that self-interest is the engine of the system and individualism, its official religion; but they reject Marx's equation of a regime built around economic self-interest with exploitation and wilding. Marx was wrong, in fact, to assume that capitalism inevitably destroyed community and social values. In some national contexts, including Confucian Japan and social-democratic Sweden, the individualizing forces of the market are cushioned by cultures and governments that limit exploitation and help sustain community.

In the United States, however, rugged individualism has merged with raw capitalism, creating a fertile brew for wilding. A Marxist view of institutionalized wilding—and of political and business elites as carriers of the wilding virus—helps correct the Durkheimian hint of wilding as deviance. Durkheim, in a major oversight, never recognized that egoism and anomie can themselves be seen as norms, culturally prescribed and accepted.

This point is a theoretical key to understanding wilding in America. Wilding partly reflects a weakened community less able to regulate its increasingly individualistic members. In this sense, the American wilder is the product of a declining society that is losing its authority to instill respect for social values and obligations.

But Marx's view of institutionalized wilding suggests that wilders can simultaneously be oversocialized, imbibing too deeply the core values of competition and profit seeking in American capitalism. The idea of over-socialization suggests not the failure of social authority but the wholesale indoctrination of societal values that can ultimately poison both the individual and also the society itself. As local communities weaken, giant corporations, including the media, advertising, and communications industries, shape the appetites, morality, and behavior of Americans ever more powerfully. For the rich and powerful, the dream of unlimited wealth and glamour, combined with the Reagan and Bush II revolution of corporate deregulation and corporate welfare, opens up endless fantasies and opportunities. As Durkheim himself noted, when the ceiling on ordinary expectations is removed, the conventional restraints on pursuing them will also rapidly disappear. This situation produces socially prescribed anomie and wilding among elites that is based on unlimited possibilities.

A different version of socially prescribed wilding trickles down to everyone else. For those exposed to the same inflated dream of wealth, glamour, and power, but denied the means of achieving it, illegitimate means provide the only strategy to achieve socially approved goals. Whether involving petty or serious wilding, such behavior gradually permeates the population. Sociologist Robert Merton wrote that crime is a product of a disparity between goals and means. If that disparity becomes institutionalized, crime and other forms of deviance are normalized, and antisocial behavior becomes common practice. Wilding itself becomes a societal way of life.

New economic realities, including the fact that the coming generation faces the prospect of living less well than its parents, could trigger a healthy national reexamination of our values, and the pursuit of a less materialistic and individualistic life. The polarization of wealth and opportunity could also prompt, before it is too late, a rethinking of our class divisions and economic system. But without such a rescripting of the American Dream and our ruthless corporate capitalism, the new circumstances could create the specter of an American nightmare reminiscent of the Ik.

3

Conversational Narcissism and Sociopathic Talk

"Conversation indeed," said the Rocket. "You have talked the whole time yourself. That is not conversation."

"Somebody must listen," answered the Frog, "and I like to do all the talking myself."

"You are a very irritating person," said the Rocket, "and very ill bred. I hate people who talk about themselves, as you do, when one wants to talk about oneself, as I do."

—Oscar Wilde, from "The Remarkable Rocket"

Individualism has a counterpart in American psychology. People tend to seek attention for themselves in face-to-face interactions. This attention-getting psychology reflects an underlying character structure of "self-orientation" that emerges in highly individualistic societies. Erich Fromm has theorized that a shared character structure develops in each society, a "social character" that is a response to the requirements of the social order and best suited for survival and success within it. The self-oriented character type develops a highly egocentric view of the world and is motivated primarily by self-interest. To cope with social and economic insecurity bred by individualism, he becomes preoccupied with himself. His "attention-getting" psychology is thus rooted in a broad self-absorption engendered by social conditions highly developed in contemporary America.

In informal conversation, the self-oriented person repeatedly seeks to turn attention to himself. This "conversational narcissism" is closely related to the individualistic norms already discussed. Attention is allocated according to norms in which each individual is responsible for himself, and is free, within limits of civility, to take as much as he can. These norms legitimate focusing on one's own needs in informal talk and are consistent with the effort by self-oriented conversationalists to gain predominant attention for themselves.

The Forms of Conversational Narcissism

Conversational narcissism is the key manifestation of the dominant attention-getting psychology in America. It occurs in informal conversations among friends, family, and coworkers. The profusion of popular literature about listening and the etiquette of managing those who talk constantly about themselves suggests its pervasiveness in everyday life; its contemporary importance is indicated by the early appearance of these problems in Emily Post's etiquette manual.

In observations of ordinary conversations, I have found a set of extremely common conversational practices that show an unresponsiveness to others' topics and involve turning them into one's own. Because of norms prohibiting blatantly egocentric behavior, these practices are often exquisitely subtle; ritual forms of civility and face-saving have evolved to limit the overt expression of egoism in social life. Although conversationalists are free to introduce topics about themselves, they are expected to maintain an appearance of genuine interest in those about others in the conversation. A delicate face-saving system requires that people refrain from openly disregarding others' concerns and keep expressions of disinterest from becoming visible. Practices of conversational narcissism are normally, then, driven underground and expressed in disguised forms where they are not readily discerned by any member of the conversation.

To explore the narcissistic practices that occur most often, we must distinguish between two kinds of attention-response: the *shift-response* and the *support-response*. The shift- and support-responses are alternative ways one can react to others' conversational initiatives. The differences between the two can be seen in the following examples:

JOHN: I'm feeling really starved.
MARY: Oh, I just ate. (shift-response)
JOHN: I'm feeling really starved.
MARY: When was the last time you ate? (support-response)

JOHN: God, I'm feeling so angry at Bob.
MARY: Yeah, I've been feeling the same way toward him. (shift-response)
JOHN: God, I'm feeling so angry at Bob.
MARY: Why, what's been going on between the two of you? (support-response)

JOHN: My mother would pack me melted cheese sandwiches every day.
MARY: My mom never made me a lunch I could stand to eat. (shift-response)
JOHN: My mother would pack me melted cheese sandwiches every day.

MARY: Hey, your mother was all right. (support-response)

JOHN: I saw Jane today on the street.
MARY: I haven't seen her in a week. (shift-response)
JOHN: I saw Jane today on the street.
MARY: Oh, how's she doing? (support-response)

JOHN: I just love Brahms.
MARY: Chopin's my favorite. (shift-response)
JOHN: I just love Brahms.
MARY: Which is your favorite piece? (support-response)

The shift-response and support-response are both commonly used. They are superficially so little different that few conversationalists notice the distinction. Yet they affect the flow of attention and the development of topics in markedly different ways. When Mary uses the shift-response, she temporarily shifts the attention to herself and creates the potential for a change in topic. When using the support-response, she keeps the attention and topic securely focused on John.

Of the two responses, only the shift-response changes who is the subject of the conversation. For example, if Mary says to John, "I'm going to the movies tonight," John can temporarily make himself the subject with any of the following replies:

That reminds me, I've got to go home tonight.

I'm sick of movies these days.

Gee, I wonder what I'm going to do tonight.

With each of these shift-responses, John introduces the dilemma of whether the conversation will continue with Mary as the subject or will turn to him. Alternatively, he could offer the following kinds of support-responses:

What movie?

Great, you deserve a break.

Are you feeling good enough to go?

These support-responses are attention-giving ones not in competition with Mary's initial assertion. They keep the conversation clearly focused on her and give her license to continue as the subject. Support-responses, unlike shift-responses, cannot normally be introduced to transfer attention to the self.

Conversational narcissism involves preferential use of the shift-response and underutilization of the support-response. We can distinguish between active and passive narcissistic practices. The active practices involve repeated use of the shift-response to subtly turn the topics of others into topics about oneself. The passive practices involve minimal use of support-responses so that others' topics are not sufficiently reinforced and so are terminated prematurely.

Active Practices

The shift-response is the one response to another's initiative through which one can introduce one's own topic. While it does not necessarily change the topic—and is frequently not so intended—it nonetheless always creates the possibility. The following dialogue illustrates how the shift-response is typically used by self-oriented conversationalists to bring attention to themselves:

MARY: My summer place has been such a blessing this year.

JOHN: I know, I sure would like a place like that, the way I've been feeling, but I've got to earn the bread first, you know?

MARY: Yeah.

JOHN: I figure that if I work enough this year and next, I'll be able to check that place out in Vermont again and maybe....

Although John appears, in his first response, to have expanded on Mary's topic, he has subtly shifted the attention to himself. He has not responded directly to her feelings but has shifted the conversation to his own state of mind, his problems with money, and his desires for a summer place of his own. Rather than returning to her topic, Mary then responds with a support-response allowing John in the following turn to consolidate his earlier topical initiative.

While changing the topic, John links his response to Mary's and prefaces his own with an acknowledgment of hers. The preface is a token gesture of recognition of what the other has said. Numerous other prefaces such as "oh really," "huh," "isn't that something," "same here," and "I can't believe it" recur in conversations. They soften the transition in topic and help to protect the individual against charges of unresponsiveness. A preface acknowledges that one is paying attention to the previous statement and adds legitimacy to an assertion in which the individual suddenly introduces himself as the subject. It also presents the interjection of oneself as not simply an effort to gain attention, but rather a form of responsiveness to share personal experience or information.

Although important for maintaining civility, a shift-response does not require a preface. For example:

JOHN: I've got such a huge appetite.
BILL: I couldn't eat a thing.

JOHN: My father would take me every two weeks to a game and I spent every minute looking forward to it.
BILL: I remember the first game my father took me to. I made so much noise that he didn't want to take me anymore.

Here, the shifts in focus are legitimized by the appearance of a topical connection. The subtlety of the shift-response is that it is always based on a connection to the previous subject. This creates an opening for the respondent to shift the topic to himself while still preserving the "face" of the other.

While repeating the shift-response is the most common way self-oriented conversationalists seek attention, it does not always imply conversational narcissism. The shift-response can serve either as a sharing-response or as a narcissistic topical initiative. The major difference lies not in introducing the shift-response, but in the intent and the statements that follow. When serving narcissistic ends, shift-responses are repeated until a clear shift in subject has transpired. When meant only as sharing-responses, interjecting oneself is temporary and is quickly followed by returning to the original topic. In these instances, the shift-response only briefly brings attention to oneself as a means of furthering the conversation.

The effectiveness of the shift-response as an attention-getting device lies partly in the difficulty in distinguishing immediately whether a given response is a sharing one or a narcissistic initiative. At a certain stage in the development of another's topic, it becomes appropriate to introduce information about oneself, but normally not until the other has introduced most of his information or narrative. The earlier the initial shift-response, the more likely it foreshadows an effort to seize the conversation. This is illustrated in the following conversation:

MARY: I saw the most beautiful rainbow today.
JOHN: Wow, I saw a lovely one just last week.

At this point, Mary cannot know whether John actually is interested in her experience or in simply turning the talk to himself. His statement is connected to hers and may well represent an honest attempt to share his experience or to highlight hers. But it may also signal a narcissistic initiative, which would be confirmed if he persists in using the shift-response.

MARY: I saw the most beautiful rainbow today.
JOHN: Wow, I saw a lovely one just last week.

MARY: It had such a magnificent blend of blues and golds.

JOHN: Huh, the one I saw was all reds and yellows.

John's repeated shift-responses have now become a competing initiative that make it more difficult for Mary to sustain her own subject. A decisive topical shift occurs in the next turn as Mary, despite her option to continue with her own topic, accommodates John's initiative with a support-response:

MARY: I saw the most beautiful rainbow today.

JOHN: Wow, I saw such a lovely one last week.

MARY: It had such a magnificent blend of blues and golds.

JOHN: Huh, the one I saw was all reds and yellows.

MARY: What time of day did you see it?

JOHN: Early afternoon. I was walking near the river and. . . .

The active narcissistic practice always follows some variation of this pattern, in which repetitions of the shift-response turn the conversation to oneself. The shift-response functions as a "gaining initiative," which introduces one's own topic. It sets the stage for a topic competition that will persist as long as each conversationalist continues to use a shift-response. The self-oriented conversationalist triumphs in this competition when his shift-response succeeds in eliciting a succession of support-responses from others, thus securing their acquiescence to his topic.

Incessant use of the shift-response is not typical because it is too baldly egoistic and disruptive. A more acceptable—and more pervasive—approach is one where a conversationalist makes temporary responsive concessions to others' topics before intervening to turn the focus back to himself. The self-oriented conversationalist mixes shift-responses with support-responses, leaving the impression that he has interest in others as well as himself.

JIM: You know, I've been wanting to get a car for so long.

BILL: Yeah. (support-response)

JIM: Maybe when I get the job this summer, I'll finally buy one. But they're so expensive.

BILL: I was just thinking about how much I spend on my car. I think over $2,500 a year. You know I had to lay out over $750 for insurance. And $850 for that fender job. (shift-response)

JIM: Yeah, it's absurd. (support-response)

BILL: I'm sick of cars. I've been thinking of getting a bicycle and getting around in a healthy way. I saw a great red racer up in that bike shop on Parkhurst Ave.

JIM: I love bikes. But I'm just really feeling a need for a car now. I want to be able to drive up the coast whenever I want. (shift-response)

BILL: Uh huh. (support-response)

JIM: I could really get into a convertible.

BILL: Oh, you can go anywhere on a bike. I'm going to borrow John's bike and go way up north next weekend. You know, a couple of weekends ago Sue and I rented bikes and rode down toward the Cape.... (shift-response)

The narcissistic initiative and the ensuing topic competition is subtle here. From a casual reading of the transcript there appears to be a responsive exchange with no readily discernible egocentricity. But a more careful examination reveals the familiar narcissistic pattern. Bill responds initially to Jim's topic with a support-response that indicates acknowledgment and at least minimal interest. Most of his subsequent responses, however, are shift-responses that change the topic from Jim's desires for a new car to a discussion of his own car and then to his own interest in bicycles. Jim makes several efforts to steer the conversation back to his original concern, but Bill's attention-getting initiatives are successful. In the end, he launches into a story about his bike trip, which decisively shifts the topic to himself.

This interchange exemplifies the pattern of active conversational narcissism. One conversationalist transforms another's topic into one pertaining to himself through persistent use of the shift-response. The topic-shift is accomplished prematurely, before the first speaker has had the opportunity to complete what he regards as the full development of his subject. Yet it is accomplished without violation of the ritual obligations of responsiveness and occasions no blatant injuries of face.

Passive Practices

Passive practices constitute a more subtle expression of narcissism, characterized not by the grabbing of attention but by miserliness in the responses given to others. Such practices involve underutilization of the support-responses that normally allow others to pursue their topics. The effect is to let the other's topics die through lack of encouragement, thereby opening the floor to the initiation of one's own topics.

To analyze the passive practices which recur most frequently, we must first distinguish among three different kinds of support-responses, which I call: *the background acknowledgment, the supportive assertion,* and *the supportive question. Background acknowledgments* are abbreviated responses such as "uh huh," "yeah," "oh really," and "umm." They are the weakest of the support-responses, but their use is important because they give the appearance that one is listening and wants the speaker to continue. *Supportive assertions* are complete declarative responses to the topic initiatives of others and include evaluative statements ("I think that's great"), comments ("I never would have thought of him"), and suggestions ("You must see her right away"). A supportive assertion is a stronger response than the background acknowledgment, for it not only confirms that one is listening but indicates active engagement in the topic. *Supportive questions* are queries that draw out a speaker on his topic. They are the most encouraging of all support-responses and the most active way of assuring that another's topic will be sustained.

Passive practices involve *minimal use* and *differential use* of these three types of support-responses so that the topics of others are prematurely concluded. Minimal use contributes to the termination of a topic by withholding or delaying support-responses. Differential use means that a weaker support-response is chosen when a stronger one could be used.

Minimal use. Conversationalists cannot refrain from making any support-responses in the course of a conversation, as this would indicate too blatant an indifference to the other's topic. Minimal use entails, then, a subtle unresponsiveness, where there is compliance with ritual expressions of attentiveness, but nevertheless a relative neglect of support-responses.

The most devastating form is the avoidance of the supportive question. While not all topics depend on such questions for their perpetuation, a high percentage are carried, particularly in the early phases, by others' queries. While a topic can be aborted at any point by lack of interest, a lack of support and interest when it is first initiated most effectively kills it. One can speak of the take-off points or critical thresholds that shape the life expectancy of the topic. If, in the first several turns of talk, the topic reaches take-off, it is far less vulnerable to derailment by minimal use. Prior to take-off, topics die if they do not elicit either enthusiastic background acknowledgments or responsive questions that give explicit indication of support and interest. A string of supportive questions at the opening of a topic will normally guarantee a respectable life-expectancy for the topic, while the absence of any questions at this stage can be an ominous sign which signals premature termination.

Despite their importance, supportive questions are typically discretionary; under most circumstances, conversationalists are free to ask questions but are also at liberty not to. While there are certain initiatives that call for a mandatory response (if someone says, "I'm feeling so terrible," a supportive question like "What's wrong?" would normally be expected in return), most initiatives allow for far greater discretion. If John makes a topical initiative by saying, "I saw my friend Bill today," Jim can show active interest with a supportive question such as "How's he feeling?" or "How did it go?" He commits no offense, however, if he simply offers a background acknowledgment such as "hummm" or volunteers no support-response whatsoever.

Passive conversational narcissism entails neglect of supportive questions at all such discretionary points and extremely sparse use of them throughout conversation. Listening behavior takes place but is passive. There is little attempt to draw others out or assume other forms of active listening. This creates doubt in the others regarding the interest of their topics or their rights to attention while, however, providing no clear basis for complaint about either inattentiveness or narcissism.

A second very common minimal-use practice involves the underutilization or delay of background acknowledgments. Although weaker than supportive questions, background acknowledgments such as "yeah" or "uh huh" are nonetheless critical cues by which speakers gauge the degree of interest in their topics. A variety of studies suggest that background acknowledgments facilitate the unfolding of topics and that their absence or delay can easily disrupt the development of the speaker's topic.

Ritual restraints preclude withholding all background acknowledgments. Every conversationalist is expected to extend such minimal support even when he has no interest whatsoever in the topic. Speakers can exploit this expectation by interjecting expressions such as "you know," subtle requests for immediate affirmations that indicate the other is paying attention. This is a way that conversationalists insecure about others' attention or interest can actively solicit support.

Despite the ritual constraints, there is sufficient freedom to permit a potent form of minimal response. While this can involve avoiding the background acknowledgment, it most often assumes the form of a delay in its insertion so that the speaker does not receive the immediate reinforcement that permits smooth continuation of his line of thought. Studies have shown that background acknowledgments can be placed with precision timing and are often perfectly inserted during split-second pauses of the other's speech. Conversationalists who delay their responses for up to several seconds after another speaker has paused can throw him off-balance, disrupting his flow of speech and causing him to wonder whether his listeners are genuinely interested. Repetition of the delayed response creates more gaps in the rhythm, slowing the momentum of the conversation further and suggesting the need for a change in topic. Such passive narcissism is rarely a conscious device to gain attention but is nonetheless a common means by which self-oriented conversationalists "underrespond" to the topics of others and thus open the floor to their own.

Differential use.   Differential use involves the offering of the weakest support-response consistent with the demands of civility. By exercising his discretion to select the least encouraging support-response, the self-oriented conversationalist hastens the termination of others' topics. This is often accomplished by the use of background acknowledgments where far stronger responses, especially a supportive question, might be more appropriate:

MARY: Oh, I had the most awful headache all day. Tom was awful at work and, uh, just kept bothering me and bothering me. And Louise, too, more of the same. I'm so sick of it.
JOHN: Yeah.

In this instance, Mary has opened with a complaint calling for a stronger, more supportive response than the one offered. Typically, with such openings, a supportive question to draw out the speaker's feelings or experiences sets the stage for fully playing out the topic. By substituting the minimal acknowledgment where a question could have been asked, John discourages Mary's initiative. She has the option to continue but will find it difficult to do so in the face of repeated discouragement of this form.

Different conversationalists vary in their vulnerability to such discouragement, depending on their assertiveness, security, and other personality factors affecting their need for responsiveness from others. Those most vulnerable are those dependent on the strongest support-responses, on being drawn out through supportive questioning. Differential use will effectively silence these speakers. At the other extreme, the most aggressive conversationalists will pursue their topics even when their initiatives elicit only weak background acknowledgments or none at all. The only effective narcissistic practice with such speakers is an active one, through aggressive use of the shift-response in one's own behalf.

Successfully aborting others' topics does not always ensure a turning of conversation to oneself, but, at minimum, prepares the stage for this possibility. At topic termination any speaker may seek to initiate his or her own topic. A second topic competition can then follow which may or may not reproduce the characteristics of the one just completed. In the pure narcissistic pattern, a conversationalist will act to discourage every topic and initiate continuing competition until he or she succeeds in securely establishing his or her own. In practice, few conversationalists remain unresponsive to *all* topics of others but will exercise selective discretion, reinforcing with support-responses a limited number that are of interest and discouraging the others with minimal and differential use.

4

Newtown Is Just the Tip of the Iceberg

On December 12, 2012, the rampage in Sandy Hook Elementary School in Newtown, Connecticut, killing twenty beautiful, innocent children between the ages of five and ten, shook the nation. Americans felt grief and fear in their bones. No event more viscerally communicated the meaning and reality of the terrifying sociopathy in our schools, workplaces, churches, and streets.

Newtown was no isolated event. Mass shootings, such as at Virginia Tech, Columbine High School, and Aurora, Colorado, are iconic, defining a new Wild West (but hardly restricted to the US West) of ferocious violence, rage, and destruction. Liberals pin the problem on guns and lack of serious gun control; conservatives blame mentally ill people and Hollywood.

Newtown, though, symbolized a deeper crisis, starting with the reality that mass shootings and rampages are just the tip of the iceberg of broader violence, and especially gun violence, that defines the US social landscape. Guns and shootings happen in towns and cities every day, at a rate many times higher than that of any other developed nation. Guns are everywhere, with estimates ranging between about 90 guns for every 100 people, or about 300 million guns in US households, to low-ball estimates of 100 million guns.

An armed population is defined as not just legal but a revered constitutional right. Laws give people the right to carry concealed weapons into schools, workplaces, and bars. The Florida "Stand Your Ground" law—used as a legal defense in the 2012 killing of an innocent seventeen-year-old African American, Treyvon Martin, by George Zimmerman, a Neighborhood Watch Volunteer—affirms the right to shoot others in everyday circumstances subjectively perceived by an individual as threatening, a right viewed by many as integral to the morality of a free people. *This view of gun ownership and armed violence as a sacred legal right and social norm is a frightening sign of the culture of a sociopathic society, with everyday interactions always bearing the risk of socially approved violent behavior.*

Sociopathic society is marked by a more encompassing sociopathic culture, which breeds nonviolent harms, such as conversational narcissism and routine cheating. But our constitutionalized and morally celebrated gun culture is its most transparent and violent expression. It is an integral part of US history and culture, including our concepts of private property, personal liberty, defense against government tyranny, and the cultural individualism and self-reliance widely seen as the heart of the American Dream.

As shown throughout this book, it is impossible to separate the culture from the intertwined economic, political, and military sides of sociopathic society. Our gun culture is an engine of—and driven by—vast profit, especially for the huge gun companies and manufacturers, such as Freedom Group (which owns Remington, Bushmaster, and others), Colt, Smith and Wesson, and US Repeating Arms. The NRA is essentially a trade association of these gun corporations, funded by the industry to protect their right to sell all their brands of guns, ammunition, and other accessories.

The gun companies, like the tobacco companies, are among the most sociopathic corporations, putting profits over the most socially harmful products. They see recruiting new young shooters as "imperative to the survival of the industry" and have moved aggressively in recent years to capture the youth market, sponsoring gun programs for elementary and high schools, the Boy Scouts and Girl Scouts, 4-H groups, and even church groups—and encouraging family trips to the gun range and gun show for fun, self-defense, and character development. The targets include children as young as four or five, although the prime marketing, carried out through industry-supported print media such as Junior Shooters, targets teenagers between eight and eighteen, with the older kids seen as "peer ambassadors" to enlisting younger siblings or friends. Industry-supported magazines discuss the imperative of getting youngsters involved early in "shooting anything," perhaps moving from archery to firearms, including semiautomatic weapons. One ad in a sports shooting industry-funded magazine directed at kids says "Maybe you'll find a Bushmaster AR-15 under your tree some frosty morning," the semiautomatic high-capacity magazine gun used by the shooters at Newtown, Aurora, and Columbine.[1]

The NRA, as one of the nation's most powerful lobbying groups, symbolizes the political sociopathy of gun violence in sociopathic society. Polls show that a majority of the public favors stronger gun control laws, including bans on semiautomatic weapons and on high-capacity magazines. Yet, even after Newtown, while President Obama proposed limited bans, Congress seems incapable of any serious gun control legislation banning universal background checks or the sale of even military-style assault weapons. The failure to pass such laws epitomizes political sociopathy, since political elites prioritize the profits of their corporate patrons over the safety of children and the larger public interest. It is perhaps no coincidence that the leading congressional—mainly Republican and Tea Party—conservatives rising after the 2010 elections called themselves the "Young Guns."

Finally, the military side of sociopathy plays a huge role in our gun crisis that has drawn little public discussion from either liberals or conservatives. Historically militaristic societies involved in imperial foreign policy and wars have cultivated an armed public and the arts of shooting as essential parts of their culture. Boys in empires or superpowers have to be raised to be warriors, a "civic virtue" much touted by presidents such as Teddy Roosevelt, who criticized universities such as Harvard for going soft and failing to develop in their curricula and campus culture the fighting skills of his own "rough riders."

While a later chapter discusses the relation between violence abroad and at home, the moral legitimation of both forms of violence deserves special attention in any discussion of sociopathic culture and everyday life. US wars are wrapped in lofty moral rhetoric of spreading liberty and defeating evil enemies, whether communists or terrorists. Defining unjust wars—for example, in pursuit of oil or power in the Middle East—as good and godly puts a halo around mass violence at home as well. Young Americans, even without a draft, know that soldiers their age are celebrated as heroes for gun violence in wars such as Iraq or Afghanistan, leaving at minimum great confusion about how they should view the morality of guns and gun violence. There is no easy boundary drawn between the military and civilian sides of our culture, since the same gun corporations manufacture arms and ammunitions for both soldiers and civilians, and military bases in every congressional district of the United States are deeply involved in the schools, civic groups, and community economies around them. Military culture—and its sociopathic ideals—is a root cause of a sociopathic society that places high moral and constitutional value on guns and gun violence.

Part III

Sociopathic Capitalism

Introduction to Part III

Is US Capitalism Antisocial?

In Chapter 1, I showed that the overriding goal of the founders of modern social theory—Marx, Weber, and Durkheim—was to understand the new industrial capitalism taking shape during their lifetimes. It was a new system with great promise but also a structural "poison pill" because of its frightening sociopathy.

The nineteenth-century theorists, especially Marx and, secondarily, Weber, felt that human liberation would require another transformation toward a more social and democratic political economy. But that transformative analysis has largely faded in the United States, just when we most need it. My purpose is to try to help revive it.

I do so in Part III with chapters on the sociopathic DNA that molds US corporate capitalism today. The first two chapters focus on capitalism itself, going to its greatest critic. In 2009 I went to London's Highgate cemetery, where Marx is buried. I report on my night-time conversation with his ghost about how to understand the 2008 Wall Street meltdown and the broader sociopathic dangers of twenty-first-century corporate capitalism. The ghost reaffirms precisely why US capitalism is systemically sociopathic and how it endangers its own survival.

The second chapter in this section shows that a newly intensified problem of "surplus people" is one of the great sociopathic capitalist crises. The United States is no longer a manufacturing economy, but it manufactures a huge surplus population of people. This includes not only the official unemployed and underemployed but millions of students, prisoners, soldiers, and retirees. The surplus crisis hits the young especially hard, and it bodes ill for the future.

The modern giant global corporation is the center of power in the United States. The third chapter looks at the corporation as it developed since the

Gilded Age, when corporate Robber Barons such as John D. Rockefeller and J. P. Morgan created its modern form. They crafted an institution in their own image: a much-admired institutional "robber" run by industrial and financial barons who steal from workers and make money by weakening society.

As in the Gilded Age, the United States now operates on corporate values and under corporate control. Corporations increasingly own or help fund and manage giant media empires, huge hospitals, great universities, the largest churches, and government itself. Government is a marriage of corporate and political elites that I call a "corpocracy," sociopathic because it erodes democracy and weakens society to serve the rich. In the fourth chapter of Part III, I define such a thoroughly corporatized society as a "corporate regime," where corporate power exceeds popular power and profits trump people.

The last main chapter in this part focuses on globalization. The US capitalist system has moved decisively toward the global theater, and its leading actors—the giant corporations—are all global. Globalization has virtues, but its current form is sociopathic, subjecting most of the world's workers, resources, and nations to the control of a global, predatory corporate elite. I explore the history of globalization and discuss three myths that have obscured the sociopathic DNA in the bedrock of corporate or neoliberal globalization.

Part III ends with two short essays on the sociopathic deformation of an American political system run by unlimited corporate money, bending government to serve corporate profits while abandoning the needs of what 2012 plutocratic Republican candidate Mitt Romney called the parasitical "47 percent."

5

Capitalist Crises and Capitalism against Society

The Ghost Talks Crisis and Systemic Risk

The ghost paused again. "But we are getting ahead of ourselves. Let's focus a bit more on the Great Recession in the United States that nearly wiped out Wall Street and the whole world economy. In late 2008 US economists and politicians were so scared they started talking about nationalizing the banks, insurance companies, car companies, and other corporations. In fact, George W. Bush, of all people, started down that path with those multibillion-dollar bailouts of AIG, Goldman Sachs, and Bank of America. The government took over majority ownership of AIG, General Motors, and other big companies." The ghost suddenly stopped and seemed to smile at the irony. "What does it tell you when President Bush follows my dictates and begins to socialize the biggest banks? When the government owns AIG and GM becomes Government Motors?"

The ghost didn't wait for my answer. "Suddenly, everybody is talking about 'systemic risk,'" the ghost said with evident satisfaction. "The elite suddenly realized that one or two huge financial companies such as AIG or Citibank could go down and take the whole system with them. For a world addicted to TINA, that is hugely significant."

Specter of Collapse: From Marxist to Mainstream

In 2008 the fear of collapse was so great that the government bailed out AIG with $180 billion, the biggest bailout in history. By early 2011, the Federal Reserve had pumped more than $3 trillion into the system to try to save it.

"The roller coaster is scary," I agreed, "but what exactly are you getting at?"

"When the idea of 'systemic risk' enters the daily vocabulary," the ghost smiled in his spooky way, "then suddenly people are thinking about the survival of the whole system—and whether it will actually self-destruct."

"What are you getting at?"

"This is new in a 'There Is No Alternative' (TINA) world because it suggests that there is indeed an alternative world to our capitalist one. In fact, several! One is collapse and no system at all. A second is a more just and democratic alter-capitalist or post-capitalist system. A third alternative possibility is the scariest, a new neo-fascist or theocratic state."

"I don't follow you," I said argumentatively. "Just because capitalism is very unstable doesn't mean that some new alternative will emerge. The current system could muddle through."

Crises and Barbarism

Marx wrote, "It is enough to mention the commercial crises that by their political return put on its trial, each time more threateningly, the existence of the entire bourgeois society. In these crises a great part not only of the existing products, but also of the previously existed productive forces, are periodically destroyed...." Marx concludes that society reverts to deeper states of "barbarism" with each new crisis.

The ghost looked at me as if I were an idiot. "You're missing the point. For one thing, each new crisis is unbelievably destructive—and we're not talking about creative destruction. In the 2008 Wall Street implosion, trillions of dollars vanished in thin air. This led to trillions in new public and private debt, making the United States almost bankrupt. In 2010 and 2011, 15 million Americans were unemployed, and your workers face the terror of long-term permanent joblessness. Talk about terrorism!!! Half the US population worries about losing a job, a pension, or a house. The prospect of a jobless recovery and the double dips of the huge housing and financial crises are serious concerns even among mainstream economists."

"Well, such crises are not exactly new—and capitalism bounces back each time." I wanted this ghost to admit how wrong he's been about the resiliency of the system.

"True enough," the ghost acknowledged. "Capitalism, especially in the United States, always has business cycles and systemic crises—and it *is* resilient. Far more so than I imagined. But just look at the last half century to see the trend. The crises seem to be coming now almost every decade—and each recovery has seen weaker job growth and more wage stagnation, what mainstream economists call a pattern of jobless recoveries."

The ghost stopped to absorb this reality and continued, "These have all been massive system failures with human costs almost too great to calculate. In each case, jobs come back more slowly and wage levels decline. These crises with jobless recoveries hit one or two times in each of the last few decades."

"True," I had to acknowledge, "crises are coming fast and furious. But what does that prove?"

"A system characterized by such frequent crises is a system in deep trouble. As capitalism matures, its crises inevitably come even faster and deeper—a recipe for complete system failure sometime down the road. That is unacceptable, really unbelievable, in a TINA world that says there is no alternative to the system we have now."

The Real Truth about the Great Recession of 2008—and the Secret of Capitalist Crises

The ghost was in his element now, fired up by one of his favorite subjects, capitalist crises destined to bring down capitalism itself!

"But to understand the 2008 Great Recession and the crises coming up, you have to remember," the ghost said, "that capitalism and crisis have always been linked at the hip—inseparable! If you look at the history of capitalism," the ghost reminded me, "its revolutionary spurts forward have always produced crises of enormous destruction that shake the system itself. Crises are in the DNA of capitalism."

"You always said," I told him, "that capitalism is the most astonishingly productive, revolutionary system in history. But you also said it is the most destructive, and doomed to deeper and deeper crises of its own making that would undermine it."

"Yes," the ghost said. "This helps define capitalism—the contradictory mix of creativity and destruction, of growth and stagnation, all intertwined in the system's DNA."

"I was never," I said truthfully, "persuaded by your views of the inevitable self-destruction of capitalism. Yes, crises will always recur, but capitalism has always rebounded. Your arguments for inevitability of a terminal crisis always seemed something of a wish-fulfillment instead of credible analysis."

The ghost looked at me with dismay. "It's hard to believe that you have not grasped the essence of my crisis arguments. They are so critical to understanding and changing the system. They are, if I can say so myself, a key foundation for the survival of humanity. You seem to not grasp them because you are a bit of a TINA believer yourself. Must I repeat them for you?"

"I wish you would. So much depends on whether you are right."

The ghost looked like an exasperated teacher. He couldn't quite believe my

Capitalist Crises Coming Faster and Faster

- A huge stagflation crisis in the late 1970s and a big recession of the early 1980s.
- The financial crisis at the end of the 1980s, including the S&L catastrophe that some feared would bring down the entire US economy.
- The 1990s Wall Street mania leading to the high-tech boom and a shattering stock market crash in the late nineties.
- The 2008 Great Recession that threatened total collapse.
- The 2010 spread of the financial crisis to Greece, Ireland, Portugal, and other EU countries that are closely linked to Wall Street and the larger US economy.

Marx's Ode to Capitalism

"The bourgeoisie, during its rule of scarce one hundred years, has created more massive and more colossal productive forces than have all preceding generations together."

Marx on the Crisis on Main Street

"In these crises there breaks out an epidemic that in all earlier epochs would have seemed an absurdity—the epidemic of over-production.... Capitalists must accumulate while the mass of producers (workers) must be restricted in their consumption of subsistence.... The last cause of all real crises always remains the poverty and restricted consumption of the masses...."

skepticism. "I'm disappointed in you. I made these points over and over again, with great clarity. Go back and read some of my twentieth-century disciples such as Paul Sweezy and Paul Baran, American Marxist professors and writers who got it right in their classic book *Monopoly Capital*. Maybe they'll straighten you out."

I remembered reading the book in graduate school. "Yes, I was impressed by their work," I acknowledged. "They argued that you had foretold that capitalism's natural state was stagnation as the system matured. Stagnation and overproduction—crises on Main Street and in the blue-chip corporations—become the norm. There would be fewer opportunities for profitable investment as industries and technologies matured and became less dynamic, markets saturated, jobs were lost, and wages pushed down, reducing the buying power of workers. Big corporate monopolies become ever less innovative and can't sell enough as workers become poorer. They turn to financial speculation to make big money. And they create easy credit for workers, leading them into big, unsustainable personal debt in order to spur them to buy more houses, cars, and goodies at the mall. All to boost the economy, just as it happened in 2008 in the Great Recession."

"Yes," the ghost said, "I had seen even in the nineteenth century that monopoly, stagnation, growing unemployment and inequality, and, finally, financial casinos were the irreversible long-term trend. *The Wall Street crises follow the crises in the 'real economy,' not the reverse as is usually thought. At the heart of the matter is the jobs and wage crisis, inherent in capitalism itself, as jobs are eliminated, unions destroyed, and wages keep falling, undercutting consumer demand, increasing the gap between rich and poor, and threatening the entire system. The financial and debt crises are a response to long-term stagnation on Main Street, reflecting a desperate effort by capitalists to keep profits high as workers' jobs vanish and wages stagnate or fall over many decades.*"

It's Capitalism, Stupid

Marx wrote, "Monetary phenomena make crises possible; they do not cause them."

"This is exactly what caused our current crisis! Thirty years of stagnation in US workers' wages, as unions were destroyed, unemployment grew, and wealth ever more concentrated among the rich." I remembered that US wages for all but the very rich had been stagnant for decades.

"Now you're seeing capitalism's heart of darkness." The ghost was pleased.

Low Wages: American Capitalism's Dirty Secret

While US workers have been working harder and harder over the last several decades, their real wages have been stagnant and declining.

Average Real Wages of US Workers (in 2008 dollars)

1972	$20.06
1979	$18.76
1993	$16.82
2008	$18.52

US wages were lower in 2008 than in 1972, despite significant economic growth. Who got the money? The rich. The richest 1 percent claimed 23.5 percent of all national income in 2007, the most since 1928.

Nickel and Dimed: Yes, It's Capitalism, Stupid

"What do you mean?" I asked.

"The Great Recession of 2008, like all capitalist crises, is the inevitable sour 'dessert' following the capitalist 'main dish.' Greed on Wall Street did not cause the crisis, although it is part of the story."

"What is the real story then?"

"The Great Recession arose from capitalism itself; it was wired into its DNA. It is the inevitable result of the way capitalism operates routinely, for decades before the crisis explodes."

"You're saying the secret of the crisis is that capitalism is really permanently in crisis, a crisis below the radar screen in 'normal times.' It is just the inevitable result of the inner laws of capitalism itself, even when things seem normal and nobody is worried about crisis."

"Yes, precisely," the ghost nodded.

"Please explain."

"Let's keep it simple. You remember," the ghost asked me, "the big 2001 best seller *Nickel and Dimed,* by the journalist Barbara Ehrenreich?"

"Yes," I recalled, "she went undercover and took jobs as a waitress, a cleaner, and other low-income positions. People in these jobs were ripped off by their employers, who used every trick in the book to keep from paying them a decent salary."

The ghost nodded. "She said they were 'nickel and dimed,' all true. But the bigger story is that nearly all US workers got nickel and dimed over the last several decades. This is the real story of capitalism—and it is the real cause of the 2008 Great Recession. No wonder Ehrenreich is a socialist and has been president of the Democratic Socialists of America."

"So the media call it a financial and Wall Street crisis, but you're saying 'It's capitalism, stupid.' It's the capitalist way and it will keep happening because of the way capitalism's DNA is designed."

"Yes, and it's not just about wages, although that's crucial. It's about the nickel and diming of most Americans—not just low-income waitresses and maids—as the middle classes sink in all aspects of their economic and social lives while a tiny rich elite cream off the wealth, creating a massive class division, just as I predicted."

Capitalism against Society: Extreme Inequality and Social Breakdown

"Let's look at the big picture before the Great Recession," the ghost continued, "because it's the only real way to understand what happened in 2008 and in future even greater crises to come."

"What big picture?"

"The picture of capitalism as it evolves over centuries. The truth is that as capitalism matures, it creates great wealth but also a growing class division between the rich and everyone else that eats away at society itself. It becomes increasingly a system of extreme inequality and of permanent crisis for the majority of workers. These long-term class divisions and deepening social crises are under the radar screen, ignored by the media until they lead to the super-explosions such as the 2008 Great Recession that the media cannot ignore."

"So great crises are like world wars that are simply exaggerations of small wars and that are festering and growing all the time as capitalism develops?"

Bi-Polar Depression

Marx wrote, "Society as a whole is more and more splitting up into two great hostile camps, into two great classes facing each other: Bourgeoisie and Proletariat." The result was inevitable class war as the economy veered toward depression and collapse.

"Yes, you can say that the great crises are simply inevitable results of the growth of capitalism itself, as extreme inequality and great class divisions intensify. Society polarizes between great corporate monopolies whose great wealth helps them control the state—and everyone else. The corporations launch class warfare backed by government: starting with an intense attack on unions and the buying of politicians. President Reagan's first act as president was to destroy the Air Traffic Control Union (PATCO), the beginning of the Reagan revolution's assault on the labor movement. A blizzard of social and economics problems increasingly plague most workers—from job insecurity, unemployment, and low wages to indebtedness, homelessness, hunger, and poverty—and they just get worse and worse. Society itself begins to fracture and fall apart."

"But capitalism has increased the well-being of workers over the centuries," I protested. "American workers live in big homes, drive big cars, and have many televisions and computers. How can you deny capitalism's great wealth creation? More than any system in history," I said defiantly.

"True, capitalism generates great wealth—I always said it was the most remarkably productive system ever seen. Workers have gotten some real creature comforts and improvements in their standard of living, in fact more than I thought possible. *But over time, just as I predicted, overproduction and stagnation set in and class divisions hardened and worsened, and class warfare intensified with the attack on unions and public services, making for an epidemic of social problems threatening not just workers but capitalism and the existence of society itself.* Consider the trends just since 1980."

"Which ones?"

"We have seen that, with the rise of globalization and the attack on unions, wages stagnated and declined for the majority of

Capitalism and Wealth: Marx Was Right

In 2009, the bottom 80 percent of Americans owned only 12.8 percent of the nation's wealth. The richest 20 percent owned 87.2 percent. This is the greatest concentration of wealth in the rich since the 1920s, and follows Marx's prediction of a growing bi-polar wealth distribution between the rich and everyone else.

US workers since the 1970s, despite real growth in the economy and national wealth. While the top 1 percent more than doubled their family income in the last 30 years, the bottom 60 percent saw almost no growth in their family income in the same long period, despite working many more jobs and hours per household." The ghost paused and added, "The problem for the majority is even worse when it comes to wealth. Over many decades, wealth has continued to concentrate to the point that in 2007, the 400 richest US families had net assets of $1.6 trillion, approximately the same wealth as the bottom 50 percent, or 150 million people. *The bottom 50 percent of the population keeps losing wealth. They now own only 2.5 percent of the nation's total wealth. They also now own less than 1 percent of all the stocks and bonds and mutual funds assets in the United States.*" The ghost was visibly agitated.

"Why does this bother you so much?"

"It's a moral scandal—this concentration of wealth in the very richest 1 percent and the relative bankrupting of the working and middle classes. Most of the politicians and media ignore it or lie about it, even though the elites helped create the problem by a ferocious attack on unions and buying out politicians on the make. Such extreme inequality undermines the basis of society itself. Most people worked longer and harder over the last generation while they kept losing income, power, and self-respect, even as the economy kept growing. A tiny corporate elite creamed off the wealth that everyone else produces, throwing the population into debt and extreme insecurity even before the Great Recession. Extreme inequality, the inevitable trend as capitalism matures, is the root of social breakdown. Decades of what we might call normal 'capitalism' in America tore apart the social fabric, breaking society apart and laying the grounds for the Great Recession while creating huge social problems."

"Ok, I can see that wages kept falling for decades and wealth became more and more concentrated in the very rich. Extreme inequality is the new normal. But what other social problems got worse since 1970 as a result of these long-term trends in 'normal capitalism'?"

The Corporation as Sociopath

The Corporation, a popular documentary film, puts the corporation (now treated as a legal person by the Supreme Court) on the psychiatrist's couch. The diagnosis: sociopath, with a strong narcissistic streak, as it always seeks more money at the expense of workers and the general public. Marx saw capitalist corporations as hardwired to commit violence against society.

Mature Capitalism Equals Social Problems on Steroids

"The ultimate social problem is the breakdown of society itself, which people are feeling in their bones as they talk about the decline of America into a Banana Republic. Like any Banana Republic, America has now experienced long-term problems of growing joblessness, inequality, poverty, hunger, homelessness, debt, and isolation. Many of these problems are now extremely severe, and they are all symptoms of the crises that capitalism inevitably breeds as it evolves over decades and centuries."

The US as Banana Republic

In a 2010 *New York Times* column, columnist and Nobel Laureate economist, Paul Krugman, wrote, **"Banana Republic, here we come."**

"So these great social problems are inherent in capitalist growth and development and manifest themselves even before the system melts down in great crises such as the Great Recession or Depression?"

"Yes, although the pattern varies by nation, with the worst social problems in the harshest capitalist systems."

"And this accounts for the huge array of social problems in the United States, which has been keeping US sociologists busier and busier as US capitalism 'develops'?"

"Yes, the United States is the paradigm case. In a 2010 comparison of 30 of the most advanced countries in the world, based on official government data, the United States had the third highest level of inequality. It had the highest level of food insecurity. It had the highest level of incarceration in prisons. It had relatively low performance in math and verbal academic performance by students. It had one of the highest unemployment rates. These 'normal' US social problems have all been developing over decades."

"So US capitalism has long been the cause of extreme social problems?"

"Yes, the United States has long suffered, for example, extremely high poverty levels, now especially among children as discussed earlier. Official overall poverty levels have remained relatively stable for several decades, at about 12 percent, or 35 to 40 million poor people, although in 2009 the official rate had climbed to 14.9 percent, or *43.6 million people*. But," the ghost reminded me, "official numbers underestimate the real poverty levels by a factor of two."

I was guessing that few ghosts keep track of the way poverty is measured, but Marx's ghost was one.

"You're right," I said. "Poverty analysts describe a 'Twice Poverty' rate (the percentage of Americans living below twice the official level) as the more accurate measure of real poverty. The official government calculation is deeply flawed because it is based on a 40-year-old, outdated view of the relative cost of food, housing, and other basic necessities. In 2011, a family of four making just over $22,000 is not considered officially poor, an absurdity in most parts of the country. This is part of the way capitalist elites control ideas—by manipulating the concept and measurement of poverty to make it appear to be a modest, manageable problem, when it is a disaster. Another form of 'false consciousness.'"

The ghost nodded soberly. "Yes, real poverty has been hovering at about 30 percent of the population for the last 30 years, an astonishing figure in a rich nation. *It means almost one in every three Americans—or close to 100 million Americans—hover near poverty in capitalist 'normal times.'*"

"This does seem to confirm your view of the 'pauperization' of the working class."

Marx nodded. "Yes, but I can't take any great pleasure in it because I suffered it personally, and I know how horrible it feels. And because high poverty causes so many other terrible social problems that millions of Americans suffer."

"Like what?"

"Hunger." The ghost spoke the word with a very grim tone. "My own kids were hungry when we lived in London, and they got sick from malnutrition," the ghost reminded me again. "Britain was the most advanced capitalist country of my day—and still all those hungry souls begging and sleeping on the streets. That is why I wrote so much about class division and immiseration."

"How bad is the hunger problem?"

"As capitalism has matured, it has reached very high levels in recent decades, much as I predicted. Your own government data show this."

I knew this was true, but simply waited for more information.

"Since 1995," the ghost explained, in a slightly professorial manner, "the US Census has been surveying households about 'food insecurity,' a term that includes both families which experience chronic hunger and those lacking enough money in certain days of the month to get enough food to meet basic needs. The percentage of 'food insecure' Americans has been hovering at slightly above 10 percent—over 30 million Americans—and after the 2008 Great Recession spiked up to about 15 percent, or about *45 million Americans confronting hunger*. If you look at households with children, more than 20 percent were 'food insecure' in 2008."

Real US Poverty Levels ("Those living under an income double the official poverty level")	
1979	31.3 percent
1989	31.4
1995	33.6
2000	29.3
2007	30.5

All these data are recorded in years before the 2008 Great Recession, reflecting "normal capitalism."

Hunger in America: Percent of "Food Insecure" Americans	
1998	11.8
2000	10.5
2002	11.1
2004	11.9
2006	10.9
2007	11.1
2008	14.8

If you look at households with children, the percentages hover at over 15 percent, and spike to over 20 percent—1 in 5—in 2008.

"The Forbes 400 have enough wealth—now $1.6 trillion in assets—to feed all these people for many years," I said. "The American story is now a tiny fabulously rich elite living in the midst of millions of hungry people. Sounds like El Salvador or Haiti or the Congo. No wonder that commentators such as Arianna Huffington write about the United States as the newest 'Third World Country.'"

The Great Recession: Is It the End of Capitalism as We Know It?

I wanted to return to the Great Recession, one of the Super-Nova explosive crises that emerge out of the normal long-term, never-ending capitalist crisis. He had said it started with the crisis of low wages, the heart of darkness that he claimed envelops most blue-collar and white-collar workers as capitalism evolves.

"I want to go back to your views of what caused the Great Recession," I said.

"The first thing to recognize," the ghost said, "is that crises are part of the DNA of capitalism. And they get increasingly worse over time. This may now seem a little obvious, but most of your mainstream neo-classical economists have been thinking just the way David Ricardo, Jean-Baptiste Say, and James Mill did in my own day. They thought markets were rational and self-correcting, much like Milton Friedman and Alan Greenspan have argued today. The Great Recession showed how wrong these classical economists were—from my time to yours."

"Yes, Greenspan has acknowledged deep flaws in his thinking about this."

"The whole classical school of Smith, Ricardo, Say, Mill, and others all felt capitalism would never go into intractable crises. I spent much of my life arguing against them, showing that crises were inevitable."

"Because of the polarization of classes, leading to depressions?"

"Yes, and because of the crises of overproduction and stagnation and declining wages we've already discussed."

"You're talking about what I think of as the *wage paradox*," I responded, eager to see if Marx would like my term. "Each individual company seeks to keep down wages and jobs to increase its profits, a rational move for that firm. But when all firms do the same thing, what is rational for each corporation becomes irrational for the system since the general wage and employment levels sink, preventing workers from buying the goods that they must consume to keep the system going."

Marx and Henry Ford

Marx realizes stagnation occurs despite workers' need for goods—goods they can't afford on their squeezed wages. "The mass of producers are absolutely excluded from the purchase of their own products."

Henry Ford saw Marx's point, inflating his workers' salaries to $5 a day so that they could afford to buy his cars.

"You've got it exactly, and I wrote all about it in my book *Theories of Surplus Value* and also in parts of the three volumes of my major work *Capital,* where I focus on crises. My focus on the system deflating from inadequate demand is not because workers do not want or need goods, either in the United States or in the developing world. It's because hundreds of millions even in high-growth economies such as China remain too poor to afford them. Profit maximization requires firms to use every means at their disposal to keep wages low. It's what globalization and global capitalism are all about, and it is self-destructive to capitalism itself. But the low wages also reflect another inexorable capitalist reality."

"Which is what?" I ask. I sense the ghost wants me to understand a truth at the heart of the current US crisis and those to come.

"Something closely related to stagnant wages and inherent to capitalism itself. And now you're seeing it in the United States in its full terrible dimensions. I'm talking about the inevitable growth of the unemployed—what I call the 'industrial reserve army.' From 2008 into 2011, it hovered around 10 percent in the United States—that is *15 million unemployed US workers*—with much higher percentages of unemployed in many cities. In fact the real employment rate is closer to 20 percent nationally, if you count workers too discouraged to look, underemployed workers, and those in temporary jobs. The dirty little secret of American capitalism is that corporate leaders feel they can maximize profits and their own wealth and income by turning a huge proportion of the US population into 'surplus people' who can be replaced by robots or foreign workers. Life in the reserve army is misery, with people deprived not only of food to put on the table but also of their basis for self-esteem and social connections. The reserve army grows because capitalists benefit by firing many workers and then overworking the others grateful to still have jobs. As the reserve army expands, wages decrease. Both the overworked and underworked lose the capacity to buy and keep the economy afloat, as you're seeing today."

"So unemployment, low wages, and stagnation in the real economy shift corporations into the seductions of financial business where they can make money by gambling with other people's money and handing out credit like candy to beleaguered workers. Main Street stagnates further as the unemployed and low-paid workers become super indebted and eventually become too scared to spend. They fear job loss or permanent low wages will force them into bankruptcy."

The Reserve Army

Marx writes, "The whole form of the movement of modern industry depends, therefore, upon the constant transformation of a part of the labouring population into unemployed or half-employed hands ... an ever-growing reserve army of unemployed develops.... The condemnation of one part of the working-class to enforced idleness by the over-work of the other part, and the converse, becomes a means of enriching the individual capitalists and accelerates at the same time the production of the industrial reserve army..."

The "Reserve Army" is much bigger than the official jobless number. Government numbers do not count the hidden unemployed, those too discouraged to keep seeking work, or the underemployed, those working part time who seek full-time work. Do the math for June 2009:

- Official Unemployed: 14 million
- Hidden Unemployed: 6.5 million
- Underemployed: 9 million
- Total Unemployed 28.5 million
- Real Unemployment Rate: 20 percent

"Yes," Marx agreed, pleased with the slow but awakening student I seemed.

"Jobless recoveries and the wage paradox lead inevitably," the ghost continued, "to *the financialization, speculation, and debt crises* that are the second key element of all serious capitalist crises. Your 2008 Wall Street meltdown is the perfect model. Companies turned to financial services, traded toxic securities like drunken sailors, played fast and loose with toxic financial instruments, and seduced workers into debt they could never pay. The seductions included ridiculously loose credit card loans and even looser—and often fraudulent—home and mortgage financing. It set workers up for foreclosure and bankruptcy, and left the banks themselves with worthless mortgage securities."

Marx Anticipates the Wall Street Crisis

"In every stockjobbing swindle every one knows that some time or other the crash must come, but every one hopes that it may fall on the head of his neighbour, after he himself has caught the shower of gold and placed it in safety. Après moi le déluge! is the watchword of every capitalist and of every capitalist nation."

"So the 2008 Wall Street implosion was the inevitable end-result of a financial scheme to prop up profits, which was itself the inevitable result of Main Street stagnation, itself the inevitable result of capitalism itself. Just the beginning of things to come?"

"Yes," the ghost agreed. "It is the paradigm of future twenty-first-century economic crises, rooted in a stagnant 'real economy' and a corrupt financialized economy built on paper money rather than tangible goods. It creates unsustainable public and personal debt. The system has to bankrupt itself to survive."

"A lot of this makes sense," I said. "But I still feel this idea that capitalism must stagnate and die in the agonies of a long crisis actually ignores rather than confirms history—and you haven't persuaded me. Productive government spending and good regulation can help capitalism solve these crises, as in the Great Depression."

"As I just said, it was only World War II that ultimately got America out of Depression—and it will take even more costly and dangerous wars to keep the economy going." The ghost was clearly annoyed at my persistent

Marx's Core View on Capitalist Crises

1. Capitalism is doomed to self-destruct.
2. This is due to class warfare against workers and inevitable and deepening stagnation in technology, profit, and workers' wages as capitalist markets mature and saturate.
3. Stagnation means business sees a lower and lower profit from producing real goods and services, leading toward recessions in the "real economy."
4. Stagnation leads to financialization, as businesses turn to financial schemes to make money they can't make producing real goods.
5. Financialization leads to institutionalized gambling that creates bubbles that eventually pop, creating financially induced crises.
6. Nothing can prevent these crises from eventually undermining the capitalist system itself; it digs its own grave.

skepticism about capitalism's collapse. "Sounds like you've been indoctrinated with TINA more than I thought."

"No," I said, "I just don't think you've proved capitalism's collapse. I don't believe in TINA but not because I feel certain that a crisis will take down the whole capitalism system anytime soon."

We had come to be a bit of a stalemate, and both of us suddenly became silent. I felt a bit proud that I had argued Marx's ghost to a standstill.

6

Manufacturing Surplus People

The Surplus American

An economic neutron bomb is exploding in the nation. The neutron bomb is an explosive developed by the United States that has the peculiar characteristic of killing people while preserving property. What a convenient truth: with this economic weapon, money can be made without the workers.

We dub this emergent United States a society of "surplus people." The economic neutron bomb does not necessarily kill all the people, but it makes most of them redundant. They are not needed in the current system, as designed by those in power. The economy functions profitably without them. The great majority constitutes a mass surplus population.

This does not mean that there is not much important work to be done in America. In a different economic system, it would be entirely rational to hire these workers in useful—indeed essential—new jobs. The United States could and should put millions of people to work in creating a new social, economic, and environmental infrastructure. Creating this infrastructure is crucial to the well-being of the nation. Unemployment and surplus people could be reduced drastically in a rational course to save the nation itself. But the current American political economy has committed itself to a different path—and it would take something approaching a revolution to change it.

Surplus people, then, are "surplus" only within a system that has made them so. A more rational and sustainable economy, organized on the basis of human need and social rationality, could employ all Americans. Americans are becoming surplus by design, a form of contrived or artificial surplus, a casualty of short-sighted greed. There are entirely rational, indeed vital alternatives and solutions that could employ all Americans who want work in useful and necessary jobs, and could even bring profit to elites in the long term. Americans would not be surplus and the nation would prosper, but the current American political economy does not permit this utterly rational and essential change to happen.

In a sense, then, the term *surplus people* could be misleading. It might suggest that there is something wrong with the people or that there is no way to employ them usefully. Since exactly the opposite is true, and we can and need to employ them for the very survival of our country, they are not existentially "surplus." Rather, we call them *surplus* because the deeply irrational system we live in has condemned them to a surplus position and refuses, against all reason, to offer them essential work. Surplus people, then, is a label appropriate only to highlight the irrationality of the current order, and to spotlight the human tragedy of rendering surplus a population that desperately needs to be employed if the country and, in fact, the planet, is to survive.

At the heart of this problem is the calculation by elites that they can make more profit by radically reducing reliance on US workers and US infrastructure, using instead foreign workers or replacing workers with robots or other new technology, while relying on infrastructures in other nations. Turning Americans into surplus workers is utterly irrational when so much useful work must be done immediately in America—for example, to create an entirely new and clean environmental and social infrastructure at home. But the current system and its leadership do not permit this rational course to be pursued.

In the end, this reflects something deeply irrational but central to US capitalism. The core concern of corporate elites is profit, not jobs. And if more profits can be made by shifting production abroad, elites will take that path. Doing so brings massive short-term profits at the cost of jobs and domestic infrastructure, but it is profoundly irrational, even for elites in the long term, because it will produce massive domestic deterioration and revolt. Nonetheless, it is the decision—one of short-term profit-seeking over long-term social health and full employment—that US employers have made.

The irrationality of the current "surplus system" cannot be overstated. But such irrationality is manifest throughout our public life. For example, the suicidal disregard of climate change is the most irrational set of decisions that any society could make. Yet, the United States continues in denial and rejects the climate change decisions that could actually make money, employ workers, and save the planet. The irrationality of making a surplus population under current circumstances is thus just one expression of a political economy that is irrational to its core.

Another name for the political economy of the United States is, of course, corporate capitalism. American capitalism has repeatedly created deep crises of mass surplus people, a crisis that gets worse and worse as the system globalizes, militarizes, matures, and declines. The irrationality of creating a mass surplus population cannot be disentangled from the irrationality of the larger economic system, nor can it be solved until that larger systemic irrationality is fixed.

The analysis of surplus is thus a window into the history and crises of the US economic and political order. There is a long tradition of political economy, a field devoted to critical analysis of Western corporate capitalism that has gone largely silent in the United States. But the severe economic problems of the US Great Recession, and especially the new surplus people crisis it has produced—along with the crises of the Eurozone and the larger global economy—require an intellectual revolution and revival. We have found there is no way to understand the surplus crisis without delving once again deeply into the irrationalities of a now globalized US capitalism that brings deep inequalities between a super-affluent 1 percent and a 99 percent increasingly destined for surplus.

Let us be clear: the problem of surplus is the most glaring example of a systemic irrationality that is catastrophic in its consequences. Capitalist political economy creates not only a surplus crisis but also crises of inequality, militarism, and climate change that threaten the abilities of most people not just to find work but to survive with a civilized lifestyle on a habitable planet. We focus, then, not just on surplus people and the elites who control their fates, but on corporate political economy. We pay special attention to the elites who have made surplus an integral part of an unsustainable economic and social future for people everywhere, including eventually for the 1 percent themselves, for the path they have chosen puts them unwittingly on a suicide mission.

Since the systemic roots and causes of the surplus crisis remain largely invisible, political leaders are unable to truly grasp the dimensions of the problem, failing to recognize that capitalist irrationality prevents reintegrating surplus people back into the economy with a meaningful life. It is also likely that many leaders do not want to see the depth of the problem because acknowledging it could undermine their legitimacy, wealth, and power. In February 2011, President Barack Obama met with Steve Jobs shortly before Jobs died. He asked Jobs why virtually all the 70 million iPhones, 30 million iPods, and 59 million other Apple products are made outside the United States. Couldn't some of Apple's remarkable digital-age miracles be made at home? Jobs, whose software and hardware infrastructure is entirely globalized, told the president, "Those jobs aren't coming back," a sentiment also expressed unequivocally by Michael Dell, the founder of Dell, Inc., and representing the global mind-set of the entire corporate elite.

This reflects the way globalized corporate capitalism works today and shows that the very problems it creates cannot be fixed within capitalist boundaries. The consequences are dire. Surplus people are not a happy lot. People, after all, need to be needed. Without a role in society, they lack meaning and the means of survival. As long as politicians are committed to serving corporate interests, they are incapable of solving the problem because they must blind themselves to the crises' underlining roots and cannot propose solutions that ultimately threaten the 1 percent. The result is inevitably mass social discontent as the crisis grows worse. In our imagined dystopia of 2020, millions of people are in open revolt, converging on Wall Street to express their outrage and despair.

We wrote our first draft just months before the Occupy Movement exploded in the United States in 2011. As experienced writers, we were accustomed to analyzing history. But we were not in the habit of predicting the future. Here, we had written a book scripted around a conflict between elites and protesters on Wall Street before it had actually occurred.

The Occupy Movement reinforced certain underlying truths. One is that the problem stems from an innate irrationality, which can only be addressed through deep changes in the entire economic and political system. A second is that the seeds of the future lie in the present. The year 2020, as we initially conceived it, was an eerie extrapolation of what was about to happen today in the United States. That helps explain why our analysis proved prophetic. But our present circumstances—in which the reality of surplus populations was becoming too great and painful to ignore—were an extrapolation of forces unfolding over hundreds of years, at least since the end of the Middle Ages. Our dystopia was actually a history and an account of today's events, as well as a prognosis of things to come.

Buckle your seat belt. The story of surplus people—and of the deeply irrational system that has scripted it—is more stomach churning than a roller-coaster. But, as in the carnival, the experience should be exciting and enlightening.

Who Are the Surplus People? They Are the Unemployed but They Include Many Other Unfortunate Souls

How to define surplus people? Doing so is not as easy as it might seem, nor is there a theoretical tradition in social sciences that has made the idea precise, familiar, or even plausible. After all, a society that has determined that it doesn't need its people is hard to grasp. Society is its people, is it not? For most readers, an economic neutron bomb that eliminated the people would no longer be a society. It would be the absence of society.

This may make a "surplus people" seem nonsensical, but consider this: while it is hard to imagine a society without people, it is much less difficult to imagine a society with a vast unemployed population. We suspect that many readers might already have identified "surplus people" as those who can't find a job, and millions of American workers already suspect that US elites have embraced an economic strategy destined to increase mass unemployment.

A focus on unemployment understates the catastrophic magnitude of the surplus people crisis. True, the unemployed are a core group in the surplus population, the one that is nakedly surplus. They have no economic role in the current social order and appear to be an unwanted burden on society. They are growing rapidly in the United States, with striking, tragic growth in the long-term or permanent unemployed, a group that has grown bigger after each business cycle and has become almost 50 percent of the total official unemployed after the 2008 meltdown. Even though there is much useful work to be done, as emphasized above, US elites have determined that it is better to utilize workers abroad and use new technology to maximize short-term profit, even though the cost of sustaining and controlling a "surplus people" nation is high, especially in the long run.

The unemployed are not just those officially counted as such. Those too discouraged to look for work are not counted, but they are part of the unemployed surplus. Discouraged workers are one segment of a larger number of workers defined as "marginally attached"—those who want a job and have looked for work during part of the previous year but are not counted as unemployed because they haven't looked in the previous month—who also are surplus. So, too, are the underemployed—those working less than they want or need to get by. These include mushrooming numbers of involuntary part-timers. We will call the unemployed, underemployed, and marginally attached workers the "Category 1" surplus population, much larger than registered in the official unemployment rate. And, among minorities, young people, those not college educated, and those from low-income backgrounds, the unemployment and larger Category 1 rate is dramatically higher than the official national rate—approaching 50 percent in the case of young male African Americans.

The unemployed are the radioactive core of the surplus population but just one of six surplus groups. We will use "Category 2" to refer to those who have been forced or induced to leave the labor force. This includes prisoners and mental hospital inmates, and also many soldiers, college students, and elementary and high school students who were legally required to stay in school as part of an effort to end child labor. Also within this category are women who were seduced into becoming housewives so they would not compete with male workers, as well as retired workers, who would otherwise be competing with younger workers for scarce jobs.

Not all students, housewives, or retirees count as surplus people. If members of any of these groups do not want to work and choose voluntarily to stay permanently out of the labor force, they are not surplus. The surplus are those who *want* to work but because of shrinkage in the labor market—due to decisions made by US economic elites—are not able to get jobs. Students who have chosen education because it is a reliable way into the labor force should not necessarily be seen as surplus in the long term. In Germany, students, even while in school, are integrated into paid apprentice work and thus cannot be considered surplus. Because US employers offer far less on-the-job training, and outsource training to schools, they are able to keep students out of the labor market for a temporary period. For many students, this increasingly leads to long-term unemployment. If the economy were organized on a different and more rational foundation, focused on social development rather than short-term profits, all these students could be put to work.

Similar considerations apply to retirees, the largest number of people in this second surplus category. Before 1986, most US workers were required to quit by age sixty-five, thus forced into surplus status and preventing even greater competition for scarce jobs between younger and older workers. There would be plenty of useful work for all if elites put the US economy on a different foundation. But by pursuing the current economic strategy of short-term profit, based on foreign labor and new technology, large percentages of older people must be lured out of the labor force. Many may have wanted to retire and might thus not be considered as surplus. But what about those who want to continue to work? Their exclusion from the labor force allows employers to fire them and hire cheaper younger workers who would otherwise be surplus and more disruptive, thus saving money by creating a pool of senior surplus workers.

Many members of Category 2 are invisible or masked surplus people who have been sucked into what we call "surplus-absorption" institutions: the military, the police, prisons, the schools, old-age homes, and mental institutions. For many housewives, the family itself is a major "surplus-absorption" institution, something that the feminist movement and writers such as Betty Friedan implicitly realized when they described the housewife role as the "problem with no name."

Surplus-absorption institutions are overwhelmingly important in a society with a mass surplus population, such as the United States. As the surplus population grows, the police and prisons, the military, and the schools siphon off mass discontent and revolt. They offer people the illusion of purpose and hope, and pluck them out of the wasteland of naked unemployment into a fantasy world of purpose and possibility.

The third major surplus group are those involved in "make-work." They are all those employed primarily for the sake of having them working rather than because their labor is needed to yield profit or social value. This is a very large and diverse group, including many people hired by government simply to create jobs, even though the jobs create no profit or value. It also includes government bureaucrats working largely to build and feather their own nest or enforce meaningless rules. And it includes managers and administrators in the private sector who are carrying out entirely unprofitable or unnecessary labor.

To be specific, members of Category 3 include some employed in Keynesian public works; conductors on completely automated elevators, buses, planes, and trains; cashiers continuing to be employed when their activity is completely automated by scanners; and some artists, teachers, social work-ers, government bureaucrats, and record keepers. For these individuals, to be unemployed would be destabilizing, so it is better to give them some-thing to do and make them think they have a purpose. This is problematic, however, because it is expensive. You must pay them more than you would if they were idle.

A fourth surplus group is people who are hired to control the unemployed and manage the surplus-absorption institutions. They work simply to keep the other groups of surplus people in line, functioning as a "worthy" surplus population employed to control the "unworthy." They include police, military officers, prison guards, many teachers, many therapists or managers in mental hospitals, and managers of government make-work projects. Yet they all fit into the large pool of surplus people and are a way of dividing and conquer-ing, managing one sector of the surplus population by the other and thus killing two surplus birds with one stone.

The fifth category of surplus people is more controversial. Category 5 contains people hired by corporations or smaller businesses who carry out profitable labor that is either socially unnecessary or harmful. From a capi-talist perspective these people are not surplus, because they contribute to profitable enterprise. But from a larger societal perspective, they are indeed surplus since they are doing a form of make-work, intended to enrich small elites but not contributing to real social needs or the sustaining of society itself—and very often contributing to its decline.

This fifth category is an enormous group, since so much of the American economy is devoted to socially destructive or unnecessary labor. It includes people in food services who create or serve dangerous or unhealthy food substances such as trans-fats; cigarette company executives, employers, and tobacco growers; owners, managers, and employers in dirty coal plants; engineers devising fracking oil technologies; and endless others.

A key subset of Category 5 is jobs created by the financial sector. The 2008 financial meltdown made clear that while the current financial system generated huge wealth and employment before the Great Recession, it was unsustainable and both socially and economically destructive. It generated many jobs both on and off Wall Street through leverage and bubbles, but, as we discuss later, these can be viewed as surplus "bubble jobs," absorbing surplus people but only for a short period until the bubble pops. Bubble jobs are staffed by a crucial and large group of disguised surplus workers, whose jobs create an impression of increasing employment in periods before a bust, and also the impression that employment is going up when it is really declin-ing, as we show in our historical discussion.

There is a sixth group who might be considered surplus, although their status is ambiguous. This group includes everyone whose jobs are created or whose pay is artificially inflated to boost consumption and thus stimulate the economy and boost profits, or to control discontent and stabilize the economic regime.

This Category 6 surplus is a disguised surplus group, with many jobs that are unnecessary from a capitalist perspective and many workers who are paid more than their labor is worth to their employers. Their jobs exist primarily to give them a sense that they are not surplus but have a social role, through which they can live well enough to consume. Of course, we are talking here about the lucky among the surplus population. There are others who are locked up or live near destitution.

Considering these six categories, we can define *surplus people* as including all the following: (1) those who lack work entirely or lack sufficient work to eat and live; (2) those forced or pressured to leave the workforce and are warehoused in custodial or surplus-absorbing institutions; (3) those who work only to control those who lack work; (4) those who do "make-work," that is, jobs that have no real economic or social value; (5) those who engage in profitable work with market value but with jobs that are socially unsustainable and destructive; and (6) those whose jobs are unnecessary, often with inflated pay, and are a disguised surplus population. This already encompasses the majority of Americans. Our dystopia of 2020 America—a nation of surplus people—has arrived.

How to Make Money from the Creation of Surplus People: The 1 Percent's Strategy to Maximize Profits by Minimizing US Employment

Why has the surplus people crisis erupted? What is it that creates an America made up of millions of surplus people? And why have the numbers of such people mushroomed so radically in our recent history?

The answer is that the American capitalist economy is, by its nature, inherently surplus-producing. Its main product is twofold: first is very high short-term profits based increasingly on global production, and second (and related to the first) is the rising mass of US surplus people themselves.

The production of surplus people is not new. It has existed for centuries, taking its modern form with the rise of Western capitalism itself. In later sections we will trace the history of the American economy, to show the key forms and phases that surplus people production has taken.

But let's now focus on the grim realities of today—explaining why America faces a super-crisis of surplus populations. Mass surplus people production is a mark of mature capitalist systems: as economies "age" they produce more and more surplus people. This is connected to long-term tendencies in capitalist economies toward protracted crises and decline as well as short-term profit-seeking strategies taken by current US elites. It is also connected to contemporary shifts in the global economy, and to the decline of the United States relative to other rising economic powers.

The contemporary crisis represents a novel phase. The US elites have embraced a comprehensive business strategy that transforms the nation itself into a surplus people. Profit today has become inseparable from the manufacture of American surplus populations, already representing a majority of the American people. This is not a rational long-term strategy for the country, nor even in all likelihood for US elites. But corporate leaders have committed to it and government allies have made it stick, despite the enormous short-term and long-term costs.

Why would government leaders embrace such an irrational and destructive course? Corporate leaders can do so for obvious reasons: they can make immense short-term profits and do not have to incur the short-term or longer-term social costs. All these costs—whether of high unemployment or prisons or poor health—are borne by the government and the population itself.

Why would the government embrace this decision when it has to confront the enormous costs to the society and the population? This question is a major theme of our work, and it relates to the power of money in politics. Government has become, to a frightening degree, a wholly owned subsidiary of the corporate elite. Politicians follow policies benefiting corporate elites even when they harm US voters and people. This is not new in capitalism, but the control of money over politics has deepened and led to far more lethal consequences for the nation and US workers in a globalized age.

US corporations now seek profits and become profitable largely through mechanisms that increase all six of the surplus groups delineated in the previous section. This represents a potentially terminal social as well as economic phase. If it is not reversed through major social movements of the surplus people, such as the Occupy Movement, it will lead inevitably to rapid and permanent decline of the United States itself.

We will show that this strategy is institutionalized and extremely difficult to reverse. Corporations, political leaders, and the media are all complicit. And it is part of a worldwide economic transformation that has developed its own inexorable momentum.

Before we describe the nature and roots of this "surplus" corporate strategy, we need to say something about corporate and other elite motives. The key motive is nothing new; it is making money, always the driving engine of the US economy and always creating surplus people.

Nonetheless, the current phase involves a shift toward mass surplus people production tied to a new globally systemic profit strategy. It carries more lethal consequences, namely, the creation of a "surplus nation" in which, in the language of the Occupy Movement, the 1 percent render the 99 percent of America "surplus."

In describing this "surplus strategy," we need to offer three caveats. First, 99 percent are unlikely to become surplus; the number will be a large majority of the population if current trends continue, but it won't include everyone. Certain productive jobs will remain in the American "surplus nation."

Business elites and many mainstream economists, it should be noted, will applaud the redistribution of jobs from the United States to poor nations as both efficient and socially just. American companies will continue to employ some American workers while raising their own efficiency by reducing labor and regulatory costs and outsourcing the majority of jobs to global workers who desperately need and deserve them. Outsourcing creates pain in the United States but a whole world of new opportunity to escape poverty in the impoverished nations of Africa, Asia, and Latin America.

True, corporate globalization helps create new jobs in the developing world and can contribute to infrastructure development. It also creates cost savings for giant global firms that contribute to efficiency in the short term. But over the long term, all poor nations will be subjected to the same outsourcing and surplus people production as the United States today. Companies are outsourcing not to help the desperately poor masses of the world, but to exploit their vulnerability and squeeze grotesque profits through abuse of sweatshop workers who will accept horrific labor conditions to avoid starvation. Most of these workers will work during their youth and then be disposed of for even younger and cheaper workers, often in yet other countries.

The long-term effect is not to elevate workers in the rest of the world or build their economies in a sustainable greater good. Quite the contrary. The foreign investment of US transnationals will extract the cheapest labor and the most valuable natural resources in poor nations while subjecting them to US corporate dominance and policies, deeply compromising their sovereignty. This form of globalization—often called "neoliberal"—will create in the Third World countries dependency in the short term, vast inequalities in the mid-term, and abandonment and collapse in the longer term.

While the argument of global benevolence on the part of US globalizing companies is a self-serving myth, it leads to our second caveat: the current "surplus strategy" is not rooted in some perverse new demonic motivation by US elites. The 1 percent knows what it is doing—creating an American mass surplus population—but this is all in the service of their historic commitment to profit maximization. The 1 percent also knows that in abandoning US workers it is not creating paradise for the poor workers and nations of the world. But today's elites are not greedier or more sociopathic than their predecessors. Their new actions simply reflect new conditions that make mass surplus people production a prime condition of profitability today. This willingness to subordinate the well-being of the mass populace to profit is hardly new; it is simply taking place on a larger and more dangerous scale.

Third, this is not an elite conspiracy. It is not a fully conscious strategy, nor are executives the all-knowing possessors of the consequences of their own individual or even class-wide economic strategies. The elites are following a semi-conscious plan that appears to ensure major short-term profits and long-term effects that are largely ignored. They are prepared to grab the profits at hand even as the long-term risks, especially for US society itself, appear increasingly ominous. While hardly morally laudatory, this is no major deviation from the historical strategies US elites have embraced since the beginning of the nation.

Nonetheless, let's not underestimate the elite hypocrisy involved. The elites never acknowledge their surplus strategy even as they downsize and outsource with frenetic enthusiasm. Their talk is all about creating jobs, jobs, jobs. While their motives may not be new, the gap between rhetoric and action could not be higher.

In our emerging surplus nation, all elites claim to be totally united in the production of jobs for US workers. The jobs mantra dominates the business rhetoric of executives and the political leaders of both main parties. Meanwhile, all the leaders are carrying out precisely the policies that are undermining the prospects for job creation at home. They are destroying jobs in the name of creating them. And this will remain the case, since to admit the truth would create a social revolution.

The Four Roots of Surplus People Production

The new surplus strategy, with its lethal long-term social consequences, is connected with four major forces that in the past actually created productive jobs rather than destroying them. They are globalization, technological innovation, the intensification of corporate control over politics and economic policy, and the erosion of national stewardship that might protect the US economic infrastructure from terminal destruction and US society itself from the ruins of a surplus mass populace.

All four forces grow out of a new economic phase, in which corporate and political elites seek to maximize profits by disengaging from the US workforce. More broadly, this phase represents a decision to disinvest in the United States itself, leading to the rotting of American infrastructure and the decline of the nation, but saving elites the costs of rebuilding it. Greater profits can be realized by investing in new technologies that dispense altogether with the need for workers as well as investing abroad in a cheaper and more compliant global workforce. Elites hunger for and help build the more modern, gleaming infrastructure that supports cheap labor in Shanghai, Abu Dhabi, or Rio.

All of this reflects the inherent tendency toward stagnation and declining profits within mature capitalist economies such as the United States. Markets become saturated, infrastructure ages and erodes, technological innovation slows, regulations increase, and domestic workers become more expensive and less compliant than their counterparts abroad. Domestic profits can still be generated at home from domestic labor, especially as anti-labor and anti-regulatory policies are implemented, but the real money is in labor-saving machinery and foreign investment and production. The profit centers of the world have moved east and south, to Asia (especially China and India) and to Latin America (think Brazil).

This points to the core role of globalization. Corporate globalization is at the heart of the American surplus crisis. The threat posed by neoliberal globalization to the jobs of US workers is widely understood, leading to mass discontent on both the Right and Left with "free trade" treaties and with the entire corporate globalization agenda. Polls show that millions of Americans fear that their jobs may be outsourced and downsized in favor of production abroad. US unions have understandably made reform of neoliberalism and "free trade" a top priority.

But even opponents of today's globalization have not grasped fully its new dimensions. It is not just that jobs today are being outsourced faster than anyone imagined a few decades ago. It is that the loss of such jobs will be more permanent than anybody in the United States wants to believe.

This is because outsourcing jobs is connected with the bigger change of dismantling the US economic and social infrastructure. Might this be the first time in history that economic elites have abandoned their nation's own physical and social foundation? In a sense, globalizing elites today are burning their own nests because they have new homes everywhere across the globe. The cost of maintaining the original declining nest has been abandoned in favor of creating new nests everywhere else.

Globalization has been happening for centuries, largely under the umbrella of colonialism's self-legitimating civilizing project. But globalization today takes a new form. In earlier stages, globalization was part of a project of developing the domestic infrastructure of the globalizing home country. Looting colonies provided the raw materials to build early capitalist countries into models of capitalist prosperity, never seen before.

Such earlier colonial globalizations thus were a way of creating domestic jobs and building the home nation. They involved "in-sourcing" rather than outsourcing. When the British Empire conquered India, England did not outsource its budding textile industry to its new Indian colony. Instead, it shut down India's relatively advanced textile business, thus opening the door for its own domestic industries and workers. Globalization in the eighteenth and nineteenth centuries was part of a larger strategy to fuel domestic development and absorb surplus people at home.

Many orthodox neoclassical and neoliberal economists argue that corporate globalization today will ultimately also turn out to be a form of insourcing rather than outsourcing. As foreign nations develop, they will presumably create great demand for high value–added products and services that only advanced countries can create. But this orthodoxy overlooks the fact that nations such as China and India already have millions of highly skilled workers and many high-tech industries, capable of producing components for Intel, Microsoft, and similar companies at far lower wages than highly skilled US workers. Investment funds to promote the high-tech infrastructure in such nations—both from their own governments and from the US companies—are booming, even as disinvestment in the US infrastructure by both the US government and US companies accelerates. This helps explain why the head of Intel has said that his company could thrive with no US workers at all.

Surplus people are being created at all skill levels. This grim reality punctures the orthodox fantasies of both conservatives and liberals, who argue that education will resolve the current surplus people problem. American educated workers may do relatively better than the nation's uneducated workers, but both will see their fates suffer. Education, as a panacea held up for all surplus people, is a myth. The rise of the Occupy Movement, bulging with highly educated students who can't find jobs to pay back their bloated student loans, is testimony to that reality.

Technology is a second force driving the new crisis. Mainstream wisdom is that technological innovation is actually a solution rather than a cause of the surplus problem. However, while innovation can create jobs and absorb surplus people, current forms of innovation are now eliminating more jobs than they are creating, particularly in the United States. Between 2000 and 2009, more US manufacturing jobs—numbering 6 million, or one of every three—were eliminated through technological displacement than all the manufacturing jobs created in the United States in the previous seventy years.

This has not always been the case. Earlier waves of technological innovation—creating the steam engine, the locomotive, or the automobile, for example—displaced people from the land and threw out of work hordes of earlier transport and craft workers, but they also created huge numbers of new jobs in the nascent oil and steel industries and textile factories. Technologically driven displacement and job creation were more balanced, with technologically inspired economic growth creating millions of new jobs to absorb those displaced.

Things have changed. This is partly because financial and electronic innovation helps free corporations to move offshore and pluck cheaper workers. The Internet, arguably the greatest innovation of recent decades, is unquestionably one of the great drivers of globalization, thus contributing to mass outsourcing and surplus people production.

The globalization of technology is an important factor here. New technologies in the United States are now rapidly diffused to other nations, partly because they are essential to the production of US companies abroad. Moreover, the decline of US economic hegemony makes it very difficult for the United States to protect its own technological innovation. As China's strength grows, it has insisted on technology sharing as a precondition of accessing its vast market. Even if new American technologies create jobs, they are more likely to be utilized to produce jobs in China than in the United States.

Another factor is the nature of the new technology. Robotics serves as the paradigm case. Obviously, robots replace workers; but robotics take technological innovation in a new direction, threatening to eliminate the majority of workers of all skill levels. This leads to entirely robotized auto plants at Toyota that create cars without a worker (or manager) in sight. And to forms of medicine and education and accounting that allow far fewer professionals at home to carry out services online to any corner of the world, while outsourcing much of the actual work to offshore producers or online consumers who may be part of the surplus masses.

Robotics offers spectacular possibilities of labor-saving social advances but leaves in its wake vast numbers of surplus people. This reflects not just the awesome power of the inventions but also the new determination by corporations that profit is greater when human workers are disposed. Robots are more efficient, more reliable, and less rebellious than humans, the paradigm innovation for a "surplus nation."

Of course, if such labor-saving technology could be linked to social redistribution permitting a good life for all, this could be a major advance in human society. Liberation from work, even Karl Marx argued, could end the cold alienation of capitalist society. But all depends on the people in power who design and implement the new technology and determine the social consequences. The intention of American leaders is anything but to allow the surplus masses to get a piece of the profits.

This brings us to the third surplus-creating force: the corporate takeover of Washington, DC. There's a good reason we talk about "political economy." Economics is never separate from politics. In twenty-first-century America, corporations and government, business and corporate elites have never been closer, joined at the hip, a corruption at the heart of concern among both Tea Partiers and Occupiers.

The economic forces producing surplus people are not inevitable consequences of either globalization or new technology. Far more humane models of globalization and new technology are easily imaginable. But they seem utopian or out of reach because people with wealth have gained increasing control over government, and thus over the design and implementation of both globalization and technological innovation.

Corporate takeover of Washington drives the crisis in multiple ways. Corporate politicians design and implement the neoliberal policies, offshore incentives and subsidies, and trade policies that send jobs abroad. They carry out the foreign policy and regime changes abroad that create friendly low-cost environments abroad for US business. They aid and abet the disinvestment in American infrastructure by describing the infrastructure itself as socialism.

They also block the prospects of domestic reconstruction that might reverse the surplus crisis. Massive domestic public investment, which would require controls over the flow of capital and vast government involvement in the economy and taxation of the rich to fund new US infrastructure and jobs, is impossible in a corporate-run state. A Green New Deal has no realistic political future in the US corporate regime, since it would threaten the hegemony of the fossil-fuel corporate establishment, the military, and the ideology of laissez-faire.

The disinvestment in the US infrastructure has been so prolonged and deep that even if the political will to reconstruct could be created, success would be dubious. Keynesian liberals and members of the Obama administration argue for renewing America through public investment and incentives for private-sector domestic job creation, with substantial attention to twenty-first-century energy infrastructure. This could help create some jobs in the short term. But the reality is that the infrastructure has been so degraded already, Keynesian remedies that are sufficiently large to make an enduring difference will never be accepted by political elites. And even with major progressive political change empowering liberals, public investment advocated by Keynesians—though far preferable to current policies—is unlikely to solve the surplus people crisis.

This leads to the fourth driving force of the crisis, the erosion of any sense of national stewardship among elites. Global US-based elites have largely abandoned national loyalties, despite their dependence on the US government for their survival and profits, through massive corporate welfare, tax subsidies and giveaways, assault on labor, globalization policies, and so forth. This is arguably the American elite with the greatest dependence on the US government and the least sense of commitment to the government or the tax-paying workers who support them.

Rejecting the nation for a global perspective could be a liberating global policy. But corporate elites look to other nations simply as profit-making opportunities, a form of leveraged buyouts. Their policies may help create jobs abroad in the short term, but each nation and foreign workforce will be abandoned as soon as offending foreign workers seek dignified, well-paying work or the offending foreign country seeks regulation and respect for its sovereignty or environment. The corporate rejection of nationalism is not an embrace of global humanity but an escape from the need to conform to civilized codes of behavior enforced by any country.

Stewardship is the other abandoned virtue. We suffer from the rule of the most myopic, short-term obsessed elites in the history of recent centuries. The United States has historically had business leaders, particularly in the financial sector, that looked out for the longer-term interests of the national economy. No longer.

In fact, the concept of the long term is vanishing. Money travels too fast, financial markets demand immediate return, the future is too precarious to believe in or care about, and time itself has accelerated and telescoped into a disregard for anything beyond tomorrow. Executives know their tenure is short and want to cash in now. There is nothing in place to support the longer-term vision that would create a passion for rebuilding the degraded infrastructure, revive the nation, and solve the crisis of mass surplus people.

How Many Surplus People Are There in the United States?

The US government has no official records of "surplus people." For obvious reasons, it is not a legal or official category, since just to discuss it would create mass discontent. Even if elites wanted to collect such data, it would be difficult. There are, of course, data on the number of unemployed people, but even these are flawed. Accurate data on many of the other categories of surplus either do not exist or are hard to operationalize and count accurately. Nonetheless, since our whole argument rests on the notion that the United States is moving toward a majority of surplus people, we shall proceed with a conservative approach—one that clearly understates the real surplus population but offers validation of the huge size of those surplus populations that are counted in government reports.

We can offer official records or relatively reliable estimates of the number of Category 1 surplus: the unemployed, underemployed, and marginally attached workers. We will also report numbers of Category 2 surplus populations: prisoners, soldiers, and conservative estimates of the percentage of students and retired people who should be counted as surplus. Because the other categories are not reported by official agencies, we will not include them in our count of the surplus workers.

The following chart is one estimate of the total number of surplus people in the United States in 2010–2012, relying only on official numbers reported by government agencies and not counting the surplus populations in Categories 3–6.

Category 1

Unemployed	15.3 million
Underemployed (involuntary part-time)	8.2 million
Marginally Attached Workers (including discouraged)	2.8 million

Category 2

Prison and Jail Inmates	2.3 million

Probation and Parole	4.9 million
(by conservative estimates, 25 percent are surplus = 1.25 million)	
College and University Students	19.7 million
(by conservative estimates, 25 percent are surplus = 4.9 million)	
Retirees (by conservative estimates, 25 percent are surplus = 9.3 million)	34.4 million

The total of our conservative estimate is 45.6 million. It represents 34 percent of the civilian nonfarm labor force, which was slightly more than 132 million as of December 2010. Because it does not include four of our six categories of surplus people, all of whom are officially counted as employed, this total radically under-states the true surplus people population.

Introducing the History of Surplus People

The surplus crisis of the 2010s was a long time in coming. Its roots were planted in the very foundation of capitalism—maybe even earlier. Capitalism is notorious for going through cycles of boom and bust, which may cause the expansion and contractions of surplus population throughout history. Or perhaps, depending upon how you define it, the surplus population doesn't really contract, but sometimes, surplus status is disguised and surplus people are allowed to live in moderate comfort. Other times, their situation is made blatant and they face misery.

One of the biggest problems for the 1 percent is how to contain and control the surplus population. We can refer to two approaches as "the carrot" and "the stick," although throughout history there has usually been a mixture of the two, with some surplus people getting more carrot and others more stick. However, depending on circumstances, there will be periods of greater seduction and others with more brutality. To understand the surplus crisis of the 2010s, we need to trace the history of surplus people and how they have been treated, beginning with the very emergence of capitalism. The fate of surplus people is not determined in a vacuum; it is a reflection of broader circumstances, which vary when the state and the 1 percent feel threatened and secure. Therefore, we will not be able to present this history by referring to surplus people alone; instead, we have to discuss the relevant historical contexts, including the birth of capitalism, the age of the robber barons, the appearance of a consumer economy in the 1920s, the Great Depression and the New Deal, the world wars, the height of American prosperity in the 1950s and 1960s, and the beginnings of America's decline in the 1970s.

Indeed, examining the fate of surplus people is actually a window for understanding the entire history and structure of capitalism. We cannot look at recent traumas alone, but instead must write about political economy, economic history, and political, economic, and social theory. In a past crisis, particularly around the time of the Vietnam War, people on the left routinely thought and wrote about such issues. They were prominent concerns among college students and in university courses. Scholars such as Paul Baran and Paul Sweezy, in books like *Monopoly Capital,* tried to update Marx and account for how capitalism was transformed since his death. The loss of this tradition is a tragedy that we hope to overcome.

Among the most important changes since the 1970s is the Reagan counterrevolution, which shifted the discourse and squelched discussion of fundamental problems within capitalism. As a consequence, it became difficult for anything more critical than Keynesian liberalism to get an audience in mainstream academia and the mainstream media. Organizations such as URPE, the Union of Radical Political Economists, carried on, but were seldom heard. It is our hope to help bring their perspective once again above ground. It appears a time for a revival is ripe, and we are not acting alone. The Occupy Movements of 2011 suggest the torch has been passed to a new generation, and we offer our understanding as a tool they can use in their classrooms, their living rooms, and their demonstrations.

7

The New Robber Barons

On July 31, 1995, the Walt Disney Company, America's most famous entertainment company, announced it would acquire ABC, America's premier news network. A month later, two of America's most powerful financial institutions—Chase Manhattan Bank and Chemical Bank—decided to merge and become the nation's largest bank. Two months after that, Time Warner proclaimed that it was acquiring Ted Turner's Turner Broadcasting Network, thereby marrying the world's biggest media company and the nation's biggest cable system. Just three years later, those gigantic mergers would look almost puny, dwarfed by the 1998 Nationsbank merger with Bank of America, the Chrysler/Daimler Benz merger, and the merger between Citicorp and Traveler's Group, the biggest in history.

Mergers and takeovers, orchestrated by financiers such as junkbond king Michael Milken, had become the symbol of greed and power in the roaring 1980s. In sheer volume, however, the merger activity of the 1990s makes the eighties look tame. Concentration is a tidal force in banking, insurance, utilities, aerospace, pharmaceuticals, telecommunications, health care, and many other industries. The years from 1994 to 1998 set successive records as the biggest merger years in American history.

While merger mania has periodically seized the American economy, the current frenzy hints at a surprising historical precedent for the current period: the Gilded Age, which extended from shortly after the Civil War to the earliest years of the twentieth century. It was an era when captains of industry and finance such as John D. Rockefeller, Andrew Carnegie, and J. P. Morgan knit American business into national corporate fiefdoms of enormous power. Like today, it was a time of explosive change, fierce competition, and mass mergers, culminating in the famous "trusts" first put together by Rockefeller in Standard Oil.

With the 1990s came a second hint of a new Gilded Age: the revelation that the United States had become the most unequal country in the developed world—with the gap between rich and poor growing disturbingly vast. By the mid-nineties, not only was the gap the largest in fifty years, but as the United Nations reported, "the United States is slipping into a category of countries—among them Brazil, Britain, and Guatemala—where the gap is the worst around the globe."

The Gilded Age, likewise, was marked by the accumulation of great wealth in the midst of overwhelming poverty. While Rockefeller and Morgan were becoming the nation's first billionaires, most Americans, including millions of impoverished immigrants and poorly paid workers, worked twelve-hour days just to stay alive. A hundred years later, America was moving again toward a great divide of vast wealth and mass poverty. In 1998, *one* rich man, Bill Gates, had personal wealth of 50 billion dollars—more than the combined net wealth of the bottom 40 percent of the US population, or 100 million Americans. In 1996, the richest 1 percent of the population enjoyed a median net worth of several million dollars and had accumulated 40 percent of the nation's wealth—the highest proportion since the 1920s. At the same time 40 million Americans—including *one of every four children*—had fallen into poverty, also the highest percentage in decades.

Building a Bridge to the Gilded Age

When President Clinton ran for reelection in 1996, he told Americans he wanted to build a bridge to the twenty-first century. The nation had to prepare for the millennium, he explained. According to the president, entering a brave new world of burgeoning technology meant that we would all have to get on the information superhighway, and travel together across the millennial bridge.

But in a revealing interview at the end of 1996, Clinton hinted that another bridge that we might cross leads straight back to the Gilded Age. Talking with James Fallows in the *Atlantic*, the president spoke of remarkable similarities between the end of the last century and the end of our own. Among the striking comparisons the president described were "labor turmoil, boom-and-bust economies, ethnic changes wrought by immigration of that era and other shocks" that transformed the country. Clinton suggested that just as the Gilded Age saw a shift from an agricultural and craft-oriented economy to an industrial one, today we are "changing our industrial paradigm—we're going from the industrial age to an information-technology age, from the Cold War to a global society." Clinton also observed that, like today, the Gilded Age was a period of contradictions, simultaneously opening up dramatic new economic opportunities while threatening to leave millions of people behind. Then and now, "vast fortunes are being made—people are having opportunities they never dreamed of. But a lot of people have been dislocated."

Clinton's historical speculations deserve serious scrutiny. The great differences between the Gilded Age and the present—including the rise of a large middle class and a vast regulatory state—make clear that we do not live in a clone of the Gilded Age. But the president has hit upon something more fundamental than he was able to flesh out in that *Atlantic* interview. Some of the nation's defining qualities—its corrupted democracy and social Darwinist thinking—seem to have leapfrogged from the end of the last century to the end of this one.

Historian Arthur Schlesinger Jr. has written of American political history as cyclical. The political pendulum's swing from Gilded Age conservatism to the liberal reaction of twentieth-century progressives to the counterreaction of the Reagan-Gingrich era is part of the picture. But the historical parallels with the Gilded Age go far deeper. They involve seismic shifts in the organization of markets, shocks to traditional notions of fairness and community, the rise of a new culture of greed, and a radical rewriting of the contract between corporations and workers. In both eras, the balance of power in the nation shifted drastically, with corporations gaining great new power relative to contending forces such as unions. Both periods were golden ages of business.

The Gilded Age brought both hope and tragedy. It ushered in the American century, with the United States emerging as the new industrial power that would replace Britain as the guardian of a new world order. Americans— among them millions of immigrants who dreamed of a better future—were never more hopeful about their prospects for prosperity. The booming new industrial economy created by the robber barons—the popular name given to Gilded Age business leaders—allowed many citizens to realize their dreams, and the Gilded Age showed the remarkable potential of American business to harness the resources of the nation.

Yet millions of Gilded Age Americans worked in sweatshops, and the intensity of economic and social exploitation wrought by the robber barons became legendary. The growth of urban slums, the concentration of new monopoly power in the trusts, and the scandalous corruption of politics made many turn-of-the-century Americans feel their nation was losing its democratic promise.

Today's new Gilded Age order stems from an economy fueled by revolutionary advances in market scale and technology. It is dominated by dynamic corporations larger than any in history, and run by men possessed of power, business networks, and personal fortunes far exceeding those of the robber barons. It is defined by a democracy in which popular sovereignty is eroding. And it features a culture in which old-fashioned "virtues" like laissez-faire economies, social Darwinism, and accumulation of wealth are enjoying redoubled popularity. Despite some central differences, the new order and the old reveal parallels at almost every level.

Robber Barons of the Information Age

Every year a group of America's most influential men assemble at the ranch of financier Herbert A. Allen in Sun Valley, Idaho. Most are heads of famous global media and technology corporations: Microsoft's CEO, Bill Gates; Sumner Redstone, chairman and CEO of Viacom; Michael Eisner, CEO of Disney. They are part of a group of business leaders who have been dubbed the "new establishment." "Call them the swashbucklers of the Information Age," writes journalist Elise O'Shaughnessy, "or the highwaymen of the infobahn: they are the leaders of the computer, entertainment, and communications industries, whose collective power and influence have eclipsed both Wall Street and Washington."

The new establishment actually extends well beyond the elites of Hollywood, Silicon Valley, and the telecommunications world. It includes Wall Street financiers and the chiefs of giant industrial Fortune 500 companies such as GE and GM. It encompasses descendants of the robber barons themselves, including some members of the Ford, DuPont, and Rockefeller families, many of whom remain part of the Forbes 400 list of richest Americans and still run their ancestral companies, banks, or foundations. The new establishment is neither so new nor so exclusively information-oriented as popular accounts have suggested. Today's most powerful corporate leaders from across the economic spectrum have joined forces in such influential groups as the Business Roundtable. The unofficial executive committee of the new establishment, the Roundtable includes the heads of the largest US banks, industrial conglomerates, insurance companies, retail chains, and utility corporations—and together they are closely aligned with policy elites and political leadership in every branch of government.

In matters of personal style, the new elites are hardly the charismatic masters of their age that the robber barons were. Today's corporate leaders tend to be anonymous, gray-suited organization men, absorbed within an institutional system larger and more powerful than themselves. While they have great power, their charisma and personal ownership stakes matter far less than those of a Rockefeller or a J. P. Morgan, and they are to a far greater degree the captives of financial markets they do not fully control and of the interlocked business networks over which they preside. The personal power of the robber barons has been subsumed into a global corporate web. While they speak the language of entrepreneurialism, the new business elites are far from the rugged individualists who strode across the Gilded Age landscape.

And yet these two sets of business barons have much in common. Like the robber barons, today's business elites have radically restructured the economy in ways that promise both dynamic technical progress and frightening social polarization. Despite the current rhetoric of social responsibility, they, like their descendants, are presiding over supercharged corporate systems that will be remembered for their irresponsibility.

Like today's new business leaders, the robber barons saw the possibilities of a new economic order and took dramatic action to bring it about. Carnegie, for example, though ruthless in his costcutting and technological restructuring strategies, also deserves credit for almost single-handedly midwifing America's steel industry into becoming the world's dominant producer. Such enduring economic achievements—including laying the economic foundations for a prosperous middle class and a century of growth—help explain why the robber barons are admired by many Americans as icons. Though they came to symbolize greed and power to much of the nation, their legendary business success has nevertheless become part of the American creed.

It is the transformation of their society—not just its economy but its politics and its morals—that is the most important parallel between the Rockefellers and Carnegies and America's new corporate establishment. Beyond their economic exploits, the barons of steel, oil, and pork remade the politics and values of their era. "Like earlier invading hosts arriving from the hills, the steppes, or the sea," a leading Gilded Age scholar wrote in the 1940s, the robber barons "overran all the existing institutions which buttress society...." We must understand "how they took possession of the political government, of the School, the Press, the Church, and how finally they laid hands upon the world of fashionable or polite society ... as well as over the manners and opinions of the people." The same holds true of business leaders today—and, more precisely, of the great corporations they run. Their economic power is linked to far-reaching political influence, and they have had remarkable success in imprinting pro-business values on our collective conscience.

The Corporate Web, Then and Now

President Rutherford B. Hayes, himself a former railroad lawyer, exclaimed in amazement about the Gilded Age: "Shall the railroads govern the country or shall the people govern the railroads? ... This is a government of the people, by the people and for the people no longer. It is a government of corporations, by corporations and for corporations." In the Gilded Age, and again in our time, the corporation has become the country's economic engine, private government, and holy shrine.

For all practical purposes, late-nineteenth-century leaders invented the modern corporation. They radically changed the pre–Civil War institution they inherited, turning it into one of the world's models of efficiency. In conjunction with the government and the judicial system, Gilded Age elites shifted constitutional powers from the public to corporations and their leaders—a legal and political transformation that continues today in subtle yet alarming ways. The result was a tension between corporate and popular sovereignty that exploded violently in epic riots and strikes at the end of the last century—but is being played out today largely off the public radar screen.

Then as now, corporate elites cooperated to plan joint economic initiatives and worked together to influence legislation. One of today's corporate leaders acknowledges that most of them "talk to each other or have a meal with each other all the time, whether they admit it or not. They are engaged in a constant dialogue." This is more than idle chatter: their intricate network of connections constitutes what is, in essence, a new worldwide corporate web.

Corporations, at base, are legal devices for concentrating capital of the many in the hands of the few. Today as in the Gilded Age, though, capital is concentrating furiously, beyond the limits of any individual corporation. Merger mania is just the most extreme symptom of a much broader dynamic that joins corporations into far-flung networks of economic and political cooperation. The new corporate web has unprecedented, intriguing potential to create a new global family of all peoples. But by turning dominant competitors into increasingly intimate partners, it suggests a Gilded Age–style set of dangers as well.

The corporate web of today is a byzantine mix of interlocking board directorships, strategic alliances, and contracting networks that link virtually every Fortune 500 corporation with every other. John Malone, CEO of TCI, one of the great cable and media giants, describes his relation to Rupert Murdoch as that of variously "competitors or partners or co-schemers." What bonds them, says one veteran observer of America's leading executives, "is a sense of interlocking ventures and relationships ... they're inextricably tied with one another because of the deals they've made."

The Gilded Age saw the formation of the first great corporate web. Rockefeller sat on thirty-seven corporate boards, Morgan on forty-eight. Railroad barons such as Commodore Vanderbilt and Jay Gould constantly realigned themselves with each other and with financiers like Morgan in shifting alliances to gain competitive advantage, corner the market, and advance their collective power. The trend was toward ever-larger systems of alliance, building toward huge systems of concentrated power. The culmination came with the marriage of the Morgan and Rockefeller corporate families at the beginning of the twentieth century. By 1912, the Gilded Age web involved 341 interlocking directorships linking more than a hundred of America's top corporations, including Standard Oil, U.S. Steel, Chase National Bank, AT&T, Westinghouse, General Electric, and the country's leading railroads.

Today's new corporate web, like the corporate network a century ago, expands economic cooperation while concentrating corporate power. It can increase both efficiency and profits, and has the potential to create a socially useful form of industrial planning. But as in the Gilded Age, it is also an instrument for controlling markets and leveraging political power for business ends.

Executives today, as in the Gilded Age, constantly reshuffle and expand their partnerships in the corporate dance for power and market share. As financier Herbert Allen says, "It's no different than fighting over railroads." A colleague speaks of John Malone as a new J. P. Morgan, driven by the philosophy that "I'm going to have a piece of everything. Some of it may not work out, but I'm going to have a piece of everything." The fallout for the rest of the population, as in the Gilded Age, is more ambiguous. The new entangled giant corporations bring the promise of wealth in the context of permanent economic insecurity and mass poverty.

Economic Insecurity, Poverty, and the Assault on Labor

As outgoing labor secretary Robert Reich was leaving Washington in 1997, he wrote enthusiastically about the 11 million new jobs created during the first Clinton administration. As in the 1890s, America's leaders could take pride in the economic resurgence of America after many had forecast its collapse. Reich argued strongly that the new global order led by American corporations would bring a new century of affluence.

But Reich was clear about the social costs of success. "The unfinished agenda is to address widening inequality. Almost 18 years ago, inequality of earnings, wealth and opportunity began to increase, and the gap today is greater than at any time in living memory." As Reich commented on the breakdown of the old corporate contract that held that "as companies did better, their workers should as well," he plaintively asked, "Are we, or are we not, still in this together?"

The sad answer is no. The social disuniting of America is the most important parallel between the Gilded Age and today. We may have a much larger and more affluent middle class today, as well as some safety nets that did not exist a hundred years ago. America's class structure and standard of living have changed dramatically. But once again today we are in the grip of a perverse form of economic growth that polarizes America into increasingly separate worlds.

The richest 1 percent of Americans today own more than $4 trillion in assets, enough to pay down the national debt themselves. The bottom 80 percent own only 6 percent of the nation's financial wealth. To find a comparable wealth gap in American history we have to go back before the New Deal era, when new policies were implemented to alleviate poverty and inequality. A leading scholar at the turn of the last century concluded that the poorest "seven-eighths of the families hold but one-eighth of the national wealth, while but one percent of the families hold more than the remaining ninety-nine percent." The 1890 census data suggested that the richest 1 percent of Americans owned 54 percent of national wealth, compared to about 42 percent today.

Wealth became the great corrupting symbol of the Gilded Age, with robber barons, such as the Vanderbilts, Rockefellers, and Fricks, aping the lifestyles of European aristocrats. Their estates were replicas of palaces like Versailles; at their parties one might see "monkeys seated between the guests, human gold fish swimming about in pools, or chorus girls hopping out of pies."

Richard Hofstadter writes that the Gilded Age's wealth and economic dynamism were achieved at "a terrible cost of human values.... The land and the people had both been plundered." In slums like Pittsburgh's Painter Mill, people cooked in dark cellar kitchens in houses without ventilation or drinking water. Neighborhoods in New York City had higher population density than that of Bombay, the most densely populated city in the world. More than 80 percent of the Gilded Age workforce was poor.

Today, while the nation's official poverty rate is only 15 percent, it is much higher than in any Western European country or Japan. The parallel with the Gilded Age is especially notable in the huge scale of child poverty, with a million children expected to become newly poor as a result of welfare reform. Dr. Deborah Frank of Boston City Hospital reports that it has become common in the city to see malnourished poor infants "whose mothers were diluting their formula with water because they couldn't afford more." The main cause of poverty, as in the Gilded Age, is not unemployment so much as very low wages; 70 percent of today's poor have jobs. The corporate social contract, while far more protective today, is moving back, as Reich hints, toward the Gilded Age model. The pattern includes not only low wages but the creation of a disposable workforce, harsh working conditions, and a relentless assault on unions.

The bloody 1894 strike at Carnegie's Homestead Steel, which dealt the labor movement a crushing defeat, rightly became a notorious symbol of the Gilded Age, much as President Reagan's 1981 busting of PATCO, the air traffic controllers' union, came to symbolize a new union-free era a century later. After destroying the Homestead union, Homestead's chief executive officer, Henry Clay Frick, sent an exuberant cablegram to Carnegie: "We had to teach our employees a lesson, and we have taught them one that they will never forget.... Do not think we will ever have any serious labor trouble again." Carnegie, the sometime robber baron idealist who ten years earlier had angered other robber barons by his acceptance of unions, joyously wired Frick: "Congratulations all around—life worth living again."

The aspiring middle class of 1900 was full of hope for the future, but it was also a very anxious class. It could prosper in booms but in other times its members were not even assured of food or lodging. John "Bet-a-Million" Gates—head of the Steel and Wire Trust—introduced the idea of the "disposable worker" a century ago, laying off thousands of workers during periods of prosperity to create fear in his labor force. Gilded Age workers, like millions of employees today, could never feel confident that their jobs would be there tomorrow.

The consequences for workers of the Gilded Age attack on unions were not surprising. Many worked in sweatshops. The life span of a mill worker in Lawrence, Massachusetts, in the 1890s was twenty-two years shorter, on average, than that of the owner. More than 700,000 workers were killed in industrial accidents between 1888 and 1908; "a brakeman with both hands and all of his fingers was either remarkably skillful, incredibly lucky or new on the job." America's working class today is better off by far than its Gilded Age equivalent. But the current assault on unions, the creation of a new contingent workforce, and the tidal wave of downsizing have combined to make contemporary American workers not much more secure than their Gilded Age forebears.

The Best Government Money Can Buy

When President Clinton spoke about today's parallels with the Gilded Age, he did not mention how his own presidency has helped to make his point. Clinton has privately called himself an "Eisenhower Republican," making the balanced budget his highest priority, ending welfare, and announcing that "the era of big government is over." Such Republican goals might seem curious for the Democratic Party, but they reflect, as in the Gilded Age, the nature of American politics in a time of corporate ascendancy.

Clinton was elected president exactly one hundred years after President Grover Cleveland, arguably the nation's first "new Democrat." Cleveland and Clinton are Democrats who won reelection only by embracing the national political agenda of big business. In 1892, railroad baron Jay Gould telegraphed Cleveland that "I feel … that the vast business interests of the country will be entirely safe in your hands." Cleveland, for his part, assured corporate America that "No harm shall come to any business interest as the result of administrative policy so long as I am President." He proved himself by repeatedly using the Sherman Antitrust Act to outlaw labor strikes, which at that time were the only recourse for workers seeking to negotiate a living wage. In 1894, in the famous Pullman strike, he sent in federal troops to attack the workers. Said the president "to those who pleaded on behalf of the workers: 'You might as well ask me to dissolve the government of the United States.'"

Politics was safe for business, no matter who ruled. A Gilded Age business leader wrote, "It matters not one iota what political party is in power or what president holds reins of office." The barons had no sentimental loyalty to either Democrats or Republicans because both had become parties of business, a pattern increasingly in evidence today.

At Clinton's second Inaugural, a protester carried a sign calling the administration "The best government money can buy." Even before the sexual scandals of his second term, Clinton was mired in multiple financial scandals, from Whitewater to possibly illegal domestic and foreign White House campaign solicitations. In the astonishing $2 billion spent on 1996 campaigns, Clinton had showed that Democrats could hold their own with Republicans, winning contributions from most of America's large corporations.

The Clinton protester could just as well have waved his sign one hundred years ago. "Washington was a bad joke. Congress was 'transformed into a mart where the prices of votes [were] haggled over, and laws, made to order, were bought and sold.'" President Grant's administration, known as the Great Barbecue, presaged the Gilded Age administrations to come, blatantly doling out favors to the highest bidder.

Gilded Age politics, according to Secretary of State William Seward, had turned the political party into "a joint-stock company in which those who contribute the most direct the action," and as today, the corporations had by far the most to give. The robber barons flooded politics with big money. To elect President McKinley in 1896, GOP chairman Mark Hanna, a business leader himself, raised millions of dollars from corporations—then an unprecedented event and a foreshadowing of the scandalous role of corporate money in politics a century later. Beyond filling the campaign coffers, Hanna also virtually invented the hired lobbyist, who came to assume a defining role in the Gilded Age. Bribery and lobbying allowed the robber barons to write legislation and shape vital commission reports or political platforms. Republican senator Joseph Foraker of Ohio got about $50,000 from Standard Oil during the six-month period he spent preparing the antitrust planks of the Republican Party.

The robber barons virtually reinvented politics. Had they been only wealthy captains of industry, they would be today simply a fascinating historical curiosity. But because their economic achievements were based on a political reconstruction of the corporation that eroded the sovereignty of the public, they had a profound and enduring impact on American democracy.

Gilded Age politics can be defined simply: It used the language and machinery of formally democratic government to weaken real democracy. The Gilded Age suffered "a government of Wall Street, by Wall Street and for Wall Street," in the heated 1890 rhetoric of populist orator Mary Ellen Lease. While the robber barons preceded Ronald Reagan in denouncing big government as evil, they quietly expanded the intricate web of connections that linked the corporation and the government, and in the process broke down the barriers between economic and political power on which capitalist democracy presumably rested. Corporations became private governments with quasi-public powers, while government itself became a servant of private interests.

The corporate undermining of democracy was so blatant in the Gilded Age that it gave rise to the Progressive Era and its "clean politics" reforms. While hardly hostile to business, Progressivism and the New Deal restored a modicum of democracy, eliminated the most outrageous corruption, and created a Democratic Party not entirely under the sway of business.

"God Gave Me My Money."

We live in a period of moral fervor. The Christian Right, calling for restoration of discipline and faith, wields vast power in the Republican Party. President Clinton increasingly uses his bully pulpit to call for V chips, school uniforms, and a general return to "family values."

A new rhetoric of personal responsibility is transforming American politics. The discourse of responsibility has become a central part of President Clinton's lexicon: We all must take responsibility for our own lives, he argues. The focus is on each individual's moral development. This new ethic is seen by many to offer the hope, in this most materialist of ages, of a great moral awakening.

The new politics of responsibility has both liberal and conservative poles. Among liberals, it is associated with personal growth, the revival of civil society, and a grassroots renewal of blighted neighborhoods and a return to community-level democracy. Among conservatives, it takes a more traditional focus on religious revival and a new entrepreneurship. The almost messianic quality of this vision among mainly conservative officials in Washington invests their efforts to cut off welfare with a sense of moral rectitude: The poor should take responsibility for themselves, the argument goes; America's great social programs, including Social Security, should be privatized. Now it will be each person responsible for herself or himself.

Such moralism is hardly new in American life. It has roots in American Puritanism, and is strongly linked to rugged individualism and the American Dream. The rags-to-riches success story is one of America's most enduring myths—it was already familiar by the time the Horatio Alger stories codified it during the Gilded Age—and it constitutes one of the common threads between the new politics of responsibility and the old politics of business. Particularly in its conservative manifestation, the new morality is linked to broader philosophies of individualism and social Darwinism dominant in the Gilded Age.

Gilded Age culture saturated Americans with the morality of business and individual responsibility, equating wealth with virtue. Robber-baron morality might seem an oxymoron; the greed and corruption of the nineteenth-century industrialists set a new low standard in American life. Yet the robber barons were among the nation's most moralistic leaders. They draped themselves in the lofty rhetoric of social Darwinism, which framed the workings of the free market as a blessing from God and subjected the unwashed poor to a religion-fueled moral indignation. John D. Rockefeller, for example, readily used Darwinist language: "The growth of a large business is merely a survival of the fittest ... it is merely the working-out of a law of nature and a law of God." Rockefeller could conclude that "God gave me my money."

Social Darwinism dominated the thinking of the Gilded Age. It made poverty, competition, and exploitation all part of the natural struggle for existence. Said one railroad baron, "Society as created was for the purpose of one man getting what the other fellow has." Social Darwinism and rugged individualism intertwined to create a theology that gave spiritual meaning to the terrible gulf between rich and poor. The robber barons' conversion of their own ill-begotten wealth into a symbol of God's favor, and reading of God's mysterious purposes into the misery of the poor, was the great spiritual accomplishment of a passionately commercial and otherwise notably non-spiritual age. It helped engender the public worship of wealth and acceptance of poverty that is among the cruelest of the robber-baron legacies.

Social Darwinism comes to us today in far more nuanced terms. President Clinton is more communitarian than rugged individualist. His "I feel your pain" style of moralism has little resonance with the robber baron approach. Clinton's style is therapeutic rather than punitive. He urges responsibility for one's fate as a means of personal growth, not as divine retribution.

Even the Gingrich Republicans, the most militantly social Darwinists of contemporary politicians, are careful to blame poverty not on God but on the welfare system. Republican representative Dan Mica of Florida brought this transformation home in a single image: Hailing the looming demise of welfare, he nodded to the familiar sign "Don't feed the alligators," suggesting that any poor family, like a family of zoo-bound alligators, should be able to feed itself when left to fend for itself. The open view of many social Darwinists in the Gilded Age had been that the poor would simply die off; today, more politically canny figures such as Mica exhort the poor to liberate themselves from their politically created dependency to exercise their God-given potential.

Today, as in the Gilded Age, we live in a world where a morality of personal responsibility rubs shoulders with a culture of greed and of flagrant social irresponsibility. Now as then, business has shed its collective responsibility for employees—just as government has for its citizens. Yet this threat to the common good is organized in the name of nurturing responsibility itself. The politics of personal responsibility offers a public moralism that does not disturb the culture of greed or existing relations of power. Making money is again a sign of personal responsibility while the failure to do so suggests a moral lapse.

The specter of moral breakdown that permeates our own times also lingered nearby during the Gilded Age, a sure product of the cynical rhetoric of personal responsibility and the erosion of public hope for social change. Yet such demoralization never gripped much of the population in the Gilded Age, an era of explosive rebellion by labor and populist movements. The populist and labor movements of today are quieter, less incendiary—yet they are resurfacing, and they are, once again, a source of hope.

8

Sins of the Corporate Regime

When American leaders talk about regimes, it is usually about the evil governments of Iraq, North Korea, Iran, Syria, or Cuba. As US power brokers see it, a regime is a horrible government somewhere else in the world that the American public ought to distrust. Regime change, by the same logic, is about how the United States can rid the planet—as it claims it did in Iraq—of a government that it views as a threat to civilization.

The dictionary defines a regime as "a manner, method, or system of rule or government." If we take this literal approach and view any "system of rule" as a regime, then the US government is also a regime, and the history of the United States—as of other nations—can be seen as a succession of regimes. American regimes, I argue, are entrenched systems of power and ideology. Regime changes at home, while not revolutions, are great dramas, creating seismic shifts in power and social values. Regime changes are political earthquakes that deeply affect the personal lives of ordinary Americans and can steal power away from the people—or return it to them.

Our current regime is a corporate one, and I start by describing what a corporate regime is and how it has subverted our democracy. This is the third corporate regime in American history and, while more global and hazardous than its predecessors, it is not entirely new. Its roots lie in the Gilded Age of John D. Rockefeller, who helped shape the first corporate regime, and in the Roaring Twenties of Warren Harding, Calvin Coolidge, and Herbert Hoover, the leaders who presided over the second corporate regime. I tell the story of each of these regimes and how they have cumulatively contributed to the crisis in our nation today.

Fortunately, corporate regimes have not been the only forms of rule in America. Both the first and second corporate regimes ended in regime changes led by progressive and New Deal movements. The systems of rule turned power back toward the people.

Today, more than ever, we need regime change at home, better than the ones before. To achieve it, we need to understand how brave, earlier generations of Americans toppled the corporate regimes of their day. Regime changes do happen in America and, sometimes, they light up our lives.

The Sins of the Regime

"Regime" has a nasty ring to it. We hear about Saddam Hussein's regime, the North Korean regime, Fidel Castro's Communist regime, the radical clerical Iranian regime, or the Syrian dictatorial regime. You get the idea. A foreign government that is repressive, and that US leaders would like to see eliminated, will get branded in the United States as a "regime."

That is why the idea of an "American regime" seems so strange to Americans, who have been conditioned to think of regimes as bad governments somewhere else. Have *you* ever imagined the term can be applied at home? Maybe not, but the dictionary makes clear that the term applies to any "system of rule," at home or abroad. Europeans, Africans, Latin Americans, Middle Easterners, and Asians talk frequently about the "American regime," which they fear and mistrust.

Certificate of Birth

Name:	Third Corporate Regime
Date of Birth:	Election Day, 1980
Father:	Ronald Reagan
Mother:	Corporate America
Headquarters:	Washington, DC
Current Caretaker:	George W. Bush

Brief Biography

The regime is twenty-five years old. It took form under the Reagan administration. The regime consolidated itself under Bush I, secured legitimacy from democrats under President Clinton, and radicalized itself under Bush II. The aim of the regime is to shift sovereignty from citizens to transnational corporations, and to transform government into a business partner committed to maximizing global profits for a small number of global executives and shareholders. It is showing signs of age and is viewed by much of the world as dangerous. Caution is advised.
Registry of Regimes, Washington, DC

Regimes are institutionalized systems of power, good or bad, that rule a nation. Every regime is like a political house built around five great pillars. The pillars usually support the ruling elites, but in democratic regimes they can empower the people. The architecture of the house and the design of its pillars reflect the underlying balance of power in society. The groups or organizations that control money tend to design and run the "house."

Meet the Pillars

1. **A dominant institution** (e.g., the corporation, the government, the church) that ultimately controls the house
2. **A mode of politics** (e.g., corporate sovereignty, theocracy, representative democracy) that determines how the house is run
3. **A social contract** (e.g., the welfare state, laissez-faire, libertarianism) that sets the terms for the tenants
4. **A foreign policy** (e.g., isolationism, empire, multilateralism) that dictates the relationship to the neighbors
5. **An ideology** (e.g., social Darwinism, socialism, individualism, democracy) that spells out the creed of the household

---

President Bush is the United States' most recent and extreme regime leader. He has done some expensive renovation of the pillars, in collaboration with the big monied interests that helped put him in office. He has changed the façade of the regime but not its underlying structure or aims.

Who Is George W. Bush?

Let's be clear: Bush should not be treated as a power unto himself. He is simply the most militant custodian of a regime that preceded him and will likely persist after he is sent back to Texas. Nonetheless, regime change looms because of Bush's extremism and the underlying terminal cracks in today's aging regime.

Regimes cling to power, claiming that God or nature has ordained them. A nineteenth-century regime leader, John D. Rockefeller, said, "The growth of a large business is merely a survival of the fittest ... the working-out of a law of nature and a law of God." This sort of rhetoric is popular in the current regime, with neoconservative ideologues from the Reagan to the Bush administration portraying the American "free market" system as part of nature, and corporate capitalism as the highest stage of social evolution. One of the regime's favored thinkers, Francis Fukuyama, a former Reagan administration official and now professor of public policy at George Mason University, calls the current American order "the end of history," evidently God's and man's most perfect creation. But while the new corporate regime is deeply entrenched and controls the public conversation, it has not ended history, which in the United States consists of a never ending contest between the existing regime and those seeking regime change. America's first ruling elite was the British colonial authority, a victim of the most dramatic politics of regime change in the nation's history: the Revolution. Under George Washington's first presidency, a Hamiltonian business regime warred with and ultimately triumphed over Jeffersonian Republicanism, to be followed by a succession of new regime changes.

A Brief History of US Regimes

US Regimes	
First Corporate Regime	
Built by the robber barons	1865–1901
Progressive Regime	
Led by trust-busting President Teddy Roosevelt	1901–1921
Second Corporate Regime	
Brought to you by presidents Warren Harding and Herbert Hoover	1921–1933
New Deal Regime	
Designed by President Franklin Roosevelt	1933–1980
Third Corporate Regime	
Sponsored by global corporations and presidents Ronald Reagan, George Bush Sr., Bill Clinton, and George W. Bush	1980–????

While you won't read about regimes in most history books, American history is a series of fascinating regimes and regime changes. The modern history of US regimes began immediately after the Civil War, when the earliest American corporate regime was born. Art Garfunkel sang *"Don't know much about history,"* but if you want to understand the current regime and how it uses power against you, you have to know its history.

The First Corporate and the Progressive Regimes

The *first* corporate regime was born with a bang after the Civil War. John D. Rockefeller, J. P. Morgan, and other robber barons built America's first great national corporations in one of the world's most impressive bursts of economic dynamism and abuse of power. The regime developed as a marriage between the robber barons and the presidents of the era. Republican presidents Grant, Harrison, Garfield, Arthur, and McKinley and Democrat Grover Cleveland all carried water for the new captains of industry. The robber barons dominated American society from the end of the Civil War until 1901.

Sound familiar? The parallels between this first corporate regime and the one today are haunting. The late-nineteenth-century robber baron regime created many of the historic companies, such as Chase National Bank (now J. P. Morgan Chase), First National Bank and National City Banks of New York (now Citigroup), Standard Oil (now called Exxon), and U.S. Steel (now called USX), which, after various mergers, still dominate America. It was the first regime to flood politics with corporate money and create all-powerful corporate lobbies in Washington. Rockefeller's aides, with briefcases literally stuffed with greenbacks, worked in the offices of senators, who wrote legislation on oil, banking, and other industries. It's no secret why they were called "robber barons." They used their influence over presidents to send in troops when workers tried to organize, and they helped write tax laws that created a huge and growing gap between the very rich and everyone else. We live in a born-again robber baron regime, with the corporations bigger and more global, and their domination of Washington even greater.

Despite its awesome power, this first corporate regime faced a radical challenge by the Populists, fiery farmers and plainspoken people from the heartland who created the People's Party in 1892, captured the Democratic Party in 1896, and launched one of the country's most important politics of regime change. They proclaimed in 1892 that corporations were being used "to enslave and impoverish the people. Corporate feudality has taken the place of chattel slavery." While the Populists melted away with the 1896 presidential defeat of their candidate, William Jennings Bryan, they helped give rise to the reform movement of the Progressive Era under the "trust-buster," President Theodore Roosevelt. In 1907, Roosevelt called for "the effective and thorough-going supervision by the National Government of all the operations of the big interstate business concerns," a direct challenge to the "free market" regime discourse of the robber barons. Roosevelt was no revolutionary, but he did engineer his own regime change politics, culminating in his effort to create a Bureau of Corporations that would put limits on the strongest Rockefeller, Morgan, and other robber baron fiefdoms. Corporations had to restructure themselves and embrace a measure of public accountability, as the Progressive Era consolidated political power in a new regulatory regime quite different from the robber baron order. The eminent historian of the Progressive Era, Gabriel Kolko, labeled the resulting government-led regime "political capitalism." The Gilded Age corporate regime passed into oblivion.

> Like earlier invading hosts arriving from the hills, the steppes or the sea, [the robber barons] overran all the existing institutions which buttress society, taking control of the political government, of the School, the Press, the Church, and ... the world of opinions or of the people.
> —Matthew Josephson,
> *The Robber Barons*

The Second Corporate Regime and the New Deal

The Bush administration resembles not just the Gilded Age presidencies but also the Republican presidencies of the 1920s, which presided over the nation's *second* corporate regime. The Harding, Coolidge, and Hoover administrations abandoned the regulatory impulse of the Progressive regime and turned Washington back to big business. While less constitutionally extreme than the Gilded Age presidents, they created a regime of corporate hyperpower, dominated by an ideology of corporate self-regulation and paternalism. They proclaimed a union-free world known as *Plan America,* a vision of corporate paternalism in which big business would house and educate workers and provide them with medical care and retirement. Plan America was a vision of a whole society wrapped in a benign corporate cocoon, without need for government regulation or unions, previewing some of the views about corporate responsibility fashionable in the current regime. President Hoover said that the government "owes nothing" to himself or any citizen, since the business world had created opportunity for everyone and could police itself. The Roaring Twenties saw an era of overwhelming corporate dominance enlivened by booming prosperity, scandals such as Teapot Dome, and a huge stock market bubble that popped in 1929. The regime ended with market collapse and the victory of President Franklin Roosevelt in 1932.

Spurred by the Depression and the recognition that capitalism could be saved only under a different order, Roosevelt created the New Deal, a regime that established basic rights for labor, codified in the Wagner Act, and created an entirely new social welfare system built around Social Security. The New Deal did not end corporate power, but it turned the government into a limited agent of countervailing power and sought to preserve a public sphere, whether in the health system or in the post office, safe from corporate predators. Economist John Kenneth Galbraith wrote at the height of the New Deal that the federal government's main peacetime role is to rein in corporate power, a statement that no established thinker or politician could have entertained in the Gilded Age or Roaring Twenties regime.

The Greatest American Regime

The New Deal regime was the longest and most important in modern American history. It lasted several decades after Roosevelt's death in 1945 and still gives hope to many ordinary Americans. By realigning government with ordinary workers and citizens, it created foundations for economic growth and a middle class who could make good on the American Dream. While the New Deal was not a revolutionary anti-capitalism regime and was far from an ideal democratic order, it resurrected the democratic dreams of the Declaration of Independence, reversed the corrupting legacy of two earlier corporate regimes, and demonstrates to skeptics today that US regime change can take back the government from the corporate moguls.

Enter, the Third Corporate Regime

The New Deal regime survived almost fifty years, profoundly changed the nation, helped enshrine the labor movement as a new force, and redefined the Democratic Party. But it, too, succumbed, as neoconservative radicals in the 1970s spurred a politics of regime change leading to the election of Ronald Reagan in 1980. As a new generation of robber barons entered into a marriage with the Reaganite political clans in Washington, they created a regime whose power is now compared with the Roman and British Empires. It rules not only America but much of the world.

The third corporate regime is the house we live in today. George W. Bush is just the current master of the mansion. The basic design of this regime was established by Reagan a quarter-century ago.

Meet the Pillars of the Third Corporate Regime

Dominant Institution—The Transnational Corporation
Corporate plutocrats own this house.
Mode of Politics—Corpocracy
Wealthy residents run the house, although all tenants have a vote.
Social Contract—Social Insecurity
Tenants have no long-term lease.
Foreign Policy—Empire
The house rules the neighborhood.
Ideology—The Corporate Mystique
The house claims tenants are free and announces it is open for business.

The Transnational Corporation

The foundation pillar of the regime is the transnational corporation, the biggest concentration of cold cash in human history. The companies dominating the regime—giants such as Wal-Mart, General Motors, General Electric, Exxon, Citigroup, Bank of America, Verizon Communications, Phillip Morris, and Microsoft—are wealthier than most countries. Citigroup has total assets of over a *trillion* dollars, to be precise *one trillion, one hundred eighty-seven million!* Wal-Mart employed 1.3 *million* workers in 2003. General Motors' annual sales in 2000 were larger than the gross domestic product (GDP) of Hong Kong, Denmark, Thailand, Norway, Poland, South Africa, and 158 other countries. Of the one hundred largest economies in the world in 2001, fifty-one were corporations, and only forty-nine were countries (based on a comparison of corporate sales and country GDPs). Big business has existed under every US regime since the Civil War, but the third corporate regime is creating a world where companies are replacing countries as the superpowers. They make the corporations of earlier regimes look like pygmies.

Two hundred corporations sit at the heart of the regime, led by the Top Ten. These Top Ten alone have *assets worth about $4 trillion.* That is $4,000,000,000,000! But you'd have to add on GM, Ford, J. P. Morgan Chase, Microsoft, and scores of other behemoths to get the picture. Four trillion dollars is just a fraction of the wealth controlled by the two hundred intertwined giant companies that control the regime.

Corporate Superpowers

Here are the Top Ten US corporations in 2003, ranked by *Forbes* magazine according to a Super-Index of sales, profits, assets, and market. I have listed only assets here.

THE TOP TEN	A$SETS
1. General Electric	574,274,000,000
2. Citigroup	1,097,190,000,000
3. ExxonMobil	152,644,000,000
4. AIG	547,295,000,000
5. Bank of America	660,458,000,000
6. Wal-Mart Stores	94,552,000,000
7. Fannie Mae	887,257,000,000
8. Verizon Communications	167,468,000,000
9. IBM	96,484,000,000
10. Altria Group	87,540,000,000

These firms' size reflects the rise of a truly transnational corporation, whose unique global character is uniquely threatening for US workers. We have long had global corporations, but never the transnational form of company that—at lightning speed and on a mass scale—can transfer abroad production of virtually every good and service. Not just the size but also the distinctive reliance on foreign labor and the approach to global profits differentiate transnational firms and the third corporate regime from previous incarnations. Today's corporation has turned "trade" into something quite new: a way to use US capital to employ cheap foreign labor at the expense of American jobs. Trade becomes an internal transfer within the global corporation itself, maximizing profit by uniting US capital and technology with foreign workers unprotected by labor laws or regulations. This inevitably produces the mass outsourcing of jobs that has now exploded into one of the great political issues of our time, and it serves notice that the core economic interests of the third corporate regime will increasingly diverge from the interests of American workers and citizens.

Two hundred corporations, eighty-two of which are American, dominate the global economy, producing 27.5 percent of the world's total economic activity. The regime serves the US companies most directly but promotes global trade and investment rules benefiting all the top two hundred. Their combined sales are now greater than the combined economies of all countries minus the biggest ten, and eighteen times the combined annual income of the 1.2 billion people (24 percent of the total world population) living in "severe" poverty.

What do all these numbing numbers mean? For one thing, huge inequality. The top three shareholders of Microsoft own more money than do all six hundred million people in Africa. Bill Gates and Warren Buffet, the two richest corporate moguls, have more wealth than the poorest fifty million Americans. Beyond this, corporations make out like bandits in many ways. *The share of federal taxes paid by corporations dropped from 23.2 percent in 1960 to 11.4 percent in 1998. In 1998, Texaco, Chevron, Pepsi Co., Enron, WorldCom, McKesson, and the world's biggest corporation, General Motors, paid no federal taxes at all.*

In the third corporate regime, we are all corporate constructions. We get our dreams and opinions from corporate media such as Fox or Disney; our children's education is based on curricula provided by Microsoft or AT&T; our food comes from Phillip Morris and Wal-Mart, the world's largest grocers; our credit cards and mortgages are granted by one-stop superbanks such as Citigroup or J. P. Morgan Chase. Corporations pry away from government anything that is profitable and increasingly deliver our education, health care, social services, and even law enforcement. Everything is for sale since the regime's purpose is to promote profit above all else.

As they seek to make the entire social order profitable and marketable, corporations are remaking everything in their own image, including government itself. Governments look and act more like companies, and corporations present themselves more as governments. Governments act to protect profits, and corporations speak the language of social responsibility. Business takes on the planning and rule-making roles of government, and government becomes increasingly about money.

Corpocracy

OK, it's not a pretty word, but it describes an ugly reality. To understand corpocracy, look at George W. Bush's cabinet, a Who's Who of corporate America.

PRESIDENT GEORGE W. BUSH
Former CEO of Texas Rangers and Board of Directors of Harken Energy
VICE PRESIDENT RICHARD CHENEY
Former CEO of Halliburton, Inc., the huge energy and defense conglomerate

SECRETARY OF DEFENSE DONALD RUMSFELD
Former CEO of General Instrument Company and of the drug giant G. D. Searle and Co.

FIRST BUSH SECRETARY OF TREASURY PAUL O'NEILL
Former CEO of Alcoa and of International Paper Co.

SECRETARY OF THE TREASURY JOHN SNOW
Former CEO of CSX, the railroad giant, and Chairman of the Business Roundtable, the leading big business group in America

TRANSPORTATION SECRETARY NORMAN MINUTA
Former Corporate Vice President of Lockheed Martin

LABOR SECRETARY ELAINE CHAO
Former Vice President of Bank of America

AGRICULTURE SECRETARY ANN VENEMAN
Former Board of Directors of Calgene, Inc., a subsidiary of Monsanto Corporation

Bush's cabinet illustrates the marriage between big business and big government that is the second pillar of today's corporate regime. Corporations are the senior partners in the marriage, dominating the political class because of their control over election funding and the media and the general triumph of big money over all major social institutions. I call the marriage "corpocracy," since it represents corporate rule in a constitutional democracy and turns a formally democratic government into a vehicle for corporate ends. To be blunt: call it "pseudo-democracy."

Give due credit to Reagan for this second pillar. Despite Reagan's rhetoric that "big government is the enemy," he hugely expanded the vast, unaccountable federal government, a body so entangled with big business as to be indistinguishable from it. Reagan's cabinet of former CEOs, like Bush's, functioned as a Board of Directors for corporate America. True, Reagan dismantled much of the government created by the New Deal regime in the name of returning power to the people and the states. But he simply shifted government control and resources in a new direction: the system annually funnels billions of dollars in subsidies to corporations, whose financial power dominates the president's cabinet and congressional cloakrooms.

Corpocracy works like a Las Vegas slot machine, but one with a sure-fire chance of winning. Take the pharmaceutical industry as an example. In 2000, the industry put millions in the Washington slot machine to help reelect Bush. The industry then used its lobbyists in the House of Representatives to draft the huge Medicare overhaul bill passed in 2003. Yes, you're right, this bill prevents government bulk purchasing of pharmaceuticals, which might reduce prices and drug-company profits. And it will privatize Medicare, adding billions of dollars in profits to HMOs and private health insurers. And for good measure, the industry will give

---

The Regime and Mad Cow

After a "mad cow" was discovered in the United States, in December 2003, Alisa Harrison, the spokesperson for Agriculture Secretary Ann Veneman, told the American public **not to worry**—American beef is safe. She didn't say that she used to be public relations director of the National Cattlemen's Beef Association. In fact, the Department of Agriculture, which is supposed to protect the public from mad cow disease and other health risks, is packed with cattle and former ag-business lobbyists. Dale Moore, who is Veneman's chief of staff, was previously chief of staff for the National Cattlemen's Beef Association. And another high-ranking Department of Agriculture official used to be president of the National Pork Producers Council.

---

millions more in 2004 to help reelect the president and ensure the profits go where promised.

The New Deal remade government to serve and empower ordinary people, but today's regime is turning American democracy into a system of corporate

---

The Corpocracy Game

Rules for Drug Companies

1. Give Bush $21 million during his 2000 campaign.
2. Spend $100 million in contributions, entertainment, and lobbying of Congress between elections (2000–2004).
3. Use 467 lobbyists on the Hill to pressure representatives and draft the Medicare Overhaul Bill, which returns billions in new profits to pharmaceutical companies.
4. Spend $100 million in 2004 to reelect the president and make sure that the new Medicare program delivers the goods.

Of course, the game is not played just by pharmaceuticals. With all corporations pulling together, it's even more fun and profitable.

Rules for All Corporations

1. Give Bush $2 million during his 2000 campaign.
2. Get back $300 billion in corporate welfare.
3. Draft the laws on energy, trade, media, pharmaceuticals, and health care.
4. Laugh all the way to the bank with a trillion-dollar tax bonanza.
5. Spend $3 billion in 2004 to reelect the president.

---

sovereignty, creating a massive divide between rich and poor in political power as well as wealth. Corporations control the political agenda of both parties, and money washes away the people's voice. Citizens became consumers and couch potatoes, spectators of the show in Washington or indifferent to it. Workers lose their voices and, increasingly, their jobs.

Just as troubling to a functioning democracy as classic quid pro quo corruption is that danger that officeholders will decide issues not on the merits or the desires of their constituencies, but according to the wishes of those who have made large financial contributions valued by the officeholder.
—US Supreme Court, in a 2003 decision upholding campaign finance reform

Social Insecurity

The regime is systematically dismantling the social contract of the New Deal that promised social security to a generation traumatized by the Depression. That contract was expensive and protected people by regulating corporate excesses. The current regime seeks a new social contract—its third pillar—that trades the social security of workers and citizens for profit maximization.

Social insecurity begins with the job. The regime now aims to abolish the very concept of a job, the secure full-time form of work that prevailed in the mid-twentieth century but now is seen as an unacceptable limit on profits. "What is disappearing," writes organizational analyst William Bridges, "is not just a certain number of jobs—or jobs in certain industries ... but the very thing itself: the job. That much sought after, much maligned social entity, a job, is vanishing like a species that has outlived its evolutionary time."

Jobs that survived in the new regime lost their government or union protections. This required all-out assault on the New Deal Wagner Act, which enshrined unions, and President Reagan was up to the task. The regime wasted no time in busting unions, with Reagan's first act being the dismantling of PATCO, the air traffic–controller union. Reagan then began what is now a long-standing regime policy of breaking unions: he made anti-union appointments to government labor boards, encouraged companies to break union contracts and demand concessions, and facilitated the ultimate corporate weapon against labor, exit power. As companies under the new regime fled overseas for cheap labor, aided by Reagan's tax breaks for companies operating overseas, massive downsizing became the regime's signature. Thus, the regime created the breed of contingent and outsourced jobs that has turned America's "middle class" into an "anxious class."

Meet Allen Mardsden

In my interviews I talked to many downsized and outsourced workers. Allen is a forty-year-old software engineer freelancing for computer companies in the United States and living in Boston. Allen told me that his father "was a salesman for an electrical company, and he worked for the same company his whole life." But Allen, although well educated with graduate degrees in business and accounting, has worked for about forty companies," and, he says, "Fifty percent of the employees on the pay-roll are temp or contractors like me. The companies don't want to pay benefits, and they're greedy." Allen claims his father's era is finished, and Allen does not expect to ever get a permanent job.

By stripping away the protections and security of the New Deal job, the current regime is endangering the middle class. Allen declares flatly: "The middle class is disappearing." Allen says his own American Dream is shrinking. "Lots of things I thought I was going to have I may never have. I may never own a home. I may never marry, and I definitely will not have children." Allen is thinking not just of his own difficult economic circumstances but of his brother and sister-in-law, who have four children and are not making it. His brother has been downsized twice out of well-paying corporate jobs. Allen says, "My brother is on his second wife and was never in a position to afford even one."

In a transnational corporate regime, corporate globalization becomes the ultimate hammer for beating down US job protections and security in the name of "free trade." But, as noted earlier, "trade" has become simply a vehicle by which US transnational companies use American capital and technology to employ foreign rather than US workers, outsourcing jobs and using the threat of future outsourcing to erode the benefits, protection, and security of the American worker created by the New Deal regime. The US social contract is dragged down toward the horrendous social contract that has long prevailed in Third World countries, thereby globalizing the third corporate regime's social contract on terms that favor the transnational corporation at the expense of workers in both rich and poor countries.

Along with the loss of secure jobs and benefits, a horrendous social contract emerged from the slash-and-burn approach to the New Deal social welfare system. Reagan started the process by taking a sledgehammer to domestic social spending, arguing that the New Deal's welfare system undermined the entrepreneurial spirit at the heart of the new regime. He bled nearly every domestic program, education, health care, food stamps—to finance his huge tax cuts for the rich and his bloated military spending.

Reagan's social policies continued under Bush Sr. and into the Clinton years, when Newt Gingrich spearheaded the Contract for America, which proposed cutting nearly all social spending and leaving a government devoted entirely to corporate welfare and the military. Clinton did his part by calling for "the end of welfare as we know it." Clinton targeted one hundred thirty federal programs for extinction, many for education, scientific research, or the environment, and he proposed to abolish or radically downsize the Department of Housing, the Department of Transportation, and other agencies devoted to social ends. One Washington observer noted, "You expect to see Republicans when they are in power doing this—it's what they've been pushing for years. But to see the Democrats doing it, and to see the competition between the White House and the Congress as they race to privatize—it's amazing."

Bush is pursuing the regime's social contract in yet more brazen ways, openly promoting permanent tax cuts for the rich worth trillions of dollars while underfunding virtually all vital social programs, including his own touted education act, "Leave No Child Behind." The regime's contract of Social Insecurity is moving, under Bush, toward its ultimate conclusion: privatizing and ultimately eliminating Social Security itself. The collapse and scandals of the financial markets postponed Bush's plans until his second term, but he proposed privatization in his 2004 State of the Union address, and his advisors are candid that they remain committed to privatizing Social Security and turning it from a scheme of social insurance into a private system of investments. That system not only threatens the retirement security of millions of lower- and middle-income Americans but also guarantees a multibillion-dollar bonanza for the Wall Street managers who are salivating about the profits to be made on your retirement money and mine.

Empire

As it revolutionizes life at home, the corporate regime is bent on transforming the rest of the world, distinguishing itself from the corporate regimes of the Gilded Age and Roaring Twenties. The foreign policy aim of the current regime—its fourth pillar—is to shape a global corporate order under the political and military direction of the United States. That aim reflects the globalization of the economy, the increasing dependency of American corporations on profits abroad, the post–World War II collapse of the European empires, and intractable global crises that require military solutions. These elements combine to create a militarized corporate system, breeding a new form of empire and a system at home eroding classic American civil liberties.

Empire has a long American history, but the current regime is pulling out all the stops, dismantling much of the multilateral framework and the system of international law created under the New Deal. Remember that Roosevelt helped create the United Nations, and his regime successors, such as Truman and Eisenhower, pursued global power with some deference to multilateralism and UN conventions. Reagan was impatient with international treaties and other multilateral restraints on American power. He rejected the entire New Deal international framework, openly expressing contempt for the United Nation, arms control, and restraints on military spending. The new regime's corporate patrons encouraged Reagan's inclination to use American power unilaterally, including efforts to change regimes throughout Central America and elsewhere in the Third World, to open the world up to their own global greed.

President Bush has simply accelerated the regime tendencies begun under Reagan and pursued more quietly under Bush's father and Clinton.

Maintaining Reagan's disdain for international law and his fondness for interventions and regime changes abroad, Bush has used the post-9/11 climate mainly to institutionalize these long-standing regime policies in an even more transparent model. Former White House advisor William A. Galston described the regime's current approach in its more extreme form: it "means the end of the system of international institutions, laws and norms that the US has worked for more than half a century to build." Princeton political scientist Richard Falk, one of the nation's leading scholars on international law, writes that the preemptive invasion of Iraq "repudiates the core idea of the United Nations charter.... It is a doctrine without limits, without accountability to the UN or international law."

While the United States remains a constitutional system, the current US regime already involves military expansion in the name of a war against evil, a fevered culture of patriotism and resurgence of religious nationalism, a system of growing repression and secrecy to protect "national security," the rise of a Homeland Security Department and a culture of surveillance, a weakening of traditional checks and balances, integration of corporations and the military, and the rise of a master ideology and political culture organized around "spin" and deception. These tendencies have been most developed by the Bush administration but are consistent with the regime's enduring aims of global dominance. They have raised serious alarms not just among liberals, but among many conservatives, from former Nixon advisor Pat Buchanan to the international financier George Soros, who see the specter of an Orwellian future. It is easy to see their point.

Have You Had This Experience?

While driving in Boston recently, I saw a big, official-looking sign posted on the back of a city bus. It showed images of duct tape, flashlights, and water bottles, and it featured a face with a large eye looking right at me. The sign read, "Help everyone be safe by keeping your eye on the system." I felt a chill run down my back as I realized the sign was really saying, "Keep an eye on your neighbors," a Homeland Security directive right out of Orwell's *1984*.

The Corporate Mystique

Free markets! Free trade! Free people! Free Iraq! Free world! Free after-Thanksgiving sales! Freedom is the seductive mantra of the third corporate regime. Most Americans buy it.

Liberty, of course, has always been at the heart of American ideology. What is new is a rhetoric of freedom for all that translates into unimagined freedom for big business, and big problems for the rest of us. The expansion of freedom for the First Citizens of this regime (that is, the corporations) is now equated with personal freedom. When we increase the freedom of corporations to speech or privacy, we increase our own. If we limit corporate free speech by limiting corporate campaign contributions, we threaten the cherished First Amendment speech rights of citizens.

It is all part of the corporate mystique, the regime's ideology telling us that a "free market," based on unfettered corporate liberty, is the best of all possible worlds. The mystique says there really is no other way. The market's freedom is the cornerstone of every citizen's freedom, and a free corporation is the precondition to a free society. The corporation is the golden goose, but it needs free range. When freed to do what it wants, it delivers the goods. If we shackle it, we shackle ourselves and our prospects for the good life. Kill corporate freedom and we kill off democracy.

The mystique, while rhetorically embracing personal liberty, in truth nourishes one form of personal freedom: the right to splurge at the mall. Consumerism! It is the highest form of freedom in the corporate mystique, and the regime encourages us to use our plastic cards to keep consuming long after we can afford to. Consumerism replaces citizenship as the operative value in the regime. *I buy, therefore I am. I am what I buy!*

The freedom dreamed of by the Founders is at high risk. Citizen choice in this regime is the right to decide between Coke and Pepsi. The regime argues that choice at the marketplace is the most powerful act of citizenship. One dollar, one vote. That is the democracy of the corporate mystique.

The regime then gets away with its frightening restraints on personal civil liberties, symbolized by the notorious Patriot Act. Citizenship is redefined as freedom in the mall, not the town hall. A corporate regime is seductive since we grew up as kids addicted to magical corporate goodies, whether Disney films or PCs. Creature comforts are the great blessings of the regime, and they are not easily dismissed by anyone, especially a population brought up on Toys "R" Us and wild about Big Macs. How can you challenge the producers of the Magic Kingdom, who have brought you happiness your whole life? How can you challenge the makers of Mickey Mouse, your best friend for life?

The corporate mystique, and its consumerist brand of democracy, was born in the first corporate regime and turned into a national religion in the second corporate regime of the Roaring Twenties. But in the earlier corporate regimes, leading ideologues were busy enough persuading the ordinary American to embrace the corporation and get serious about consuming. Now they have to persuade the rest of the world. Globalization is the spread of the corporate mystique as the universal religion of the planet, and it is the cutting edge of the third corporate regime's ideology.

One of the chief ideologues of globalization, *New York Times* columnist Thomas Friedman, writes, "So ideologically speaking, there is no more mint chocolate chip, there is no more strawberry swirl, and there is no more lemon-lime. Today, there is only free-market vanilla." Nobody puts the regime's line better than Friedman. Corporations are not good and necessary for the happiness only of Americans but of everyone in the world. And even if you don't like it, you better learn to, because the train is out of the station and can't be turned around. "I feel about globalization a lot like I feel about the dawn. Generally speaking, I feel it's a good thing that the sun comes up every morning.... But even if I didn't much care for the dawn there isn't much I could do about it.... I'm not going to waste my time trying."

This is the corporate mystique as God's way. The regime aims to make everyone on the planet a believer.

The Six Regime Sins

Six trends have hit the headlines under Bush that reveal the long-term basic aims of the larger regime. If the pillars of the regime create the design of the "house," these sins are the design flaws that will lead to its inevitable destruction. We have here a mansion with a luxurious upper floor and a deteriorating foundation. Even as the architects are busily expanding the mansion, walls are crumbling, plumbing is rusting, and the roof is leaking. All these things hint that the regime, or political house, is beginning to implode and decay.

1. Hooverism Redux

Bush is the only American president other than Herbert Hoover to preside over a net loss of jobs in the economy, at this writing 2.6 million of them. The mass loss of full-time unionized manufacturing jobs, along with long-term wage stagnation and the relentless stripping of overtime, pensions, health care, and other benefits, has been a defining feature of the regime for the past quarter-century. As it did under Hoover, the regime trusts in business as it moves the country and the world toward a speculative financial capitalism, chronic macroeconomic instability, erratic growth, and potential systemic deflation or depression. In this sense, Hooverism is the economic Achilles heel of every corporate regime, expressing itself now in global deregulation, overproduction, and financial instability.

2. The Red Shift

One of the key signs of systemic erosion is the scary red shift in the national accounts. Reagan led the way when he cut taxes and increased military spending, creating huge new debts. The Bush administration has created the biggest budget deficits in American history, amounting to $378 billion in fiscal year 2003 and projected to be almost half a trillion dollars the following year. The current Bush deficits are bigger, as a share of GDP, than those of Argentina when it melted down in 2002. Combined with massive trade deficits, the budget deficits put into serious question the fiscal credibility of a country depending on Japanese, German, Chinese, Saudi, and other foreign investment to finance its multitrillion-dollar national debt. The regime's priorities of high military spending, giant corporate subsidies, and enormous tax cuts ensure growing long-term debt. Bush pushes tax cuts, military spending, and deficits to the limits, thereby endangering the health of the economy and the regime he represents.

3. Reverse Robin Hood

Every corporate regime is Robin Hood in reverse. The deficits from Reagan to Bush Jr. grew out of manic tax cutting to achieve the corporate regime's main aim: transferring wealth to the rich. Trumping Reagan's, Bush's successive income tax cuts, projected to amount to several trillion dollars over the coming decade, are the most spectacular giveaway to the rich in American history. The top four hundred families, under Bush, gained the highest percentage of national income in more than half a century; the top percent of the US population control 40 percent of the wealth, their biggest slice of the American pie since the 1920s. During the first twenty years of the regime, "the gap between rich and poor more than doubled from 1979 to 2000.... The gulf is such that the richest 1 percent of Americans in 2000 had more money to spend after taxes than the bottom 40 percent." Between 1973 and 2000, average real income of the bottom 90 percent of Americans fell 7 percent. The top 1 percent saw their income rise 148 percent, the top 0.1 percent had a 343 percent income rise, and the top 0.01 percent had a 599 percent income rise. America looks increasingly like Third World economies made up of corporate aristocrats and paupers.

4. Good-Bye Social Welfare, Hello Corporate Welfare

Bush has accelerated the regime's twenty-five-year trend toward brutally cutting social services—including education, Social Security, and health care, privatizing the shrunken remains, and redirecting federal savings to corporate welfare such as farming subsidies, mining and timber giveaways, research and development breaks and subsidies for big pharmaceuticals, depreciation breaks, and huge contracts to military companies. By the mid 1990s, according to the conservative Cato Institute, the regime was already spending approximately three hundred billion dollars a year on corporate welfare, reflecting the cronyism at the regime's heart. The biggest service cuts and corporate welfare are still to come, laid out in the Bush administration's plans to privatize Social Security, Medicare, and the other programs at the heart of the New Deal. The Bush plan will turn over billions to the Wall Street houses that invest the new privatized retirement accounts, and to the health care companies that take over administration of Medicare, thereby undermining the retirement nest egg and key health care needs of most Americans as they age. But the war at home does not discriminate against the elderly; young people are the fastest growing group of poor in the twenty-five years of the regime, reflecting ever deeper cuts in education, child care, and welfare.

5. Corporate Constitutionalism

Rewriting the Constitution to protect corporations rather than people has been a dominant theme of corporate regimes since the Gilded Age. Under the First, Fourth, Fifth, Sixth, Seventh, and Fourteenth Amendments, the Supreme Court has been extending constitutional protections to corporations, securing the corporate right to spend literally billions of dollars, through political action committees (PACs) and "soft money," on political campaigns and Washington lobbying, immune from public scrutiny. In the Reagan years, this was the perfect breeding ground for the savings and loan scandals and for huge corruption in the Pentagon and other government agencies. Today, the rash of Enron accounting scandals, Putnam mutual fund fraud, and Wall Street currency trading scandals reflect the same regime tendencies that weaken regulation and corporate accountability. Bush's new frontier involves coercively exporting legal protection for corporations to the rest of the planet under the auspices of the World Trade Organization (WTO), which encompasses in its trade rules a planetary version of inviolable corporate rights in the name of free trade, development, and the war against terror.

6. Global Imperialism

The United States has been expansionist since its beginning, but the third corporate regime has been the most imperialist and militarist on a planetary scale. Reagan massively built up the military and the military-industrial complex and engineered multiple regime changes abroad—most famously in Nicaragua, Grenada, and other Central American countries—in the name of anti-Communism. While his backers claimed that Reagan's policies created regime change in the Soviet Union itself, the Soviet Union, much like the Roman Empire, crumbled from within mainly because of its own corruption and inefficiency. After the Soviet meltdown, Bushes I and II both warred in Iraq to create a world order run solely by the United States. A long-standing regime aim is to integrate the petroleum reserves in the Middle East and elsewhere; the overarching goal is to increase the global profitability of American firms by preventing the rise of rival empires or trading blocs. Geopolitics and planetary greed meld in the new military-corporate regime, which now justifies its global imperialism in the name of a permanent war on terrorism.

9

Romney's "47 Percent" Blunder Reveals the Hidden Heart of His Agenda

Charles Derber and Yale Magrass

Obama may have failed to nail him for calling nearly half the nation parasites, and Romney may have beat a hasty retreat from the beans he spilled in a private moment among rich friends, but Americans should heed the core truth it revealed.

If President Obama wins re-election, historians may view Mitt Romney's now infamous "47 percent dependent" remark as the decisive turning point. But the comment has deeper implications than the election outcome.

It weakens the long-term credibility of right-wing political discourse on dependency and welfare. And it will help transform the public's understanding of capitalism, as Americans see that those most dependent on government are corporate elites, turning upside down our ideas of who is parasitical.

In the first debate, Romney never mentioned the 47 percent and Obama, in a devastating blunder, never called him on it. And just two days later, Romney did his ultimate etch-a-sketch and said his comments had been "completely wrong."

But the now-infamous comments will not fade away since they are the heart of right-wing philosophy and Romney's agenda. They tell the core conservative narrative of "producers versus parasites" and they reveal the nasty realities of capitalism crucial to understanding our economic system and decline.

Romney defined the 47 percent as those Americans who feel entitled to government benefits, don't pay income taxes and are parasitical in the sense that, "I'll never convince them they should take personal responsibility and care for their lives."

The potent right-wing narrative on which Romney builds is that society is always divided between a class of producers or "strivers," and one of parasites. The producers are private sector employers and their workers, who create wealth. The parasites are government workers and the needy depending on government benefits, especially welfare.

It has now become dogma among Republicans that the government is inherently incapable of generating wealth, that it can only be a leech, draining resources away from private individuals and corporations, who, if unfettered, would bring untold prosperity to all.

The Republican anti-parasite narrative teaches that society can prosper only when the producers dominate the parasites and keep them from destroying wealth, progress, the work ethic and the broader health of society. In an economic crisis, the 47 percent, specifically white workers, could turn against their corporate employers and even capitalism itself. However, the narrative tells them the source of their troubles are government, the Left and shiftless parasites.

In the United States, the history of the "parasite" narrative is inseparable from Republican politics. After the 1929 crash, President Herbert Hoover refused to give massive government aid to the unemployed, claiming that it would reward sloth and bankrupt the government, a theme taken up in the 1930s by big business critics of the New Deal, like the American Liberty League and by Right populists like Father Charles Coughlin.

The moocher discourse regained prominence in the 1950s and 1960s, in the presidential campaign of Barry Goldwater and the immensely popular novels of Ayn Rand, who explicitly wrote about the war between "productives" and "moochers." Rand became a hero to the new generation of young conservatives that included Paul Ryan, who helped lead the "New Right" to build a base among white workers, especially in the South.

Under Ronald Reagan, the right-wing charge of parasitical dependency became mainstream. Welfare "queens" and government social programs were demonized to rally hard-pressed workers against liberals. Reagan's success transformed US politics, weaning the white blue-collar class from the Democratic Party and creating a blue-collar class of white "Reagan Democrats" whose anger at employers was replaced by an ironic solidarity with bosses in the struggle against the "parasites." Herein lies the answer to the question of "What's the matter with Kansas?"—why workers act against their own self-interest.

Mitt Romney underwent a magical metamorphosis since being Massachusetts Governor, explicitly embracing the moocher narrative, believing that this would secure his majority among white workers, his swing base most resonant to the parasite story.

But Romney made a fatal error. Parasites had always been defined as a minority of America, mostly African Americans. But with the "47 percent," he suddenly turned a huge percentage of whites into "parasites." This deeply alienated the millions of whites who had always gained self-respect by identifying with the class of the "productives" or "creatives," a world apart from the minority parasites.

Romney turned his most important swing base—white workers—against him, and, in the long-term, gave them reason to question the legitimacy of the entire parasite narrative.

But it gets worse. By defining half the country as dependent on government, Romney suddenly opened up the question of who was not dependent. And a series of stories about Romney, Bain Capital, and Romney's taxes began to make clear a revolutionary truth: that the corporations and richest Americans, such as Romney himself, were actually the most dependent, the most parasitical.

The 47 percent began learning some startling truths about Romney and Bain, the company that Romney founded and made him rich. Bain subsidiaries, Holson, Staples, Steel Dynamics and GST Industries received millions of dollars in grants and tax exemptions from communities where they built plants and offices. To encourage Steel Dynamics to build a plant in DeKalb County, Indiana, the county and the state gave $37 million to the company in subsidies, which was paid by raising taxes for DeKalb residents by 0.25 percent, a direct transfer of wealth from the working class to the corporate elite.

Bain executives such as Romney also owe much of their wealth to special tax laws that allow them to redefine their income as "carried interest," on which they pay much lower rates than on normal income. Romney and other Wall Street executives are also dependent on tax shelters in paradises like the Cayman Islands, where Bain Capital has organized 138 funds.

In the 1990s, Bain was spared from possible collapse when the Federal Deposit Insurance Corporation forgave $10 million of over $30 million that Bain owed.

The 47 percent did not have to work hard to see that Bain Capital is hardly the only recipient of "corporate welfare." As of March 31, 2012, the federal government has given investment bankers $4.6 trillion in TARP bailouts of which only $1.3 trillion has been paid back.

The bailouts had become a sore point among white workers and other believers in the parasite narrative. Wall Street bailouts have opened them to the larger story of corporate welfare, something likely to become a leading story as the issue of "who is dependent" blows open.

The money the government gives annually to corporations runs into hundreds of billions. These include tax breaks, depreciation allowances, submarket sales of land and natural resources to mining and oil companies. Energy companies receive about $78.8 billion annually in subsidies. Under the Mining Act of 1872, $230 billion worth of federal land was given to mining companies from 1872 to 1993. Federal subsidies to agribusiness may have totaled $245.2 billion from 1995 to 2009.

The 47 percent already knows that government spending brings billions in profits to defense contractors such as Lockheed Martin, General Dynamics, Raytheon, and Boeing. In 2011, the top 100 military contractors received a total of about $117.5 billion from the Pentagon. Lockheed Martin alone received $17.4 billion, Boeing $8.4 billion, Raytheon $6.2 billion, and General Dynamics $5.5 billion.

The white workers in the 47 percent will have to ask if big military companies, like the banks, aren't "dependents."

After the election, the new debate about "dependency" will expand. The 47 percent will inevitably learn that corporate dependency is hardly new. Right from America's beginning, state public works projects underwrote the private economy. Throughout the nineteenth century, the railroads were built with largely public money, but the profits went to private robber barons. The federal government handed over 19 million acres in land, as well as about $1.1 billion in 2010 dollars in grants to the Union Pacific and the Central Pacific, the "private" companies that built the transcontinental railroad.

Nobody would drive Ford's Model T or Romney Sr.'s AMC Rambler without roads built by the government. While praising the achievements of private entrepreneurs, Mitt Romney proclaims, "We once built the interstate highway system and the Hoover Dam," neglecting to mention that these were massive public works projects. The 47 percent are more likely to see through this now.

They may also be more ready to see that the corporation itself is an invention of the state, an artificial person, who is entitled to have its private property protected by the government, no matter how many billions it is worth.

Romney's 47 percent blunder—and the huge debate it unleashed—has exposed two deep and subversive realities that could reshape US politics after the election. One is that the rich are parasitical and have always mooched much of their wealth from the state.

The trillions spent on welfare for the rich could unleash mass anger against elites like Romney who claim to have made it on their own. The hyperindividualistic rhetoric of the 1 percent will begin to sound absurd, especially to the white workers in the 47 percent who have been taken in by these deceptions for so long.

The second subversive reality is that capitalism is a form of state welfare for the corporations, undermining the most basic idea of capitalism itself.

If the corporations and the richest Americans are government-dependents, then capitalism looks to the 47 percent who believed in the "free market" myths as an outrageous lie. Their anger could still be trained on welfare recipients, but this time the corporations could bear the brunt of their sense of betrayal.

Of course, there is no inevitability that the dependency debate will lead in this hopeful direction, even if the 47 percent are now more receptive. It will take concerted action by progressives after the election to make good use of this new "teachable moment." The Occupy movement started this education, and deteriorating economic conditions will continue to feed public discussion about "free market" dogmas and the statist realities of capitalism, in which government helps the largest companies dominate the market and that 100 percent, but especially the rich, are government-dependents.

If the American government is to serve 100 percent of the American people, not the 1 percent in the corporate elite, it is necessary—but not sufficient—to defeat Romney. What happens after the election is crucial. Obama and the Democrats have been co-perpetrators of many of the myths about "free market" capitalism. Obama will not blow away these myths, but it will be easier for the movements to educate the public if the Democrats, who share skepticism of Republican "dependency" and "parasite" rhetoric, are in power.

After the election, mass campaigns like the Occupy movement, focusing on removing money from politics, ending most corporate welfare, expanding social welfare and creating true democracy, must continue and expand. The government, even an Obama-led government, must know the people will never be quiet until it becomes a government of the people, not the corporations.

10

Sociopathic Globalization

Sacred cows make the tastiest hamburger.

—*Abbie Hoffman*

History supplies little more than a list of people who have helped themselves with the property of others.

—*Voltaire*

Maybe it's because I teach in a Jesuit school, but I often find myself talking about trinities. There are three things at the heart of globalization: the building of a global economy, politics, and culture. They are the three pillars of a new world system and are completely intertwined. You can't build and integrate (1) new global markets without (2) new rules administered in a political system of global rather than national sovereignty that depend on (3) globalized cultural beliefs. If you cut off one leg of this three-legged stool, it will soon buckle.

A body of misconceptions surrounds this trinity, and they have become so widely held that I refer to them as a new "common sense." However, as is often the case, this common sense is deeply flawed and does not reflect what researchers have learned about both modern and ancient globalizations. Whether the new common sense is sensible has become a serious puzzle for thoughtful US citizens today. I will now return one more time to globalization's ghosts to see how history can help us decide what is sense and what is nonsense.

Consider the first leg of the stool: the making of a global economy. It has many names, from "free trade" to "economic integration" to apple pie, equivalents in US parlance today. The new common sense states that global economic integration is (1) new, (2) inevitable given the new technology, and (3) one of those rare earthly joys: a win-win situation.

This is far from nonsense. Yet listen first to this Bangladeshi worker, whose story, told in 2001, suggests how strange and mythical these ideas must seem to her.

My name is Samima Akther. I am twenty-one years old. I have been working in garment factories for three years. Since February I have been working in Shah Makdhum as a sewing operator.

I produce shirts including Disney's "Pooh" label. My operation is joining the side seams of the shirt. In my factory, each line has thirty-three machines. Each line produces 120 shirts per hour, a total of 1,320 shirts a day if we work eleven hours.

Until recently, I had to work from 8 AM until 10 PM each day. We get only two days off a month. I walk to work and back because I cannot afford to take a bus or bicycle rickshaw, which would cost 450 *taka* a month. In dollars that would be $7.84, or 27 cents a day. The factory is three kilometers away, and it takes thirty minutes to walk. I normally get home at 10:30 PM.

I get a regular wage of 1,650 *taka* a month, not counting overtime. In dollars this comes to $28.75, or 14 cents an hour.

Because we have to work very long hours, seven days a week, we have no family life, no personal life, no social life.

Samima wants to keep her job. This tells us that the win-win story of globalization may not be entirely wrong, despite her sad life. Let us first look at why Western economists and leaders see hope for Samima, and what cautionary wisdom our ghosts may offer. After all, the lives of these wretched workers, we now know, are intertwined with our own; until Samima can eat and feel safe, our own prosperity and safety cannot be assured.

The win-win view has been called the Washington Consensus, because every president in the last twenty years has bitten deeply into the apple and pronounced it delicious. President Clinton embraced globalization with the same untutored schoolboy's enthusiasm as did Ronald Reagan and the two George Bushes. All presidents since 1980 have proclaimed free trade as a centerpiece of their presidencies. Just weeks after September 11, President George W. Bush traveled to a Southeast Asian summit to declare that free trade remained the key to peace and prosperity in an age of terror.

The reasons seem simple enough. Globalization is good for American business because it creates overseas markets and a field of dreams for investment. It's good for US workers because, while some lose jobs, others get better ones from the export opportunities. It's good for poor countries because they get desperately needed foreign investment. It's good for rich and poor countries because of export-led prosperity. It's good for the world economy because it makes for efficiency above all else, and it's good for world peace because trade helps link nations together. The websites of the president's Office of Trade and the World Trade Organization spell out all of these benefits with pictures, carefully chosen examples, and statistics.

For those who worry about sweatshops and Samima's or Nisran's poverty, the Washington Consensus has soothing and persuasive messages. MIT economist and *New York Times* columnist Paul Krugman tells a story: "Could anything be worse than having children work in sweatshops? Alas, yes. In 1993, child workers in Bangladesh were found to be producing clothing for Wal-Mart, and Senator Tom Harkin proposed legislation banning imports from countries employing underage workers. The direct result was that Bangladeshi textile factories stopped employing children. But did the children go back to school? Did they return to happy homes? Not according to Oxfam, which found that the displaced child worker ended up in even worse jobs, or on the streets—and that a significant number were forced into prostitution." This sentiment underscores the apple-pie argument that mainstream economists make about trade and global markets: trade is a form of mutual gain or economic safe sex. Any international economics textbook, in the chapter titled "Comparative Advantage," will tell you that it makes economic sense for Portugal to specialize in its most efficient product, wine, and for Britain to stick with its most efficient good—let's say clothing—and then trade with one another. This is true even if the clever British can make *both* wine and cloth cheaper and more efficiently than the Portuguese. While it might seem better for the British to make their own wine too, they will make more money by specializing only in clothes, shutting down their vineyards and buying the wine of the less efficient Portuguese.

Early formulations by the great classical economists Adam Smith and David Ricardo appear to support this perspective. Trade, Ricardo says, "binds together, by one common tie of interest and intercourse, the universal society of nations throughout the civilized world. It is this principle, which determines that wine shall be made in France and Portugal, that corn should be grown in America and Poland, and that hardware and other goods shall be manufactured in England." The message here is that trade is a win-win for the world, because all nations are better off doing only what they are naturally equipped to do best—and engaging in trade or economic intercourse for the rest.

While something akin to biblical text in mainstream economics, it ignores certain assumptions by both Adam Smith and David Ricardo and leaves open the idea that both Smith and Ricardo might be offering now at least half a cheer to the Seattle protesters. Smith assumed that the "invisible hand" of the market worked only when "moral sympathy" binding local communities was strong and capital had deep local roots. Ricardo said that free trade was a win-win only under very limited circumstances: particularly when capital could not travel from high-wage to low-wage countries and when unemployment was low and trade balanced. Today's cheerleaders for free trade make other flawed assumptions, including the idea that each country has "natural" cost advantages in certain products or industries. This assumption sounds reasonable, but it ignores the fact that countries create "natural" advantages through subsidies and other political incentives. Nonetheless, conventional international trade analysis does what good academic theory does; it is rigorous within its own assumptions, and it has an intuitive commonsense nature about it.

But it is blind to history. This is not surprising since economic history is out of fashion with today's economists. Colonialism was obviously a system of economic integration and trade, but hardly a win–win proposition entered into, as Ricardo writes, by "a common tie of interest." The colonies went along because they had a chain around their necks with a very short leash. Colonialism led to bloody anticolonial revolutions and wars, and some who see globalization as a new form of colonialism have already begun to pick up their guns.

The most powerful evidence against the win–win view comes from the school of "world system theorists" who have studied a range of ancient glob-alizations, of which colonialism is only one form. The reigning figure is Immanuel Wallerstein, who believes that Westerners have been looking at the world with the wrong set of glasses for about the last five centuries. We look through the glasses of our respective nations, seeing national economies, national interests, and feeling like a member of our own country. I am an American, we say proudly. Or a Brazilian or French. Wallerstein suggests we are seeing an illusion when we see the world in this way. Or more precisely, we are missing the forest for the trees. For several centuries now, he argues, the nation has been simply an interdependent part of a much larger reality of economically integrated world systems. It's these systems that we must acknowledge. The nation doesn't stand alone or have a true autonomous identity, but we hang onto it for dear life as if it's everything.

World system development has been going on for at least seven hundred years: some believe that the process actually goes back almost to the dawn of civilization itself. Through much of history, what we might call "global-izing projects" have knit together distinct tribes, city-states, or nations. The knitters are most often traders—like the Venetian merchants who traveled the famous Silk Road to join Europe with the exotic markets of the Orient. But whether they are ambitious traders, conquering generals like Alexander the Great, bold explorers like Christopher Columbus, or ruthless entrepre-neurs like Cecil Rhodes, they help build a large integrated market and a new regime. In the more successful of these ancient globalizations, a world system is created that may not actually encompass the whole world (in fact, it can be only a small geographic slice of the earth), but that blooms into a far greater order than the tribes or societies comprising it. Examples range from the Renaissance Mediterranean economy built around the city-state of Venice to the British Empire. Some believe that the first world system and global economy was Mesopotamia in 3000 BC.

The punch line here should be very sobering to the apple-pie thinkers of today and to all of us concerned about the relation between global inequality, poverty, and violence. The historical research finds one universal idea: that all globalizing projects through history have created world economies polarized into "cores" and "peripheries," winners and losers. If the scholarship is as accurate as it is voluminous, all ancient globalizations have historically been wired more as a win-lose than a win-win proposition—and often degraded into wars and sickening violence between the core and the periphery.

Distinguishing the core and periphery is not rocket science. In the Roman Empire, Rome was the core, and all its far-flung dominions the periphery. In the "world-economies" of the Italian city-states such as Venice, Florence, and Milan, the core was the center City itself, and the periphery its smaller and weaker trading partners. In the British Empire, London was the core, and the colonies (from India to Palestine to South Africa) the periphery. Colonialism can be defined as a world system in which the core and periphery are legally and militarily linked as colonizer and colonized in an exploitative division of labor. But, and this is perhaps the more telling historical conclusion, virtually all ancient globalizations seem to have been built around some variant of the core/periphery divide.

Core and periphery are historically intimate partners that function a bit like spouses in what the Oprah-world calls a codependent relationship. There is a deep and unhealthy interdependency. Like dysfunctional marriages, world systems wed economic partners on troubling terms but create binding ties and constraints that make it difficult to exit. Codependency, however, suggests a kind of equality or eager mutual complicity that is misleading when it comes to ancient globalizations. Core and periphery are not created equal; the inequality is raw and naked in colonialism, but it recurs in mild to virulent forms in virtually every world system. "Unequal exchange," which history suggests is a more apt phrase in globalizing projects than "free trade," has polarized core and periphery from the Egyptian Empire of the pharaohs, to the Renaissance Italian city-states, to the last colonial empires of the twentieth century (whose vastly extended peripheries included much of diamond-rich Africa and the oil-rich Middle East).

Today, globalizing projects continue to integrate and divide the core (the developed nations of Europe, Japan, and the United States) and the periphery (the Third World). The core uses skilled labor, while unskilled and cheap labor dominates the periphery. The core enjoys high profits and accumulates capital rapidly relative to its periphery. The core is higher on the "commodity chain," meaning that it tends to rely on its periphery for raw materials and to reserve for itself the production processes requiring the most sophisticated technology and skill. Net wealth tends to flow from the periphery to the core rather than vice versa. Not surprisingly, then, the end result is a wider and more tragic wealth gap between core and periphery than existed when the globalization project took off.

Let us personalize this depressing line of analysis by thinking again of Samima. Bangladesh is the periphery, and if history tells us anything, it is that Samima and her fellow Bangladeshis are not going to see their living standards get closer to ours or even take them out of abject poverty. The Western core countries, if history repeats itself, will take more money out of Bangladesh than they will bring in unless Samima and her fellow workers gain a new voice in deciding how the global economy works and who runs their factories.

But why do globalizations seem to always polarize in such tragic "unequal exchange," with such serious potential for violence and war? Trading partners start at different levels of development. They are often integrated through conquest, as colonialism illustrates. Even before colonialism, trade was often historically intertwined with military tribute or forced expropriation of property, raw material, or profits from the periphery. Free trade, the mantra of today, has almost always involved rules and terms of trade imposed by the more powerful trading partners.

And power is the key idea here. It is absolutely central and yet constantly neglected in the apple-pie free-trade conversation. History teaches us that you never ever have trade without power. Trade in oranges, oil, sneakers, or microchips is always shaped by the power of the businesses and the governments selling the sneakers or buying the oranges. In trade between core nations—for example, France and Germany—the power balance can be relatively equal. But when the core (the United States) trades with the periphery (El Salvador), the power imbalance calls to mind the dominatrix in black stockings holding the whip over her prostrate partner.

The core/periphery distinction is now being de-territorialized. That is, we find large parts of the periphery increasingly in the core. Think of all the impoverished immigrants from Mexico, China, Pakistan, or Nigeria who work in the sweatshops of New York or Los Angeles under conditions very similar to those of Samima and Nisran. And we find more members of the "core" in the Third World: superwealthy business leaders in Saudi Arabia, Thailand, Chile, or Mexico who are part of a new globalized plutocracy. This denationalization of core and periphery is one sign of the end of a thousand years of national sovereignty and the rise of a global sovereign that makes today's globalization a radical departure from all former systems.

The power difference between the core and periphery today (still largely a distinction between the First and Third Worlds) is immense, and the deeper the power imbalance, the more the risk of exploitative trade. Yet the win-win idea of trade fills the airwaves. Only two things can explain this out-of-touch discourse. One is that it simply reflects our desire to ignore how our own power stacks the odds in our favor, something that Third World nations have been trying to tell us for two centuries. The second is that our beliefs about trade are rooted in economic theories that never talk about power. Go to any leading international economics text, and search the index for *power*. Look in the table of contents for chapters on the historical power imbalances that shape trade. You will come up empty. This scandalous intellectual dereliction has made much of economics irrelevant to a real world discussion of globalization.

Despite this gloomy picture, trade can be good and mutually beneficial. Even in the context of great power imbalances, it can bring gains to the weaker party. In the Roman Empire, for example, many regions were eager to gain the privileges that Roman protection and investment brought. The lesson is to recognize that those who make the rules will reap the spoils. The danger is that the periphery will resent, hate, and then rebel, and the core will never feel secure.

John D. Rockefeller (J. D.) has something important to add about the economic dimension and its mythology. When we think of the Gilded Age economy, a globalization within the United States, we see two key stories. One can be called "go sweat," and the other is "grow the gap." Both reinforce the world-system historical perspective about why Samima and Nisran are likely to be losers rather than winners.

The famous Gilded Age muckraker, journalist Upton Sinclair, ventured into the terrifying meat factories of Chicago. In his classic 1906 book *The Jungle,* he described a world of sixteen-hour workdays, paying pennies per hour, in slaughterhouses making meat rotting with blood and hair. A century later, Sinclair's graphic look at the sweatshop economy still scorches the brain and shapes our understanding of the nature of the robber-baron economy.

The Upton Sinclair of today's global economy is Charles Kernaghan, the New York–based muckraker most famous for his exposé of sweatshops producing the Kathie Lee Gifford line of clothing for Wal-Mart. Mostly young girls worked at the factory in Honduras. Wendy Diaz was one of them. At a press conference in Washington, Diaz described her seventy-hour work week for approximately 31 cents an hour in an ovenlike plant where the bathrooms were kept locked. She told of nights of forced overtime, threats, physical abuse, and sexual harassment.

Ground zero of the global workshop is China, with its one billion-plus workers. In 2000, after numerous trips to Chinese factories, Kernaghan writes: "When you see an Ann Taylor suit on sale for $198, do you ever imagine twenty-year-old women in China being forced to work ninety-six hours a week, from 7 A.M. to midnight, seven days a week, and being paid just 14 cents an hour? When you think of Ralph Lauren or Ellen Tracy do you imagine women in China being paid 23 cents an hour to work fifteen-hour shifts six days a week?" Global companies, he writes, "are actually lowering standards in China, slashing wages and benefits, extending forced overtime hours, and weakening respect for human rights while relocating their work to a growing sector of unregulated foreign-owned sweatshops in the south of China."

The harsh reaction against unions is a defining mark of global free-trade zones, evoking memories of the robber-baron hatred of organized labor. After crushing the Homestead union and killing many strikers in the infamous 1894 labor dispute of the Gilded Age, Homestead Steel robber baron Henry Clay Frick wrote to his boss, Andrew Carnegie. "We had to teach our workers a lesson and we have taught them one they will never forget.... Do not think we will have any serious labor trouble again." Carnegie, who had been the only robber baron once supporting the ides of unions, joyously wired back, "Congratulations all around, life worth living again."

As in the Gilded Age, any force that gets in the way of cheap labor must go, leading to an all-out assault on unions throughout the world's global export zones. The struggle of workers to associate freely and form independent unions has become the new civil rights movement. While most nations have agreed to this right as codified in the UN's International Labor Organization, global production is increasingly organized to escape or crush unions. Companies flee to safe union-free environments such as China, El Salvador, or Honduras, which typically also offer the freedom to pollute and avoid regulations on health and safety, sexual harassment, or working hours and conditions.

Listen to Nisran, whose story suggests that the "go sweat" rule, especially the virulent opposition to unions that marked the Gilded Age economy, has reemerged in force:

> In my factory the supervisors treat us like dogs. I would like to be treated as a human being. If we try to make any demand or to argue, the supervisors threaten us and say they are going to fire us, or they fire us immediately without our severance pay. For this reason we cannot make any demands, we have no power, we have no possibility to organize. We would like to form a union, but for all these reasons it is impossible for us to organize.

The robber barons viewed their immigrant workers as just a step above animals or inanimate objects, more like children, and thus developed "scientific management" to shift all mental decisions from the workers to engineers and other managerial experts. They completely rejected the view that such "undeveloped" workers should unionize or have a voice.

Listen now to Samima's story:

> I cannot support myself with the wage I am getting. I have rice and lentils for breakfast, rice and mashed potato for lunch, and for supper rice and vegetables. I eat chicken once a month when I get paid, and maybe twice a month I buy a small piece of fish.
>
> If we want to use the bathroom, we have to get permission from the supervisor, and he monitors the time. If someone takes too long for any reason, the supervisor shouts at her and humiliates her, calling her names. If someone makes a mistake, the supervisor docks four or five hours of overtime wage, or lists her as absent, taking the whole day's wage.

In my factory there is no day care, no medical facilities. The women don't receive maternity benefits. The overtime is mandatory, but we are always cheated on our overtime pay. The supervisor makes us sign two separate payroll sheets. One tells the truth—that we worked four or five hours of overtime each day. The other says that we only worked two hours of overtime a day, as our labor law requires. That is the one they show to the buyers.

Our lives have been stolen. We are treated like animals, and any workers who attempt to get together a union are fired immediately and may be black-listed. We feel we have been born only to serve the needs of the owners.

As in the Gilded Age, the antiunion regime is a prescription for exploitation masked by the eagerness of workers to participate. In 1890s America, desperate Polish, Italian, or Russian immigrants waited in line to work in Carnegie's steel mills in Pittsburgh or in horrific sweatshops in Manhattan. Now, Samima and Nisran still want their jobs, and Mexicans flock to work in Mexico's forty thousand foreign assembly plants, like the Kukdong plant at Atlixco that produces sneakers for Nike. An international human rights team found that the factory refuses to pay legally mandated sick pay and maternity benefits, denies workers five hours' wages each week, and forces workers to eat in a plant cafeteria where food is spoiled. It imposes a company union while beating and firing workers seeking to organize an independent union. At another sweatshop, an Alcoa employee, Isidro Esquivel Sanchez, who clings to his job in Ciudad Acuña, Mexico, said, "They work us like donkeys, and we come back to this," pointing to his one-room, dirt-floor hovel. His coworker, Oscar Chavez Diaz, showed a *New York Times* reporter a weekly pay stub for $60; Diaz lives with his wife in the rusting shell of a school bus and says he lacks money for food and clothing. Economist Ruth Rosenbaum, who has studied purchasing power in eleven border communities where foreign plants proliferate, says the misery is getting worse. "You study these wages for a while," she says, "and it makes you sick to your stomach."

Yet the workers keep coming, prompting influential scholars and journalists to conclude that even the worst sweatshops are better than the feudal conditions in the countryside. Harvard's Jeffrey Sachs suggests that the only problem with sweatshops in poor countries is "that there are not enough of them." Sachs is right that millions in the new global workforce are clamoring to work at and hang on to sweatshop jobs. Says one Mexican female sweatshop worker, "Without these jobs, we would have nothing. We would have no food, and our children would die." But this reveals globalization as a system organized to take advantage of extreme human vulnerability, with the new captains of industry as eager as the old to capitalize on it. We make a terrible mistake if we think that the sweatshop workers desperate to hold on to their job are grateful to us. Nisran and Samima are fighting for their humanity and their survival, and these gentle souls, while not disposed to violence, will not go softly into the night.

"Grow the gap" could have been the slogan of the Gilded Age, and it too has come back to haunt us. In 2000, the three top shareholders of Microsoft owned more wealth than do all six hundred million people living in Africa. The three richest people in the world have accumulated more wealth than the combined GDP of the forty-eight poorest countries. The UN reports that 458 global billionaires have acquired a combined wealth equal to that of half of humanity.

A huge gap between rich and poor defined the Gilded Age. When John D. Rockefeller became the country's first billionaire, more than 90 percent of Americans lived in poverty. In the 1890s, when millions of poor people in Philadelphia, Chicago, and New York were living in some of the most densely populated slums in the world, robber barons were building their fabulous summer palaces in Newport. A leading scholar in the 1900s concluded that "the poorest seven-eighths of the families hold but one-eighth of the national wealth while but one percent of the families hold more than the remaining ninety-nine percent."

Splendid economic growth and high employment did not close the gap. Eighty percent of Gilded Age workers, who toiled twelve to sixteen hours a day, stayed poor. The reason was very low wages that robber barons created by exploiting the huge immigrant labor pool and successfully destroying unions. The combination of low wages and high profits grew the gap until the Progressive Era's reforms in wages, working conditions, and progressive taxation finally ended the Gilded Age.

Globalization resurrects the Gilded Age growth model that spectacularly increases wealth while expanding poverty. The wealth gap today is growing between and within nations. The average income in the world's richest twenty countries is thirty-seven times the average in the poorest twenty, and the per capita income gap between rich and poor nations *tripled* between 1960 and 1993. Globalization might someday level the huge differences between the First and Third World, but by the present rules it does just the opposite. As experts say, instead of win-win, the name of the game is "divergence." Could anything be more dangerous in our already deeply polarized world?

At the tear-gassed 2001 Quebec trade summit, the leaders of the Americas laid down their new battle cry: "Globalization = Democratization." The new US ambassador to Canada, Paul Cellucci, said, "The purpose of the summit is to help democracy. We want to strengthen democracy, the rule of law...." President Bush repeated that free trade is the foundation of freedom. He said he was putting his money where his mouth was by backing an "action plan" of $20 billion to build up democracy in every nation joining up with the massive new free-trade zone forged at Quebec.

Like the idea of trade as apple pie, the mythology of globalization as democracy has become part of the new common sense of the day. But is it true? Is globalization the brave assassin of African dictators or oil-rich sheiks of the old authoritarian world? After the events of September 11, the new spotlight on Middle East politics raises serious doubts. We are painfully aware that unreconstructed oil monarchies that give their increasingly discontented people no vote and hardly any free expression are as much a part of the globalization system as are liberal democracies. And we are newly aware that our support of antidemocratic Mid-East regimes that keep the oil flowing in the global economy has opened us to new and terrible dangers. At the 2001 antiglobalization Quebec protests, protesters saw the hated ten-foot-high chain-link fence keeping them out as a symbol of the "un-freedom" of globalization. If globalization is the spirit of democracy, why do they need to build a "wall of shame" to keep the people out? Said one protester, "This fence is an offense to justice and freedom. Tell your Dubya Bush he can cringe but he cannot hide behind this barrier." Nonetheless, there is reason for hope: globalization has supported new "emerging democracies" in many parts of the world, even if it bolsters other ancient repressive regimes. The relation between globalization and democracy is the most contentious and important of all questions in today's world—and it does not reduce to simple formulas.

The neglected lessons of former globalizations are important here. Remember that all globalizing systems throughout history have three dimensions, and while the economic one holds our attention today, the historical record shows that the political one may be the true father of any "world system" trinity. No one reminds us more of this than J. D. I have said that the robber barons were "globalizers in a single nation"; the new vast US market they created was bigger and richer than many European colonial empires. But while the robber barons are most famous for building Standard Oil, U.S. Steel, and the Morgan banks and making fabulous profits by ruthlessly breaking up unions and exploiting immigrant workers, their greatest accomplishment was rewriting the Constitution and changing the entire balance of sovereign power in American democracy. The Gilded Age is a historical window into a brave new form of corporate rule.

In 1892, tycoon Jay Gould telegraphed the new president, Grover Cleveland, a Democrat, this message: "I feel ... that the vast business interests of the country will be entirely safe in your bands." Cleveland assured corporate America that "no harm shall come to any business interest as the result of administrative policy as long as I am president." Republican president William McKinley succeeded Cleveland in 1896 with an even deeper commitment to a new corporate democracy. His campaign manager and close adviser, Mark Hanna, one of the most famous robber barons, staged huge fund-raising parades down Wall Street and raised millions to pay for McKinley's election.

With McKinley's 1896 knockout blow to the populist Democrat William Jennings Bryan, the robber barons sealed the political side of their own "globalization within a nation." As they knit local economies into a national US economy, sovereignty shifted in two directions: (1) from the states toward a newly powerful federal government and (2) from the people toward the large corporations and financiers. The new system of American government, essentially federalized democracy with a corporate logo, was described bluntly by 1890s populist, Kansan activist Mary Elizabeth Lease, as "a government of Wall Street, by Wall Street and for Wall Street." As the robber barons integrated the economy from New York to California, they deformed democracy and unhinged the social order. A leading Gilded Age scholar makes clear that the robber barons led not just a business crusade but a wholesale societal and political transformation. "Like earlier invading hosts arriving from the hills, the steppes, or the sea," he wrote, the robber barons "overran all the existing institutions which buttress society ... they took possession of the political government, of the School, the Press, the Church." Business, that is, began to absorb all of society into itself.

The unexpectedly swift rise in the size and power of large corporations helped create this revolution. Before the Civil War, corporations had been local businesses, and they were balanced in power by craft guilds, state legislatures, and other organs of community or citizen power. But after the Civil War, the robber barons beefed up their businesses to conquer the emerging national markets, while labor and community groups found themselves struggling to survive in the new scale of enterprise. Corporations had become businesses on steroids with huge concentrations of capital never seen before, while contending popular forces of unions and governments remained small in scale.

When you hear "balance of power," you no doubt think about Congress checking the president and the Supreme Court checking both. But the more fundamental balance of power is in society itself, involving the balance between business, on the one hand, and the "countervailing" forces of ordinary citizens and their unions, communities, and governments on the other. Democracies always require a delicate balance here and are undermined when the balance shifts too far in one direction. Democracies also require that popular forces remain supreme, even though they must respect important rights of property.

One lesson of the Gilded Age is that "globalizing" projects tend to tilt the social, and then political, balance of power dangerously toward corporate and financial entities. Money can move a lot faster than people. The information revolution has made investment capital astonishingly mobile, with General Motors or Sony able to shift operations across borders with a few flicks of the computer key. There are no emotional roots or family bonds to tie money down, but one can hardly say the same of the workers left behind or the organizations that are supposed to protect them. Unions are largely local or national affairs, as are governments that are stuck in fixed territories. They are contending with global corporations, the most exquisitely mobile large organizations in history. We can say that corporations are now jet streams, while unions and government are still quicksand organizations.

As anyone in a marriage knows, one of the great sources of power is the freedom to exit. In any relationship, the person who can leave has enormous leverage over the person who has to stay because he or she lacks the emotional or financial resources to leave. Now extend that way of thinking to globalization. Corporations enjoy huge new forms of exit power. By threatening to leave, they can exact enormous concessions from unions or governments. In the 1980s and 1990s, companies such as General Motors, AT&T, and Ford repeatedly forced frightened unions to open up contracts and "give back" wages or benefits. Entire countries confront the same extortion. For example, if El Salvador doesn't lower its taxes or change its environmental regulations or labor standards, the Gap will relocate to Guatemala. This is globalization as the proverbial "race to the bottom," with corporate exit options shifting the balance of power in every society away from the quicksand organizations to the jet streamers.

The Gilded Age offers an ominous warning of the implications for democracy. Exit across state lines by the big robber-baron companies became a corporate craze. In the 1890s, thousands of New York companies threatened to move across the Hudson River to New Jersey, a neighbor who offered not only lower taxes but far less restrictive corporate charters. In 1896, New Jersey created a revolutionary new charter, which permitted unlimited corporate size and market share, removed all time limits on the corporate charter, and legalized new mergers and acquisitions for Standard Oil and other companies already big as an octopus. Corporations were so pleased that by 1900, a total of 95 percent of big US companies decided to become New Jerseyites.

This triggered a furious bidding war among states not unlike the one going on between countries today. New York, Maine, Delaware, Maryland, and others competed to see who could shed fastest any hint of corporate public accountability in their charter. "For a state to be conscientious," wrote one law-school commentator, "would be synonymous with cutting its own throat." The eventual winner of this suicidal competition was Delaware, which, as one legal commentator put it, was "determined to get her little, tiny, sweet round baby hand into the grab bag of sweet things before it is too late." Virtually all big corporations began slowly migrating to this tiny state in the twentieth century, after it passed a revolutionary new general incorporation law that turned the corporation into the lord of the kingdom, a sovereign accountable mainly to itself.

"The certification of incorporation," the new law said, may "contain any provision which the incorporators may choose to insert." As Ralph Nader notes, "These little words literally turned corporate law inside out." States had previously retained for themselves all powers not expressly given to the corporation. Delaware blew away this fundamental tenet of state sovereignty by allowing corporations to define their own powers and make their own laws as long as they didn't go against explicit state prohibitions. This Delaware law was the Magna Carta of modern corporate sovereignty.

It succeeded, but far more important, Delaware inaugurated the *political* race to the bottom that profoundly changed democracy in America. For a hundred years, the United States had used its state charters to keep companies in check and harness them to the public interest. Before the Civil War, companies were subjected to harsh limits on acquisitions, capitalization, debts, land holdings, and even profits. Moreover, they had to show that they were contributing to the civic well-being, or they would be dismantled. In fact, Americans since Jefferson had been so afraid of concentrated financial power that many states in the pre–Civil War era limited banks to ten-year life spans.

But this kind of popular sovereignty went the way of the buggy whip when the robber barons economically integrated the nation. Using their exit power, they forced states into a madcap rush to free them of the slavery that Jeffersonian democracy had imposed. This is a ghostly preview of globalization's new politics that would make J. D., the greatest robber-baron power wielder, shiver with delight.

The creation of corporate sovereignty in the Gilded Age required a retooling of the American Constitution and was part of the great shift of sovereign power from the states to the federal government. Earlier globalizers such as John D. Rockefeller and J. P. Morgan triumphed not just by creating a race to the bottom among states but also by subordinating local and state authority to a more business-friendly, federal sovereign government. This globalizing of sovereignty within the nation eerily foreshadowed the secret of today's globalization.

Rockefeller and Morgan unleashed a constitutional revolution that blessed corporations as citizens of the republic, endowed them with protection under the Bill of Rights, and turned them into legal "persons" who would be kings of the castle. The property rights of these new "corporate citizens," enforced by the federal government, would come to reign supreme and trump the human rights of flesh-and-blood citizens. What the Gilded Age ultimately achieved was the reconstruction of democracy to fit a corporate world. Gilded Age constitutionalism is a precautionary tale of the legal revolution led by the World Trade Organization, today quietly drafting a new property-centered constitution for the world.

George W. Bush seems like a plain-spoken man to most Americans, and he says that globalization is just plain common sense. It's good for the United States, good for the Americas, good for the world, good for democracy, good for hungry people, good for economic growth, and good for civilization and peace in an age of terror.

But is his common sense right in this case? Our friendly ghosts Cecil and J. D. remind us again that earlier globalizations also created their own common sense. And while there is much to praise about globalization, a peek into history suggests that globalizers have tended to think a bit too kindly about their own enterprise. Globalizers always create a set of cultural values and beliefs by putting the best possible light on what they are doing. The cultural system props up the globalization trinity and creates a third mythology crucial in sustaining the new world order.

Cecil haunts us with the memory that the colonialists defined their endeavor as a moral responsibility. Rudyard Kipling's 1899 poem, "The White Man's Burden," is generally regarded as colonialism's creed. It begins as follows:

> Take up the White Man's burden
> Send forth the best ye breed—
> Go, bind your sons to exile
> To serve your captives' need

Throughout Kipling's poem, the refrain of sacrifice by a more advanced race in the service of a less-developed people recurs. He says the colonial globalizers "seek another's profit and work another's gain." The primitive state of those being served demands a heavy moral responsibility and lays a "heavy harness" and "weariness" on the colonizers:

> To wait, in heavy harness,
> On fluttered folk and wild—
> Your new-caught sullen peoples,
> Half devil and half-child.

> Take up the White Man's burden—
> Ye dare not stoop to less
> Nor call too loud on Freedom
> To cloak your weariness.

Not all the elites of the time bought into this "common sense" of sacrificial colonialism. Ernest H. Crosby, in the *New York Times,* wrote an 1899 rejoinder, "The Real 'White Man's Burden,'" that begins:

> Take up the White Man's burden;
> Send forth your sturdy sons,
> And load them down with whisky
> And Testaments and guns.

> Throw in a few diseases
> To spread in tropic climes,
> For there the healthy niggers
> Are quite behind the times.

Crosby ends his parody, for good measure:

Take up the White Man's burden;
To you who thus succeed
In civilizing savage hoards
They owe a debt, indeed;

Concessions, pensions, salaries,
And privilege and right,
With outstretched hands you raise to bless
Grab everything in sight.

But if more than a few skeptics remained, virtually all the business, political, and intellectual leaders of the European nations were fervent believers and avid propagandists for their global expansion. Cecil Rhodes spread far and wide their view of colonialism as impassioned idealism. As a young man, in 1877, Rhodes wrote a famous "Confession of Faith," in which he proclaimed, "I contend that we are the finest race in the world and that the more of the world we inhabit the better it is for the human race." Although he got fabulously rich through his global businesses, Rhodes always portrayed colonialism as both sacrifice and "duty." In establishing the criteria for Rhodes scholars, he talks repeatedly of "duty, sympathy for and protection of the weak, kindliness, unselfishness and fellowship." He established the scholarships to create a cadre of leaders who would put into practice his view of colonial globalization as a grand civilizing endeavor. This idea, in new language, has become part of globalization's creed today.

J. D. reminds us that the robber barons had cultural myths essential to their "globalizing" endeavors. When Rockefeller said, "God gave me my money," he was expressing the Gilded Age common sense that the robber barons were carrying out a divinely inspired plan. Like the colonists, the robber barons were religious men who saw their own ancient globalization as serving the highest moral ideals. The religion of the Gilded Age was couched in the rhetoric of social Darwinism, a distinctively American common sense. It made poverty, competition, and exploitation all part of the natural struggle for existence. Said one railroad baron, "Society as created was for the purpose of one man getting what the other fellow has." Rockefeller frequently used Darwinist language: "The growth of a large business is merely a survival of the fittest.... It is merely the working-out of a law of nature and a law of God." In other words, the integration of a national market, the robber barons' globalization within a nation, was entirely in harmony with nature and God. Like global business leaders today, the robber barons believed that the market was not a creation of people but part of a natural order of things. As markets expand and larger businesses swallow up smaller ones, business leaders are simply acting out the age-old morality of evolution.

Globalization today has softened its self-justifying rhetoric. Business leaders, backed by the world's most respected economists, continue to see global markets, commerce, and trade as part of the natural order of things. To refrain from globalization today would be to stand against the laws of economics and nature. But today's globalizers do not tend to read God's mysterious purposes into the misery of the poor. Rather, the new common sense is that globalization is the only viable way to bring the world's poor out of poverty.

Consumerism and the mystique of the market have replaced social Darwinism as the common sense of today's globalization. To challenge it seems to challenge the sovereign right of all the world's peoples to consume burgers at the golden arches or to dream of driving a Mercedes. Those who raise doubts tend to be viewed, at least within the United States, as just as strange as those a century ago who questioned social Darwinism or the white man's burden. When those outside of the United States, like Islamic fundamentalists in the Middle East, attack the new cultural creed, they tend to be viewed as relics of a doomed premodern era.

Some view this cultural revolution as the real explanation for the terrorist attacks on New York and Washington. Samuel Huntington has written of a new "clash of civilizations" now exploding between Islam and the West and pitting globalization against traditional values all across the world. It is a powerful idea, but not the prime source of the conflict between the Islamic world and the West. But without question globalization *is* an explosive cultural and secular force that exports the American dream and melds the idea of consumerism and freedom. Global culture is immensely seductive, even in the Middle East where anti-American elites mimic the lifestyles of the rich and famous, watching reruns of *Dynasty* and sipping Pepsi even as they decry US values and policy. The cultural magic is most explosive among the global poor, awakening desires for earthly comforts that they will never enjoy.

The culture of globalization is based on the vision of billions of people newly liberated to make their own choices in a market offering dignity and endless delights. Even when you recognize that it is a fantasy for most of the world's people, you see the seduction while walking down the main drag in the Sanjuku district of Tokyo at night. The hundred-foot-high, brilliant neon lights of thousands of well-stocked stores and boutiques selling brands from all over the world illuminate the nocturnal landscape. Engrossed shoppers rush around frantically, buying and buying as if making up for centuries of deprivation and serfdom. It makes you a believer and makes clear that globalization will not disappear until a new, even brighter vision takes root.

11

Kochamamie Democracy

Cockamamie: *adjective.* 1. Of poor quality, inferior 2. Silly; ridiculous

Texan oil and gas magnates David and Charles Koch, and a few other billionaires and multi-millionaires, such as Las Vegas casino tycoon Sheldon Adelson, are each pouring hundreds of millions of dollars into the elections, mainly to try to elect Mitt Romney as president and to ensure a Republican Congress. The unprecedented tsunami of big money into political campaigns—expected to total between $6 and $7 billion in the first presidential electoral season since the 2010 Citizens United Supreme Court case removed any limits on contributions—marks a qualitative shift from Constitutional Democracy toward what might be called "Kochamamie Democracy."

In Constitutional Democracy, the guiding principle is one person/one vote. In Kochamamie Democracy, it is one dollar/one vote.

One dollar/one vote is the legal principle governing US corporations, with each shareholder entitled to the number of votes corresponding to his or her number of shares, deviating from the Constitutional principle that each citizen is entitled to equal voice, whatever their wealth.

Kochamamie Democracy thus represents the corporatization of American democracy. Billionaires such as the Koch brothers, who own the second largest privately held US corporation, Koch Industries, have pledged $100 million of their own money as well as to bundle at least $300 million more in their Super Pac, Americans for Prosperity, to elect Romney and help consolidate corporate control over US elections and the US government.

One dollar/one vote has been the established system of corporate governance for over a century, enshrined during the 1890s Gilded Age. Whatever its economic merits, it is a degraded system of national political government and helps explain why a 2012 international Commission on Elections, Democracy, and Security, headed by former UN secretary general Kofi Annan, singled out the United States as the most important example of a rising trend of "uncontrolled, undisclosed, illegal, and opaque" political and election financing that is deeply corrupting, comparing the United States highly unfavorably to other advanced democratic nations such as Canada.

Kochamamie Democracy has the following core attributes:

- **Massive contributions from a tiny plutocratic elite.** A study by the Center for Responsive Politics of political contributions in 2011–2012 showed that the 100 top donors to Super Pacs, mostly super-wealthy individuals, were 3.8 percent of all givers but accounted for more than 80 percent of all political contributions in the current race. Beyond the Koch brothers, Adelson has said that he will spend "whatever it takes" to defeat Obama and elect Romney, already contributing more than $100 million and suggesting he may spend two or three times that amount.
- **Extreme low voter turnout.** The United States now has the lowest voter turnout of all advanced democratic nations, with about 60 percent expected to vote for president this year. The other 40 percent, comprising more than 80 million adult Americans, mostly low income and the working poor, who support President Obama over Governor Romney by about 2 to 1 according to a recent Suffolk University poll of nonvoters, view the system as hopelessly rigged and believe the act of voting has become pointless.
- **Corporate control of both major political parties.** Despite all the talk of extreme partisan polarization, the Republicans and Democrats are both captives of big business, the parties of Bush and Bush Lite. Parties that break from corporate priorities are unable to harvest the billions of dollars necessary to win elections.
- **Corporate control of government policy.** An infamous, secret clique of top oil executives and corporate lobbyists shaped the Bush-Cheney energy policy. This was emblematic of Kochamamie policy making. Corporate lobbyists on K Street, from Wall Street, trade associations, and the Chamber of Commerce, draft much of the legislation on finance, energy, pharmaceuticals, agriculture, trade, environment, and even national security.

Corporate influence has been a major force since the 1890s Gilded Age, but we are entering a new electoral regime, where both political parties toe the corporate line. Both President Obama and Governor Romney work within the corporate consensus, with Obama saying that "I am an ardent believer in the free market," and that "my administration is the only thing between you (the CEOs) and the pitchforks." But even a whiff of populist sentiment by Obama in this election has turned Wall Street—which helped elect him with huge money in 2008—toward support of Romney, who personifies the corporate "1%."

If Governor Romney wins, the explanation is Kochamamie Democracy. Because of the long-rising corporate takeover, the image of America as champion of constitutional democracy is already fading abroad and at home. Romney and the Republican Party—the most loyal political partners of Wall Street, corporations, and their agenda—are committed to Kochamamie Democracy because it is their only way to win when their core policies hurt the majority and are not embraced by the majority of voters, as Romney acknowledged in his 47 percent comments.

Changing this degraded system will require reversing the United Citizens decision, creating public financing of campaigns, redistributing wealth, passing iron-clad laws limiting lobbying and separating corporations and government, and breaking up or nationalizing the nation's biggest companies, while rechartering corporations to ensure that business serves the people, not the reverse.

Part IV

War and Sociopathic Foreign Policy

Introduction to Part IV

Sociopathy and Empire

Sociopathic societies tend toward mass violence both internally and externally. Historically, militarism is a defining trademark of large and powerful sociopathic societies. In the most powerful—Rome, Britain, and now the United States—it gives rise to empire.

Imperial foreign policy—and especially wars of conquest by empires or hegemonic powers—are sociopathic because they kill or injure large numbers of innocents while undermining the integrity or survival of entire societies, including the imperial hegemon itself.

What moral philosophers call "just wars," such as those aimed at preventing genocide or for legitimate self-defense, may not be sociopathic. But wars carried out by an empire aim to secure profit and power. This is sociopathic behavior at its worst, exemplified by colonialism or neocolonialism. Imperial wars epitomize sociopathic behavior enshrined within the legal code of the sociopathic society itself.

The main chapter in this section demonstrates, first, that the United States is, in fact, an empire. America has developed a new neocolonial model differentiating it from European and other past empires. This chapter identifies five stages of US empire, each manifesting sociopathic values and conduct integral to the nation as it developed.

Second, this chapter shows that the American empire, as was also the case with the Roman and British empires, has been cloaked in lofty moral and religious discourse, with conquest justified as good or sanctioned by God. In the United States, the moral and religious justifications—including slogans such as "Manifest Destiny"—have been persuasive to many Americans and constitute a form of *"immoral morality"*: evil done in the name of good. The strength of this moral discourse in the United States makes it particularly difficult for Americans to see their own nation's foreign policy as sociopathic. The intense moralism and religiosity of the US discourse is, itself, a form of sociopathy, reducing resistance to unjust wars in the US public.

Four short chapters following the main chapter look at recent examples of US political discourse and sociopathic policy around militarism and imperial violence. They show that Martin Luther King's effort to critique the war in Vietnam made many see him as a traitor, while the storm about President Obama's relation to his Chicago pastor, Reverend Jeremiah Wright, symbolized the risks of defining American violence abroad as sociopathic. That led John Kerry, an anti–Vietnam war activist inside the military, to choose to run for president in 2004 as a "war hero" rather than a "peace hero," a term that barely exists in our political vocabulary. Kerry's choice symbolizes how difficult it is to speak of the sociopathy of US foreign policy. The final short chapter shows that militaristic societies almost always bring their wars home, offering a new perspective on the sociopathic crisis of gun violence on our own streets and in our schools, malls, and workplaces.

12

American Empire and Its Moral Big Stick

Charles Derber and Yale Magrass

If we cannot muster the resolve to defeat this evil in Iraq, America will have lost its moral purpose in the world.

—*George W. Bush, March 28, 2007*

Americans see themselves as a "shining city on the hill," a moral beacon for all humanity, but not an empire. The British, while recognizing their empire, shared some of this blindness. Salman Rushdie observed wryly, "the British don't know their own history because so much of it happened overseas."

But Americans have been particularly reluctant to see themselves as an empire—a startling fact given that the United States is the most powerful nation in history. While showing classic signs of overstretch and imperial decline, the United States remains a military, economic, political, and cultural colossus astride the world. Its power makes Rome and Britain, at their height, look pitifully weak.

The reluctance to acknowledge empire is also surprising because US expansion and intervention have been so continuous and violent throughout its history. True, much of American imperial force has been exercised through what Harvard political scientist Joseph Nye has called "soft power," including economic and diplomatic influence; and the United States has been anticolonial in its strategic approach to world power. Empires based on soft power that do not acquire formal or legal colonies are still empires. Political scientist Dimitri K. Simes agrees, observing that empires, which are defined by their transnational exercise of "great authority over large and varied territories"—an obvious trait of America—"rely on a broad range of tools and incentives to maintain this dominance: political persuasion, economic advantage, and cultural influence where possible, coercion and force when necessary."

But the American Empire has been based on hard as well as soft power: hard power so brutal, persistent, and expansive that the pervasive denial of empire remains puzzling. In a recent book, former *New York Times* journalist Stephen Kinzer details fifteen different regime changes forced by American intervention, often through the CIA, and involving overthrows of democratic governments replaced by US-supported dictatorships, from Iran in 1953 to Guatemala in 1954, to Chile in 1973 to Iraq in 2003. American scholars and pundits all across the political spectrum have chronicled the endless imperial US interventions, regime changes, and wars. On the Left, these include great historians such as Charles Beard and William Appleman Williams, and contemporary analysts such as Noam Chomsky, Chalmers Johnson, and William Blum. In the center are historian Andrew Bacevich and Kinzer, and on the Right are Niall Ferguson, Pat Buchanan, and the neoconservatives Max Boot and Robert Kagan. Their work leaves little room for doubt about America as an empire. Yet in a 2006 survey of students on my own (Derber's) campus, a plurality of students, and a vast majority of those identified as conservative, say they do not believe that America is an empire, which national polls also confirm.

American denial of empire is startling for yet another reason: it has been an empire with increasingly global aspirations since its founding. In 1783, George Washington characterized the colonies as "a rising empire," and nearly all the Founders saw America as destined to become one of the world's great empires. After 9/11, American leaders and neoconservative intellectuals defined America as a new kind of democratic empire called on by God and the world to defend civilization, spread freedom, and combat terrorist barbarism. Of course, this moral story was not new at all since it mirrored the immoral morality of both Rome and Britain and is part of the American moral fairy tale.

From the beginning, Americans saw themselves as a chosen people destined for greatness. They were also always intensely moralistic, their moralism and religiosity a defining trait of the Puritans who arrived on the Mayflower as well as the early slaveholders in Jamestown. Because of its radical individualism, the United States also had special needs for the glue that the identity of a winning team provides. America's triumphant morality made a group of enterprising immigrants without strong roots or safety nets more secure about themselves and their community. Moreover, the ruthlessness and acquisitiveness of American capitalism intensifies the need for an immoral morality that moralizes global greed and global power.

While George W. Bush is often seen as the creator of the American Empire, nothing could be further from the truth. American capitalism and the religious and moral ideology of the Founders created an empire project that has defined the nation since its beginning.

American history is actually the story of *five* American Empires, each reflecting the capitalist imperatives of the era, as well as a particular story of immoral morality.

First Empire: The Fledgling
Constitutional Empire, 1776–1828

In 1776, Americans began a revolution to free themselves from the British Empire and to recreate themselves as an independent and great power. Alexander Hamilton, a leading architect of the US Constitution, argued the thirteen colonies should unite to create an empire: "one great American system, superior to the control of all trans-Atlantic force or influence, and able to dictate the terms of the connection between the old and new world." As noted earlier, Hamilton's boss, George Washington, saw America as "a new empire rising." A South Carolina planter of the era, William Henry Drayton, foresaw "a new empire, styled the United States of Americas, that bids fair, by the blessing of God, to be the most glorious of any upon Record."

The Revolution led quickly to melding the colonies into a new, vast nation. In its first fifty years, the United States would expand southward and westward with stunning speed and violence. The milestones after 1776 included the following:

- In 1783, in the Treaty of Paris, Britain ceded its territory south of the Great Lakes and east of the Mississippi River to the Americans.
- In 1803, President Jefferson completed the Louisiana Purchase, the biggest expansion in the New Empire's history, adding 526 million acres that constitute 22 percent of the land territory of the modern United States, including not just present-day Louisiana, but also "parts or all of present-day Arkansas, Missouri, Iowa, Minnesota west of the Mississippi River, North Dakota, South Dakota, Wyoming, and Colorado east of the Rocky Mountains" and parts formerly of Canada.
- In the War of 1812, the United States tried to take all of Canada from the British but failed.
- In 1821, Andrew Jackson conquered Florida since slaves were escaping there to gain Spanish protection.

By 1789, virtually all of America's Founding Fathers had weighed in to support a vision of empire. The Founders drew on America's creation myth of a "city on the hill," a Godly beacon of freedom to the world pronounced by John Winthrop as the Pilgrims' creed and repeated by Jonathan Edwards, who said that "God might in [America] begin a new world in a spiritual respect." In 1778, George Washington issued a proclamation from Valley Forge that it has "pleased the Almighty Ruler of the universe to defend the cause of the United States...." Washington added in his inaugural address to Congress in 1789 that "every step" of the new nation "seems to have been distinguished by some token of providential agency." John Adams wrote that the colonial era was just "the opening of a grand scheme and design in

Providence for the illumination of the ignorant, and the emancipation of the slavish part of mankind all over the earth." America was mythically born, like Christian Rome and Livingstone's Britain, as an empire constituted by God to serve His will, an imperial America that Ronald Reagan and George W. Bush, among many other presidents, would repeatedly call "God-blessed."

But as suggested by Adams, in his reference to "the illumination of the ignorant, and the emancipation of the slavish part of mankind," this early Constantine vision of a Godly American Empire was tightly linked to an equally ancient secular immoral morality, expressed in the British Empire as the White Man's Burden and earlier in pagan Rome as the moral obligation to spread civilization to the barbarians. The American Founders created their own version of empire, stressing freedom and the Constitution. We shall call it the Constitutional Code, and it has prevailed to this day as a central creed of American imperial, immoral morality.

Today's Constitutional Code, as we will soon see, speaks of America's moral obligation to bring freedom and constitutional government to the Islamic nations, as well as the rest of the world. Its core message is:

1. Americans are a free people on a free land.
2. Americans inherited the rights of Englishmen and are destined to develop them further, including rights of religion, conscience, expression, and equal rights under the law.
3. The Constitution is sacred and may have been sanctioned by a higher power.
4. All Americans have the constitutional right to freely contract with others and to protect and accumulate property.
5. Freedom, including the right to property, requires a state to protect it. However, the state should intrude upon that freedom as little as possible.
6. Freedom requires prosperity. Resources must expand, and the state must be prepared to help citizens acquire, trade, and market their goods everywhere.
7. Americans must be prepared to help people everywhere who cannot develop freedom and prosperity on their own. The truly unfit and dangerous may have to be eliminated.
8. As a beacon for the rest of the world, America has a manifest destiny to extend from sea to sea and, in fact, beyond the oceans.

As will be shown soon, the Constitutional Code evolved through all five American Empires. The Founders, while sharing the assumption (indeed creating it) that America radiated universal values of freedom and constitutionalism, did not embrace the rights of all Americans, such as slaves or Native Americans. They also had a particular focus, arguing that American

Empire was necessary not just to bring freedom to the world but also to preserve liberty in America itself. As early as 1751, Benjamin Franklin wrote that expansion for surplus land was crucial to creating prosperity and liberty, and to avoid domestic corruption. James Madison, the author of the US Constitution, vigorously espoused this argument. Inverting the French political thinker Montesquieu's notion that freedom was possible only in a small country, Madison argued precisely the opposite, as paraphrased by Williams, that "empire was essential for freedom." In a letter to Thomas Jefferson, Madison wrote that a republic "must operate not within a small but an extensive sphere." An expansive and expanding state would acquire the new, surplus land and resources necessary for prosperity, cohesion, constitutional rights, and freedom: "Extend the sphere, and you take in a greater variety of parties and interests; you make it less probable that a majority of the whole will have a common motive to invade the rights of other citizens."

Here, Madison is using a version of the Constitutional Code that justifies a strong and expanding state as necessary to preserve the universal moral values of liberty and rights enshrined in the Constitution. But Madison's critics in the 1780s and beyond saw the immoral morality built into Madison's reasoning. Fellow Virginian John Taylor wrote that Madison's argument was leading to an "iron government" of an imperial nature. "The executive power of the United States is infected," wrote Taylor, "with a degree of accumulation and permanence of power, sufficient to excite evil moral qualities." Taylor especially feared the executive branch's license in war making, reminding his friends Madison and Jefferson that "War is the keenest carving knife for cutting up nations into delicious morsels for parties and their leaders."

Taylor did not prevail, but his critique worried Jefferson, who had moral doubts about empire but overcame them. In arguing for the Louisiana Purchase, Jefferson wrote that the people of Louisiana "were as yet incapable of self-government as children." And in 1809, Jefferson wrote that "no constitution was ever before as well calculated as ours for extensive empire and self-government." Jefferson's startling idea that the Constitution's supreme moral virtue of self-government required and justified empire is the core of the immoral morality in the Founders' Constitutional Code.

The colonists and Founders assembled both Godly (Constantine) and secular (constitutional) high morality to justify an imperial project rooted in mundane commercial interests. Expansion westward and southward offered both Northern merchants and Southern planters endless horizons of wealth. To disguise acquisitiveness in the discourse of Christian mission and liberty was, itself, a classic sign of immoral morality. But the most serious form of immoral morality among the colonists and Founders, as in Rome and Britain, was superimposing these high moral arguments on the dirty business of conquering, removing, and killing large "savage" populations, which in America consisted of more than twelve million Native Americans as well as enslaving millions of Africans. Since the commercial interests driving empire ultimately required what can only be described as genocide and terrible crimes of slavery, it is impossible to deny the immoral morality with which the colonists and Founders, and the Constitution itself, will be forever tarred.

Both colonists and Founders coped in ways borrowed from the Romans and the British. The colonists and Founders were deeply steeped in Roman classical history and moral philosophy and were British subjects, using long-standing British moral sophistry and self-deception integral to immoral morality. One involved the lie that much of the land was empty. The dimensions of that lie continue to grow as historical research shows that the size of the Native American population and African slave community were far greater than scholars have traditionally known, while also showing that Native Americans and slaves were key, by virtue of their skills and labor, to building America itself.

Another approach involved simply denying the humanity of the Native Americans and slaves, treating them as agents of the Devil or as animals. European Christians had often seen darker peoples—including Muslims, Africans, Asians, and Indians—as primitives or Satanic, and the Devil was always portrayed as black. Killing or enslaving was morally construed as "a sign of the Grace of God." Both religion and racism played a role in this form of "hard imperialism" that could take the religious form of destroying Satan or a crude secular Social Darwinism that justified genocide and slavery as a form of natural law and the triumph of the morally fittest.

Another approach was "soft imperialism," which did not deny the humanity of the Native Americans and Africans, "acknowledged their achievements," and "considered it possible and desirable to elevate the Noble Savage into at least partial civilization." Soft imperialism, a classic immoral morality of both pagan and Constantine Rome, and at the heart of the White Man's Burden, moralized conquest as religious or civic salvation, a moral service to the conquered. America's "city on the hill" radiated soft imperialism, both of the religious and secular variety. Winthrop's Christian community would deny the legal claims of Native Americans to their land but would treat them as potential converts. The Founders' Constitutional Code would treat self-government as a potential ideal for the undeveloped savages and justified conquering them as exposing them to civilization's highest blessings.

Second American Empire: Manifest Destiny Continental Empire, 1828–1898

In the Second Empire, America expanded westward all the way to the Pacific Ocean, annexing a good chunk of Mexico in the south and west and uniting a vast continent under one government. All this was done to acquire land, spread American Gilded Age capitalism from coast to coast, and create a beachhead for economic expansion across the Pacific. But the expansion was dressed up in eloquent immoral morality, the famous creed called Manifest Destiny, drawing on the Chosen People motif of the Romans, the White Man's Burden code of the British, and America's own vision of spreading democracy and civilization.

Nobody symbolized the immoral morality of the Second Empire better than General Andrew Jackson, whose rise to the presidency in 1828 inaugurated the new era. In this swashbuckling fighter, we see all the imperial populism and brutalism of the age. Jackson promoted violent expansionism mainly to help the Southern plantation economy that was depleting its own land and needed more. Jackson inaugurated the pre-bellum phase of the Second Empire, which unsuccessfully sought to reconcile expansionist interests of Northern capitalism and the Slave South.

Jackson expelled Native Americans from all land east of the Mississippi, but he did not always bother to provide moral justification—a reminder that empire sometimes uses raw force without pretenses. In 1833, Jackson told Congress without any high moral rhetoric that the Natives "must necessarily yield to the force of circumstances and ere long disappear." While Jackson was describing genocide, his lack of moral posturing was almost refreshing since there is nothing more morally odious than the use of high moral arguments to slaughter indigenous peoples.

Nonetheless, Jackson could not keep removing and killing without resorting to high principles and creating his own immoral morality. In annual addresses to Congress from 1829 to 1836, he used several different moral arguments that later became integral to Manifest Destiny. One was virtually a clone of the British White Man's Burden, with the Indian Removal Act of 1830 discussing how "removed Indians" would, under US guidance, advance "from barbarism to the habits and enjoyments of civilized life." Jackson told Congress of his own desires to uplift the Indians: "Toward the aborigines of the country no one can indulge a more friendly feeling than myself, or would go further in attempting to reclaim them from their wandering habits and make them a happy, prosperous people."

In another congressional address in 1831, Jackson proclaimed about Indian removal, "It is pleasing to reflect that results so beneficial, not only to the States immediately concerned, but to the harmony of the Union, will have been accomplished by measures equally advantageous to the Indians." Jackson then offers this classic version of immoral morality: "That those tribes can not exist surrounded by our settlements and in continual contact with our citizens is certain. They have neither the intelligence, the industry, the moral habits, nor the desire of improvement which are essential to any favorable change in their condition." Jackson concludes that they must accept their removal and control by the "superior race," for it will teach them the virtues of a civilized nation.

Here, Jackson describes Indian removal and subordination as service by Americans to an inferior race. This is extermination framed as moral education and civilizational uplift. The racism echoes the British White Man's Burden, but the emphasis on the obligation to help barbarians become civilized goes back to Rome.

Jackson melded this civilizational theme with motifs of self-defense of America against Indian aggression. In 1832, after a particularly brutal assault that killed numerous Cherokees who resisted removal, Jackson told Congress this: "Severe as is the lesson to the Indians, it was rendered necessary by their unprovoked aggressions, and it is to be hoped that its impression will be permanent and salutary." Here, Jackson equates Indian resistance to extermination as aggression and the US fight against such "aggression" as honorable self-defense. This was analogous to the nineteenth-century imperial British, who defined Africans resisting colonization as "terrorists." The British viewed their war against such terrorists as the protection of civilization itself and thus essential to the survival of morality.

Three years after Jackson completed his second term, and the Indians had largely been eliminated east of the Mississippi, John L. O'Sullivan would expand on the larger meaning of Jackson's accomplishments. A prominent diplomat, journalist, and editor, O'Sullivan coined the term Manifest Destiny to explain America's great moral mission as a new hemispheric empire. In 1839, in an essay called "The Great Nation of Futurity"—one of the classic American doctrines of immoral morality—O'Sullivan argued that the United States was unlike any past nation or empire. "On the contrary," O'Sullivan argued, "our national birth was the beginning of a new history, the formation and progress of an untried political system, which separates us from the past and connects us with the future only; and so far as regards the entire development of the natural rights of man, in moral, political, and national life, we may confidently assume that our country is destined to be the great nation of futurity."

America, O'Sullivan said, is destined for something entirely new—and far more moral than any prior nations or empires. "We are entering on its untrodden space," wrote O'Sullivan, "with the truths of God in our minds, beneficent objects in our hearts, and with a clear conscience unsullied by the past." But while O'Sullivan emphasized American exceptionalism, he actually makes the case for a new American Empire that sounds much like earlier empires—and has the hint of Orwell: "The far-reaching, the boundless future will be the era of American greatness ... its floor will be a hemisphere, its roof the firmament of the star-studded heavens, and its congregation an Union of many Republics, comprising hundreds of happy millions ... who will, what can, set limits to our onward march? Providence is with us, and no earthly power can [stop us]."

America's Manifest Destiny is power over all the hemisphere of the Americas, and O'Sullivan suggested this is just the beginning of a providential guidance by America of all nations of the world. This vision of US power makes both the Roman and British empires look small, but theorists of Manifest Destiny, such as Stephen Austin, who led US colonists into Texas to take it from Mexico, sees this as a moral mission, a principled obligation, in almost exactly the same sense that the Romans and British did. "It is so destined," Austin proclaimed, because America's principle of "equality is perfect, is universal." Here, in pronouncing the radical newness of America, Austin and other Manifest Destiny moralists return to the argument of pagan Rome: that its values are universal. They are, Austin wrote, "the self-evident dictates of morality." As in Rome, and as reinterpreted by Madison, Jefferson, and other Founders, this universality of America's moral vision of liberty and equality—as codified in the US Constitution—gave it both the right and the "duty" to expand its influence around the world.

Manifest Destiny was a reformulation of the immoral morality of the Founders' Constitutional Code, justifying endless American expansion to spread freedom: "We must onward to the fulfillment of our mission [i.e., spreading across the Continent and to all nations] of . . . the principle of our organization—freedom of conscience, freedom of person, freedom of trade and business pursuits, universality of freedom and equality. This is our high destiny, and in nature's eternal, inevitable decree of cause and effect we must accomplish it."

This secular moral imperialism became a license for US expansion in the Second American Empire, involving war against Mexico and persistent extermination of Native Americans after the Civil War. Stephen Austin argued that "Texas was a wilderness, the home of the uncivilized and wandering Comanche and other tribes of Indians," and he wrote that it was necessary "to restrain these savages and bring them to subjection." His great moral justification for taking Texas from Mexico by force was "that it was due to the great cause of liberty, to ourselves, to our posterity, and to the free blood which I am proud to say, fills our veins." Here, we see the immoral morality of *justifying a war to expand slavery in the name of liberty.* Austin explicitly links this to the civilizational and Constitutional Code of the Founders: "Our cause is just, and is the cause of light and liberty—the same holy cause for which our forefathers fought and bled to resist and proclaim war."

Austin portrayed the Mexican war as deeply moral, not only to spread freedom but also to guarantee the security of the United States. In 1846, President James K. Polk, who led Americans in the Mexican war, proclaimed that US security required annexing not just Texas but all of Mexico, leading much of the public and Congressman Abraham Lincoln to oppose Polk's war as "imperialist." But invoking the Monroe Doctrine and the right of self-defense, Polk rallied Congress to support the war. Polk raised "national security" to a high moral imperative, his main contribution to American history.

Manifest Destiny, the Second Empire's main moral story, also carried echoes of the Constantine Syndrome, with America's great power, like that of Rome, seen as ultimately sanctioned by God. In defining Manifest Destiny, O'Sullivan wrote: "All this will be our future history, to establish on earth the moral dignity and salvation of man—the immutable truth and beneficence of God. For this blessed mission to the nations of the world, which are shut out from the life-giving light of truth, has America been chosen."

The language evokes the constitutional secular moral code of the Founders. But the Second Empire emphasized that America is carrying out God's will, with O'Sullivan saying, "America has been chosen" by God. In O'Sullivan's seminal essay on Manifest Destiny, he continues, "In its magnificent domain of space and time, the nation of many nations is destined to manifest to mankind the excellence of divine principles; to establish on earth the noblest temple ever dedicated to the worship of the Most High—the Sacred and the True."

It is thus not just the US Constitution but God who has ordained American Empire. In the Second Empire, American elites discovered, like Constantine, that divine will is the most compelling argument for military intervention, something that remains central in American immoral morality all the way up to President George W. Bush.

Manifest Destiny opened up the entire US continent as a wild frontier. As Americans in their covered wagons rode across that "virgin land" in the last phase of the Second Empire, a new Frontier Code emerged. It justified the final taking of the West and was a marriage of the Constitutional Code and Manifest Destiny:

1. People, especially men, prove their goodness through valor, courage, and hard work.
2. Good men are entitled to their property, the fruit of their labor, but must be prepared to defend it.
3. Good men protect their family while they should expect respect and obedience as patriarch and provider.
4. Good people should bond together to form a law-abiding prosperous community, obeying the community's rules and leaders or sheriffs.
5. There are outlaws and savages, including rebellious Native Americans, who do not accept the rules. They are apt to cheat, steal, and resort to violence.
6. Men of courage and honor must control the outlaws, using violence if necessary, and removing savages who prevent expansion of law and order across the frontier.
7. Good men have a manifest destiny to bring civilization to the wilderness, even though it has a rustic beauty, which should be preserved as much as possible.

The Frontier Code masculinized the imperial impulse and became the American blueprint for heroes from Buffalo Bill and Wyatt Earp to John Wayne and George W. Bush. The American cowboy was born as an imperial hero. Teddy Roosevelt imprinted his own stamp on it in the Third American Empire.

Third American Empire: Allied Global Empire, 1898–1945

In the Third Empire, the United States expanded its reign from the continent to the world. Manifest Destiny was globalized and American leaders described their new empire as the source of the first truly moral global order. The Third Empire's contribution to immoral morality was to build global American dominance in the name of a new world, free of the evils of colonialism and enshrining universal values of American democracy.

This vision cloaked the economic interests that drove the Third Empire in high moral principles—the classic mark of imperial immoral morality. By the end of the nineteenth century, when financial crises and class struggles were destabilizing and saturating the domestic market, US agricultural and industrial firms were already investors in Latin America and were hungrily eyeing trade in the Pacific and in China, as well as expanding trade in traditional European markets. America's imperial drive was fueled by commercial greed and interest like that of the Europeans, even as it claimed a moral rather than self-aggrandizing end. But the United States was not yet ready to displace the British or other great European empires. Instead, it rhetorically challenged European colonialism in order to supplant European influence, while also allying temporarily with Europeans in imperial wars that could expand US access to resources and "free trade." The "open door" policy announced by Secretary of State John Hay under President Teddy Roosevelt became the economic mantra for free trade and US expansion, but the broader argument for the Third Empire remained fundamentally moral. Presidents Grover Cleveland and William McKinley attacked the morality of Spanish and European colonialism, inaugurating a new thread of "humanitarian" argument for expansion; Theodore Roosevelt defined the morality of US war and global policing as "civilizing" and essential to world order and "national security"; and President Woodrow Wilson defined a new American global order that would replace European colonialism, spread democracy and liberty, and a century later would become the hallmark of the neoconservatives and of the immoral morality of George W. Bush.

The Spanish-American War of 1898 over Cuba and the Philippines marked the beginning of the Third Empire. By the 1890s, the United States had already invested deeply in Cuban sugar plantations as Cuba's relation with Spain—its colonial master—became increasingly conflictual. The

Monroe Doctrine and Manifest Destiny had already made clear that the United States claimed a high moral imperative to prevent European colonialism from taking root anywhere in the Americas. The Third Empire began with an American assault on Spanish colonialism and on the backwardness, cruelty, and evilness of the Spanish control of Cuba, thus implicitly invoking a contrast between greedy European empires and democratic American globalism. American Empire would be the anti-Empire, a conceit central to American immoral morality.

In 1896, President Cleveland, moving toward a war footing with Spain, noted the US economic interests, observing that "$30 million to $50 million of American capital are invested in plantations and in railroad, mining, and in other business enterprises on the island." But Cleveland quickly shifted the discourse from economics toward morality, saying, "The people of this country always feel for every struggle for better and freer government," and proclaimed that America would act out of "considerations of philanthropy and humanity in general." Cleveland joined the growing chorus of newspapers and pundits calling for America to help "liberate" insurgent Cubans from a despotic Spanish rule. In 1898, joining the "yellow journalism" of William Randolph Hearst, who was selling newspapers by railing against the Spanish as brutal torturers and imperialists, the *New York Times* described the Spanish national character as blending "civilization and barbarism." The polarity between American goodness and European colonial evil was the new American gospel. So, too, was the identification of the American anti-empire as a new form of global humanitarianism.

In his first State of the Union Address, in 1897, President William McKinley announced his intention to intervene against the Spanish for it is America's "duty imposed by our obligation to ourselves, to civilization, and humanity to intervene with force." Here, McKinley aligned himself four-square with the "civilizing" ethos of Rome, Britain, and the American Founders, invoking the Constitutional Code by saying that the United States seeks "to see the Cubans prosperous and contented, enjoying that measure of self-control which is the inalienable right of man." Beyond echoing the Founders, McKinley adds the humanitarian thread: "Intervention upon humanitarian grounds has not failed to receive my most anxious and earnest consideration"—a theme that would become part of the standard immoral morality of American imperial intervention from Woodrow Wilson to, most prominently, George W. Bush.

Along with the constitutional and humanitarian secular arguments, though, McKinley added two other classic themes of immoral morality. One was an echo of Constantine, with McKinley arguing that Spanish cruel rule over Cuba and the Philippines "called forth expressions of condemnation from the nations of Christiandom." God, McKinley was suggesting, would be on America's side in its war on barbaric Spain, and he recounted praying about what to do in the Philippines: "We could not leave them to themselves—they were unfit for self-government—and they would soon have anarchy and misrule over there worse than Spain's was; and ... there was nothing left for us to do but to take them all, and to educate the Filipinos, and uplift and civilize and Christianize them, and by God's grace do the very best we could by them, as our fellow-men for whom Christ also died."

Here, McKinley melded the secular theme of "uplift and civilize" and the sacred theme of "by God's grace," the two classic themes of imperial immoral morality since Rome. But there was also a third increasingly central pillar: the morality of imperial self-defense, a concept that expanded to encompass moral protection of anyone within the empire or moral attacks against those resisting it. Like President Polk in the Mexican war, McKinley emphasized that US national security was at stake, especially after the explosion that blew up the *USS Maine* in Cuban waters on January 15, 1898. McKinley argued that war against Spain was necessary "when the lives and liberty of our citizens are in constant danger"—the Third Empire's first effort to frame its expansionism as honorable self-defense against aggression. The famous war slogan "Remember the *Maine*" turned the Third Empire's early overseas adventure into (1) a moral evocation of the need to protect Americans and the honor of fallen US sailors, thus strengthening the national security religion developed in the Second Empire; (2) the expansion of "self-defense" into a moral doctrine protecting the Cubans, expanding the Monroe Doctrine that had already seen defense of South America as part of America's moral duty; and (3) a new symbol of American civic goodness versus European colonial evil, with the *Maine* coming to represent, as Brad Bauer put it, "the vessel of the democratic ideals of the nation," essentially a re-evocation of the Constitutional Code of the Founders.

Defeating Spain in 1898, and securing dominance over Cuba, the United States acquired Guam, Puerto Rico, and the Philippines, gaining such a visible and initially embarrassing global imperialist profile that Andrew Carnegie offered to buy the Philippines for $20 million and give it its freedom. Mark Twain, initially a fervent American nationalist, now railed against the flagrant "imperialism" of his beloved nation. But the Third Empire's expansionism was unstoppable, fueled by US corporate needs for overseas markets and for uniting the population around a nationalist "winning team" identity as class conflicts intensified under the robber barons.

The two most important Third Empire leaders were Teddy Roosevelt and Woodrow Wilson, who layered new, seductive, progressive, and immoral morality on American Empire. Roosevelt was to the Third Empire what Andrew Jackson was to the Second, a self-proclaimed warrior who championed bold new American expansionism without initially seeming to dress it up in morality of any form. Roosevelt had graduated from college and gone immediately to the Badlands of South Dakota to ride horses and shoot guns. In 1898, when the Spanish-American War began, he immediately resigned his assistant secretary of the navy position to volunteer as a Rough Rider. Leading a regiment up a Cuban hill into battle, without waiting for the approval of his commander, Roosevelt became a new American hero after his swaggering, bravado performance in what he famously called this "splendid little war."

As early as 1895, Roosevelt had written that the "greatest boon" he could bring America was "an immediate war with Great Britain for the conquest of Canada"—a line that seemed consistent with a man who later became famous for the line, "speak softly but carry a big stick." In writing about the Spanish-American War and the Rough Riders, Roosevelt acknowledged that "I had preached, with all the fervor and zeal I possessed, our duty to intervene in Cuba." While this might just seem naked warmongering, his use of language signals Roosevelt's evolving recognition that war and imperialism required strong, moral argument. Note that he says "duty to intervene," *making clear that his enthusiasm for the war reflected a moral obligation rather than simple lust for battle.* Roosevelt was explicit that the "duty to intervene" arose from the moral necessity "to take this opportunity of driving the Spaniard from the Western World," which became known as the Roosevelt Corollary to the Monroe Doctrine. American intervention was a moral imperative, the only way to protect the Americas against the colonialism of the Europeans. Here, Roosevelt, like Cleveland and McKinley, made European Empire his enemy and American Empire a moral crusade against the evils of the Old World. Expansion as honorable protection and self-defense—of both US citizens and the millions in other nations requiring American protection—became Roosevelt's theme song and his legacy to the empire.

In his corollary to the Monroe Doctrine, Roosevelt wrote that "chronic wrongdoing or an impotence which results in a general loosing of the ties of civilized society may ... in the Western Hemisphere—force the United States, however reluctantly ... to the exercise of an international police power." As corporate leaders close to Roosevelt spoke forcefully of their need to capture markets both in Latin America and in Asia, specifically China, only seven hundred miles from the Philippines, Roosevelt extended his vision of moral sheriff from the Americas to the world as a whole. When the Spanish-American War started, he sent a telegram to Commodore Dewey to strike the Spanish fleet in the Philippines immediately. Historian William Appleman Williams concludes that "Roosevelt did not restrict that police power to Latin America, noting explicitly that America's efforts 'to secure the open door in China' were part of the same effort to protect and extend (in TR's own words) 'the interest of humanity at large.'"

Here, Roosevelt uses not just the Monroe Doctrine but also the ancient immoral morality of Rome, proclaiming the universality of the moral values and interests that American expansion would protect. Roosevelt seemed so entranced with warfare as the highest form of civil and moral conduct that he whimsically, but approvingly, quoted one of his fellow Rough Riders who asked for a haircut before battle, saying, "Don't want to wear my hair long like a wild Indian when I'm in civilized warfare."

But Roosevelt was uncertain that Americans would maintain the character to pursue "civilized warfare." In a 1907 speech to the Harvard Student Union, after Harvard President Charles William Eliot proposed abolishing football at the school, Roosevelt pronounced, "We can not afford to turn out college men who shrink from physical effort or a little physical pain." For the nation needed men with "the courage that will fight valiantly against the foes of the soul and the foes of the body." His athletic references helped him create a new character code for the Third Empire, synthesizing Manifest Destiny and the Frontier Code, which we now call the New American Team Code:

1. The team/nation is sacred and is destined to prevail over its adversaries and protect deserving peoples.
2. The nation's goodness, both military and non-military, is sanctioned by higher powers and is proven through victory.
3. Personal morality and the team's honor are intertwined and all-important.
4. A few who are especially strong or valorous—the nation's leaders and military—have been chosen to represent and protect the group in a dangerous and threatening world.
5. People prove their goodness through valor, honor, courage, hard work, and dedication to the team.
6. Everyone must identify with the team and see it as their representative and symbol.
7. Being chosen for the team is a special honor. Honor is an ineffable quality, which must be defended at all times.
8. The entire community must support the team. Anyone who doesn't should be ostracized or perhaps punished more severely.
9. A victory for the team brings glory to the entire community/nation.
10. Do not question authority or think for yourself in ways that might endanger the unity of the team/nation.

This was Roosevelt's original contribution to moralizing the Third American Empire, helping bring the experience of every boy's playing field to the battlefields of America's new empire. American boys would play to win but in the service of the highest moral values. Roosevelt came to symbolize a vision of American global policing to end the evils of European colonialism. But like McKinley and Cleveland before him, Roosevelt failed to disclose honestly the urgency of the self-interested economic interests driving Third Empire expansion. In 1901, McKinley had admitted, but downplayed, the economic motives: "Incidental to our tenure in the Philippines is the commercial opportunity ... the legitimate means for the enlargement of American trade." Roosevelt also acknowledged the role of trade, but in his emphasis on moral policeman he did not forthrightly state the intensity of the US corporate interests involved. The corporations themselves were more forthright. US Assistant Secretary of the Treasury Frank A. Vanderlip—later president of National City Bank—said in 1900 of the Philippines:

> It is as a base for commercial operations that the islands seem to possess the greatest importance. They occupy a favored location not with reference to any part of any particular country of the Orient, but to all parts. Together with the islands of the Japanese Empire, since the acquirement of Formosa [Taiwan] by Japan, the Philippines are the pickets of the Pacific, standing guard at the entrance to trade with the millions of China, Korea, French Indo-China, the Malay Peninsula and the Islands of Indonesia to the south.

Chauncey Depew—a financier who worked for Cornelius Vanderbilt and became a corporate-friendly US senator—was also more forthright, speaking at the Republican National Convention in 1904:

> The American people now produce $2 billion worth more than they can consume and we have met the emergency, and by the providence of God, by the statesmanship of William McKinley, and by the valor of Roosevelt and his associates, we have our market in Cuba ... in Puerto Rico, in Hawaii ... in the Philippines, and we stand in the presence of 800 million people, with the Pacific as an American lake, and the American artisans producing better and cheaper goods than any country in the world.... Let production go on ... let the factories do their best, let labor be employed at the highest wages, because the world is ours.

Nonetheless, despite the undeniable role of Roosevelt in promoting US global expansion through classic forms of American immoral morality, his contributions ultimately appear restrained relative to Woodrow Wilson. Roosevelt became more cautious in his imperialist view over time, actually being the only candidate in 1912 to argue for withdrawal from the Philippines. In contrast to the crusading Wilson, Roosevelt evolved toward "realism," committed to expanding America's sphere of influence through what he described as "step-by-step" pragmatism.

An ongoing current debate about Roosevelt's role does not really bring into question his role in facilitating America's global expansion or his contribution to the moral discourse, but it does highlight the more important role played by Woodrow Wilson, particularly constructing the modern forms of immoral morality that underlie US foreign policy. Journalist Fareed Zakaria has written, "Almost every American president in the past half century has been, at least rhetorically, a Wilsonian." Wilson not only crystallized the moral story of the Third Empire but shaped the moralism guiding US empire ever since.

On April 2, 1917, in his speech to Congress in which he declared war, Wilson proclaimed, "The world must be made safe for democracy." This became a Wilsonian trademark and came to define both Wilson and America as "idealist." Wilson enthusiastically embraced this label: "Sometimes people call me an idealist. Well, that is the way I know I am an American. America, my fellow citizens—I do not say it in disparagement of any other great people—America is the only idealistic nation in the world."

While echoing traditional ideas of American exceptionalism—a nation unlike all others dedicated to moral ideals—Wilson is actually repeating, here, much of the rhetoric of the British and even the Romans, who also defined their power as an expression of exceptional idealism and universal moral values. What Wilson accomplished was to take these classic Roman and British themes, integrate them with those of the Founders and the Manifest Destiny creed, and create both a secular and sacred American immoral morality suited for the modern age.

Wilson accomplished this synthesis in his 1917 war declaration to Congress:

> It is a fearful thing to lead this great peaceful people into war, into the most terrible and disastrous of all wars, civilization itself seeming to be in the balance. But the right is more precious than peace, and we shall fight for the things which we have always carried nearest our hearts, for democracy, for the right of those who submit to authority to have a voice in their own governments, for the rights and liberties of small nations, for a universal dominion of right by such a concert of free peoples as shall bring peace and safety to all nations and make the world itself at last free.

In a senseless war of European colonial empires that were killing off their own citizens for greed and glory, Wilson framed the anti-colonial American argument for jumping into the war. While joining the Allies, Wilson was making an immoral moral argument for US global power, as a nation playing by different rules than the Old Powers, one standing not for colonial greed or exploitation but "for the principles that gave her birth." Here, Wilson embraced the Constitutional Code of the Founders and made it an argument for twentieth-century American world dominion. America would fight this war—and remake the world—"for the things we have always carried nearest our hearts, for democracy," for the right of all peoples "to have a voice in their own governments," all to "make the world itself at last free."

This, again, is empire as anti-empire: remaking the world to ensure that all peoples enjoy the universal moral values of self-determination and rights codified in the US Constitution. It is imperial power as moral service. This is classic immoral morality, cloaking self-interest in the rhetoric of moral sacrifice. The hypocrisy is on display in his own view of a genuine peace: "Only a peace between equals can last. Only a peace the very principle of which is equality and a common participation in a common benefit." Yet, at the signing of the Treaty of Versailles after World War I, when Wilson helped other European leaders carve up the crumbling Ottoman Empire and redraw the map of the world, it was anything but a "peace between equals." This was a victory dictated, as always, by the victors, and not just over the Germans and Japanese. It was a cruel peace in which the lack of generosity helped lead to World War II. The signing of the treaty also created a fraternity of wealthy nations—especially between the British and French—who cooperated with America, as historian William Appleman Williams writes, "to control the poor in return for the rich [Europeans] accepting the American rules for the international marketplace." The poor nations, of course, had no voice at all, betraying the immoral morality of Wilson's proclamations of a "peace between equals" and a commitment to "the rights and liberties of small nations."

While Wilson largely expressed himself in the secular immoral morality of the Constitutional Code, he also embraced the Constantine Syndrome: "There is a spirit that rules us.... I believe that men are emancipated in proportion as they lift themselves to the conception of providence and of divine destiny, and therefore I cannot be deprived of the hope that is in me—in the hope not only that concerns myself, but the confident hope that concerns the nation—that we are chosen and prominently chosen to show the way to the nations of the world how they shall walk in the paths of liberty."

Fourth American Empire: The Good Empire versus the Evil Empire, 1945–1991

In the Fourth Empire, America justified its rise to global superpower as the only alternative to what President Ronald Reagan dubbed the "Evil Empire." In the face of new Soviet evil, America redefined itself as the indispensable free and good society, which became the core moral premise of both the Fourth and current Fifth empires. The Fourth Empire's contribution to American immoral morality was to announce a new titanic moral struggle between good and evil, aligning America with an unquestioned cosmic goodness, while covertly cooperating with the Soviet enemy and using Soviet barbarism as moral cover for its own imperial expansion. The Fourth Empire updated the Roman tale of empire as the only moral defense against barbarism, all the while disguising America's own increasingly savage global power.

The two bookends of the Fourth Empire were presidents Harry Truman and Ronald Reagan. In 1947, soon after the end of World War II, Truman announced the Truman Doctrine, which assumed America's "goodness" (a matter discussed shortly) and clarifies the unsavory truth that Truman created *a morality of self-defense that instantly became a morality of global intervention-ism.* Truman called for intervention in Greece and Turkey since "the very existence of the Greek state is today threatened by the terrorist activities of several thousand armed men, led by Communists, who defy the government's authority." In the name of fighting Communism (loosely defined as supporters of Marxism and the Soviet Union), Truman led an intervention that would install an American-friendly, quasi-fascist Greek regime—a paradigm for the immoral morality that emerged in the Cold War. In the speech outlining the Truman Doctrine, the president laid out the underlying morality of this new "security"-driven intervention: "We should not realize our objectives, however, unless we are willing to help free peoples to maintain their free institutions and their national integrity against aggressive movements that seek to impose upon them totalitarian regimes. This is no more than a frank recognition that totalitarian regimes imposed on free peoples, by direct or indirect aggression, undermine the foundations of international peace and hence the security of the United States."

Of the reactionary Greek regime he was supporting, Truman would acknowledge only that "No government is perfect." Truman, like most of his Fourth Empire successors, would accept the dictatorial impulses of the leaders (in this case Greek generals) he was aiding in the name of the all-important containment of Communism. The immoral morality here is at least triple: (1) the United States expanded its power projection and its right to intervene anywhere in the name of honorable self-defense against global Communism, (2) it put in place an authoritarian military regime in the name of democracy, and (3) it extended the sphere of corporate-friendly puppet regimes in the name of self-determination. Fourth Empire US interventions that followed were all built on the model of Truman's Greek intervention. Examples of such interventions consisted of the following: the 1953 CIA overthrow of the democratically elected President Mohammed Mossadegh in Iran, replacing him with the Shah; the CIA overthrow of the democratically elected President Jacobo Arbenz of Guatemala in 1954, replacing him with a series of brutal dictators; and the overthrow and killing of the democratically elected President Salvador Allende of Chile in 1973, installing the dictator Augusto Pinochet. But these interventions added a fourth dimension to the immoral morality, claiming that intervening was self-defense against Communism when none of the governments involved were Communist or Communist allies. Such successful deception ensured that the Fourth Empire could expand anywhere, in the name of security and self-defense, as part of a moral crusade against Communism.

In 1950, Truman signed NSC 68, a National Security Council document that solidified Truman's view of the Cold War as a moral emergency: "The issues that we face are momentous, involving the fulfillment or destruction not only of this Republic but of civilization itself." NSC 68 proclaimed that the aim of the Soviet Union was "the complete subversion or forcible destruction of the machinery of government and structure of society in the countries of the non-Soviet world and their replacement by an apparatus and structure subservient to and controlled from the Kremlin.... The assault on free institutions is world-wide now, and in the context of the present polarization of power a defeat of free institutions anywhere is a defeat everywhere."

The last phrase locks in Truman's imperial definition of global interventionism as honorable self-defense. The entire NSC document reinforces the Fourth Empire's moral obligation to police the world since "a defeat of free institutions anywhere is a defeat everywhere." This was precisely Truman's language in the Greek intervention, but NSC 68 heightens the moral stakes involved, conceiving the new world as a cosmic struggle between good and evil. America is the bastion of goodness because of its Constitution and the unquestioned commitment to freedom that America represents. America's purpose, made explicit by NSC 68, is

> to maintain the essential elements of individual freedom, as set forth in the Constitution and Bill of Rights; our determination to create conditions under which our free and democratic system can live and prosper; and our determination to fight if necessary to defend our way of life, for which as in the Declaration of Independence, "with a firm reliance on the protection of Divine Providence, we mutually pledge to each other our lives, our Fortunes, and our sacred Honor."

Here, NSC 68 returns to the Constitutional Code of the Founders as the basis for certitude about fundamental American goodness, while also adding an allusion to the Constantine Syndrome and America as God's chosen. Truman had also seen the American system as God-blessed, saying, "The basis for our Bill of Rights comes from the teachings we get from Exodus and St. Matthew, from Isaiah and St. Paul." In contrast, the Soviet Union is the polar antithesis, a demonic slave system at war with the American ideal of liberty: "Being a totalitarian dictatorship, the Kremlin's objective in these policies is the total subjective submission of the peoples now under its control. The concentration camp is the prototype of the society which these policies are designed to achieve, a society in which the personality of the individual is so broken and perverted that he participates affirmatively in his own degradation."

NSC 68 set the stage for *Star Wars*, with the Soviet Union portrayed as the evil Darth Vader. American elites thoroughly digested and embraced this stark morality, but since NSC 68 was a policy document for experts, it took a popular president to bring this moral message to the public. That president was Ronald Reagan. In his famous March 8, 1983, "Evil Empire" speech, Reagan spoke of a father he had heard reacting to the fear of Soviet aggression: "Communism and our own way of life were very much on people's minds. And he was speaking to that subject. And suddenly I heard him saying, 'I love my little girls more than anything.' He went on: 'I would rather see my little girls die now, still believing in God, than have them grow up under Communism and one day die no longer believing in God.'"

Reagan added, "There were thousands of young people in that audience. They came to their feet with shouts of joy. They had instantly recognized the profound truth in what he had said, with regard to the physical and the soul and what was truly important." Reagan said this father of three girls had also recognized the most important truth of our day: that the Communists "are the focus of evil in the modern world."

Reagan then honed in on morality as the central issue in the world, with the Soviets repudiating "all morality that proceeds from supernatural ideas—that's their name for religion—ideas that are outside class struggle." Quoting the writer C. S. Lewis, Reagan said "the greatest evil" now is created by these Godless Communists, bureaucrats who operate "in clean, carpeted, warmed, and well-lighted offices, by quiet men with white collars and cut fingernails." Reagan then warned that the greatest danger is "to ignore the facts of history and the aggressive impulses of an evil empire, to … remove yourself from the struggle between right and wrong and good and evil."

These were the Fourth Empire's most important words. You cannot remove yourself from the new all-consuming struggle between good and evil. Nor is there any questioning the Soviets' evil or the Americans' good because the president has already firmly rooted these moral certitudes in God. Reagan proclaimed that the basis of moral "ideals and principles is a commitment to freedom and personal liberty that, itself, is grounded in the much deeper realization that freedom prospers only where the blessings of God are avidly sought and humbly accepted." Reagan melded God, morality, and global American policing in a seamless concept of American goodness. American Empire became a Godly imperative to expand US military power across the planet in the name of fighting evil. The emphasis on God as the foundation of morality itself and of American goodness, as well as of building American military dominance, is especially notable, particularly in Reagan's Evil Empire speech. "The great triumph of our Founding Fathers," said Reagan, was "voiced by William Penn when he said, 'If we will not be governed by God, we must be governed by tyrants.'" And Reagan cites Alexis de Tocqueville's famous quote: "Not until I went into the churches of America and heard her pulpits aflame with righteousness did I understand the greatness and genius of America." De Tocqueville's conclusion: "America is good. And if America ever ceases to be good, America will cease to be great."

In this reference to de Tocqueville, Reagan makes America's moral goodness (in perfect contrast to Soviet evil) the center of US foreign policy, roots morality in God, and connects America's morality with her Godliness. It is America's belief in God and God's belief in America that make her good. *America's moral obligation is to defend the world against the Evil Empire and to spread America's own divine and democratic Goodness.* Reagan has joined Madison and Constantine in his version of America's hegemonic immoral morality. This melding of God, freedom, and the American way in a global contest of good versus evil—requiring American boots on the ground all over the planet—would be taken up with urgent intensity by George W. Bush in the Fifth and current empire.

The Fifth Empire: World Hegemon, 1991–Present

In 2002, John Bolton, who became George W. Bush's ambassador to the United Nations, proclaimed, "We are an empire now, and when we act we create our own reality." In 2004, George Bush himself said, "I trust God speaks through me." These words announced the coming of age of the Fifth American Empire, the most powerful empire in history.

The Fifth Empire began with the collapse of the Soviet Union in 1991 and assumed its most militaristic and moralistic form under President George W. Bush from 2001 to 2008. Whether President Obama will preside over the end of the Fifth Empire is something we take up in the concluding chapter. Here, we cover the Fifth Empire from its inception through the Bush Jr. years. The novelty of the Fifth Empire's immoral morality was (1) a synthesis that managed to integrate virtually all the classic themes from Rome and Britain as well as those of the earlier four American empires, and (2) the intensity of contradiction between its lofty moralism and religiosity and its actual global conduct, which increasingly mirrored that of the terrorists it fought.

When the Soviet Union collapsed in 1991, it ended not only the Soviet Empire but also the American Fourth Empire. The two had existed as spouses in a codependent marriage, fueling each other's survival and sense of moral purpose. While they hated each other, they couldn't live without each other. Soviet aggression—sometimes real, usually exaggerated, and sometimes fabricated by US leaders—gave the American Fourth Empire its main moral justification for global expansion and intervention. Likewise, "Yankee imperialism" gave the Soviets their moral argument for holding on to Eastern Europe and keeping tight control over their own people.

But while the Fourth US Empire was so morally tied to the Soviet Union that it could not survive without her, the death of the Soviet Union created a unique opportunity. For the first time, there was no nation that could check American power. All obstacles to America's Manifest Destiny seemed to have been overcome. American elites now set about the business of creating the fifth and possibly final American Empire, reaching its greatest power ever, yet possibly, ironically, beginning its inevitable decline. Just as many had viewed the 1898 Boer War as the beginning of the end of the British Empire, America's war with Iraq could possibly be the beginning of the end of its reign.

The immoral morality of the Fifth Empire rests on classic forms of American imperial dishonesty. The Fifth Empire was driven in large part by corporate aims to radically increase profits through globalization. With the collapse of any Soviet deterrent, corporate elites were eager to exploit cheap labor everywhere on the planet, using the threat of outsourcing to break down the costly high wages, job security, health care, and pension plans that American workers had built up since the New Deal was put in place by President Franklin Roosevelt. But Fifth Empire leaders defined America's new power as a high moral imperative—for spreading democracy and saving civilization itself—rather than a ticket to huge profits for global corporations. This was greed disguised as God's will and moral sacrifice.

The key to the Fifth Empire was the view, largely associated with neo-conservatives, that America must become permanently and overwhelmingly militarily dominant. But the first leader of the Fifth Empire was no neoconservative but President Bill Clinton. Instead of creating a "peace dividend" after the Soviet fall, Clinton built the foundations of an even greater empire, arguing that economic and military aims had merged and that the new globalization could only succeed if America dealt decisively with new global security threats of drugs, international crime, rogue states, failed states, and terrorism. "The very openness of our borders and technology also makes us vulnerable in new ways," the president said. Clinton's national security advisor, Samuel Berger, proclaimed that, after the Cold War, virtually everyone now "believes we need a strong military to protect our interests in a world of continuing if shifting dangers." As military historian Andrew Bacevich wrote, Clinton combined this premise with two others to define his foreign policy: first, "that the United States must possess military capabilities enabling it to prevail over any conceivable combination of adversaries," and the United States must proactively change the world in America's interests, thereby transforming, in Bacevich's words, "the Department of Defense . . . into a Department of Power Projection."

After the Soviet collapse, Clinton would keep one hundred thousand forces in both Europe and the Asian Pacific, as well as thousands more in the Persian Gulf. In 1999, he proudly proclaimed, "We have people on the sea, people in foreign countries, all over the world on every continent. We are everywhere."

Clinton had the honesty to discuss the US economic stakes involved, speaking frequently about globalization and the benefits for US companies and economic growth. Nonetheless, since empires are ultimately about the power to control and kill, a higher level of morality is required to legitimize them. This explains the persistent immoral morality of the five American empires, all fueled by a capitalist economic system whose greed and profits cannot be honestly acknowledged as the basis of US foreign policy. A president cannot say, "We are killing for Exxon and to lower the price of oil." He must find a moral ideal lofty enough to justify war and sophisticated enough to compel belief.

Only after September 11, 2001, did the immoral morality of the Fifth Empire come into full view, preached to ordinary Americans by George W. Bush. Bush's moralizing of US aims was not new, having its roots in the intensely idealistic and religious rhetoric of Ronald Reagan, Woodrow Wilson, and many other earlier presidents. But no other president has put immoral morality on such spectacular and stark display. Bush divided the world after 9/11 into heaven and hell. On the one side was an America that represented God and His fundamental Goodness, embodied in liberty and American democracy. On the other were terrorists, who embodied the evilness of Satan and who were out to destroy all civilized values. In the immoral morality of the Fifth Empire, one could challenge a particular war, but any challenge to America's basic goodness became religious heresy—an opposition to God and to His plan of liberty.

Bush's immoral morality was that of a crusade, a word he used in several of his speeches on Iraq and the War on Terrorism. "This is a new kind of—a new kind of evil.... And the American people are beginning to understand. This crusade, this war on terrorism is going to take a while."

This new titanic struggle between good and evil of the Fifth Empire is familiar. Terrorists became the new Communists, and the relationship between Bush and Osama bin Laden was a codependent marriage much like that built by the Fourth Empire between American and Soviet leaders. Bush despised bin Laden but needed him as a symbol of evil to rally Americans and to build support for US intervention anywhere in the world. Bin Laden and al-Qaeda gave America a moral justification for any war that served US economic or strategic interests, since US leaders could always allege, as in Iraq, that their motives were to attack evil terrorists. Likewise, bin Laden had contempt for Bush but found him splendidly useful, a poster boy for jihad. American imperialism was the best possible recruitment tool for radical Islam, and Bush played the role perfectly.

To seek global dominance is immoral, but to do so in the name of fighting evil is worse—hypocrisy that is classic immoral morality. Bush repeatedly defined the War on Terrorism—his umbrella policy to expand US global power—as a pure moral struggle to destroy evil and assure the triumph of goodness: "We're taking action against evil people.... Our war is a war against evil. This is clearly a case of good versus evil, and make no mistake about it—good will prevail."

Bush repeatedly used the phrase "Axis of Evil," making clear that any future wars against Iraq, Iran, and North Korea would be part of his morally driven war on terrorism. And intervention, which expands the empire, is seen as the only moral way to protect the world against barbaric terrorists. In the process, Bush redefines global policing and expansion as honorable self-defense: "In a time of testing, we cannot find security by abandoning our commitments and retreating within our borders. If we were to leave these vicious attackers alone, they would not leave us alone. They would simply move the battlefield to our own shores. There is no peace in retreat. And there is no honor in retreat."

If this imperial redefinition of honorable self-defense against global barbarism is Bush's first pillar of immoral moralism, the second was his focus on spreading freedom and liberty, the heart of America's moral goodness. As Bush was reducing freedom at home and working with murderous dictatorships abroad like in Saudi Arabia, Pakistan, and Egypt, his rhetoric on freedom itself intensified. He proclaimed, "I believe that freedom is the deepest need of every human soul." When weapons of mass destruction were not found in Iraq, he ratcheted up further his focus on liberty, saying that the war was driven by his "moral clarity" to bring freedom to Iraq and the whole Middle East. And this, he repeatedly said, stemmed from the historic truth that freedom was the moral value uniting all Americans: "America has never been united by blood or birth or soil. We are bound by ideals that move us beyond our backgrounds, lift us above our interests, and teach us what it means to be citizens."

Here, Bush is returning to the civilizational claims of Rome and Britain, and especially the Constitutional Code of the Founders, updating it for the Age of Terrorism. The terrorists, Bush said, hated America most because it was the world's "beacon" of Constitutional freedoms: "Americans are asking 'Why do they [terrorists] hate us?' They hate what they see right here in this chamber, a democratically elected government. Their leaders are self-appointed. They hate our freedoms, our freedom of religion, our freedom of speech, our freedom to vote and assemble and disagree with each other."

Bush added sacredness to America's secular creed of liberty, putting a particular stress on freedom as being God-given. In his 2003 State of the Union Address, Bush preached that "God has planted in every human heart the desire to live in freedom." God is the third pillar of Bush's immoral morality, as no president has made more frequent reference to God or to His embrace of the freedom that America embodies. While he was careful not to say publicly that God chose America, Bush said repeatedly that the liberty America practices is a gift from God and one that God intended for all peoples. He thus crafts his own version of the Constantine Code: "Americans are a free people, who know that freedom is the right of every person and the future of every nation. The liberty we prize is not America's gift to the world; it is God's gift to humanity."

This is Bush's way of aligning America with God in the War on Terrorism and the new American world order. But what is distinctive about Bush is not his belief in God or his view that the United States embodies God's will, and thus has a moral obligation to spread US values through wars and global dominance, the classic form of immoral morality expressed by many presidents. The unique element is the intensity of his view that God speaks through him personally, as highlighted by Republican presidential counselor and critic Bruce Bartlett: "I think a light has gone off for people who've spent time up close to Bush; that this instinct he's always talking about is this sort of weird messianic idea of what he thinks God has told him to do.... He truly believes he's on a mission from God."

This personalization of the Constantine Syndrome makes it yet more dangerous. The Constantine Syndrome is one of the most ancient Roman pillars of immoral morality. If Bartlett is correct, Bush moved toward a view preceding Constantine, one more like the Egyptian pharaohs who saw themselves as the Sun God. Bush does not see himself as a God, but his belief in himself as God's vessel was the foundation for new extreme forms of immoral morality leading toward an Empire that would control the world in the name of God and liberty, while breeding frightening political and religious authoritarianism at home, in the name of securing freedom in America.

13

The "Wright Problem"

Charles Derber and Yale Magrass

The US mainstream media has been nearly unrelenting in its condemnation of the Reverend Jeremiah Wright, forcing Senator Barack Obama to distance himself from someone he considered a mentor. But Obama's "Wright problem" reveals a largely ignored national problem: the narrowing of public debate to exclude the possibility of speaking truthfully about the US role in the world.

Wright's rhetoric and his inflated ego are doing serious damage to Obama's campaign. Wright seems now mainly interested in his own newfound celebrity. The media have been correct to point out his recent buffoonery, to denounce his view that the US government infected blacks with AIDS and to dismiss his idolization of the Reverend Louis Farrakhan, but it has inappropriately discredited everything he has said, including the nuggets of truth he has exposed and that are worth hearing, even from such a flawed messenger.

His insights have come with brutal bluntness: "The U.S. is the No. 1 killer in the world." But the substance of this message is little different from the assessment offered by Martin Luther King Jr. during the height of the Vietnam War: "I could never again raise my voice against the violence of the oppressed in the ghettos without having first spoken clearly to the greatest purveyor of violence in the world today—my government."

King went on to speak of a basic American "malady": that the United States would repeat catastrophic ventures like Vietnam until it changed its basic aim, wrapped in lofty ideals of spreading liberty, to dictate to the rest of the world. This is the beginning of real "peace talk," but today, in both political parties, there is only "war talk" that does not get to the root of the problem and offer solutions.

We Americans need urgently to redraw the boundaries of respectable public debate. This is especially crucial for Obama. Even as he distances himself from Wright, his campaign is deeply bound up with changing the terms of debate.

Today, it is possible to be a respectable critic of the Iraq war, but one must judge the war's failures as "mistakes" or problems in "execution." One cannot reject—or even speak credibly of—the aim to dictate to the world.

Since the terrorist attacks on September 11, 2001, the Bush administration has moved the boundaries of debate so far to the right that even the peace movement often calls Iraq a "mistake" rather than a sign of America seeking illegitimate dominance cloaked in idealism.

That leaves the mainstream conversation today full of different variants of war talk and no genuine peace talk.

The conservative version of war talk is to promote US global supremacy, enforced by unilateral military intervention when necessary, as a moral imperative in a "transcendental" war on terrorism. John McCain is running for president on conservative war talk.

The liberal version of war talk is to promote US global "leadership," enforced by multilateral institutions, partnerships and greater reliance on soft power.

Obama has hinted at a new foreign policy vision but seeks a bigger military footprint in Afghanistan. Hillary Clinton is even more aggressive, strongly focused on a bigger global US military force and the potential need to invade Iran.

Yet the US public may be hungering for a new peace talk after the Iraq debacle. A February 2007 Gallup poll asking about what role the United States should play in the world indicated that only 15 percent said "the leading role," a rejection of American global dominance. This hints that Obama could find a new path to peace talk that better aligns him with voters' values.

Without authentic peace talk, there can be no real movement toward peace. Obama's greatest skill is as a rhetorician, and in his recent speech on race he proved that he could speak truthfully, in a new and unifying way, about this most charged American subject. In this same spirit, he will be a transformative leader and make a lasting contribution if he moves to resurrect the authentic peace talk of Martin Luther King Jr.

14

What Does It Mean to Call McCain a "War Hero" Candidate?

Charles Derber and Yale Magrass

McCain is running as one, but those who oppose dishonorable wars are also heroes.

"624787." In his first national campaign ad for president, John McCain is shown reciting his rank and serial number as he lies in a Vietnamese hospital bed as a prisoner of war. The ad describes him as "a real hero."

Let's be clear: Senator McCain is running for president as a war hero who plans to win the campaign based on character and honor. On the surface, it seems churlish to critique the idea of a war hero. And criticizing a tribute to courageous and self-sacrificing soldiers *would* be disrespectful.

But inextricably tied to the idea of the war hero for president is a discussion that goes beyond individual soldiers or prisoners of war, such as McCain, to the wars they fight and what their role in the war says about their moral merits as national leaders. This turns out to be surprisingly problematic.

We need to distinguish the war hero from the war. Fixed ideas about war heroes get into what we call "morality wars," crucial struggles about which values should prevail, who should be admired and for what qualities.

When we call McCain a war hero, we engage in moral discourse about the Vietnam War and now Iraq. We also give McCain—currently the country's most celebrated war hero—the ultimate political weapon: power by virtue of heroism and the ability to discredit opponents as weak or unpatriotic.

The public has treated McCain's record in Vietnam and his status as a war hero as something unchangeable. But placing his sacrifice beyond the pale of criticism also implicitly places the cause he served beyond the pale, and that hushes important dialogue.

McCain's heroism stems entirely from Vietnam. McCain was brave in captivity, but he and his fellow pilots dropped more bombs on Vietnam than all those dropped in World War II, leading to the conclusion that "we had to destroy Vietnam in order to save it." But he did not acknowledge the war itself as immoral. Had he engaged in such "straight talk" about the war itself, or if we had a more enlightened concept of heroism, he might not be getting so close to becoming the next president.

This language of war heroism is used unfairly to confuse unjust wars and their architects with the honor of brave soldiers. By promoting the idea that Vietnam was an honorable war and denigrating antiwar Democrats as too weak to "stay the course," Richard Nixon won the election in 1968. He then kept the war going for another five futile years, sustained by that myth.

Playing the war hero card has long been a political strategy to elect Republicans; legitimize imperial wars; and portray Democrats and peace activists as weak, cowardly, or traitorous. John Kerry, also a courageous soldier, was swift-boated as a traitor because he became a peace activist in Vietnam.

Republicans even did the same to Daniel Ellsberg, a real hero of the Vietnam era. Ellsberg was a war planner who turned against the war and in 1971, at great personal risk, released to the *New York Times* the "Pentagon Papers," the military's internal and damning history of the war. But as there are no peace heroes, only war heroes in the American moral discourse, President Nixon tried to indict him and many *still* brand him as a traitor.

Ten out of eleven presidents after the Civil War were Republicans, the majority of whom were generals who ran as war heroes. In the twentieth century, Republicans continued to serve up war-hero candidates like Teddy Roosevelt, Dwight Eisenhower, and George H. W. Bush, a strategy that has worked for tens of decades. And now we have John McCain.

If the Democrats are to win elections in the twenty-first century, the key is to finally engage in straight talk about war and war heroes.

First, they must renounce the morality of militarism.

Second, they must be clear that the architects of unjust wars are not honorable or heroic but immoral moralists, those who wage evil in the name of good.

Third, they must create a new language of heroism. Brave soldiers in just and unjust wars may be heroes, if we refer purely to personal courage and sacrifice in battle. But it is critical that we recognize that those who oppose dishonorable wars are also heroes. Surely, *their* courage should also qualify as a character virtue for the highest office in the land.

The peace hero—even more than the war hero—should be the ultimate moral force in the world we now inhabit.

15

When Wars Come Home

Charles Derber and Yale Magrass

In the flood of commentary about the Newtown massacre and broader US gun violence, liberals tend to blame failures of gun control while conservatives blame the mentally ill and Hollywood. But they are both missing one important and overlooked explanation: the domestic consequences of a militarized superpower engaged in chronic wars around the world.

The United States spends more money on the military than the next ten countries together. It also has the highest level of domestic gun violence in the developed world. Highly militarized societies cannot compartmentalize foreign from domestic violence. They cannot prevent wars—and guns—from coming home.

Christopher Dorner certainly brought the war home. On February 3, 2013, he began a killing rampage, shooting his lawyer's daughter and her fiancé, firing at three police officers, killing one, and issued a manifesto, threatening to kill at least twelve more. Dorner is a former navy lieutenant, a specialist in undersea warfare, rifle marksman, and pistol expert, who lost his job in the Los Angeles police department. The L.A. police announced that the weapons training Dorner received in the navy made him a very serious threat.

Europe provides a clear contrast to the United States. Since World War II, as the United States became the sole superpower, the nations of Europe largely renounced militarism and war. Demilitarization is one of the reasons why many European countries, such as Sweden, have high levels of gun ownership for hunting and sports but have one-tenth the US level of gun violence. Demilitarization weakens the cultural foundation of violence in civil society—if violence is not acceptable abroad, it can hardly be seen as honorable at home.

US analysts tend to focus on the growing separation of the military and its values from the larger society. The liberal MSNBC cable television host Rachel Maddow argues in her book *Drift: The Unmooring of American*

Military Power that American civilians have little connection with soldiers or military culture, making it easier for them to detach from the grim realities of war. Civilians and soldiers are living in a separate cultural universe. Neo-conservatives, such as Robert Kagan and Max Boot, agree that Americans are focused on their own lives at home and have little engagement with the military values and threats that support US wars.[1]

But the assumption that the military is increasingly walled off from civil society needs to be reexamined. True, the lack of a draft and the rise of a volunteer military distance young people from war today, very different than during the Vietnam conflict. Even without a draft, though, ideas, values, and profits emerging from the war sector flood civilian society, a torrent that a draft would only increase.

A militarized society develops a culture and institutions that program civilians for violence at home as well as abroad. War celebrates the heroism of soldiers who use the same style of weapons and ammunition used by the mass shooters at Newtown, Los Angeles, and Columbine. A warrior society values its armed forces as heroic protectors of freedom, sending a message that the use of guns is morally essential. Such messaging can easily confuse youth, and particularly angry or distressed young men such as the shooters in school rampages like Newtown or Columbine, who tend to see themselves as moral avengers and martyrs. It can lead many more Americans to see gun violence as honorable on the home front.

Mass killers often obsess over the military, even if they are not soldiers or veterans. At several school rampages, the killers were fixated on military equipment, war stories, and the military bases near their school. This was demonstrated by Michael Moore in his film *Bowling for Columbine* (2002). One of the Columbine shooters had earlier lived on an air force base that displays a plane with a plaque proclaiming that it killed Vietnamese villagers on a Christmas Eve. Moore asks, "Don't you think the kids say to themselves, 'Dad goes to work everyday. He builds weapons of mass destruction. What is the difference between that mass destruction and the mass destruction over at Columbine High School?'"[2]

New war technologies and policies may inspire even more. Drone warfare, as carried out by the Obama administration, targets and kills "enemy combatants, whether foreign or American," without judicial oversight. Each week, John Brennan, Obama's new head of the CIA, brings Obama a "kill list," with the names of people to be "eliminated." If the president can kill Americans in the name of honor and security, with nobody empowered to question his judgment, other Americans may decide they too can shoot to kill based on their own morals and view of the threat. As President Nixon declared, "When the President does it, that means that it is not illegal."[3]

The military has been directly involved in shaping cultural attitudes for centuries. Since 1916, Junior ROTC, for example, which now operates in

1,645 high schools, has tried to mold civilian society and bring military moral messages to America's young. JROTC defines its mission as "The study of ethics, citizenship, communications, leadership, life skills, and other subjects ... focusing on character building and civic responsibility ... being presented in every JROTC classroom."

The power of military culture in civilian life is not lost on the gun industry. It knows that 50 percent of all sporting rifle owners in the United States are present or former veterans or in law enforcement. The industry is now actively working to increase that percentage, targeting veterans and their families with advertising, particularly for the kinds of assault guns vets used in the service—which the industry argues are both necessary for the safety of family in your neighborhood and for fun in civilian life. The ads highlight that gun use is part of the fabric of US constitutional and moral values, and makes our society morally exceptional.

As spelled out in *Shooting Industry* magazine in July 2012, the industry praised the social network of "America's modern veteran," involving "hundreds of thousands of dads, brothers, uncles, wives, sisters, aunts, cousins, and extended family and friends, who served or are serving in Iran and Afghanistan. They are respected and admired. They carried firearms to protect our country. That factor, that imagery, has had a huge positive impact on how firearms are viewed in our country."[4]

The military does not act alone in causing gun violence. Gun violence is partly a response to poverty, but it also has roots in American culture. America enshrines gun ownership as a fundamental right in the Second Amendment. The gun culture is particularly important in the South and the West, where it evolved largely to keep blacks and Native Americans in their place. In fact, one of the motives for passing the Second Amendment was to establish patrols to capture escaped slaves. Today, the South and the West are the regions that have the highest rate of domestic gun violence and the largest percentage of their population in the military, with the most military bases and strongest support for military adventurism.

A militarist state must raise boys, ready and able to commit violence enthusiastically, providing it is directed against peoples whom their rulers deem enemies. As the typical American boy grows up, the media inundates him with violence. For generations, boys have been watching John Wayne Westerns, showing how lawmen must conquer outlaws and the land must be purged of savages. Bomber pilots, like John McCain, are upheld as paragons of heroic moral virtue. The same day as the former navy lieutenant and police officer was on his rampage in Los Angeles, CNN broadcast a long segment praising Clinton Romesha, a newly minted winner of the Congressional Medal of Honor, as the "bravest of the brave," who directed the killing of over thirty Afghani "enemies" in a twelve-hour battle, which left eight Americans dead.

Military societies cannot reproduce themselves without sustaining the commitment to guns and the morality of gun violence in the larger society. In his farewell address, President Dwight Eisenhower warned of the dangers of the penetration of the values and economic interests of the "military-industrial complex" into the heart of civil society. The Newtown massacre and the L.A. police officer's rampage are powerful reminders of Eisenhower's understanding of how the military inevitably shapes the morality and conduct of civilians and companies, always threatening to bring wars home. As Martin Luther King Jr. lamented at the height of the war in Vietnam, "I could never again raise my voice against the violence of the oppressed in the ghettos without having first spoken clearly to the greatest purveyor of violence in the world today—my own government.... The war in Vietnam is but a symptom of a far deeper malady within the American spirit."[5]

PART V

Climate Change as Sociopathy

Introduction to Part V

Violence against the Earth

Destruction of the environment has long been a feature of sociopathic societies. We now face the catastrophic prospect of environmental change that not only would destroy US civil society but also threatens the survival of humans and many other species on the planet.

In this section, I focus on climate change as the ultimate sociopathic threat. Historically, the United States has been the largest perpetrator of the problem, and even today, US per capita greenhouse gas emissions are much larger than those of any other nation. Unless the United States drastically shifts course, it will undermine the chance for other nations to solve or even mitigate the crisis.

The main chapter in this section shows that US capitalism is one of the prime causes of climate change. In the United States, capitalism is seen by many environmental theorists and advocacy groups as the solution, the best hope for technological innovation that can solve the problem. I argue, however, that climate change is part of the DNA of US capitalism, and that despite US innovative and entrepreneurial strengths, many elements of the American political economy create global warming and prevent change.

My analysis shows that climate change, despite its extreme gravity, is fundamentally a symptom of our corporate regime and unsustainable way of life. Climate change—both because it threatens to destroy our society while also an outcome of our system—is the most terrifying dimension of our sociopathic society, creating an unprecedented tragedy of the commons.

The second short chapter in this section looks at Superstorm Sandy as a reflection of "climate sociopathy" and the infrastructure crisis of our sociopathic society. It shows Sandy can be seen as a harbinger of twenty-first-century disasters reflecting a tragedy of the commons, bred by a society that denies climate change and fails to create the new green infrastructure that would begin to change our fossil-fuel capitalism and heal our sociopathic society.

The third chapter looks at consumerism as a root cause of climate change, and argues that to consume is becoming a sociopathic act. It shows that if everyone in the world consumed as we did in the United States, we would need seven planets to sustain us. Despite this grim reality, I show that even in the United States, discontent with the consumer society is growing and there is hope for change.

16

How Capitalism Causes Climate Change

Solving global warming requires a revolution in our capitalist markets, politics, and culture. This solution goes beyond the energy-sector focus in much of the environmental movement itself and remains scarily outside the mainstream of public debate and Washington politics. For the sake of future generations, the public conversation must change quickly to address the causal relation between capitalism and climate change, as the window of opportunity closes.

Here, I look at how capitalism, especially the US model, creates climate change. I examine the systemic changes in capitalism required to solve the climate crisis, describing what a new sustainable politics and economic system, as well as a green American Dream, look like. I focus on the president's and the public's responsibilities in bringing these changes quickly to fruition.

Proposing big system changes seems very daunting when time is short. How can we be optimistic about change that must be both radical and fast? To use a football metaphor, it is a little like rooting for a home team that is down by three touchdowns in the fourth quarter. Boston College's Doug Flutie threw a "Hail Mary" pass to win in the last second of the Orange Bowl against Miami. But it seems as if I am proposing four Hail Mary passes to solve climate change.

Nonetheless, there is reason for hope. At this writing, we live in the deepest crisis since the Great Depression and we have elected a president with a mandate for change. The economic crisis is so serious that it opens Americans—out of necessity—to big new ideas and programs. The president has shown signs of a transformative green vision and policy, and he has deep public support. He is already making proposals to renew and remake the economy by greening America. We cannot expect miracles, but there are practical reasons to believe that this is a promising moment, making possible much of the change we need.

From Blind to Green Markets

In February 2009, the *Boston Globe* editorialized that "coal is the cheapest source of electricity. One major reason is that mining companies and coal-burning utilities have managed to pass many of its health and environmental costs—from the dust miners breathe to greenhouse gases—onto society at large." This editorial points to an urgent and systemic problem with our current capitalist system: It creates markets that ignore and are blind to the costs of environmental pollution as well as of social "pollution," such as wages keeping people in poverty. Corporations are indifferent to such costs because they do not have to put them on their books but can just let society or other individuals pick up the tab (what economists call "externalizing" the cost). If a company spews untreated sewage into a river or carbon dioxide into the air, people will get sick, but the patient or a medical insurance company, not the corporation, will pay for the cost of that illness. An "externality" is a cost that a company or producer does not have to pay itself; it can "pass the buck" on to the rest of us. It is a real cost to society, but it never has to appear on the company's books—this externality does not exist in the minds of company accountants. The cost is socialized, absorbed by the public or government; the benefit is privatized, enjoyed by the corporation.

The underlying assumption is that self-interest, or even greed, can work to better society. There is an "invisible hand" premise here, an ideological dictum integral to capitalism according to which each company and individual pursuing a selfish interest will create the best society. The assumption is that if each individual follows his or her own private individual selfish interests, the competition among conflicting needs will balance itself out and the net result will be the best for everyone. The "commons"—that is, the air, the water, the earth itself, and all the natural and social resources that the human community needs for survival and well-being—will take care of itself as long as each individual pursues his or her own goal.

This view produces a tragedy of the commons. If people look out only for themselves and pay no penalty for the consequences, then nobody has to look out for the common good and it will be neglected. This is, in fact, the deepest ideological and structural reason for the unsustainability of capitalism: It cannot protect the commons. If it could, we would not have a global warming problem—the ultimate crisis of the commons, a tragedy built on modern, distorted interpretations of economist Adam Smith, the creator of the invisible hand ideology. The common good requires a steward and cannot take care of itself. In US capitalism, there is no obligatory steward, the government abandons that responsibility, and sustainability depends on the goodwill of voluntary corporate stewards that have abdicated that role.

In *For the Common Good*, a pioneering book on environmental econom-ics, Herman Daly and John Cobb wrote: "All conclusions in economic theory about the social efficiency of pure competition and the free market are explicitly premised on the absence of externalities. The undeniable importance of externalities in today's world is therefore a serious challenge" to our whole economic way of thinking. Many did not listen then, but it has become impossible to ignore Daly and Cobb in the age of global warming. Externalities have moved from being a distraction to being a doomsday machine. CO_2 pollution is the most dangerous externality of all time, and it should lead the entire world toward green markets rather than toward our idealized capitalist "free markets."

We must cap carbon emissions and tax them in some form to ensure they reflect their real costs to humanity. There are two fundamental mechanisms: a direct carbon tax and a cap-and-trade system. The two can be melded, but both can work. Barack Obama has already endorsed a cap-and-trade system for the United States to reduce CO_2 emissions 80 percent by 2050 from 1990 levels, and in 2009 members of Congress introduced cap-and-trade legislation. Producers in this initial plan, which has been modified in the House cap-and-trade bill passed in June 2009, would have to pay the government for CO_2 emissions they spew out; this system would essentially tax carbon emissions but allow flexibility by permitting one company to sell its permits to others if it burns less carbon than allowed by its permits. The aim is to create a national (and ultimately global) cap that will be reduced over time. Scientific analysis tells us the ultimate cap must reduce global CO_2 atmospheric concentrations to less than the critical 350 parts per million (ppm) threshold. This cap is the anchor and touchstone of a sustainable America and world.

When properly designed—in a model often called cap-and-dividend that would return money raised by the program to ordinary citizens—capping carbon emissions could win majority public support, given the high stakes and the short-term economic gains it offers. As carbon analyst Peter Barnes argues, returning the money raised by the program to the population will make "the carbon cap (with monthly dividends) the most popular federal program since Social Security."

Carbon taxes, including gas taxes, are simpler than cap-and-trade systems. There is no selling of permits to pollute, no complex trading of the right to emit, just the taxing of people directly for polluting the atmosphere with carbon emissions. We know this system works—when gas prices spike up, people drive less and buy greener cars. If the political will is present, carbon taxes could be the best approach. To create the political will, a carbon tax would have to be progressive—with the rich paying more—and made palatable to a tax-resistant public. The tax would also have to be high enough to cap carbon consumption at the 350 ppm limits. Some combination of the cap-and-trade and tax may be necessary, depending on global negotiations.

There is nothing utopian about capping emissions using a carbon tax. Costa Rica has been doing it since 1997, when it put a 3.5 percent tax on carbon emissions and invested the proceeds in a fund for indigenous people to protect their forests. The Costa Rican environmental minister, who is also the minister for energy, mines, and water, has directed heavy investment in renewables as a cheap alternative to fossil fuels, whose true costs are now known. What has been the result? Costa Rica operates with 95 percent renewable energy. It has oil, but it has decided to ban drilling for it. Costa Rica has seen large economic payoffs: Tourists flock to the country's pristine waters and forests, and the full-cost accounting has led to much lower poverty rates among Costa Rica's poor.

An ambitious US cap is the core around which a US green regime must be built. It requires people to attend to the atmospheric commons and pay when they damage it. It means requiring greenhouse gas polluters to pay the true cost of their production or consumption. But to truly solve global warming—and to make the cap into a political reality that works rather than a Hail Mary fantasy—we need to create the broader political and economic transformation of our society.

Cause and Consequence: Corporate Capitalism and Climate Change

Regime change is a systemic shift in power. The third corporate regime, developed in the period from presidents Ronald Reagan to George W. Bush, has been run by a small oligarchy of capitalist and political elites, all devoted to ensuring maximum short-term profits for the nation's largest corporations. This regime must be changed because it is incompatible with essential long-term solutions to warming. To achieve success, the new green regime must be democratized, moving us from our current capitalist economy and the corporate stranglehold over politics to the popular sovereignty our leaders always talk about.

Solving climate change is impossible within our current system of corporate capitalism. But communist and other economic systems have not created solutions either. We must thus move rapidly to innovate the best blend of different economic models, including elements in the United States, Europe, and many other nations, to create a green economy. The systemic change I describe requires deep changes in the US economic model and mind-set, including the shifting of our current system of corporate-managed markets and government to a more democratic system in which business serves the public rather than the opposite. Businesses, of course, will survive, but more will be smaller and local. The large corporations that survive will be restructured and subject to greater public accountability.

Many environmentalists and climate change thinkers, as well as President Obama and many congressional leaders, say they want big change, but they have been unable to spell out the scale and nature of the systemic economic and political transformation that is at the heart of the matter. Their focus has been on a technological revolution and major new government subsidies, incentives, and regulations for clean energy. But this leaves out what will make all the other changes possible and is at the core of the green regime itself: ending corporate control of society, creating a new sustainable economy based on full-cost accounting and protection of the commons, and building a long-term culture of sustainability. We need an internal regime change that involves a fundamental shift in the power structure and short-term mentality of our corporatized capitalist society and a shift toward a new model of a social and green economy that many will view as social democracy or brand as socialist. Such change does involve a shift from capitalism as we know it but actually combines freer markets with smarter government.

Before describing the new regime, I need to raise a simple question: Why do we need regime change—indeed, basic change in the capitalist system—rather than reforms within the current order? The answer is this: The fundamental values and core institutions of a globalized US capitalism—and the scale and urgency of the climate crisis—make incremental reform a recipe for disaster. Climate change is a symptom of systemic capitalist problems that have intensified during several centuries.

Solving climate change in the United States requires changes in the short-term profit engine and speculative financial system, the corporate-driven political system, and the debt-driven consumerism that are deeply embedded in the US capitalist system itself. We need to remake the larger economy rather than create recovery for our current capitalism, a recovery that would prove neither economically nor environmentally sustainable.

The underlying problem—both in the economy and in the environment—goes beyond the greed of a few "bad apples," of the top executives on Wall Street, or of Wall Street itself. It is systemic and rooted in the intertwining of big government and big companies at the expense of public needs—all characteristic of capitalist systems in late stages of crisis. Corporations have harnessed the state as an instrument of unsustainable short-term capital accumulation tied to unsustainable consumerism that eats away at the commons and destroys it.

At least since the Civil War, the corporate rich have used the government to serve them, and the history of capitalism reeks with corporate schemes to take control of the government to repress labor and other countervailing class forces that would interfere with corporations' intention to "get rich quick." As early as the 1600s, the Dutch economy imploded after speculators paid ten times the average craftsman's annual wage for tulip bulbs. In the late 1800s, American railroad barons managed to have banks and the government finance the railroads for more than they were worth. Post–World War I credit and stock speculation for quick wealth ended in the Great Depression.

Today's sped-up and crisis-ridden capitalist model is thus not new, but it operates globally and electronically at a pace never seen before and produces environmental destruction at an unprecedented level. Our present economy is an extreme form of monopolistic and financialized capitalism. In a financialized economy, unregulated financial speculation replaces industrial productivity when too much capital flows to the financial sector, which absorbs excess profits and starves nonfinancial sectors. Short-term yield overrides long-term security, and speculative debt and credit instruments proliferate on Wall Street. Meanwhile, stagnation in manufacturing and other nonfinancial sectors creates a long-term double-whammy crisis for the economy and the environment.

Double Whammy: How US Capitalism in Crisis Creates Climate Change

Kevin Phillips, a best-selling political analyst and historian, argues forcefully that the current economic crisis is rooted in the financialization of US capitalism as the United States enters its stage of hegemonic decline. The history of capitalist empires—from the Dutch to the British—shows that as they mature, the hard work of creating long-term profits from selling real goods succumbs to the lure of short-term speculative bonanzas. Capital in the entire economy migrates rapidly, in our case to Wall Street, which has transformed itself into a high-tech, sci-fi, mathematically modeled, unregulated system of derivatives, futures, swap defaults, hedge funds, and commodity trading. Trillions of dollars are exchanged across computer screens on a daily basis; the whole financial system becomes a supercharged, superleveraged day trader. The state, meanwhile, acts to remove regulations and restraints, putting politics at the service of speculative finance.

This is a Wall Street operating on an extreme, toxic, invisible hand model. Each bank chases its own short-term interests with no concern for the effects on the larger system. There is no need for stewardship because the financial commons will take care of itself. The consequences of this reasoning are now obvious.

Phillips observes that financialization is unsustainable economically, creating bubbles, such as in the housing market, doomed to burst. But looking just at the housing bubble, we see that such speculative finance also locks consumers into their own turbocharged and unsustainable personal lifestyles, racking up credit debt and leveraged money on their inflated house values to buy second homes, cars, and other big-ticket items neither they nor the environment can afford. Speculative and excess consumerism follows inevitably on the heels of speculative finance (before the crash). As we all used easy credit and balloon, variable-rate mortgages, we were burdening the earth with an ever-heavier personal, national, and global carbon footprint.

Phillips's argument is that the United States is following a well-trodden path in which Wall Street becomes the model and center of gravity for the entire economy. As Wall Street accelerates speed, shrinks time focus, and accelerates debt-induced consumption, the larger economy is unable to respond to a longer time scale. The real economy accelerates toward the unsustainable pace of Wall Street.

Sociologist John Bellamy Foster, a pioneer in linking environmental sociology and social theory, offers a related but deeper systemic analysis of the roots of financialization—and of the larger economic and environmental crises. Foster shows that financialization is caused by an enduring stagnation in the nonfinancial sectors that is endemic to capitalism as it develops during decades and centuries. Stagnation is the unhappy but unavoidable result of many factors: a maturation of industries, growing monopolization, globalization, and increasing inequalities, with the biggest firms soaking up greater profits and paying US workers low wages in a globalized labor market. As corporations seek to lower labor costs, thereby creating greater profit for individual firms, they create a collective problem plaguing all corporations: a systemic crisis of insufficient consumer demand as wages fall and workers cannot afford to buy. In US capitalism, neither government spending nor corporate investment can solve this "demand-side" problem, although governments ratchet up military spending (military Keynesianism) to try to prime the economic pump, or restart the economy, through demand for planes, guns, and other military goods and services. Corporate investment in the United States itself, however, declines with the expectation of lower profitability as worker consumer power declines. Ultimately, the only solution is to financialize the system and introduce easy credit and debt, encouraging US workers to spend well beyond the means of their diminishing wages. Business invests in the financial sector itself as the one last, great opportunity for huge quick profits. This works for a while but leads to bubbles and unsustainable debt in households, banks, and the government, which in the current case led to the 2008 Wall Street crash.

At least six core reasons (see chart on p. 198) explain why US capitalism creates climate change and why the current crisis exacerbates it.

Mainstream economists largely ignore this analysis of inherent capitalist contradictions and the system's built-in environmental unsustainability, which are greatly exacerbated in the current crisis and in the global economy. Global US firms push down wages far more easily through outsourcing and exploiting billions of impoverished workers in Asia, Latin America, and Africa. Global sweatshops and pollution created by transnational companies in poor nations strip naked for all to see the crises of the global economy and the environment as intertwined systemic capitalist time bombs. Capitalist conflicts between labor and capital—and the squeeze on US workers facing competition in a globalized labor market—create declining consumer demand, growing inequality, slack productive investment, financialization, speculation, and accelerated financial transactions, credit, and debt. The

---

How US Capitalism Causes Climate Change

1. Blind markets externalize environmental and social costs.
2. Wall Street grows like a cancer, creates "financialized capitalism," and promotes extreme short-termism.
3. Low wages, driven down by the core capitalist drive to maximize profits, create a manic work-and-spend cycle that is unsustainable.
4. The ideological apparatus creates a religion of unlimited growth and unsustainable consumerism; Madison Avenue makes us all believers.
5. Big corporations intertwine with political elites and dominate Washington, with both parties promoting profits over people and the environment.
6. American consumer capitalism becomes entrenched in a fossil-fuel–intensive lifestyle based on cars, highways, malls, suburbs, and exurbs all rooted in hyperindividualistic values.
7. In the name of property rights, the commons are privatized and destroyed.

---

aim is to speed up short-term consumption in order to buttress a stagnating real economy and feed the financial services industry that produces the easy credit and loose debt as well as the last great profit opportunities for big business. The debt system and the short-term mentality of easy credit fuel madcap environmentally unsustainable consumption, which leads toward even more debt that is economically unsustainable and brings the economy to its knees. At the same time, workers are induced into the short-term thinking of the consumer culture that redefines excess (bigger carbon-intensive houses and cars, more "stuff") as happiness while burning up the planet. This all might be called "capitalism's bonfire," a real-world variant of what novelist Tom Wolfe called "the Bonfire of the Vanities."

Sociologist David Harvey argues that the globalization of financialized capitalism in the electronic age transforms culture itself, creating "time-space compression" that locks workers and consumers into the frenzied short-term frame of the capitalism controlling them. The whole history of capitalism, says Harvey, "has been characterized by speed-up in the pace of life." But the current time-space compression is so extreme that it engulfs and overwhelms all of life. Disposable workers embrace a fast-paced lifestyle, which is consistent with the sped-up pace of the work that they need to pay for their sped-up consumption and compensate for their own rapid skill obsolescence. The experience is "challenging, exciting, stressful, and sometimes deeply troubling," but the end result is that our own personal psychology reinforces an unsustainable economic order that is victimizing us. The personal and egoistic clock of each of us—and debt-financed, turbocharged consumerism—reinforces the financial order (now disorder) on Wall Street that keeps this new hyperaccelerated systemic clock and global warming time bomb ticking until the bomb blows up, as in our current crisis.

In short, the current corporate order is structurally incompatible with the long-term thinking, moderated consumerism, and social and environmental conditions essential for democracy and for survival of not just the planet but also the economy itself. The systemic incentives, driven by the threat of long-term stagnation, are all for short-term profits rooted in unsustainable debt and consumption. Corporations are (1) tightly wired into the short-term financialized model inspired by Wall Street, (2) addicted to fossil fuel global production to ensure short-term profitability while underinvesting in the real economy and overinvesting in the financial sector, (3) wedded to the fevered systemic advertising sales pitch that induces workers into unsustainable debt and consumption ravaging the planet, and (4) so gigantic that they have the power to impose their own policy agendas on the state, on the regulatory agencies presumed to regulate them, and on our own personal consumerism. If we are to create economic and environmental sustainability, we need to move rapidly away from a financial system organized by Wall Street, from corporate control of America, and from the current US model of global corporate capitalism itself. Some corporations with a green business vision and long-term investors (such as church and labor pension funds) can play a constructive green role, but they lack the vision and power to get the systemic change we need.

The Disappearance of Capitalist Stewards and What to Do about It

Although Wall Street has always been built on a flawed model of finance, in earlier eras such as the New Deal core capitalist elites sustained a view of their responsibility to preserve the capitalist system over the long term. These "capitalist stewards" have historically been in finance. Wall Street leaders are located at the center of the capitalist economy and have the greatest interests in ensuring that the entire system is viable. Many Depression-era financial leaders looked out for the long-term interests of the capitalist system, as had earlier financiers who believed that great power brings great responsibility. In the progressive era, J. P. Morgan helped coordinate Wall Street efforts in concert with Teddy Roosevelt to save the country and capitalism from the runaway financial panics and speculation at the turn of the twentieth century. Morgan supported the creation of the Federal Reserve and the beginning of national regulation. The capitalist stewards in the New Deal, including Nelson Aldridge, CEO of Chase National, and Henry Morganthau, secretary of the treasury under FDR, went further, supporting social welfare systems and major government regulation, intervention, and stimulus to create jobs and infrastructure. Both earlier regime changes had a very pale green tint, as discussed in later chapters, and were far from radical enough to deal with the current crisis. The stewards sought to deal with the stagnation tendencies at the heart of the problem through Keynesian measures of greater government spending and regulation—offering relief in the short and medium term—but were never prepared to carry out the deeper systemic changes necessary to solve the problem for the long term.

The extreme short-term time frame of US capitalism in decline reflects the deepening of structural stagnation and the disappearance of capitalist stewards, although there are financiers like Warren Buffet and George Soros who try to play that role. In the third corporate regime, finance intensified its focus on the short term because of new irresistible and superprofitable opportunities created by globalization and the Reagan Revolution. Reagan's deregulation and free-trade policies made possible the rise of totally unregulated global speculative instruments involving hedge funds, complex derivatives, mortgage securitization (bundling of mortgage loans into "collateralized debt obligations" for resale), and related "toxic assets," all of which escalated into a madcap speculative Wall Street house of cards, built on unsustainable leverage and debt, that had no long-term viability. Had the capitalist stewards survived and played their earlier role, the current crisis might have been deferred, but that would not have resolved the longer-term structural crisis of stagnation, short-term profit maximization, accelerated debt, and unfettered consumerism. To save business and finance, as well as the environment, we will need new economic and political stewards, not just in business but also in civil society and the larger political system, working to help build the larger green long-term economic system.

The implications are unequivocal. At the very moment when we most need a long-term sustainable vision, capitalism itself no longer breeds the sustainable conditions or stewardship ethos—not to mention the political movements and politicians seeking deeper and essential systemic change—to sustain both prosperity and the environment. The Wall Street implosion and the astonishing irresponsibility of Wall Street leaders looking out only for their own bonuses—doling out to themselves an eye-popping $32.6 billion in nine huge bailed-out banks—make this clear. The government (at federal, state, and local levels), along with democratic movements in the larger civil society, has to step in and assume the stewardship role that financial leaders have abandoned. Government, led by the president and driven by accountable empowered citizen movements, is the only institution with the constitutional authority and political power to take on the stewardship role and rapidly create the change in political and economic institutions necessary to get the job done.

The economy cannot function without business or credit; even a perfectly green economy will require both small and large businesses. The effort, rather, is to restructure the economy systemically to operate in a democratic manner with long-term vision and full and true cost-accounting. Inefficient and costly overinvestment in Wall Street will be replaced by investment in sustainable nonfinancial sectors and in local community banks. This will require major public investment and transformations of the corporate structure itself to overcome stagnation in the real economy by means that are not based on hyperconsumerism.

To summarize, we need systemic changes in capitalism toward a green economy that include the following shifts:

- from short-term profit maximization to sustainable long-term enterprise
- from externalizing environmental and social costs to internalizing them
- from monopoly corporations to smaller and midsize businesses
- from financialized Wall Street capitalism to a sustainable Main Street economy
- from corporate-controlled government to popular sovereignty
- from shareholder-owned businesses to stakeholder, labor, and community businesses
- from the invisible hand to the preservation of the commons
- from poverty and low worker wages to living wages for all
- from consumerism to quality of life
- from growth to sufficiency

17

Hurricane Sandy, Climate Sociopathy, and the Infrastructure Crisis

In October 2012, Superstorm Sandy—the largest hurricane ever to hit the US East Coast—killed hundreds of people and destroyed the homes, businesses, power grids, roads, bridges, and jobs prospects of thousands of survivors. Only Katrina was bigger than Sandy. The total cost of damages is estimated at $80 billion. As the weather warms and sea levels rise, with 52 percent of Americans living in coastal areas, millions will have to relocate. This will create population pressures inland hinting at twenty-first-century Malthusian scenarios. Climate change will erode the land, water, crops, and infrastructure available, potentially leading to serious conflicts over where future generations can live.

Scientists view climate change as a major contributor to the enormous size and wrath of Sandy, with warmer Atlantic water temperatures intensifying the winds and waves crashing on the coast from New England to Florida and the Caribbean. Sandy arrived in the hottest year ever recorded, at the end of the hottest decade. As temperatures and sea levels rise faster than scientists predicted, Sandy is a foretaste of things to come.

Natural disasters may hardly seem sociopathic. But preventable natural disasters are a different story. Since climate change is man-made, and US leaders have rejected essential policies to slow or halt climate change, Sandy lives as a nightmarish symbol of the most dangerous sociopathy of the twenty-first century.

Because climate change threatens the survival of civilization, societies that fail to do everything possible to stop and reverse climate change are sociopathic. This is especially true of the societies most responsible for creating and perpetuating the crisis. The United States is by far the largest per capita emitter of greenhouse gas pollution and the most influential nation blocking national and global change to solve the crisis. This, by itself, qualifies the United States as a sociopathic society leading sacrifice of the future for current interests.

Such "climate sociopathy" takes several forms in the United States. One is denial, championed mainly by the Republican Party, which dismisses man-made climate change, claiming the science is inconclusive. The Democratic Party engages in a softer denial, acknowledging that climate change is real and man-made, but failing to vigorously pursue the transformative policies—at home and abroad—that would permit the rapid and radical transformation urgently needed.

Behind this failure is economic sociopathy carried out by the major US corporations profiting enormously from current arrangements. The worst offenders are Big Oil and Big Coal, corporations such as ExxonMobil, Chevron, Shell, BP, and Duke Energy. They have manipulated the public with false promises about creating alternatives to oil, "clean coal," and "environmentally clean" techniques such as fracking, for natural gas, while charging full-speed ahead to squeeze the greatest profits out of oil and coal before full-scale disaster hits.

The energy companies are the tip of a larger corporate sociopathic spear. Nearly all US corporations—especially in the financial, agricultural, chemical, aviation, and construction sectors—are pursuing business as usual, with fossil fuel business models that are poisoning the planet.

Most of the rest of us are collaborators, by embracing mass consumption and suburbanized, automobile-based ways of life that are unsustainable.

Climate sociopathy is closely linked to the enormous infrastructure crisis—an intertwined sociopathic nightmare—that starts with the environment but extends into the other foundations of a sustainable society. Infrastructure is crucial to any analysis of sociopathy because it makes society itself possible. When a society disinvests in its own infrastructure, it destroys the future of its own population and ensures its own eventual collapse.

Investing in a new clean energy infrastructure—of public transit, electric cars and charging stations, solar and wind power production and distribution networks, and green homes and office buildings—is crucial to solving climate change, nationally and globally. The US failure to lead in this area is political and economic sociopathy, since it protects established interests at the expense of a survivable future. It is sociopathic as well because massive public investment in a green infrastructure, especially in the context of a more social democratic or socialist economy, would solve much of the employment crisis in the United States and provide a model for an alternative to fossil fuel economies everywhere.

Failure to create a sustainable environmental infrastructure is linked to two other types of infrastructure sociopathy. One is disinvestment in the social needs of the population, including health care, public education, natural parks and wilderness, vocational training, and community development, pouring money instead into the military, prisons, and corporate subsidies. Public investment in social infrastructure, as in the environment, would also immediately help solve the crisis of jobs and surplus people, making disinvestment in the social infrastructure a doubly compounded sociopathy.

The third infrastructure imperative is to create safe streets and public spaces on which all civil societies depend. But, even after the Newtown Sandy Hook school massacre, the United States has been unwilling to embrace the policies—on gun control, poverty alleviation, and community policing and development—that would create a new public infrastructure assuring safety for the public. As shown in earlier chapters, much of this reflects the economic sociopathy of gun manufacturers that don't want to give up their most profitable products and the political sociopathy of politicians lacking the courage to confront the corporations that fund them.

Disinvestment in all three infrastructures represents a business strategy by the largest US corporations in the age of globalization. Closely tied to the crisis of surplus people, corporations have determined that they can make more money in the short term by investing and producing abroad. Domestic infrastructure is a secondary concern, deliberately subordinated to global profits. US corporate elites are abandoning the United States itself.

Climate change and infrastructure deterioration attack the foundations of society. They will determine prospects of survival in the twenty-first century and should be front and center in theories of political economy and in the public discussion of sociopathic society and the need for transformations in capitalist economies.

18

Consumerism as Sociopathy

A quiet revolutionary struggle is brewing in the minds of the US "Millennial" generation, those between ages sixteen and thirty-four. This huge cohort of 80 million young Americans is wrestling with the fundamental edict of capitalism: buy and you shall be happy. The Millennials have not rejected consumerism but they have also not embraced it fully. They are ambivalent and see serious downsides of the high-consuming life—for reasons that go to the very heart of capitalist sustainability and morality.

In the last few years, surveys have shown Millennials—a socially progressive generation—to be more concerned than their elders about how high consumption affects the environment. But recent polls, by marketing firms and by the respected Pew Research Center, also hint at a broader issue: whether consumerism itself makes for a good life and society. They love their computers and sleep with their iPhones next to their pillow, but this has not wiped out their concerns about the negative side of consumerism.

Technology itself may be contributing to what commentators have called the "death of ownership" culture, as the issue is not owning a book or music album but having access through the Web. Technology is changing the very idea of ownership. But broader factors—including the very availability of so much "stuff"—are contributing to making consumerism less new, exciting, and "cool."

In a recent informal study of Boston-area college students, I asked them how they felt about American consumerism. Almost all of them said they would prefer to be in a society that was less consumer-oriented, because consumer culture gives them these headaches:

- It creates fierce competitive pressure to have more and newer "stuff"
- It makes them feel they never have enough
- It complicates their lives, always worrying about how to maintain, pay for, and use all the things they buy
- It distracts from a quality life with their family and friends

- It creates a "dirty" lifestyle that makes them and the planet sick
- It leads to more inequality, with people seeking more at the expense of others
- It distracts from political engagement—President Bush told them to go shopping as he was gearing up for war with Iraq after 9/11
- It leads to a life they can't escape full of products and empty of meaning

These negative feelings are reflected in changing purchasing patterns. Buying a car has been central to consumerism and the American Dream since World War II. But recent polls indicate that a much higher percentage—about 25 percent of Millennials—do not want to buy a car at all, compared to 10 percent of their parents at their age. In 1978, 67 percent of seventeen-year-old Americans had drivers' licenses compared to just 45 percent in 2010. Of course, these differences may reflect reduced family income as well as changes in consumer attitudes.

Many are also uninterested in buying their own home, the symbol of the American Dream. They prefer renting. In 2010, only 20 percent of the Millennials owned a house.

These may seem like self-indulgent whims of affluent young Americans who consume far more than most people on the planet. Or it might seem a "sour grapes" reaction to their loss of wealth during the Great Recession, as they can no longer afford to buy so much. It could also be a phase of life since young idealists too often turn to traditional consumerism as they assume responsibilities of adult life. It certainly does not suggest that young Americans are decisively rejecting consumerism.

But a quick history of American consumerism suggests something very important: that the growing awareness of its downsides can largely be explained by deep problems of sustainability and freedom at the heart of the capitalist system.

Up until the 1920s, most Americans made their own clothes, grew their own food, and bought very little. They were producers and not consumers. This changed in the 1920s, when the growth of capitalism had created large corporations that could no longer prosper simply from World War I production. They needed Americans to stop making things for themselves and to buy products instead.

The corporations hired public relations experts and launched the modern advertising industry. Retailers such as Sears Roebuck were now sending out millions of catalogs with alluring pictures of clothes, furniture, and other commodities. They began broadcasting ads on the radio. They created billboards showing happy, glamorous consumers.

This was the beginning of "coerced consumption." The 1920s early advertising blitz was primitive compared to the feverish "sales pitch" that followed World War II. In the 1950s and 1960s, Madison Avenue—the heart of the

New York advertising industry immortalized in the hit television show *Mad Men*—took over US culture. The new advertising culture was massive and irresistible. It redefined freedom in America as the freedom to buy, to choose between Coke and Pepsi.

In the half-century following World War II, Americans learned to think of consuming in the market as the only freedom that really mattered. But the Millennials now feel less free to live the lives they truly want, seeing a negative side of the corporate script of buy, buy, buy as "un-freedom."

American capitalism requires that they consume—whether they want to or not. Profit depends on ever-expanding consumer markets, and if the public loses its passion to buy, capitalism will collapse.

Capitalism thus has always coerced consumption, typically by seduction but also by harsher means. In the 1920s, Los Angeles had a huge electric trolley system that allowed people to move around in the city without cars. General Motors responded by buying the trolley system and tearing up the tracks. They then began the long process, culminating in the 1950s, of getting the US government to underwrite highways and cars. People in LA began to buy cars because other transportation choices had been ripped away from them, a perfect example of coerced consumption.

What is the solution for Americans unhappy with consumerism? Many are beginning to make changes in their personal life. Students are starting to grow food in gardens at their universities. Many Americans are living closer to work so they can walk or bike to the job. Some are looking for companies offering choice of shorter work hours, which liberates them from the work-and-spend treadmill. Some are joining the "share economy," where they share things—Zip cars and bikes—with others. Many are "downshifting," choosing to work and consume less, living a simpler life.

But these are small, micro experiments, and constraining consumerism requires changing the DNA of US capitalism. This will require limiting corporate power and rewriting corporate charters to emphasize worker rights and environmental health as well as profit. Quality must replace quantity as the measure of economic and cultural success.

This seems like a tall order. But the existential emergency of climate change and environmental destruction, along with the deep personal unhappiness and social injustice in a consumer-obsessed society, could create dramatic changes. They will not eliminate or necessarily drastically limit consumerism, even as accelerating global warming intensifies the urgency of change. But in the most optimistic scenario, they could put society on a new path toward a more sustainable, cooperative way of life.

These changes will be on the agenda of people around the world in the twenty-first century. America is the glittering symbol of a consumerism beginning to fade. Europe is already a far less consumerist society than the

United States. The BRIC nations of China, India, and Brazil are struggling with issues of environmental justice and equality that bring the issue of consumerism to the front burner. It will take a new social economy that rejects American-style consumerism to solve these problems and help save the world.

Fascism: The Ultimate Sociopathic Society?

Introduction to Part VI

Sociopathy and the Far Right

The most sociopathic of Western societies in the twentieth century were Nazi Germany and Fascist Italy. Nazism combined genocide with a brutally violent agenda of global conquest, leading to World War II and the death of many millions of people. As in all extreme sociopathic societies, its self-destruction arose inevitably out of its own grandiose and evil ambitions.

In this section, we look at fascist systems, first, because they illuminate and dramatize in extreme form the danger of sociopathic regimes and societies. Second, they pose the question of whether another grave economic crisis could lead toward a new and different twenty-first-century neofascism, in a nation such as the United States.

While the United States today and the 1920s German Weimar Republic are very different systems, there are some striking similarities. The main chapter here looks at these parallels and at the danger signs of a potential "fascism lite" arising in the United States. The possibility sounds remote to many Americans, but most Germans also thought it ludicrous in the 1920s that Hitler and his Nazi Party or other Far Right groups would take power. Today, the Tea Party, survivalist groups, and extreme evangelical and militarist Far Right groups already have a loud voice, deep pockets, and representation in the Republican Party. Their power could grow if our economic crises deepen. The chapter shows that we can already see some of the core sociopathic elements of a US "fascism lite" in the war on terrorism, propaganda driven by official lies, and growing surveillance and policing of the population.

The short chapter in this section focuses explicitly on the Weimar syndrome and the contemporary dangers it poses. It examines its form in

Weimar Germany and considers whether and how a Weimar syndrome might be crystallizing in the United States today, looking at the frightening sociopathic consequences.

19

Fascism Lite

Right after George W. Bush was reelected in 2004, thousands of Americans applied to emigrate to Canada. Immigration lawyers in Toronto and Montreal got so many requests for help that they went to San Francisco, Boston, and other bastions of the blue states to answer questions from Americans who didn't want to live in their country anymore. Most of these despairing Americans were not just upset that their candidate had lost the election. Some feared a slow-motion coup, in which a far-right Administration would tighten its grip on the nation, continue its attacks on constitutional rights, and step-by-step undermine American democracy.

We have seen hints of a fascist drift in earlier American eras, although it never created a permanent police state or fascist order. In 1917, Woodrow Wilson launched one of the worst crackdowns against antiwar protest in American history, involving unconstitutional detentions and deportations of thousands of people. The internment of Japanese Americans in World War II and the anti-Communist hysteria of the McCarthy era during the early 1950s were other such periods. McCarthy purged thousands of government civil servants, scientists, professors, journalists, and Hollywood writers and producers. The country's move toward a police state was halted only when McCarthy went after top generals in the military and he was discredited.

This chapter looks at the dangers of an unprecedented tip toward a new regime that I will call "fascism lite." Fascism has long been understood as a police state based on the union of big business and government. Such a regime suspends the most basic constitutional liberties of citizens in the name of a religious or nationalist war against civilizational enemies. I argue in this chapter that several forces could converge to create right-wing regime change toward an American brand of fascism.

In the current regime, we already see the embryonic shape of such a new hypernationalist order, foreshadowed in the Patriot Act, the Homeland Security restrictions on civil liberties, and the Pentagon's suspension of the Geneva Accords and Constitutional safeguards against arbitrary detention and abuse of terrorism suspects. This suggests a creeping authoritarianism that already functions within today's regime and could continue to sustain the current order. But, in another scenario, repressive forces could expand and accelerate to create regime change. By fascism lite, I mean a new regime that would effectively suspend much of our current rights, while still preserving the patina of formal elections and constitutionalism. It would preserve a government-corporate partnership, but, in contrast to the current regime, it would clearly subordinate corporations to the state. It would eliminate unions, formally subjugate the press to government censorship, increase the tie between religion and the state, and subject dissenters and tens of millions of ordinary citizens to the unconstitutional treatment and daily abuse now received by terrorist detainees.

Any form of fascism that might take root in America is radically distinct from the classical forms in Germany and Italy in the 1930s—and will remain a different breed. Fascism lite is not Nazism, Hitlerism, or Mussolini-style rule, and is dangerous precisely because it is likely to retain the framework of constitutional rule that Hitler and Mussolini openly abandoned. Nonetheless, parallels between the conditions in classical European fascist societies and ours today include the marriage of big business and the state, the rise of militaristic and religious nationalism, and the severe economic dislocation at home that creates an "anxious class" of workers and small businesses. Hitler exploited such social anxieties and came to power through elections, promising to respect democracy and the law. He created fascism from within a democratic, corporate order undergoing great destabilization, a situation not entirely different from our own. Both the parallels and differences between fascism and fascism lite in the European and American contexts need exploration.

Another caveat is that fascist regime change in the United States is a possibility, not a certainty. The American people have the ability to stop it if they understand the danger and how to respond. In the last section of this book, I make clear how Americans can not only prevent fascist regime change but also tip the corporate regime in the opposite direction, toward a reenergized democracy.

The Prophet of American Fascism

At the beginning of the current regime, Bertram Gross, a prominent political scientist, wrote *Friendly Fascism,* a best-selling book that was published in 1982, two years after Ronald Reagan's election. The book was a shot across the bow about the dangers posed by the new corporate order and its structural potential to transform itself into an American breed of fascism. Gross saw the rulers of this new "friendly fascist" order as "members of the Establishment or people on its fringes, who in the name of Americanism betray the interests of most Americans by fomenting militarism, applauding rat-race individualism, protecting undeserved privilege, or stirring up nationalistic and ethnic hatreds. I see pretended patriots who desecrate the American flag by waving it while waiving the law."

Friendly fascism was likely to come to America not through brown-shirted fringe elements on the streets but "as an outcome of powerful tendencies within the Establishment itself." "Big Business and Big Government," he writes, "have been learning how to live in bed together, and despite arguments between them, enjoy the cohabitation." Such cohabitation regimes—what I have called corporate regimes—have had a historical tendency, Gross noted, to slide down a dangerous authoritarian slope. "I am worried," he observed, "by those who fail to remember—or have never learned—that Big Business–Big Government partnerships, backed up by other elements, were the central facts behind the power structures of old fascism in the days of Mussolini, Hitler, and the Japanese empire builders."

But Gross did not imagine a friendly fascism in America that looked anything like the classical fascist regime. In the United States, "anyone looking for black shirts, mass parties, or men on horseback will miss the telltale signs of creeping fascism." Instead, friendly fascism would have a distinctively American form, preserving the formal constitutional framework and presided over by congenial, folksy leaders. Gross suggested a new kind of authoritarian order built on America's own most basic institutions. Instead of abolishing the Constitution and formal democratic procedures, elections would be subtly subverted, and opposition parties and the general public subtly intimidated and manipulated. Propaganda would come not through direct government-owned media but through the electronic circus of corporate cable media. Dissent would be crushed not by murderous street gangs but by professional and high-tech policing and surveillance.

Unlike classical fascism, friendly fascism arising from a corporate regime would play off the most appealing elements of contemporary American culture. "In America," Gross wrote, friendly fascism "would be supermodern and multi-ethnic, as American as Madison Avenue, executive luncheons, credit cards, and apple pie. It would be fascism with a smile. As a warning against its cosmetic face, subtle manipulation and velvet gloves, I call it friendly fascism. What scares me most is its subtle appeal."

William Shirer, in his epic chronicle of German Fascism, *The Rise and Fall of the Third Reich*, wrote that "America may be the first country in which fascism comes to power through democratic elections." Gross admitted his own very personal fear of this possibility. "I am not afraid to say that I am afraid," he wrote. "I am afraid of those who proclaim that it can't happen here."

While Gross's work points to the structural potential of our corporate regime to become fascist, fascism lite is the most likely scenario. Gross could not anticipate 9/11, or the ideology of the current American war on terrorism.

He could not imagine the blatantly unfriendly form of fascist regime change that looms now as a national nightmare. The current fascist drift already evident in the existing regime, as symbolized in the torture chambers of Abu Ghraib and Guantanamo, is far less cosmetically appealing or apple pie than the model Gross forecast.

Fascism lite is not at all friendly. True, it has a corporate flavor, and it has many of the attributes Gross predicted, including the ability to insinuate itself slowly into the American landscape without the most extreme trappings of classical fascism. But the driving thrust is likely to come not so much from the corporations, as Gross would suggest, but from the state, the military, and religion. Corporations would continue to play a major role, but the state would move toward more direct control over corporations themselves, as part of a new, radically militarized social order. Its center of gravity will be the Pentagon rather than Citigroup or Merrill Lynch. Its repression of ordinary people, particularly dissenters, minorities, and immigrants, at home and abroad, will be characterized by violence and inquisition.

Causes and Catalysts

Consider the following three potential causes of a fascist lite regime tip.

1. From Cracks to Chasms

Serious cracks in the regime could potentially destabilize it and lead toward regime change of either a progressive or a reactionary form. Fascism lite could arise from a deepening of the regime's current cracks into unmanageable chasms, leading to vast popular dissent and a decision by regime elites to maintain order by suspending normal constitutional procedures and imposing an American form of police state.

One scenario is a deterioration of the regime's economic crises, creating recessions or even a depression. Mass unemployment, spiraling debt, a collapse in the dollar with a steep rise in interest rates, and dramatic new cuts in health care, Social Security, and other parts of the safety net could trigger mass protests or riots. If the dissent looked like it might spin out of control, threatening the regime's very survival, elites might crack down with brutal new measures outside the current constitutional order, sliding toward right-wing regime change. Another possible scenario is a desperate deterioration of the military situation in Iraq and Afghanistan, or other catastrophic new foreign policy misadventures. As in the Vietnam era, these could produce a huge antiwar movement that would divide the country and threaten regime stability. New terrorist attacks on the homeland are another such eventuality, but I consider these separately because they are historically unique and probably the single most likely catalyst of a fascist regime turn.

We have already seen the rise of a popular movement against corporate globalization, and we also have seen the eruption of one of the biggest peace movements in history against the Iraqi war. The regime's response has not been reassuring. While both the antiglobalization and antiwar movements have been largely peaceful and have not threatened large-scale social disorder, regime elites have responded with growing repression. In the 1999 Seattle protests against the WTO, the police launched volleys of pepper spray and used batons against protestors, rounding up hundreds in detention centers. On the first day of protest, authorities darkened Seattle's sunny skies with clouds of tear gas. By the fifth day of protest, tanks were patrolling Seattle streets.

To deal with hundreds of antiglobalization and antiwar protests in recent years, police have cordoned off whole areas of cities, built walls with barbed wire or electronic shock devices to keep people miles away from the meetings, forced protestors to march in small cordoned areas surrounded by fences and armed guards, begun refusing to issue protest permits of any form, rounded up and detained larger numbers of protestors without charges, beat peaceful protestors violently, and launched judicial proceedings and sentencing that prevented those arrested from going out on the streets again. Before the 2002 Miami protest of the Free Trade of the Americas meeting, authorities described a military approach to "crowd control." Television cameras showed mass detention facilities, humvee-type police vehicles, and prison-like protest areas, as officials made barely disguised threats of police violence. I knew many students, labor activists, religious protestors, and others who were terrified and canceled their decision to go out of fear of being beaten, jailed, or even killed.

I have had my own experience of the new repressive climate:

I went to jail briefly for civil disobedience in support of a "Janitors for Justice" protest event in Boston in 2002. It was a very different and more frightening experience than my other experiences with the prison system during 1960s antiwar protests before the current regime. All those committing civil disobedience were arrested, fingerprinted, booked, and eventually sent to individual cells. I noticed on the walls of the police station a thick sheaf of daily postings from Washington about terrorism. After we were booked and sent to cells, the police told us that our detention was indefinite, pending word from Washington regarding whether we were suspects for terrorism. They sent our fingerprints and records to Washington to determine whether any of us might be under surveillance by the CIA or FBI. Sitting isolated in a cell, unaware of how long I would be detained and feeling that I might be deprived of my normal rights to talk to lawyers and get help, was quite different than contemplating the Patriot Act from my office. For anyone who doubts whether civil liberties and the Bill of Rights matter, I recommend an involuntary stay in a jail cell under the new conditions.

While the rise of a fascist regime would require more far-reaching constitutional and institutional changes, the assault on dissent suggests a climate where additional catalysts could create a tipping point. The most likely candidate for such a tipping point is more terrorism and an escalating war against it.

2. Terrorism and the War on Terrorism

In January 2005, Richard Clarke, the country's leading counter terrorism advisor to presidents Reagan, Bush Sr., Clinton, and Bush Jr., published the article "Ten Years Later" in the *Atlantic Monthly* about what America might look like in 2015. Clarke envisages a series of new terrorist attacks on the country beginning in 2005 and 2006. They are not dramatic disasters on the scale of 9/11 but smaller explosions like the terrorist bombs set off in Madrid train stations. They involve attacks on subway stations or commuter rails, on shopping malls, power plants, and official buildings. American officials respond to the attacks with global military campaigns that intensify anti-Americanism and create more terrorist attacks. Authorities in 2008 and 2009 seek to restore order with a massive extra-constitutional campaign of repression. Civil liberties are dramatically curtailed and the president suspends many constitutional constraints on surveillance, detention, and normal judicial procedures. Key parts of the Bill of Rights fall by the wayside. Clarke concludes with a picture of America as an Orwellian police state, suggesting essentially a regime change to a fascist model in five to ten years.

Clarke acknowledges that this is an exercise in hypotheticals, commonly used by intelligence and counter terrorism analysts to crystallize their planning. But while he takes pains to emphasize that this is only an imagined future, he also emphasizes that his analysis is based on existing threat analyses and policy responses to terror—involving surveillance of all citizens, new detention procedures, lifting of existing bans on torture, and other emergency suspensions of constitutional liberties—that are already laid out in thousands of Homeland Security, Pentagon, FBI, CIA, and Justice Department documents and procedures. He laces his *Atlantic* essay with pages of footnotes based on this official documentary record, essentially creating a fictional future that looks scarily possible based on present evidence.

Clarke's scenario is conservative by his own admission because he does not discuss nuclear or biological terrorist attacks. This is a leading matter of discussion among the nation's top intelligence analysts and political officials. American leaders have already stoked fear of such attacks as grounds for the war on Iraq and suspensions of constitutional rights at home. If a nuclear terrorist attack were actually to occur, it would be the single most likely catalyst of a fascist regime change.

Clarke also does not discuss the deeper economic and political aims of the regime that lock in a dangerous US foreign policy. The entire regime is structured today around the interests of global corporations whose interests require American global hegemony. The unilateral and militarized excesses of the neoconservatives have captured attention, but even before their coming to power in the Bush administration, the regime under Reagan, Bush Sr., and Clinton had firmly committed itself to empire. This was built into the regime's DNA, since global corporations depend on a globalization system secured by the US military that can sustain friendly governments and stabilize a global order increasingly polarized between rich and poor.

The regime's interests thus commit it to a permanent expansionist policy that is a recipe for anti-American terrorism and intensified repression abroad and at home. Empires have always faced terrorist attacks, from the Roman to the British Empires, particularly as they decline. The American Empire is no exception; Empire is a pillar of the regime, and the military has become an increasingly central player. The difference from prior empires is that technology has made terrorist attacks, even from the periphery of the Empire, far more lethal to the imperial heartland.

The war on terrorism (and its implications for a fascist turn) will continue even if the Democratic leadership, now securely integrated into the corporate regime and its foreign policy establishment, comes to power. Clarke's scenario is based on the regime's global interests, not just on the radicalism of neoconservative Republicans, and likely would play out under a Democratic administration as well. Terrorism and the war against terrorism remain the most likely catalysts for a fascist regime change under either Republicans or Democrats. Both parties are likely to pursue the regime aim of US hegemony, create blowback of repeated terrorism against America, and unleash the potential of a regime change toward fascism.

3. Regime Radicalism and Civilizational Warfare

The potential for a fascist tip is far more likely under the Republican Right governed at this writing by President George W. Bush. Bush has turned the third corporate regime into an "extreme regime," and his right-wing radicalism and pandering to his evangelical religious base is a third factor that could prove a tipping point toward a fascist regime change.

One way to see this is to look at the master narrative of the regime under Bush, which I term civilizational warfare. Civilizational warfare was also the master myth of Germany and Italy when they turned fascist. It is the most dangerous ideological myth for stabilizing a regime, since it creates the war between absolute good and evil that fascist leaders use to justify the abandonment of constitutionalism and the creation of a police state. The rhetoric of religion and race is especially dangerous, because it brings God and biology in as justifications for state repression.

Civilizational war propaganda is so dangerous because it suggests politics is now a struggle against barbarians at the gate—and against the more insidious barbarians who have already slipped in. Such barbarians are not really political opponents but devils, since they threaten everything human and everything good about America, Christianity, and the West. If we don't win this fight, we don't just lose another election but we lose thousands of years of the best that religion and human civilization have created, the kind of extreme danger that could legitimate even a fascist response.

When you declare war against an enemy that is absolute evil, the goal of destroying it justifies any means. In 1954, at the height of the McCarthy hysteria, a commission formed by the president and headed by ex-president Herbert Hoover, made exactly that claim about the new Communist threat, arguing that "traditional rules of American fair play" could no longer apply. Bush's radical language of absolute good and absolute evil justifies even more extreme measures, since what is at stake is not just capitalism but the survival of civilization itself. This helps to explain the famous secrecy and constitutional radicalism of his administration, and explains why he has brought the nation farther down the path toward fascism than any of his predecessors. His increasing reliance on religion and religious extremists waging war on judges and secular politics is especially dangerous, a harbinger of fascist possibilities.

Civilizational war propaganda has always been most dangerous in societies where large sectors of the population are economically threatened or socially displaced. Historians see Hitler's appeal as rooted in the German small-business class that was being displaced by the corporations during the terrible German economic crises of the 1920s and 1930s. Their anxieties became intense enough that Hitler's propagandists could manipulate them at will with their own version of Aryan civilizational warfare. The new anxious working class in America is suffering its own fear of social displacement, with some of the same anxieties and resentments of the German lower middle classes in Hitler's day. The black-magic propaganda of the current regime feeds on the American displaced classes with comparable power, and any further deterioration in the security of American workers, especially displaced males who have always been the backbone of fascist movements, will only make a shift to fascism in the United States that much more likely.

Fascism Today

Might we already have seen a regime tip as the third corporate regime encounters ever-deepening crises—in the context of a war on terrorism that seems tailor-made for the rise of fascism? The explosion of literature in academic circles, in the mass media, and on the Internet about fascism suggests that this possibility is on the public's mind. George Orwell is back in vogue, now required reading in classrooms around the country.

This is not the first American era when there has been widespread discussion about whether fascism "could happen here." But today's conversation is carried out by more educated elites, is marked by a less paranoid style, and is less focused on the rise of extreme right-wing fringe groups such as the KKK or the American Nazi party. Instead, the focus is on the systemic attributes of fascism and how they might arise (or might already have done so) out of tendencies within the ruling elites and the corporate regime itself.

Consider the widely circulated work of political scientist Lawrence Britt, who after a comparative, historical analysis of fascism from Germany and Italy to Franco's Spain, Suharto's Indonesia, and Pinochet's Chile, identifies fourteen defining attributes of fascist regimes.

The list should be nailed on the door of every classroom in the country. It is a generic description of a fascist regime broad enough to encompass both classical and fascist lite models. It hints clearly at the structural vulnerabilities of the current US corporate regime to a fascist turn. At minimum, it raises the question of where America is headed and whether some form of fascism could lurk in our future. At worst, it suggests that the United States is already undergoing a regime change toward its own species of "democratic" fascism.

The Fourteen Characteristics of Fascism

1. Powerful and continuing nationalism
2. Disdain for the recognition of human rights
3. Identification of enemies/scapegoats as a unifying cause
4. Supremacy of the military
5. Rampant sexism
6. Controlled mass media
7. Obsession with national security
8. Religion and government are intertwined
9. Corporate power is protected
10. Labor power is suppressed
11. Disdain for intellectuals and the arts
12. Obsession with crime and punishment
13. Rampant cronyism and corruption
14. Fraudulent elections

(Lawrence Britt, *Free Inquiry Magazine,* Spring 2003)

Many of Britt's fourteen attributes have been elements of the third corporate regime from the beginning. On most of the fourteen criteria, the current regime is clearly becoming more extreme. Look at the items on the list referring to militarism, patriotism, enemies, and national security. Ever since 9/11, these have become defining staples of the American political landscape and they are becoming ever more serious threats to American constitutionalism. Control of mass media, as discussed below, is a part of a growing official propaganda apparatus threatening an independent press in America. Much of the rest of the list relates to corporate power: the dominant role of corporations, their growing ties to government and the military, and the rampant growth of institutionalized corporate cronyism and corruption. These building blocks of the third corporate regime—particularly the tight, incestuous link between big corporations and government—have grown more blatant and far-reaching as it has aged. The suppression of labor power is particularly important, a defining feature of the regime since its birth but increasingly its ruling passion as it seeks to virtually eliminate unions from the American scene. The similarity here to German fascism is too strong to miss, since Hitler secured the support of German corporations for his own regime change by crushing the German unions, a benefit too great for otherwise reluctant German corporate elites to overlook. And the elements related to the disdain for intellectuals, obsession with crime and punishment, and fraudulent elections are other frightening signs of a regime turning to repression as it loses its ability to survive through constitutional means.

The melding of religion and government may be among the most ominous signs that Britt describes. Religious conservatives have become a driving force in the regime, pushing toward a redefinition of the classic separation of state and church. They are assaulting the independent judiciary, a classic fascist threat. Their efforts to bring Christian language, symbols, and beliefs back into the classroom and the courtroom, and to make churches recipients of government funding for social services and broadcast enterprises, dangerously blur the line between religious and political discourse and institutions. The growing dependency of the Republican Party on its religious base, and the willingness of President George W. Bush and Congressional leaders, such as House Majority leader Tom DeLay and Senate Majority Leader Bill Frist, to accommodate and even encourage extremist religious demands are truly explosive ingredients here. In early 2005, DeLay threatened "activist" judges with retaliation, after judges had been shot in the courtroom and religious conservatives themselves had threatened to remove judges who were purportedly attacking people of faith. The willingness of regime leaders to play the religion card, hinting or overtly claiming that their political opponents are enemies of God, is straying into the deep weeds of a new American fascism.

Warning Signs

Three current trends rank among the most alarming signs of the potential for a fascist regime tip:

1. Propaganda

To report the war in Iraq, America's war correspondents became "embedded." The Pentagon assigned them to combat units, and they became a new part of America's fighting forces. Their weapons were their laptops, and they reported the story like good soldiers.

The 2003 Iraqi invasion coverage was one of the great propaganda triumphs of modern times. Americans heard a war story scripted by top political leaders. It was as if the generals "embedded" the software of the reporters' brains and laptops. The programmed journalists told the official story of American liberators who would be greeted by Iraqi civilians showering G.I. Joe with roses.

In fascist regimes, the media becomes officially "embedded" in the government propaganda apparatus. Structurally, the media is absorbed into the government and "institutionally" embedded, with stories prepared and distributed by political hacks. Ideologically, this embedded press reports what it is told and reporters unconsciously parrot the official master narrative of the regime.

In the current corporate regime, the press remains officially independent of government ownership and control, but is increasingly informally embedded. The extent of today's ideological and structural embedding has been widely discussed by authoritative media critics such as Robert McChesney. As huge corporations such as GE, Disney, Newscorp, and AOL–Time Warner have bought up television stations and newspapers, and have become ever more monopolistic, structural embedding has become an obvious fact of life. Of course, the mainstream media varies in its level of embeddedness. Fox has become the model of the most fully embedded media, faithfully disseminating not just the regime's propaganda story, but becoming the quasi-official broadcasting voice of the Republican Party. Other mainstream media, such as CNN, are less partisan in terms of party politics, but uncritically accept most of the regime's underlying ideological assumptions about the virtues of US hegemony abroad and corporate power at home, reflecting corporate ownership and beliefs. The Public Broadcasting System (PBS) and National Public Radio (NPR) are the mainstream media that are more open to critical discourse, particularly on social issues related to race and gender, but are themselves operating increasingly as embedded media on core economic and foreign policy issues. This reflects their growing dependence on corporate funding, the general repression of dissent, and their continued financial dependence on an increasingly conservative Congress that views them as part of the liberal Establishment.

The coverage of the Iraqi war demonstrated the level of ideological programming throughout the mainstream media, as reporters embraced the regime's underlying premises that the United States seeks to rid the world of tyrants and terrorists while promoting freedom not just in Iraq but everywhere. Such ideological embedding is particularly important because it does not require coercive control; reporters learn from childhood to absorb the underlying regime myths and the embedded media requires no formal censorship to ensure conformity with the regime's master narrative.

Beyond the informal media embedding that characterized the third corporate regime almost from the beginning, there are new trends that hint at a shift toward the more formal embedding characteristic of friendly fascism. In January 2005, a scandal broke when it was revealed that the Bush administration paid $240,000 to a columnist, Armstrong Williams, to write columns in support of its No Child Left Behind program—and to encourage other journalists to do the same. Soon, similar secret arrangements with other columnists were revealed. This led to outrage because it crossed a long-standing, sacred line separating government and media, making it impossible to know whether a journalist is independent or on the Administration's payroll and just parroting its official line. The arrangements violated US law that prohibits this form of propaganda, although analysts noted that the Administration had devised similar arrangements to promote its Medicare reform and other policies. It was an early mark of the more formal embedding found in fascism.

In 2005, reports implicated far more influential media personalities in a different propaganda outrage. Well-known conservatives, such as Bill Kristol, editor of the influential conservative magazine the *Weekly Standard* and a regular commentator on Fox News, have helped draft speeches and policies for members of the Administration. Then, in their role as media commentators or columnists, they would praise these speeches or policies as "independent" journalists. Kristol and fellow prominent conservative journalist Charles Krauthammer were consultants to President Bush in the drafting of his second inaugural speech. In the January 31 edition of the *Weekly Standard,* Kristol lauded the speech as "powerful," "impressive," and "historical," making similar comments on Fox national news during Fox's live coverage of the event. Fox commentator Krauthammer called the speech "revolutionary," comparing it to John F. Kennedy's inaugural address. There is nothing wrong with conservatives like Kristol and Krauthammer getting involved in or being paid for speech writing. But to appear in print or on television as independent journalists without making clear when and how they have been involved in drafting the very important speech that they are commenting on moves the media closer to being the official organ of propaganda characteristic of fascist regimes.

In January 2005, the Administration required leaders and staff professionals in the Social Security Administration (SSA) to join the regime's full-court media campaign to privatize Social Security. Top Social Security administrators prepared documents about the imminent crisis of the system and the dangers of not moving quickly to privatize. But staff professionals in the agency blew the whistle, disclosing that this was false information and that the Agency was being forced to shift from its professional independence to become part of the Administration's propaganda system. The agency's professionals claimed that their integrity and that of the Agency were being destroyed, leading top Bush officials to say that the Social Security officials would not be required to advocate any specific privatization remedy. But SSA officials continued to promote the Administration's policy under reported pressure from top officials, a sign of a shift to embed not just the media but the civil service.

In 2002, reports emerged that the Pentagon was creating a new propaganda tool involving foreign media. The idea was not different from that in the Armstrong Williams scandal. Through a new internal office, the Office of Strategic Influence, the Pentagon planned to pay foreign media or columnists to run favorable stories or to write stories for them involving "spin" or demonstrably false information. As one Washington watchdog group wrote in an online piece called "Paying for Disinformation," "George Orwell couldn't have come up with a better name for a program whose yet-to-be-determined mission may include expensive public relations campaigns using the foreign news media, the Internet, and covert operations to win the hearts and minds of foreign citizens." This revelation set off intense global and domestic storms against the Pentagon's role as chief foreign propagandist.

As noted above, the Administration set the stage for the Iraq invasion of 2003 by running one of the most deceptive propaganda campaigns in American history. To justify the two key false justifications for the war, that Saddam Hussein had weapons of mass destruction and that he helped cause 9/11, the regime put pressure on intelligence officials at the CIA and other intelligence agencies to back their own story of the threat. As in the case of the Social Security Administration, this action compromised the credibility of the most important US intelligence organizations, turning them into embedded instruments of state propaganda. Senior professionals in the agencies who resisted this trend either quit or were fired.

As Baghdad fell in 2003, an Iraqi American exuberantly calls out "Thank you, Mr. Bush, thank you, U.S.A." to a television crew in Kansas City. But it turns out that the television news clip was not produced by the local Kansas City channel but by the State Department, although this was not announced to the viewing public. Some months later, another reporter in a story on US airport security described the changes as "one of the most remarkable campaigns in aviation history." This "reporter" was also fake, a public relations professional from the Transportation Security Agency. In January 2004, another story described the success of the Bush administration in opening up global markets for US farmers. This "news" was actually produced by the Office of Communications of the State Department, with the public having no way of knowing.

These government-produced propaganda pieces are just three of hundreds of precooked news segments produced by the Bush administration between 2001 and 2005, and disseminated to local news stations around the country for inclusion in their regular news programming. Typically, the fact that it was government-produced rather than regular news created by the local news department was never revealed. Karen Ryan, a former reporter for ABC and PBS, appeared as a "reporter" for seven different government agencies in 2003 and 2004. During investigations, she said, "I just did what everyone in the industry was doing."

Almost all major government agencies now have vast public relations offices creating "news" for America's home viewers. Local channels may be reluctant to become such official propaganda organs but many are hurting for funds or staff and are happy to get these free prepackaged segments from the government to insert and fill out their own news. As this remarkable pattern of formal embedding expands, it turns the broadcast media into direct extensions of the state, part of the official propaganda structure.

In fascist states, both the media and official government agencies become explicit organs of propaganda. The media and government bureaucracy in America have historically managed to avoid this fate, despite the many pressures on them to conform to official story lines. But the examples above suggest a crossing of the Rubicon. The regime is moving from cajoling and pressuring journalists and civil servants to embedding them directly into the official government propaganda apparatus, while embedding government propaganda agencies and their public relations reports seamlessly into the mass media's news. If this "deviant" pattern becomes more normalized, as many think it already has, it is a path to the complete disappearance of a free media and professional civil service, one of the hallmarks of fascist regimes.

2. Torture

The image of an American-held Iraqi prisoner at Abu Ghraib, hooded, with electrical wires attached to his arms and genitals, has been seared on the consciousness of the world. So have the photographs of naked Iraqi prisoners in a pyramid, forced to masturbate by their American guards. And we have all seen the photos of Iraqi prisoners with leashes around their necks dragged around by American soldiers. We have not seen photos of some of the beatings that have led to severe injuries and even death.

Such abuse has not been restricted to Abu Ghraib. It has been confirmed in American detention centers in Afghanistan, where US guards have used "water board" torture (strapped to a board and held under water) to threaten prisoners with drowning. In Afghanistan and at Guantanamo Bay, journalists have reported other grisly forms of torture, including dog attacks that led to severe bite wounds and beating prisoners so brutally on their legs that at least one died of a heart attack. Indeed, all these practices go well beyond the humiliation of prisoners. At least five prison detainees have been reported killed at the hands of their American guards.

While only lower-level soldiers, such as Sergeant Charles Graner at Abu Ghraib, have been officially convicted of these practices, internal Pentagon reports acknowledge that they were following orders launched from further up the chain of command. This confirms a shift toward a more official embrace of torture and a repudiation of constitutional procedures at the heart of the American system. Since the beginning of the third corporate regime (and before), the United States has supported governments from Saudi Arabia to El Salvador that have used torture and systemically rejected constitutionalism. But there are new signs that this fascist repudiation of constitutionalism—of which the direct embrace of torture is one of the most frightening signs—is becoming part of the American system itself.

After Attorney General Ashcroft stepped down, the new attorney general designee, Alberto Gonzales, refused under questioning at his 2005 Senate confirmation hearings to renounce the use of torture. Gonzales was famous as the White House counselor who had aggressively advanced the argument in 2002 that 9/11 had ushered in a new era in which the old rules of the game—such as the Geneva Conventions that forbid torture—were out of date. Thirty-six senators voted against his confirmation, observing that he was one of the principal architects of a new American policy of torture. Senator Edward Kennedy was one of many senators who explicitly argued that Gonzales's policies "have been used by the administration, the military and the CIA to justify torture and Geneva Convention violations by military and civilian officials."

The regime's religion of civilizational warfare is a recipe for torture and broader extra-constitutional measures. The prominent British journalist Jonathan Steele reported in 2005 "that the administration sees the US not just as a self-appointed global policeman, but also as the world's prison warder. It is thinking of building jails in foreign countries, mainly those with grim human rights records, to which it can secretly transfer detainees (unconvicted by any court) for the rest of their lives—a kind of global gulag beyond the scrutiny of the International Committee of the Red Cross, or any other independent observers or lawyers." The documented record of abuse and torture at Abu Ghraib, Guantanamo, and Afghan prisons makes clear that the regime sees torture as an acceptable part of the war on terrorism. The attorney general's view that the old rules do not apply—including the ban on torture—is a grave step toward fascism.

3. Election Fraud

The Constitution requires fair and free elections, and the most dangerous extra-constitutional sign of friendly fascism is the corruption or suspension of the electoral process. Classical fascism involved the direct suspension of elections, which Hitler did after the 1933 Reichstag fire. But fascism lite is more likely to take the form, as discussed earlier, of maintaining the formal procedures of elections. Systemic rigging undermines the possibility of fair outcomes, while other factors, including the incorporation of all the leading political parties into the regime, erode real, substantive democracy.

In the 2000 presidential election, in which Bush was selected by the Supreme Court rather than elected by a majority of the voters, at least the following electoral irregularities or blatant fraud surfaced:

The famous butterfly ballots in Florida

Voters, mainly African Americans, who reported being turned away at the polls

Organized crowds who disrupted recount procedures in Florida precincts

Prevention of voter registration of convicted felons who had served their terms

About 40 percent of American voters viewed these irregularities as a pattern of fraud that led them to view Bush as an illegitimate president. It spurred legislation for electoral reform, the Help America Vote Act, passed in 2002 to prevent any repetition. But in 2004, more serious charges of electoral fraud surfaced all over the country but especially in the key state of Ohio, which determined the outcome, as Florida had four years before. The new election problems in Ohio, which led to an official recount of the whole state vote, included:

Disappearance of ballots in some precincts

3,000 more votes for Bush counted than voters registered in at least one precinct

Citizens were denied legal access to voting records and lists in Ohio precincts as they tried to check the validity of the counts

Waits of up to eight hours in some, mainly African American, districts

Electronic voting without paper records, with the voting machines manufactured by an Ohio-based company, Diebold, whose CEO, Walden O'Dell, is on record as committed "to helping Ohio deliver its electoral votes" to President Bush.

While many view these irregularities as mistakes and not fraud, the very fact that the top election officials in Florida in 2000, Katherine Harris, and in Ohio in 2004, Kenneth Blackwell, were chairs of the Bush reelection campaigns in their states creates unacceptable conflicts of interest. These officials made key decisions about registration procedures, ballot types, machine selection, distribution of voting machines by precinct, and how to investigate allegations and do recounts. Harris, of course, reported to Governor Jeb Bush, the brother of the president.

Beyond the problems in Florida and Ohio, systemic national voting problems increasingly undermine the legitimacy of the American "free elections" system. The problems and their potential remedies are now widely recognized:

> Election machines, particularly electronic machines without paper records, create an unaccountable system and should be banned.
>
> Top state election officials should be prevented from serving on the campaigns of any candidate.
>
> Machines, ballots, and counting procedures should be made uniform within and across all states, with bans on providing more machines for affluent precincts, as occurred in Ohio.
>
> Counts and recounts should be transparent, preventing the shenanigans reported in Ohio of precinct officials throwing whole lists into the garbage.
>
> The Help America Vote Act should be fully funded and expanded to address all of the problems discussed here.
>
> Registration procedures that deny the vote to prisoners, felons who have served their terms, and millions of others in the entire voting age population are unacceptable. In European countries, all voting age citizens are automatically registered when they are issued passports or driver's licenses.
>
> Voting should be on a holiday, as in many other countries, so all can vote.

The regime is shifting in the opposite direction of most of these remedies, introducing more voting machines without paper ballots, creating more restrictive and difficult registration procedures, and underfunding its own voter reform initiatives. It appears to be normalizing what were seen as deviations in 2000. Should this pattern of normalizing electoral deviance continue, not only will about half the American public continue to be nonvoters, but those who do vote will doubt whether their preferences have been counted fairly. The loss of faith in free elections, and the systemic subversion of a fair electoral system, is the surest path to fascism lite.

None of this proves that we are already living under a fascist system. Instead, it shows that we have already drastically weakened or eliminated many of our most important constitutional rights and protections, and have already experienced what might be described as creeping fascism *within* the current regime. If we don't reverse course, the current path could take us toward fascist regime change. But there is nothing inevitable about this. The United States has survived prior eras, such as the 1917–1920 repression and the McCarthy period, that temporarily subverted the Constitution but did not lead to fascist regime change. Substantial freedom still remains in the United States, as evidenced by my freedom to publish this book and your freedom to read it. And cracks in the regime could equally open up possibilities for a regime change toward a more humane and democratic society.

20

History's Magic Mirror
America's Economic Crisis and the Weimar Republic of Pre-Nazi Germany

Charles Derber and Yale Magrass

Germany's economic crisis of the 1930s led to the rise of far-right populism and the Nazi Party, fueled by the corporate and military establishment. An American version of this "Weimar Syndrome" could emerge as the far Right closes its grip on the Republican Party.

Contrary to common wisdom, the ascendancy of the Tea Party, Christian fundamentalist, militarist, anti-feminist, anti-immigrant, and other racially coded right-wing elements in the Republican Party—that could gain preponderant influence over the nation in a Romney/Ryan Administration—is not new. It is the most recent example of the "Weimar Syndrome," where liberal and Left parties fail to solve serious economic crises, helping right-wing movements and policies—that lack major public support, but are groomed and funded by the corporate and military establishment—to take power.

These movements have sometimes created perilous right-wing systemic change. In the 1920s and early 1930s German Weimar Republic, the world witnessed the rise to power of far-right groups, supported by only a minority of the population, but aided by the conservative establishment. An American Weimar could emerge as far-right elements gain increasing dominance in the Republican Party. The corporate establishment, represented by Mitt Romney, feels dependent on their support and is willing to implement most of their agenda, despite Romney's sprouting strands of moderate rhetoric since the first debate to reach beyond the hard core.

The Weimar Syndrome involves the following elements:

1. A severe and intensifying economic crisis
2. A failure by majoritarian liberal or Left groups to resolve the crisis

3. The rise of right-wing populist groups feeling economically threatened and politically unrepresented
4. The decision of the conservative political establishment to ally with and empower these right-wing elements, as their best way to stabilize capitalism and prevent the rise of progressive movements against corporations or capitalism itself

The most dangerous Weimar right-wing populist movements in Germany were not anti-statist, a distinctively American approach, and were brutally violent. Moreover, they would never support a candidate offering conciliatory rhetoric to appeal to the unconverted. While thus different from US ultra-conservative elements in the Republican Party today, who do not pose now the same type of danger, they nonetheless offer alarming lessons for America today.

The disastrous defeat in World War I and the ensuing hyperinflation and collapse of the German economy spawned hundreds of far-right populist groups. The most famous Weimar populists were the Nazis, but in 1920s Weimar they were just one of many hyper-nationalist, militarist, and "family value" fringe groups not taken seriously by either the conservative or social democratic German Establishment.

The Weimar populists were "Red State" rural and small-town Germans, rooted in small business, a demographic much like the Tea Party. Their leaders expressed the insecurity and rage of these conservative traditional classes.

Rural and small-town Germans felt threatened by the humiliating defeat in the Great War and Weimar's crushing economic crises. Using racist demagoguery, the Weimar populists blamed both the military defeat and the economic crisis on Jews, the leading "traitors" concentrated in Berlin and other great cities. Under Weimar, big cities had become a cauldron of new movements for unionism, socialism and Communism, feminism, and artistic experimentation.

The leading German liberal and conservative parties dismissed the Weimar right-wing populists as extremists and lunatics. By the early 1930s, though, the conservative corporate establishment viewed Hitler as the only alternative to a liberal or Communist takeover as the economy collapsed. German conservative elites correctly believed he would dispose of the Communists but erroneously calculated that they could contain Hitler himself. So they put him in power despite his electoral weakness and funded his militaristic solutions for the German crisis, which they thought would also save German capitalism.

Right-wing populists in the United States also emerged in the Weimar era of the 1920s, involving Christian evangelicals such as Billy Sunday, as well as the Ku Klux Klan. They expressed anti-establishment religious revivalism and racist calls for restoring the traditional order and honor of the South. In the 1930s, the American Liberty League formed a Tea Party ancestor that opposed the entire New Deal as unconstitutional statism.

From the 1960s to the 1980s, the United States underwent even greater division between a counterculture tied to a Left that saw the Vietnam War as emblematic of a flawed militaristic empire against a "silent majority"—a term coined by President Nixon to suggest a majoritarian right-wing America backed by the GOP establishment—committed to American glory, free market capitalism, traditional families, the virtues of hard work, and for some, white rights and Christian values.

By the late 1970s, the Silent Majority morphed—with aid from the Republican corporate establishment—into the populist "New Right." The New Right groups embraced unrestrained capitalism as "Christian," something that evangelical movements had seldom previously done. The American corporate elite found this version of populism—which they helped shape—palatable, especially when, like the German establishment during Weimar, it confronted a threat from the Left.

The 1970s New Right was a new generation of Christian fundamentalist populists emphasizing traditional values and free markets. In 1980, the New Right helped elect President Ronald Reagan and helped consolidate the Republican establishment's hold on power, based on the odd marriage of big corporations and Southern right-wing populism.

For all the talk about how polarized the United States is now—with polarization between a minority conservative rural populace and a progressive urban demographic, a feature of the Weimar Syndrome—it was far more so from the late 1960s through the late 1970s. Then, there was a real Left that was undermining the latitude of the American military. Many within the younger generation were rejecting the capitalist consumerist society that they were supposed to inherit. Japan and Europe were showing signs of surpassing the United States economically. Some within the corporate elite, like David Rockefeller, felt it was essential to re-establish respect for traditional authority.

A few years before the rift of the late 1970s, much of the American corporate establishment would have seen the Christian Right as a "loony fringe," but like the German elite of the early 1930s, they felt a need to find someone to return order and stability. Although many were previously suspicious of Ronald Reagan, they allowed him to become president. Hitler promised German honor would be restored and Germany would never again lose a war. Reagan made the same promise to America. The German business community thought they could contain Hitler. They were wrong. The American business community hoped they could control Reagan and it turns out they were correct. Reagan built a coalition between the corporate elite and the evangelical Right. He did not enact the programs of the fundamentalists, but he gave them lip-service as their perspective gained respectability. He re-centered the political spectrum as the real Left fell beyond the edge and liberalism, which previously had been the mainstream, became the "L-word."

Reagan dissipated the crisis that he was brought into office to resolve, but his fiscal and military policies laid the seeds for the present economic catastrophe, the structural heart of a Weimar era. He doubled the government deficit as jobs and infrastructures were exported. Despite underlying instability, reflecting the beginning of a long American decline, there appeared to be a surface return to normalcy, prosperity, and patriotism and today, even some liberals remember his tenure nostalgically.

The Tea Party and the right-wing groups in the Republican Party and House, led by Paul Ryan, are the step-children of Reagan, the New Right and the latest incarnation of right-wing populism. They pose new challenges for the corporate establishment in the GOP. How they deal with the Tea Party and Ryan Republicans will shape a possible Romney administration.

Long-term decline increases the radicalism of right-wing populists and the political volatility of the population. The corporate and GOP establishment, represented by Mr. Romney, are betting the ranch that they can again contain the new Far Right populists. But they are increasingly dependent on them, as evidenced by the pick of Ryan as Romney's running mate.

Romney insists that he, not Ryan, is the head of the Republican Party, and he is shape-shifting back to the image of moderation during his Massachusetts governorship. But a look at Romney's endorsement of the Ryan budget, his electoral-season new marriage with the southern Evangelical, militarist, and racist elements in the party, and his own "severely conservative" budget and policy suggest the real Romney, in characteristic Weimar fashion, has embraced the right-wing Ryan factions and chosen to empower them.

Anti-tax guru Grover Norquist said, "We just need a president to sign this stuff.... Pick a Republican with enough working digits to handle a pen." Romney is willing. He has said he would sign the Ryan budget, the document crystallizing all the Tea Party dreams of drowning the social welfare government in the bathtub.

He has spoken for a new hegemonic American militarism and proclaimed, "This century must be an American Century ... [Obama] has chosen this moment for wholesale reductions in the nation's military capacity.... This conduct is contemptible. It betrays our national interest." He has joined anti-immigrant forces by opposing the Dream Act, while attacking Obama as a "food stamp" president and thereby appealing to all the racially coded elements in the party. This is a corporate presidential candidate adopting through most of the campaign the Weimar strategy of embracing the most Rightist elements in the GOP, and only muting his "severe" conservative tone very late in the campaign to expand his base beyond true believers.

President Obama's inability to lead the country, in FDR fashion, toward a New Deal that might solve the economic crisis, opens the door to a Weimar outcome. The corporate establishment fears even the weak populist tone that Obama has embraced during this election season, and sees both the long economic crisis and an Obama victory as eroding their power and potentially subverting capitalism itself.

The obvious lesson is that in periods of severe crisis and long-term decline, all bets are off. The establishment is risking not only the Republic, but its own survival. Only the progressive popular movements—mobilized by righteous anger at the plutocratic globalizing elites disinvesting from the nation itself as they embrace far-right nationalism and populism—can ward off a potentially disastrous repeat of the 1920s Weimar march into decay and barbarism.

Alternatives and Activism

Introduction to Part VII

Beyond the Sociopathic Society

Despite the depth of the US sociopathic crisis, there are realistic paths toward change if the population mobilizes to save itself. This final section explores new values, alternative socioeconomic systems, and social movements that might create them.

In the first of three subsections, I show that a majority of Americans have embraced new values, with roots in the social justice movements of the 1960s. The first chapter here describes it as "a new feminized majority," because women are the principal carriers of these pro-social values and have led efforts to make them the foundation of a new America. In another short essay, I use polling data to show that young people are surprisingly critical of capitalism and receptive to the idea of socialism, while in a second brief essay I show that the demographic realities of a new America reflect and create not just cultural shifts and "identity politics" but a move toward a new economic agenda. It is based on the pressing needs of the dispossessed new "majority minority." A third brief essay shows surprising views of the public on the deficit and argues that the deficit that matters is the "democracy deficit" reflected in the failure of Congress and the White House to reflect the majority agenda.

The first chapter of the second subsection looks at more democratic and egalitarian possibilities in the United States, ranging from worker-owned businesses to a new corporate charter that limits corporate money in politics and breaks up giant sociopathic corporations to a more localized economy that is environmentally sustainable and helps build community. The second chapter looks at emerging trends toward a new global democracy, integrating visions of a more localized world with those of a less hegemonic and more cooperative global system prioritizing people over profits. And in a final short essay, I summarize the challenge of creating a new less sociopathic world based on human rights rather than money.

Change ultimately boils down to whether ordinary people come together to build a new order. I conclude by examining the question of social movements and activism, especially in the United States. The first essay in the last subsection outlines twenty-five steps you can do to transform our corporate system and create a less sociopathic society. In the second and final essay, I look at three activists, including myself, exploring the personal and political motives, costs, and rewards of activism itself. It turns out that activists trying to build a less sociopathic society find surprising ways to help heal and humanize not only society but themselves, part of a new society emerging from the ashes of the old.

SECTION A

New American Values and the New America

21

Women's Values and a New America

The rising feminized majority has a different vision of America, but what is this vision and how widespread is it? In this chapter, we examine polling data about public opinion to answer these questions. In the first part, we present gender gap research concerning women's values and vision for America. It's a story about a desire for a new America, far more progressive than that currently embraced by the Democratic Party. In the second part, we prove that a robust majority of Americans already share a feminized vision for major social change. That will happen only if the Democratic Party seizes the opportunity.

Gender gap research documents our argument that: (1) men and women have different values, (2) these differing values spill over into the political arena, and (3) women's values lead to a progressive vision for economic and social transformation in America. Gender gap research also highlights how millions of men share feminized values and a progressive vision for the country. Then, we show that extensive polling research documents that the feminized majority's views resonate with a majority of American voters.

The Gender Gap

Substantial research suggests that gendered values affect the private and public decisions of men and women. This research focuses on the political "gender gap" that emerged in the mid-1980s, a phenomenon proving that men and women do not see eye to eye on many issues. The term *gender gap* initially measured the difference in the number of men and women who vote for a specific political candidate. In the 1996 presidential election, for example, a 12 percentage-point gap separated the number of women who supported Bill Clinton and the number of men who supported Bill Clinton.

The gender gap also refers to the difference in the number of men and women who support a certain position on a political issue. For example, a 2007 Harris poll found a large gender gap between the number of women and men who oppose "Don't Ask, Don't Tell" military policy. Sixty-one percent of women want the policy overturned, compared to 47 percent of men—a 14 percentage-point gender gap.

Today, few people doubt either the existence or the political importance of a large gender gap. In the last three elections, a majority of female voters *and* male voters supported different presidential candidates. In 2004, 51 percent of women voted for John Kerry, compared to just 44 percent of men. In 2000, 54 percent of women voted for Al Gore, compared to 42 percent of men. In 1996, as we noted, Bill Clinton was reelected with a large gender gap.

The 1990s are significant not only for the increasing size of the gender gap, but also because, for the first time, men and women actually voted in opposite directions. In the 1980s, by contrast, a majority of both men and women voted for Reagan. In 1980, men voted for Reagan by an 18 percent margin while women voted for him by a 2 percent margin.

A September 2007 poll suggested that the gender gap is growing dramatically. It showed that 53 percent of women planned to vote Democratic for president in 2008 compared to 27 percent who planned to vote Republican. Only 41 percent of men in the same poll said they would vote Democratic for president, while 37 percent said they would vote for the Republican presidential candidate.

Gender gap data show that women of all demographic groups are trending more Democratic. Even among traditionally more conservative women—those married and living in suburbs—a plurality of 46 percent said they planned to vote Democratic for president in 2008 compared to only 29 percent who said they would vote Republican. In contrast, in 2004, while 51 percent of women voted for Kerry, married women voted 55 percent for Bush and 44 percent for Kerry, compared to single women who voted 62 percent for Kerry and only 37 percent for Bush.

Because of their underlying values, women not only *vote* more liberally but also hold more *progressive views* than men on most political issues. Women are more likely than men to support civil unions for same-sex couples, and less likely to say that homosexuality is a choice. They are more opposed to the death penalty, especially for minors. They are more likely to support a pullout date for the troops in Iraq. These opinions put women further to the left on the ideological spectrum than most men, and much further to the left than most evangelicals.

At the same time, women, perhaps unexpectedly, are *more* religious than men. Eighty-three percent of women over fifty, and 65 percent of women under fifty, rate religion as "extremely important," compared to 59 percent of men over fifty and 56 percent of men under fifty. Women also are more likely than men (by a 37 percent to 29 percent margin) to believe that the Bible should have greater influence over American law than the will of the people. How is it possible that women are both more religious than men and more progressive?

Women are still socialized to move through life with the goal of *Together We Can*. Women's gendered values encourage them to view issues differently than men, even if they share the same level of religiosity as men. Researcher Karen Kaufmann observes, "Men who believe that new lifestyles are bad and that new moral values should not be tolerated are more likely to be conservative on social welfare issues than women who hold similar beliefs." Women with traditional moral values are more progressive than men with traditional moral values because they look at the same issues in different ways. In the case of social welfare, religious women share with other women the feminized values of community and equality and are more supportive of social programs, while traditionally religious men disapprove of welfare because they hold the masculinized values of individualism and competition. When traditional moral values intersect with feminized or masculinized values, it does not lead to the same conclusion. And, more generally, *when feminized values are applied to politics, they translate into a more progressive politics*.

Values emerge again and again as the reason women and men hold different political opinions. One study attributed political gender gaps to women's "egalitarian values" and their desire to "help others." These traits make women more likely than men to support racial and gender equality. Women are also more likely to agree with the idea that the government should have more responsibility in helping its citizens and that government is better able to handle problems than is the free market. Not surprisingly, these values make women more likely to consider themselves liberal. Egalitarian values remain statistically significant even when controlling for income, education, occupational status, and religiosity.

Men's views about the role of government in citizens' lives differ from women's views. Men are more likely to prefer a free market approach to social problems. In this sense, men's values closely align with capitalist values. Traditional capitalism was built on the values of competition, winner-take-all individualism, and inequality. The masculinized value system also includes individualism and competition—men are socialized to believe that *Alone I Will*. As government programs and a strong social welfare state restrain capitalism, they also end up at odds with masculinized values. More men than women, for example, feel that the government is "wasteful and inefficient," and would prefer a smaller government with fewer services to a larger government with more services.

It seems historically appropriate that masculinized values are closely intertwined with capitalist values. Men were traditionally socialized to believe that, with hard work, they could move up the socioeconomic ladder. They were encouraged to use capitalism to pursue their dreams. Women, on the other hand, were traditionally socialized to take care of the home, providing unpaid domestic labor that has little value in a capitalist economy. Historically, women have not had the same relationship with capitalism as men, so their values intersect with capitalism in different ways than men's values. In fact, feminized values often counter capitalist values—cooperation versus competitiveness, for example. Social programs and other liberal approaches fit into the feminized value system, whereas they encroach on the masculinized value system.

Women and men also have strikingly different opinions regarding security and force. These differences were highlighted on September 12, 2001—the day after the attacks on the World Trade Center and the Pentagon—when a *CBS News* poll asked if respondents felt that the "US should take military action against whoever is responsible for the attacks, even if it means that innocent people are killed." A full 75 percent of men agreed that the United States should take action, compared to 57 percent of women—an 18 percentage-point gender gap.

This and other polls suggest that women think about war in a very distinct way. Because women value negotiation and cooperation over force—partly reflecting the historical reality that women have been victims of so much violence and women's caretaking roles in the family—they are more likely than men to renounce violence in all spheres of life. In politics, they are much more hesitant to support violent intervention to solve international conflicts. The gender gap in the 1980 election between Carter and Reagan highlights women's reluctance to support hawkish candidates. By controlling for concerns about armed conflict, researchers found that the gender gap disappeared.

Not only are women less likely to support war as a tool to attain peace, they also have different feelings from men about acceptable codes of conduct during war. An *ABC News* poll found that 44 percent of men think that torture is acceptable in some circumstances, compared to only 27 percent of women. Fifty-four percent of men, compared with 39 percent of women, believe that physical abuse that stops short of torture is sometimes acceptable. The issue of holding prisoners at Guantanamo Bay without filing formal charges against them divides men and women. Men support the government's policies at Guantanamo Bay by a 52 percent to 40 percent margin, while women oppose it 46 percent to 37 percent. Perhaps women's feelings about Guantanamo come from their attitudes about equality under the law, the inherent humanity of all people, or sympathy for the families of those being detained. Any of these explanations are part of a feminized value system.

Toward a Feminized Majority

Gender gap data show that women are leading the way toward a more progressive politics. But they are doing more than that. They are actually creating a nation that is in line with their values: a feminized America. However, we should not assume that these trends point to a forthcoming battle-of-the-sexes ideological showdown. As more women vote in line with a feminized worldview, more men are actually *joining* them.

Feminized values are becoming majoritarian values. Bill Clinton, for example, was reelected with 43 percent of the male vote. Because a large enough majority of women supported Clinton, the progressive choice for president became the majoritarian choice. The same can be true for political issues. Men are more likely to have conservative positions on political issues, but the majoritarian view can still be progressive, as more women vote and more men hold feminized values.

Our portrayal of Americans as feminized may seem counterintuitive in a time of terrorist threats, bans on same-sex marriage, and attacks on a woman's right to choose. The global community certainly doesn't see America as having become more progressive in the past decade. If anything, the reelection of George W. Bush in 2004 showed the world that the United States is on a fast track to right-wing territory uncharted in our nation's history. Moreover, many Americans find it hard to believe that there is a progressive majority in their own country. However, countless polls from the most reputable surveying agencies prove that, despite an influential conservative minority, the majority is, in fact, more progressive than ever before. And this majority is feminized not because women are disproportionately represented but because women's values give rise to their progressive vision. This is not an interest-driven majority—seeking to advance the narrower interests of racial minorities, the working class, or even women themselves—but a morally driven community seeking to nurture the entire society in the spirit of the feminized values we have already identified.

Many advocacy organizations are catching onto the idea that Americans are far more progressive than conventional political wisdom would have us think. We draw on scores of national polls in this section. We also rely on several reports that synthesize data from multiple polls over time, including one from the Pew Research Center called "Trends in Political Values and Core Attitudes: 1987–2007." In another 2007 report, the nonprofit organization Campaign for America's Future compiled more recent polls administered by survey research organizations such as Gallup and Pew, as well as news organizations such as the *Wall Street Journal* and the *Los Angeles Times,* to examine comprehensively Americans' views on a wide range of economic, social, and military issues. The polls synthesized in these reports—and in hundreds of other individual polling studies—overwhelmingly contradict widespread assumptions about a conservative, masculinized American majority. We report on these polls in such detail because the results are counterintuitive for many people, who see a conservative country. A close look at the polls reveals that, while the government pursues masculinized policies, ordinary Americans want a feminized progressivism.

Data on support for government social programs are a good beginning point, because they are a sensitive indicator of the feminized values of empathy, equality, and community. The Pew 2007 study of core values shows that 69 percent of voters agree that "government should care for those who cannot care for themselves." Likewise 54 percent agree that "government should help the needy even if it means greater debt." In a period of high personal and public deficits, this shows a feminized majority committed to a generous safety net, but polls show a broader feminized commitment to help all citizens. For example, while men are more likely than women to prefer a smaller government with fewer services, 58 percent of Americans, reflecting millions of men as well as a majority of women, think the government should overall be doing more for citizens, not less. A 2004 National Elections Studies poll showed that twice as many Americans support more government services and more spending compared to those who support fewer services and less spending, even if it means an increase in taxes. The same poll showed that the percentage of Americans who support the feminized position of more services and spending increased from 23 percent in 1982 to 43 percent in 2004, not yet quite a majority, while the percent opposing it dropped from 32 percent in 1982 to 20 percent in 2004.

The issue of health care provides a striking example of the feminized majority's commitment to provide help for all citizens. While politicians worry that promoting a system of nationalized health care is career suicide, multiple polls show that a majority of Americans want the government to guarantee health care for all citizens—and are willing to make sacrifices to see it happen. A *New York Times/CBS News* poll taken in March 2007 found that 60 percent of Americans would pay higher taxes to ensure that all citizens had coverage. A CNN/Opinion Research Corporation poll from May 2007 asking the same question found an even higher majority—64 percent. A Gallup poll from late 2006 showed that 69 percent of Americans feel it is the "responsibility" of the federal government to provide health care coverage to all its citizens. These data suggest that a majority of Americans have adopted the feminized ideals of community and empathy and believe that the government has a responsibility to help their fellow citizens preserve their health.

A majority of Americans believe that government should do more to protect workers' wages. Increasing the minimum wage is supported by a huge majority of Americans. A December 2006 AP/AOL News poll showed that 80 percent of Americans support a government-mandated increase in the minimum wage, with only 18 percent opposed. A *Los Angeles Times*/Bloomberg poll, also from late 2006, found 77 percent of Americans want Congress to pass legislation to raise the minimum wage. A CNN poll in August 2006 found 86 percent in support and only 13 percent in opposition. These statistics reflect the feminized values of community and empathy: people should lift up their friends and neighbors and give a hand to those in need.

Americans are also uneasy about corporate power and the increasing divide between rich and poor, as reflected in their views about taxes. A Gallup poll from April 2007 showed that 71 percent of Americans feel that taxes on corporations are too low, and 66 percent feel that taxes on upper-income people are too low. A 2005 *NBC News* poll showed that 54 percent believe that corporations pay "lower than their fair share of taxes" while only 4 percent believe they pay "more." An *NBC News/Wall Street Journal* poll from 2005 found that a majority of Americans feel that Bush's tax cuts, largely serving the rich, were "not worth it." Americans are turning away from the masculinized perspective that individualism is virtuous and that the rich deserve their wealth.

Americans also support unions. A 2007 Pew poll showed that 56 percent are favorable to unions, while only 33 percent are unfavorable. A 2006 Gallup poll finds similar results: 59 percent favorable to unions compared to 29 percent unfavorable. In the same poll, 52 percent of people say they generally side with unions in labor disputes compared to 34 percent who take the side of the company. Unions embody the feminized values of cooperation, equality, and *Together We Can.*

Perhaps American workers know they are living in frightening times. The 1980s and 1990s represented an era of corporations consolidating power: Multiple corporate mergers resulted in monopolies or oligarchies; free trade legislation led to endemic outsourcing and layoffs; and stagnant wages caused more Americans to sink into poverty as CEOs reaped unprecedented bonus-laden salaries—sometimes reaching hundreds of millions of dollars even as their companies sank, as in the cases of Enron and Tyco. In the face of such greed and corruption, the feminized values of equality, community, and cooperation resonate more than ever to men as well as women.

Americans also share an increasingly feminized outlook on social issues. Comparing current polls to those from decades past shows how the country is changing on charged social issues such as gay and lesbian rights, women's rights, and affirmative action. In 1987, for example, 51 percent of Americans felt that school boards "ought to have the right to fire teachers who are known homosexuals," and a 1977 Gallup poll showed that only 56 percent believed that homosexuals should have equal job rights. In contrast, a 2006 Gallup poll finds a robust 89 percent of Americans believe that homosexuals should have equal job rights. As noted earlier, more women than men support overturning "Don't Ask, Don't Tell" military policy, but a Pew poll shows that 60 percent of *all* Americans support gay and lesbian soldiers openly serving in the military.

Support of equality for gays and lesbians, women, and racial minorities is a core marker of the feminized sensibility. On the highly charged issue of same-sex marriage, a feminized majority does not yet support same-sex marriage itself. Gallup polling in 2007 shows 46 percent in favor and 53 percent opposed. Other polls, including a 2007 Pew poll, show a smaller percentage, 37 percent, supporting same-sex marriage with 55 percent opposed. But if we look at the percentage supporting either same-sex marriage or civil unions codifying legal rights for gay and lesbian couples, a 2007 CNN poll shows that 50 percent support either same-sex marriage or civil unions. A generation ago, hardly any Americans supported same-sex marriage, because being homosexual was seen as shameful and therefore mostly hidden. For example, a 1982 Gallup poll showed that only 32 percent of Americans viewed "homosexuality as an acceptable lifestyle." Today, the feminized majority increasingly embraces gay and lesbian Americans and gay rights as an expression of its core value of equality.

A majority of feminized Americans now embrace women's rights. In 1987, only 28 percent of Americans "completely disagreed" that "women should return to their traditional roles in society." By 2007, 51 percent "completely disagreed" and 75 percent disagreed, either completely or mostly. Likewise, in 1972, a National Election Studies poll showed that only 47 percent of Americans believed that "women should have an equal role with men in running business, industry and government." By 2004, that number soared to 78 percent. A solid majority of women and a majority of men now support women's new roles and rights.

The most charged issue about women's rights is abortion. Despite continuing controversy, and the intense views of those who equate abortion with murder, a majority of Americans—57 percent, according to a 2007 *ABC News/Washington Post* poll—want to keep abortion legal "in all or most cases." An August 2007 Quinnipiac poll found 62 percent of Americans agreeing and 32 percent disagreeing with the *Roe v. Wade* decision that "establishes a woman's right" to abortion. A May 2007 Gallup poll showed that only 35 percent of Americans support overturning a woman's constitutional right to abortion. The feminized majority specifically affirms abortion as a "right" that protects not just the woman but constitutional ideals of privacy and social well-being. But the majority is sensitive to concerns about the adverse social impact of abortion on demand. A 2007 *CBS News/New York Times* poll showed that a plurality of 41 percent seek "stricter limits" on the availability of abortion even though 75 percent, a clear majority, want to retain the right to abortion guaranteed by *Roe v. Wade*.

A growing feminized majority also supports civil rights for racial and ethnic minorities. In 1987, when Pew polls asked whether "it's all right for blacks and whites to date each other," 48 percent agreed; by 2007, 83 percent agreed, with the trend unwaveringly upward and a visceral indicator of a new tolerance and feminized social egalitarianism. Affirmative action, another key expression of a feminized commitment to support and nurture the underdog, is also widely supported as in the interest of the whole society. A 2003 Pew poll regarding affirmative action—taken in the midst of a Supreme Court battle over the subject—showed that 57 percent of Americans support programs "which give special preferences to qualified blacks, women and other minorities in hiring and education."

A Zogby poll taken right after the 2004 elections asked Americans what is the most "urgent moral question" in the nation. While abortion and same-sex marriage had gathered all the headlines, and reflected the conservative religious moral agenda, only 16 percent of voters answered "abortion" and 12 percent "same-sex marriage." The majority said the "most urgent moral question" was either "greed and materialism" (33 percent) or "poverty and economic justice" (31 percent). Together, 64 percent of Americans expressed the feminized majority's real moral concerns: a focus on injustice and inequality that harms the entire society.

The most dramatic examples of feminized values becoming majoritarian emerge with issues of militarism and foreign policy. As we've noted, women are more likely to support diplomacy over force as a way to solve problems. However, a 2005 poll showed that 64 percent of Americans—again, reflecting millions of men as well as women—feel the United States "should emphasize diplomatic and economic efforts over military efforts in fighting the War on Terror." In 2007, the percentage rose to 67 percent. More broadly, a 2005 Pew poll showed that 55 percent of Americans agree that "the best way to ensure peace is through diplomacy," while only 30 percent said the best way to secure peace is "military strength." Poll numbers over time suggest that Americans are increasingly adopting the feminized position that violence is not a viable way to secure peace.

It makes sense for the feminized values of diplomacy and international cooperation to become the norm. Thousands and thousands of Americans have lost family members in the wars in Iraq and Afghanistan, yet the regions are no closer to being stabilized. Reports from Iraq suggest that the war has actually created *more* terrorists. And in the midst of this desperate situation, some fear that the Bush administration is setting up Iran as America's next military target. After the carnage in Iraq, it is not surprising that Americans are leery of using firepower to tamp down Iran's alleged terrorist support network. The masculinized view that aggression secures victory doesn't seem to fit reality.

A February 2007 Gallup poll showed that the majority of Americans not only prefer diplomacy to violence *but also are beginning to challenge American hegemony itself.* This challenge is not firmly established—the same poll finds 60 percent of Americans saying that the United States should continue to be the country with the most powerful military. But when Gallup asked a differently worded question, about what role America should play in the world, only 15 percent said "the leading role." A remarkable 58 percent majority said "a major role but not the leading role." This is an explicit rejection of American hegemony and of elite concepts of American empire.

As the situation in Iraq becomes more desperate, Americans increasingly want our soldiers out. A *CBS News* poll from September 9, 2007, showed 62 percent of Americans feel the US invasion of Iraq was a "mistake." A full 53 percent say that Iraq will "never" become a stable democracy. And poll after poll—including those from the *Washington Post/ABC News, USA Today/ Gallup,* and *CBS News/New York Times*—show that a majority of Americans want a firm deadline for withdrawing American forces from the region.

Polls also show that it will take a lot more than manipulated reports about yellowcake from Niger—one of the ways the Bush administration misled Congress to authorize the Iraq War—to gain public approval for the next war; despite a calculated fear campaign from the Bush administration, in April 2006, CNN/Opinion Research Corporation found that a full 63 percent of Americans oppose war with Iran. This is not to say that Americans support Iran creating a nuclear weapons program. Polls show that Americans, in fact, desire an end to *all* nuclear weapons programs—including that of the United States. A Pew report released in November 2005 shows that 70 percent of Americans support a "multilateral disarmament treaty." Americans want changes in international relations that will usher in a new era of nonviolence. The nuclear arms race of the cold war was a masculinized competition to see which boys had the most toys, and most Americans don't want to play that game again. An increasing number of women and men are adopting feminized ideals and goals, and are demanding a peaceful future for their children.

We argue that these changes in values show a new American majority that rejects the masculinized values from American history and supports new feminized values. This shift of major dimensions represents a threat to the historic masculinized systems of American capitalism and empire, secured by rampant individualism, and to the traditional American Dream. Our nation, constructed as an individualistic capitalist hierarchy, rewards (in theory) those who work the hardest with the biggest rewards. By pursuing feminized ideals, such as egalitarianism and nonviolence, Americans are softening the founding principles of our country.

When a country becomes inhospitable to its citizens and unwilling to help its people in need, and when an aggressive foreign policy fails and threatens citizens rather than protects them, many citizens will reexamine the values and dreams handed down to them. Feminized values lead to economic policy that gives underprivileged and middle-class Americans a chance to succeed. The *Together We Can* philosophy becomes more appealing to both women and men. Feminized values create foreign policy that values human rights and makes America a partner in the global community, again enhancing the appeal of *Together We Can* for all Americans.

Americans still pursue self-interest and profit. But as the feminized majority grows, more ordinary citizens—both women and men—believe this pursuit needs to be carried out under different rules. A feminized vision requires a fairer, more egalitarian, and less violent social order. The new feminized majority sees the need for changes in the underlying social and moral fabric, helping explain why a huge majority of Americans today say America is moving in the wrong direction under President Bush and the Republicans. As America's economic and military crises lead more men to join women in embracing feminized values, a rising feminized majority can transform not only the Democratic Party but also America itself.

22

Capitalism

Big Surprises in Recent Polls

According to the conventional wisdom, the United States is a Center-Right country. But a new poll by Pew casts doubt on that idea. It shows widespread skepticism about capitalism and hints that support for socialist alternatives is emerging as a majoritarian force in America's new generation.

Carried out in late April and published May 4, 2010, the Pew poll, arguably by the most respected polling company in the country, asked over 1,500 randomly selected Americans to describe their reactions to terms such as "capitalism," "socialism," "progressive," "libertarian," and "militia." The most striking findings concern "capitalism" and "socialism." We cannot be sure what people mean by these terms, so the results have to be interpreted cautiously and in the context of more specific attitudes on concrete issues, as discussed later.

Pew summarizes the results in its poll title: "Socialism not so negative; capitalism not so positive." This turns out to be an understatement of the drama in some of the underlying data.

Yes, "capitalism" is still viewed positively by a majority of Americans. But it is just by a bare majority. Only 52 percent of all Americans react positively. Thirty-seven percent say they have a negative reaction and the rest aren't sure.

A year ago, a Rasmussen poll found similar reactions. Then, only 53 percent of Americans described capitalism as "superior" to socialism.

Meanwhile, 29 percent in the Pew poll describe "socialism" as positive. This positive percent soars much higher when you look at key subgroups, as discussed shortly. A 2010 Gallup poll found 37 percent of all Americans preferring socialism as "superior" to capitalism.

Keep in mind these findings reflect an overview of the public mind when right-wing views seem at a high point—with the Tea Party often cast as a barometer of American public opinion. The polls in this era do not suggest a socialist country, but not a capitalist-loving one either. This is not a "Center-Right" America but a populace where almost 50 percent are deeply ambivalent or clearly opposed to capitalism. Republicans and the Tea Party would likely call that a Communist country.

The story gets more interesting when you look at two vital subgroups. One is young people, the "millennial generation" currently between eighteen and thirty. In the Pew poll, just 43 percent of Americans under thirty describe "capitalism" as positive. Even more striking, the same percentage, 43 percent, describes "socialism" as positive. In other words, the new generation is equally divided between capitalism and socialism.

The Pew, Gallup, and Rasmussen polls come to the same conclusion. Young people cannot be characterized as a capitalist generation. They are half capitalist and half socialist. Since the socialist leaning keeps rising among the young, it suggests—depending on how you interpret "socialism"—that we are moving toward an America that is either Center-Left or actually majoritarian socialist.

Turn now to Republicans and Democrats. Sixty-two percent of Republicans in the Pew poll view capitalism as positive, although 81 percent view "free markets" as positive, suggesting a sensible distinction in their mind between capitalism and free markets. Even Republicans prefer small to big business and are divided about big business, which many correctly see as a monopolistic force of capitalism undermining free markets.

The more interesting story, though, is about Democrats. We hear endlessly about Blue Dog Democrats. But the Pew poll shows a surprisingly progressive Democratic base. Democrats are almost equally split in their appraisal of capitalism and socialism. Forty-seven percent see capitalism as positive but 53 percent do not. And 44 percent of Democrats define socialism as positive, linking their negativity about capitalism to a positive affirmation of socialism.

Moreover, many other subgroups react negatively to capitalism. Less than 50 percent of women, low-income groups, and less-educated groups describe capitalism as positive.

So much for the view that Obama does not have a strong progressive base to mobilize. In fact, "progressive," according to the Pew poll, is one of the most positive terms in the American political lexicon, with a substantial majority of almost all subgroups defining it as positive.

You may conclude that this all add ups to little, since we can't be clear about how people are defining "capitalism" and "socialism." But in my own research, summarized in recent books such as *The New Feminized Majority* and *Morality Wars*, attitudes registered in polls toward concrete issues over the last thirty years support the interpretation of the Pew data, at minimum, as evidence of a Center-Left country.

On nearly every major issue, from support for minimum wage and unions, preference for diplomacy over force, deep concern for the environment, belief that big business is corrupting democracy, and support for many major social programs including Social Security and Medicare, the progressive position has been strong and relatively stable. If "socialism" means support for these issues, the interpretation of the Pew poll is a Center-Left country.

If socialism means a search for a genuine systemic alternative, then America, particularly its youth, is emerging as a majoritarian social democracy, or in a majoritarian search for a more cooperativist, green, and more peaceful and socially just order.

Either interpretation is hopeful. It should give progressives assurance that even in the "Age of the Tea Party," despite great dangers and growing concentrated corporate power and wealth, there is a strong base for progressive politics. We have to mobilize the majority population to recognize its own possibilities and turn up the heat on the Obama administration and a demoralized Democratic Party. If we fail, the Right will take up the slack and impose its monopoly capitalist will on a reluctant populace.

23

The New America Is Not about Identity Politics

The prevailing narrative is that President Obama's reelection and hopes for long-term Democratic Party control are rooted in a demographic revolution, in which Hispanics, African Americans, and other nonwhite minorities are becoming the new American majority. This view is not wrong, but it is incomplete and misleading.

The deeper narrative is economic, pointing to a socioeconomic transformation in which majorities of all races depend increasingly on government protection and public investment. The two narratives, while they agree on the demographic statistics, have different policy implications, with the current interpretation of the demographic story belying the deeper change that both parties must make.

Whites, currently 63 percent of the population, will become a minority by 2050, according to a November 7, 2012, Pew Research Center Report. Republicans, fearful of permanent minority status, are rethinking immigration policy as a way to appeal to Hispanic voters and other minorities, while also eyeing 2016 potential White House candidates such as Florida senator Marco Rubio, son of Cuban immigrants, and his mentor, former Florida governor Jeb Bush, married to a Mexican American and fluent in Spanish. Meanwhile, the Democrats consider moving immigration policy to the front burner to hold onto the Hispanic vote.

But this is where the reigning demographic story misleads. It suggests that minorities are voting identity politics, with dark-skinned candidates or immigration the key way to their hearts and ballot. And it focuses on policy toward minorities rather than toward whites, a misreading of how to win in the new America.

The economic narrative argues that minorities, like the majority of whites, while not at all indifferent to identity appeals and often promoting important identity politics agendas, are voting mainly their socioeconomic interests, especially jobs, but also broader social government protections of education, health, and the environment.

This interpretation is supported by the *New York Times* exit polling data showing that lower-income Americans of all colors supported President Obama at higher rates than higher-income voters. As shown by the Pew Report, economic logic—a strong need for government protection—helps explain why minorities, women, and singles voted for Obama and have long expressed more support for an activist government than whites, men, and married people.

But the same economic narrative helps explain crucial differences among white voters. President Obama won reelection because he held his "firewall" in crucial Midwestern states such as Ohio, Michigan, Pennsylvania, and Wisconsin. Minority turnout was crucially important, but so was the vote of working-class whites.

Unions mobilized to promote economic-based voting among culturally conservative white workers. Obama gave the unions the necessary ammunition with his auto bailout, the policy that secured his reelection. Jobs in Ohio and other vital Midwest swing states depend on the auto and auto-parts sectors. When Obama delivered a strongly progressive economic policy—temporary nationalization of GM and Chrysler, with the United States owning 61 percent of GM shares of stock in August 2010—he guaranteed Ohio jobs and gave white workers a strong economic reason to vote for him. And—according to exit polls—a majority of lower-income Ohio, Michigan, and other Midwestern white workers did vote for Obama, in contrast to upper-income whites, who voted overwhelmingly for Romney.

Obama, pushed by labor and other progressive movements, delivered activist government, helping economics trump identity politics.

Such activist government is color-blind. It is the kind of policy in the new America—a land not only of a minority majority but of surplus people of all colors looking for jobs—that will guarantee future political success. In the new America, minorities are likely to vote Democratic and support broader and deeper progressive agendas, not mainly because the Party's leaders are black or brown, but because they are more likely to promote the activist government that minorities disproportionately require.

The economic narrative means that there are no easy answers for Republicans. Their brand is based on small government and slashing entitlements. In the new America, this will not win over minorities or the necessary percentages of working-class whites, except possibly Southern whites.

The Democrats, though, cannot sit back and bask in the illusions of identity politics. As the crisis of surplus Americans intensifies, the Democratic Party will have to develop a far more robust economic policy protecting both whites and minorities, promoted aggressively by coalitions of all progressive social movements, including labor and identity movements.

This will require more than emergency interventions such as the auto bailout. It will necessitate preventive strategy—a new and profoundly ambitious new New Deal of green coloring—the most promising policy to ensure that the majority of Americans of any color in the new America will find work and prosper. It will be the foundational agenda of progressive social movements in the twenty-first century, which must lead the Democrats where they will not go on their own.

24

The Democracy Deficit Is the Real Deficit

Charles Derber and Paul Shannon

In the early 1970s, Harvard political scientist Samuel Huntington coined the term "democratic surplus" to critique the thousands of activists protesting on the streets to end the Vietnam war and fund the war on poverty. Huntington believed this "excess of democracy" undercut the experts who had the technical skills to frame rational policy on complex issues such as the economy and the budget. Today, we should be talking about a "democracy deficit," since the public's views on the great issues of the day—particularly the deficit and broader budget issues—have hardly any voice in Congress.

From the public's view, congressional focus on the deficit is misplaced. According to a CBS News/*New York Times* exit poll of voters reported on November 6, 2012, less than 15 percent of the public see deficit reduction as a top priority today. Eighty-five percent are more concerned with jobs and the economy, and on nation-building at home rather than abroad.

According to multiple national respected polls, including a May 12, 2012, poll from the Center on Public Integrity, the great majority of Americans, including the majority of Republicans, now favors big cuts in military spending, including in the navy, army, air force, marines, and nuclear weapons. Averaging Republicans and Democrats, Americans want an 18 percent cut in the military budget, freeing up money for needs on the home front.

A large majority also says a resounding no to cuts in entitlement programs and discretionary social spending. While Americans favor limited government in the abstract, majorities of both Democrats and Republicans oppose cuts whenever specific social programs are mentioned. As reported by a December 2, 2012, *National Journal* poll, majorities of about 80 percent say no to cuts to the "Big Three"—Social Security, Medicare, and Medicaid. Sixty-three percent say no to cuts in housing vouchers going to low-income families, and 51 percent say no as well to cuts in food stamps.

The democracy deficit shows up in what the Congress did—and is likely to do—on the 2013 federal budget. The majority agenda has never been put on the table. Instead, Congress passed sequestration, huge across-the-board cuts, on March 1, 2013. Future proposed actions include a new congressionally initiated "grand bargain" or "bipartisan deal" that would target specific cuts presumably more representative of the public interest. The third is the "balanced approach" elaborated by President Obama in his State of the Union address.

The sequester actually is more consistent in one respect with the public's views. It forces $600 billion of cuts in military spending, largely consistent with the majority view. But it also hammers domestic social spending programs that are favored by majorities of Democrats and Republicans.

If a congressionally initiated "grand bargain"—similar to the one considered in 2011 by President Obama and Speaker John Boehner—were to be passed, it would likely be even less consistent with what the public wants than sequestration. The Pentagon cuts would be far less than what the public wants and sequestration delivers. It would require even deeper cuts in social spending than sequestration proposed and will exclude new revenues.

Obama's "balanced" proposal, framed initially on February 5, 2013, is also out of whack with public sentiments, preserving more defense spending than the public wants while making cuts in social spending that the majority opposes. In his State of the Union address, Obama said his proposal would be the beginning of a deficit reduction "big deal." It would raise more revenues by cutting tax loopholes for corporations and wealthy individuals, which the public supports, but also make much bigger entitlement and social spending cuts, including in Social Security and Medicare, which the public rejects.

The bottom line: the public loses with sequestration or its two alternatives. The democracy deficit is baked into the current foreseeable options coming out of Washington. This is sociopathic, both because it violates the democratic will of the people and because all likely actions will cut programs essential to public well-being and increase military spending for unnecessary wars.

Is there any way out? Yes, if we take three urgent actions.

First, we need a national conversation about the real deficit that matters today: the democracy deficit. We should make this the bottom line not only of the budget debates but the 2014 elections, voting out those rejecting the public's budget priorities.

Second, Congress and the White House should be forced to take stock of the lay of the land since the Great Recession. The continuing fragile economy has transformed Americans' priorities to rebuilding jobs and infrastructure at home, funded partly through savings from large military cuts.

Third, Obama has to lead with the majority agenda, which rejects his proposed social cuts and seeks bigger military cuts. His proposals lead the public, correctly, to see themselves as paying taxes without representation, even though they favor Obama over Republicans.

This suggests we need a very different kind of Tea Party to pass the majority agenda on the budget and that we need to substitute the misplaced obsession on eliminating the fiscal deficit during a weak economy with a passion to end the democracy deficit. This is an agenda that can unite Democrats and Republicans alike.

SECTION B

Alternative Systems

25

The UN, the Barbershop, and Global Democracy

I am not an Athenian or a Greek. I am a citizen of the world.

—*Socrates*

TINA. *There Is No Alternative.* These four little words seem the most common in the world today. They are depressing, and they paralyze many people who are deeply uneasy about globalization and would dearly love to help make a better world. I bet you think TINA when you think about "reinventing globalization." But the popularity of TINA reflects a terrible ignorance of history. Reinventing globalization has been a large part of what world history has been about for at least a thousand years.

The world's first great civilizations, such as Mesopotamia and Egypt, invented "ancient globalizations." The Romans reinvented globalization when they created their great sprawling empire. The Italian city-states, such as Venice and Florence, created a merchant-driven "Renaissance globalization" that circled the world with Marco Polo. The colonial powers of Spain, the Netherlands, France, and Britain built a new globalization as they built the foundations of a worldwide industrial order. And the United States with its global business partners reinvented a new model of globalization over the last fifty years.

While much of this history is drenched in blood, the basic story line should lift our spirits. It shows that systemic change is not only possible but is a constant in history. Each time we think reinventing globalization seems farfetched, remember that it is already the reality of our times. With the collapse of colonial globalization after World War II, the reconstruction of globalization was inevitable, leading to our current Constitutional Moment.

It is precisely because we are in a new Constitutional Moment that the idea of reinventing globalization has begun to capture serious attention. We the people can sit back and allow global business and our government to design globalization as they are doing now, or we can choose to enter the fray and reform it in the spirit of our own values. Thousands in the new global justice movements have already chosen to act. Moreover, millions, perhaps billions, of other people not identified with these movements in either the First or Third Worlds are uneasy about globalization. After the events of September 11, they also want to change the world to make it safe and economically secure for everyone.

The struggle to reinvent globalization will be the dominant issue of the coming century. To succeed, it will have to offer a credible alternative and build a global mainstream social movement that can translate it into action. The alternative vision is what I call *global democracy*. I will discuss what I mean by this idea, how ordinary people are beginning to develop the vision and put it into practice, and how and why I think it will change our world for the better.

Global democracy may sound utopian, but it is pragmatic and realistic. However, this does not mean it is inevitable. In the aftermath of September 11 and the darkening global recession, it is clearly possible that the world could take the opposite path: toward a permanently militarized model of globalization rather than the democratic variety I am proposing. The world stands at a crucial crossroads. Without choosing the democratic path, globalization will survive but move rapidly toward the fortress model outlined in the introduction. This possibility looms as the great and most frightening danger of the coming era. The fortress model is a militarized globalization that puts security over freedom in order to contain growing global violence. It will sabotage the prospects for democracy at home and abroad.

The path toward fortress globalization in the United States was laid down only weeks after September 11. The threats to democracy within the United States are obvious. In a rush, Congress passed—and the president signed—a "Patriots" bill that permitted far-reaching new powers of government surveillance, wiretapping, and detention. Authorities would be able to detain illegal immigrants and prisoners suspected of terrorism without formal charges. They could be tried by military tribunals and their conversations with their attorneys could be monitored by government officials. There are sober discussions about the US government using torture against suspected terrorists. Constitutional scholars see major threats to civil liberties and warn of a looming police state.

The war on terrorism, killing many civilians and dislocating wretchedly poor people in Afghanistan even as it helps liberate the country from a horrifically repressive regime, may last for some time. This could easily incite more terrorism and lead to even more American-led military retaliation. The "peace" of globalization could be a chronic state of terrorism and military responses against it.

This would accelerate a turn toward fortress globalization. Under conditions of fear and instability, business will not close down overseas and come home. There are no safe harbors in this new war. But global firms and many frightened citizens will insist on new elaborate security measures. And this will involve a partnership between business and government that could curb political liberties that have been the pride of our society.

Since we are already seeing movement toward the fortress, why is there reason to believe that the democratic path is a realistic alternative? I see several hopes. First, fortress globalization contains the symptoms but doesn't attack the sources of global violence and instability. The fortress model is expensive and inefficient, committing the world to massive new surveillance and operational costs subverting the efficiency of the markets. The fortress will mitigate terror if billions are invested but will never eradicate it.

Second, global democracy attacks the causes rather than the symptoms of global injustice, and it works in concert with the positive sides of globalization. That is why I have called global democracy a move through and beyond globalization rather than backlash. It empowers the world's poor and pushes in more deeply democratic directions.

Third, historical movements deeply grounded in the Third World and newly explosive in the First World have already begun a struggle for global democracy. They do not share a crystal clear vision, and they remain in the early stages. But because they attack globalization's core problems and reflect the interests of the world's poor and fragile middle classes, they will be able to build a global majority for their democratic agenda.

Fourth, business itself has a stake in the democratic path. As noted in the introduction, globally extended businesses are the front lines of globalization, and the fortress will impose huge new operating and transaction costs on global companies. They will have to invest billions in new hidden cameras, cyber security, and other security and employee-safety measures, and they will face major new and costly hurdles to cross-border trade and investment. Communication at home and abroad will be slowed and compromised (think only of spreading anthrax in the mail). Whatever the costs of global democracy, they could be less for business than those of the fortress, a possible explanation for the new business rhetoric of social responsibility and "global citizenship."

Fifth, the plunge of the United States and the world into recession, in association with the economic dislocations caused by the New York attacks and the 2002 US market crisis, has changed the political debate. Free-market credos are being reconsidered as government is being asked to bail out industries, protect the public, and create new jobs for millions of unemployed or laid-off workers. Democratic governments are the only ones that will create the necessary jobs and new safety nets in dark economic times. During the US Great Depression in the 1930s, a New Deal was needed to make people feel safe. Today, only global democracy will create the new New Deal that will bring true security to American workers and the world's poor.

After September 11, the growing violence and darkening global recession set global democracy back in the short term, but they may broaden its base of support significantly in the longer term. Religious leaders have begun speaking more urgently about the importance of global justice. Toward the end of 2001, Catholic bishops meeting in Rome passed a document denouncing the growing gap between global haves and have-nots and emphasizing that "the persistence of gross inequalities between nations is a threat to peace." Third World bishops were especially vocal in critiquing global economic policy and called for "drastic moral change."

World political leaders are sounding many of the same themes. Tony Blair strongly supported the war on terror but made eloquent pleas for a new global order based on democracy and justice for the poor. In a now famous speech, Blair focused on the remaking of globalization on a just and democratic basis as the only way to free the world from terror: "If globalization works only for the benefit of the few, then it will fail and will deserve to fail. But if we follow the principles that have served us so well at home—that power, wealth and opportunity must be in the hands of the many, not the few—if we make that our guiding light for the global economy, then it will be a force for good and an international movement that we should take pride in leading." Bill Clinton and Mikhail Gorbachev made speeches with almost identical emphases on the need to reform globalization so that the poor have a new voice and a new deal. These words suggest that the world after September 11 will be one in which global democracy will get new rhetorical support from the most powerful as well as the poorest of the world.

Powerful movements for global democracy started at the end of World War II, the same time that modern globalization itself was born. Over the last fifty years, movements began to conceive the global democratic vision that is still evolving in global justice movements today. They are the foundation of the new democratic path that will help heal the crises of global poverty while promising a reduction in global violence and terror.

Global democrats have in recent years divided into what appear to be two quite different camps. One talks about a "globalization from below" that brings a democratic voice and justice to the world's poor. I call them "UN people," because they see the original vision of the UN and its 1948 Universal Declaration of Human Rights as the inspiration of global democracy. The UN camp is reincarnating the "citizens' globalism" movement discussed in the last chapter. Recall that during the big bang of our Constitutional Moment, between 1944 and 1948, President Franklin Roosevelt and many Third World leaders envisaged one world based on justice and democratic human rights. They imagined a planet free of colonialism and militarism, and capable of making the idea of global democracy meaningful. They founded the UN to be the forum and symbol of their alternative democratic world. While many global democrats have become disillusioned with the UN itself, which they see as increasingly harnessed to US-led globalization, today's global justice movements draw inspiration from the ideas of the UN founders. They see the 1948 UN Declaration and later conventions of the rights of women, children, workers, and the environment as an enforceable bill of rights for the world.

From the beginning, the UN camp embraced the revolution against national sovereignty at the heart of globalization. But it had a very different idea of world government than the WTO version. UN founders sought a new global order for peace rather than profit. After two world wars, they recognized that unfettered national sovereignty meant global anarchy and perpetual war. The UN founders also wanted what Franklin Roosevelt called global "freedom from want." This required a global constitutional vision subordinating property rights to broader human rights and especially jobs for the global poor.

The 1948 Declaration called for "positive" economic and social global constitutional rights for jobs, education, health, and welfare. These simple but revolutionary rights have become the passion of the current global justice movements. Today's UN people see a movement to secure positive human rights, especially rights to employment and free association of workers, as the starting point for a new global vision. Building democratic movements for global positive rights is close to the core of the very idea of global democracy, and it is the only way to create global and national government committed to the needs of the world's people.

This vision has begun to crystallize. It starts with an enforceable system of global labor rights, ensuring that Guatemalan peasants can organize farming cooperatives and Indonesian workers can organize independent unions without being arrested or shot. The positive rights vision also includes a call for global environmental laws. It calls for regulation of worldwide capital flow and global corporations to ensure a more equal distribution of wealth. It demands abolition of racial and sexual discrimination, with special attention to the safety and dignity of a mainly female and nonwhite global labor force.

For the UN camp, the problem with globalization is not too much global government but the influence of money over everything it does. The UN camp recognizes that desperately important human and environmental rights are possible only in a world racing rapidly beyond the old world of national sovereignty. In this sense, the UN camp runs with the tide of globalization but seeks a democratic world government and constitution that deliver positive rights to the 3 billion people living on less than $3 a day.

The second camp of global democrats that has emerged in recent decades speaks for what at first appears a blatantly contradictory idea of global democracy. Rather than stressing world government and global constitutionalism, they see democracy embedded in the revival of community and local autonomy, a way of life rooted in face-to-face connections and active citizenship rather than constitutions and laws. I call them the "barbershop camp."

Barbershops have yet to become a global corporation, and I suspect that they will always remain a community business. This inherent localism symbolizes the barbershoppers' core vision: the democratic economy and democracy itself need a strong local anchor. Once we start rigidly integrating local economies into a global system, we lose not only diversity but start a chain reaction of ecological and human devastation. Businesses get divorced from the local community, the local community gets dependent on absentee companies and loses its economic independence, and then it loses its political control to big business and big government. This undermines its ability to protect its environment and to sustain the community itself. And once community is gone, democracy is out the window, and the possibility of the good life rapidly erodes, as people try to compensate for the loss of human connection with the thrills of headlong consumerism.

The barbershoppers want to "relocalize" the world to democratize it. They see a problem with the UN camp because they do not think global human rights conventions or even the best world government can build life-affirming democratic economies and communities. Only people on the local level can do that. Only local folk can know their neighbors, come out to town meetings or tribal assemblies, and create a vision of how their community can produce a sustainable way of life. If the UN people have politicized globalization, the barbershoppers have personalized it. They see globalization as a spiritual crisis, not just a political or even social one. They consider it a threat to their own capacity to be human. The future of nature and the human soul are on the line.

Like the UN people, the barbershop people have a diverse history to draw on. They have learned from native Americans and their respect for the tribe and the earth, Mexican Zapatistas and their defense of indigenous communities, and Gandhi and his vision of nonviolence and local political autonomy. From the anarchist Emma Goldman, they have learned that how you make the revolution matters as much as where you want to go, and you have to dance while you are doing it.

The barbershoppers want to reinvent globalization by retribalizing the world. This is not just a spiritual dream but a global reinvention vision rooted in carefully designed democratic local institutions networked in new global connections. At this vision's core are not democratized global businesses but sustainable community-based businesses newly networked with other localities. It is not democratized global government but revitalized and reconnected local communities armed with a measure of sovereign autonomy. They want not so much a UN-enforced culture of peace than a peace arising from the cultures of thousands of nonviolent communities.

If there is to be a new movement to reinvent globalization, it needs a coherent vision. But that is not what the UN camp and the barbershoppers seem to offer. Instead they seem to be serving up radically different alternatives that clash with each other as much as they do with today's globalization. Yet, despite real differences, they are looking at two sides of the same global democratic coin.

Many barbershoppers fear the UN, even a perfect UN, as a deadly threat to local sovereignty. And many UN-ers see the barbershoppers' passion for local sovereignty as a huge, outdated hurdle to the global rights and rules we desperately need. But both see the threat today as the creation of a new market-driven world answering only to money. The relentless expansionism of the markets threatens the global rights and rules of the UN-ers as much as it does the localism of the barbershoppers. And they are united by their underlying horror of the global commodification of everything. What both UN-ers and barbershoppers share is a desire to preserve both the local and global community from becoming just two expressions of the same giant cash register. And they instinctively recognize that they need to work together to keep market expansion and the globalization mystique from imperializing our souls as well as privatizing every niche of local community and every nation.

Today's global democrats openly resist a single blueprint for change, and one would not want to paper over the differences in their perspective. They are not party-line people. When asked about their creed, they say "one no, many yesses." The one no is their common opposition to today's globalization. The many yesses is their view that the world cannot be reinvented using a formula. They are not going to go about the arrogant project of speaking for billions of people and laying out a formula tailor-made for all of them. They want people around the world speaking up for them. They want people around the world speaking up for themselves in a new democratized dialogue.

One starts the process of global reinvention, then, by simply moving the conversation out of the closed meetings and into the town square. What both UN people and barbershoppers clearly share is outrage at the secretive process through which elites are inventing today's globalization and imposing a corporate way of thinking on the world. That is why the activists all went to Seattle, Quebec, Washington, and Genoa. They were determined to crash the party and show that it can't be a closed country-club affair anymore. If there is going to be conversation about the future of the world, it has to be open to people and views not heard in the boardroom. And there can't be an admission charge.

In 2001, as the world's financial and political elites were planning to meet in Davos, Switzerland, the traditional site of the World Economic Forum, thousands of people from around the world came to Pôrto Alegre, Brazil, to launch a "people's" Davos. Farmers, workers, clergy, students, and teachers jammed together in huge assembly halls to talk about reinventing globalization. They talked about sustainable development, sweatshop organizing and global labor rights, rights of indigenous communities, regulation of global capital flows, debt relief to poor nations, changes in global patent law, and hundreds of other pieces of a new global agenda. The conversations were broadcast over loudspeakers to people out in the streets and sent over the net to people around the world. These reinventors did not come with a new global blueprint, but they did model a new and more democratic discussion about the future of the world. In February 2002, a second massive people's assembly gathered at Pôrto Alegre to protest the World Economic Forum held in New York City and show that the democratic alternative was more vital than ever.

Democratizing the conversation is the most important first step in creating a democratic world, the passion clearly bringing together the UN and barbershop camps. It is slowly giving rise to a view of global democracy that both camps can embrace. It imagines a world governing itself at many different levels in a robustly democratic spirit. Democracy from the barbershop level to the UN level is indivisible, and inevitably comes together in the emerging idea that neither local democratic association nor global democratic formal governance can do the job on its own. If we think of global democracy as a living organism, the UN camp is building the skeletal system, and the barbershoppers the soft tissue and blood.

Democracy is both a constitutional arrangement, a political system making government accountable to ordinary people, and a way of living that brings people together in multiple, freely formed associations to form a common identity and a way of expressing themselves as citizens. The UN camp is beginning to spell out the political arrangements necessary for this to happen worldwide. The barbershop camp is starting to create the new forms of community and participation necessary to revive the idea of local democracy while also building global citizenship.

Global democracy requires respecting differences while refashioning and integrating the vision of the two camps, something already under way. Few in the UN camp believe the UN can be activated as a democratic government for the world without building a new sense of global community and civil society outside the market itself. Nor do UN-ers believe that one institution, including the best UN possible, should be vested with anything like the full powers of a global sovereign or planetary Big Brother. They seek a pluralism of global governing institutions that are limited in their authority and strictly democratically accountable both to national and local governments and to global citizens newly organized into thousands of civic associations.

Likewise, few barbershoppers seek a world of totally insular local associations and communities. In the distant past, localities could seek total self-sufficiency and isolation, but few today want to wall off their local communities. The aim is not pure localism, but forms of democratic association that connect communities everywhere through more democratic links than the market. The aim is to revive local democracy as well as create a democratic community of communities, another name for the global government imagined by the UN camp.

Both the UN and barbershop camps are working toward a new intertwined model of local and global citizenship. They are creating new associations of labor, women, environmentalists, and other civil society groups that are locally based and revitalize local communities. But these localists also are "thinking globally" and increasingly forming global networks to create new democratic global rules necessary to save their own jobs and communities. A local labor union in Detroit understands today that it can't protect its own workers without changing the rules governing wage conditions and cross-border investment in Mexico. Increasingly, that union is beginning to form cross-national links with Mexican unions as the only way to defend jobs and dignity in both Mexico and the United States. It takes global democracy to preserve local democracy, while global democracy cannot be achieved without the revitalization of localism and civil society.

The globalizing of markets and states is being haunted by the globalizing of civil society. Over 150 years ago, Alexis de Tocqueville marveled at the proliferation of civic associations in the United States, which he saw as the basis of American democracy. If he were back today, I suspect he would turn his attention to the globalizing of these same associations, whether they are unions, environmental groups, feminist groups, educational and health groups, public interest advocates, or other new global citizens. These are the new activists of both local and global democracy, and they come equally from the UN and barbershop camps.

The barbershop symbolizes the local level of community and business. The UN is a symbol of the broadest global level of governance and citizenship. And there are many levels in between. The goal of the global democrat is neither to integrate economies nor to resist their integration. It is to democratize every level of social and economic organization to maximize participation and equity. The global democrat seeks to encourage a flowering of social connection and popular control outside as well as inside the market, and to build many different democratic levels that enhance global democracy itself.

In globalization today, the integrating principle is the market. Each level, from local to global, is more and more tightly organized around corporate power and finance. Globalization increasingly makes local communities look like miniaturized carbon copies of global markets.

The democratic alternative starts with a rejection of the global market as the integrating principle of the world. It is too radically homogenizing, and it betrays democracy in the service of money and corporate sovereignty. It is the seduction from hell—our consumer self desperately wants to buy it, but we pay the price of losing our job, our community, and our own power as citizens.

The reinvention of globalization requires the discovery of a new set of connecting and integrating principles. Today's global democrats have a few starting points.

One is the idea of "subsidiarity." It says that decisions should be made at the lowest level that can handle the problem, as well as at multiple levels to encourage a democracy that overflows the voting booth. Subsidiarity has a bias toward the local, but welcomes the global, as long as power flows from the bottom up rather than from the top down. It encourages local communities and businesses to manage their own affairs, but recognizes that they face key issues like global warming and global capital flight that they cannot manage without help at higher political levels.

The European Union has become a pioneer in working out the subsidiarity idea, and global democrats are taking note. Rather than shutting down economic integration, the Europeans are trying to get the right mix of local and European-wide communities, which is consistent with the preservation of local cultures and economies, human rights, and democracy itself. They are inching toward a European government and constitution; the idea of a European constitutional convention was floated for 2001, which would create Europe-wide rights and social protections for workers, but in a way that increases participation and pride of place within localities, regions, and nations.

A second, closely related principle is federalism, an idea dear to most Americans. It makes explicit that we need many interdependent levels, and we need to build from the bottom up rather than from the top down. The key words in a federal constitution are that "all powers not explicitly reserved for the federal government are retained by the states or localities." In other words, the upper levels cannot grab powers not delegated explicitly by the people and levels below. The federalist principle gives comfort to localists who fear a centralized Big Brother. It ensures that communities will give away only as much power as they choose, but permits the rise of global bodies that can deal with global problems.

This takes us to the most basic principle: democracy itself. Reinventing globalization is really about reinventing democracy. *Democracy* is the most used and abused word in the world today. It evokes both rituals of reverence and near total cynicism in the public. Even in the United States, which sees itself as the democratic model for the world, more than half the people don't vote. The new vision starts with the recognition that globalization has debased democracy even as it has exported the idea to every corner of the earth.

The alternative to globalization is, at heart, exceedingly simple: it is to take the idea of democracy seriously. This means vesting ordinary citizens across the entire planet with real control in an era when governments have become handmaidens of global corporations and global markets are held up as the model of democracy. Global democrats bring a few fundamental new ideas about democracy. One is that democracy is not the same as free elections.

Whether in El Salvador or Iraq, elections are rarely free, and they do not by themselves create the kind of democracy that guarantees real popular control.

We should not disregard the importance of constitutional democratic procedures, or the vital need for elections in societies that have never given citizens the vote, free speech, and freedom of association. But free elections in scores of countries are not delivering democracy serving the poor, the great majority of the population. We need a broader, deeper democracy if we are to wean governments at every level from the grip and greed of global markets. We need to move from the procedural democracy of globalization—which restricts itself to voting while societies are polarized between a tiny wealthy oligarchy and a huge poor majority—toward the social democracy that can attack global corporate power at its roots. This means vesting ordinary citizens with real control over the political and economic decisions that matter. It will involve engaging citizens not only in free and fair elections, but in active participation in local, national, and global politics through civic, grassroots, labor, feminist, and public interest associations of every stripe. We need citizens who are as passionate about political participation as they are about sports or sitcoms and who have effective rights and vehicles for holding leaders accountable.

Global economic democracy is a second new idea. Because financial markets now drastically limit the choices that any government, even the most democratized, can make, there is no choice but to take democracy directly into the world of business. In any age, but especially the age of globalization, there can be no political democracy without economic democracy. Global economic democracy means making corporations answer to citizens as well as stockholders, and making financial markets accountable to the global public as well as investors. The urgency is so great in the new era of terror and recession that it has become the great passion of citizen activists throughout the world who speak of economic democracy. But it has also become a matter of conversation among global business leaders, who, after Enron, increasingly talk about stakeholder democracy and global citizenship.

A third and most basic new idea is that democracy today has to be globalized. The biggest challenge will be empowering the majority of the world's population who live in the Third World. This will require democratic movements led by the Third World itself, both to take back their own governments and to invent new regional and global bodies that can speak for them. While poor nations claiming their rightful power is threatening to almost everybody in rich countries, democratically aroused Third World peoples are the most important allies workers and ordinary citizens in rich nations can have. They bring the desperation of the hungry and their moral authority, as well as the power of two-thirds of the world's people, to challenge the global monied powers corrupting democracy and riding roughshod over human rights.

If we can't create a democratic world forum in a body like the UN, where the world's majority holds sway, we can't expect to preserve democracy in the town hall or in national governments, and we certainly will not get a democracy taken seriously in the Third World. This leads to a fourth new idea: democracy at any level depends on democracy at all levels. The town meeting in Springfield or Jakarta and the global town meeting at the UN or the World Bank have to support each other's democratic possibilities, or they will both surrender to the "democracy of the market"—the degraded forum we suffer now.

26

Alternatives to Sociopathic Capitalism

Social Democracy in America

"We started by talking about Europe," the ghost said, "and that's because social democracy could come to the United States, too. We've already agreed social democracy is a baby step compared to the revolution you need, but it is a start."

"Social democracy, with its big government, high taxes, and vast social welfare system just doesn't seem suited to the United States."

"It will take a different form in the United States," the ghost says. "And the obstacles are great. But Franklin Roosevelt introduced a popular form of American social democracy during the New Deal. So social democracy has a history here, and many view it as one of the country's great social achievements."

"What will US social democracy look like?" I ask.

"You can see some very early outlines in both the New Deal, LBJ's Great Society, and now with Obama," the ghost said.

A Green New Deal

Obama ran his 2008 campaign on the promise of solving the economic crisis with green job creation. He has not delivered, but in 2011 called again for green investment as the cornerstone of his economic policy. The people who elected him still believe in a Green New Deal.

"FDR created the Social Security system, and he also used government to create millions of new jobs. Many of them were green, by the way, planting trees. In the 1930s, the New Deal reconstructed the American government to promote full employment and social well-being in the people's hour of need. This became the earliest foundation of a new US social democracy. LBJ passed Medicare, which became a second pillar of budding US social democracy. Now Obama has added his own health-care program, one further baby step down the path of social democracy."

"But these programs—from government job creation to social welfare—are all being seen by conservatives and many other Americans," I said, "as breaking the bank—just too expensive to maintain. They are slashing the programs that exist and will do anything to block new ones."

"They are a minority," the ghost said. "True," he continued, "the Tea Party has a big megaphone. And then there's the clout of anti-government Republicans such as Republican Budget Committee Chair Rep. Paul Ryan of Wisconsin who wrote and passed a GOP House budget that would privatize Medicare, turning it into a voucher program. But polls show that most Americans," the ghost continued, "do not want to eliminate major government programs such as Social Security or Medicare. More public spending for education, jobs, infrastructure, Social Security and Medicare, public transit, affordable housing, and job training is popular because it is the only way for millions of people to survive. The Republicans have found that attacking Medicare may be political suicide because Medicare has become a pillar of a US welfare state that 80 percent of Americans support."

"Well, I agree," I said, "and I could say the same about student loans. I notice even my conservative students find public aid to students and education, another US 'social welfare' program, appealing. Their families are hurting, they can't afford their tuition, and they feel like slaves to their student loans. But they always ask about the cost of all these programs in the era of $12 trillion national debts."

"The short-term cost is big," the ghost acknowledged. "Building on the US social democracy is going to require a major shift in the entire government budget. Massive cuts in military spending. Higher taxes on the very wealthy. And sharp reductions in the bloated corporate welfare system, meaning all the subsidies, giveaways, and tax breaks lavished by the billions every year on Exxon, Goldman Sachs, Monsanto, and Boeing."

Student Loans and Lost Dreams

I tell the ghost my students admit they take corporate jobs that pay rather than the creative or social change jobs they really want. Their student loans often are more than $50,000 when they graduate. So they give up their dreams to pay back the loans. When they hear that European students don't carry student loans, their eyes widen. They feel that social democracy might free them to pursue their dreams.

"So we already have a massive welfare state," I said. "You're just suggesting shifting all those taxpayer dollars from corporate welfare to social welfare."

From Corporate Welfare to Social Welfare

Marx mentions again the secret the US media and US politicians never tell the public. The United States is already a welfare state. But it dishes out corporate welfare to the biggest businesses and military welfare to the Pentagon rather than social welfare to the poor and workers.

"That's a good way to put it," the ghost said. "You DO already have a massive single-payer welfare system in America. Corporate welfare. It goes to support the richest Americans, corporations, and the military rather than the poor and working classes. And, by the way, a change will ultimately save money and create efficiency because if government invests in the people, they will sacrifice for the country and be more efficient and productive workers."

"You're saying," I replied, "that social democracy gets everyone to buy into the society. It makes ordinary people stakeholders with loyalty and something to lose. While it costs money, it pays back big time in reducing crime, mental health costs, and other social problems, while also increasing the skill and motivation of workers and thus improving the economy."

"You've got it," the ghost said. "Social democracy is a strategy for economic efficiency as well as social health. European economies, such as Germany, have been highly productive and efficient precisely **because** of their social democracy, not in spite of it. All Germans are stakeholders in their society, exercise some workplace power, and get a basket of human services. They give back loyalty, hard work, and social commitment."

"Sounds like the United States better get on board fast," I agree.

The Co-Op Nation, American Style

"Yes," said the ghost, "but remember that social democracy is only one of several major alter-capitalist possibilities—and it is far from visionary enough to solve the biggest crises of global warming, financial meltdown, joblessness, and war. A few other systems might be added into the mix in America. One is co-operativism."

"What do you mean by that?" I asked. "A kind of Mondragon system expanded throughout the United States?"

"Yes, it means changing a growing percentage of US businesses—especially the biggest ones—into worker-owned and community-owned co-ops. If they were organized in the Mondragon style, it would change the corporation from a top-down structure into a business run from the bottom up. US business would be reorganized as a one-person, one-vote democracy. But they must go beyond Mondragon and unite with progressive worker political parties to take state power and reconstruct property and corporations around worker self-government."

"So you're talking about a kind of economy democracy," I say. "Business of, for, and by the people, so to speak."

"Yes," the ghost replied, "as long as we're talking about a network of businesses committed to systemic political change in the larger economy and society. Mondragon has shown that democratically organized businesses—where workers are governing their own work and the entire firm—can be highly productive and efficient, in fact, world class competitors. But it can only happen successfully if the people and the government get behind co-op nation and if the co-ops

Michael Moore and Co-Op Nation

In his documentary *Capitalism: A Love Story,* Michael Moore argues for transforming capitalism. His major solution is co-operativism, turning big capitalist companies into worker-owned companies that will not outsource their jobs and dehumanize labor.

unite with militant labor parties to create a new political agenda for worker self-governance and economic democracy."

"Well, the democratic idea might sell in the United States," I concede, "because we are so committed in our national rhetoric and mythology to democracy as the best system. But it still seems a dream world, a fantasy. Corporations will resist to the end."

"Yes, but polls show 70 percent of US workers say they would like working in a co-op or worker-owned business. Actually, the United States has its own very extensive history of co-ops," the ghost reminded me. "Some of the timber co-ops out in Oregon and Washington have been highly successful over almost a century. This is true also of many large agricultural co-ops as well as some industrial and food co-ops, usually small businesses such as bakeries, bookstores, house-cleaning firms, and groceries in cities across the United States. There's a flourishing network of both producer and consumer co-ops throughout the country, and they are increasingly linked in co-op associations and with some labor organizations promoting their cause."

"You wrote," I reminded the ghost, "that co-ops will often clash with the struggle of unions to gain power. The companies can say that co-ops prove the workers don't need unions, making the co-op a pseudo-democracy that actually becomes a hurdle to real economic democracy."

"That's still a very serious concern of mine," the ghost said. "But unions are beginning to find co-ops attractive. They realize that many co-ops still need unions to fulfill the democratic dream. And they also see co-ops as a strategy to take over plants that are being shut down, with jobs outsourced and moving overseas."

"You mean," I say, "that unions see worker-owned firms as a new strategy for creating jobs themselves because global corporate capitalism is stealing them away to far-flung places."

"That's exactly right," the ghost said. "One of America's biggest unions, the United Steelworkers, you will remember, entered into a 2009 formal agreement with Mondragon to create worker-owned co-ops in the United States."

"It seems a promising development," I admitted. "But even the union admits it's an experiment, and they are moving cautiously. It will take a long time before most corporations are transformed into worker co-ops."

"You're right about that," said the ghost. "That is precisely why we need to move fast on other fronts. The big corporations are going to resist, and most will not turn into co-ops anytime soon. But the unions and other progressive groups are going to add money and promote a political agenda for a co-op movement fighting for systemic changes in Wall Street super-capitalism. This offers hope for big social transformation."

Unions and Co-Ops against Wall Street and Super-Capitalism

Leo Gerard, president of the United Steelworkers, said, "We see today's agreement as a historic first step toward making union co-ops a viable business model that can create good jobs, empower workers and support communities.... We need a new business model that invests in workers and invests in communities."

Post-Corporate America: Beyond the Corporation

"I agree completely," I said. "But what are the other ways to deal with corporations? It seems as long as they dominate the United States, we are going to have super-capitalism and the intensification of the death spiral."

"Yes, and that is why TINA is so dangerous," the ghost said. "TINA is preventing most Americans from imagining the very possibility of a world or country without American-style corporations that will remain masters of the universe."

"So any alter-capitalism or post-capitalism revolution will have to rekindle a belief in the possibility of what seems impossible: a post-corporate world?"

"There you go again, Mr. TINA," the ghost reproached me. "Actually, there are social movements all over the United States working on this very goal. Of course, there is a need for business enterprise to exist, but it doesn't have to take the super-capitalist form that we see in America, which is actually a relatively recent invention."

"US businesses, themselves," I nod, "are talking about social responsibility and the idea of stakeholder corporations, along the European model. Stakeholders, such as workers, consumers, suppliers, and the community, not just the investors, will have influence and perhaps a seat on the board of the stakeholder corporation."

"As you know, much of the social responsibility and stakeholder language is pure hype. It's just so much corporate window dressing. The real power is left in the hands of the executives."

"I think there may be more hope here than you're admitting. I know personally some of these stakeholder activists, and they want transformation in the whole system. Admittedly, the stakeholder corporation is just a first step, but the best stakeholder activists know this."

"Claptrap, mostly," he repeats. "There could be some possibilities among the most visionary stakeholder thinkers. But there's little time and you need far more radical—and rapid—transformation."

"So what do we do to start reinventing big business, beyond stakeholder ideas and supporting co-ops?" I ask. "And what is the new business model? If there is a realistic alternative," I added with more skepticism in my voice.

"US history is a good guide," the ghost said. "You know very well that the Founders of the United States—and later presidents such as Abraham Lincoln—feared that the corporation could become a tyranny that might destroy their democratic experiment. So they designed the corporate charter—the law in each state that defines

Abraham Lincoln on Corporations

"I see ... a crisis approaching that unnerves me and causes me to tremble for the safety of my country.... Corporations have been enthroned and an era of corruption in high places will follow, and the money power of the country will endeavor to prolong its reign by working upon the prejudices of the people until all wealth is aggregated in a few hands and the Republic is destroyed."

the purpose and governance of business—to try to ensure that corporations would serve the public rather than vice versa."

"The charter laws are essentially the constitution of the corporation," I said. "And it's true that the early charters defined the corporation as a creation of the public to serve the common good."

"Every American should know this secret history," the ghost said, "because the early charters offer a vision we ought to look at again today. They legally defined the aim of the corporation to serve the public interest. They permitted private profit for investors. But they said corporations were ultimately accountable to the people and their elected representatives in the legislature, not to the shareholders or investors."

"Corporations of, by and for the people, in a sense," I summarized.

"Well, they were very imperfect, but, yes, this is how we need to reinvent business today," the ghost said. "Remember, in a corporate welfare system like the United States, the people are funding big corporations because all those government bailouts, subsidies, and tax giveaways come right from the taxpayers. Corporate welfare is really a system of forced popular investment—through taxation and government subsidies—in huge companies, without popular consent. If the people finance the corporations, the corporations should be accountable to them."

"No taxation without representation," I said.

"Yes, the most revered American tradition," the ghost said. "Any true US patriot would see that the application of that principle to a corporate welfare system means that corporations should return to the original vision of the charter—of business as legally accountable to the people, with the aim first and foremost of the common good."

"So the first task is to rewrite the charter of the corporation in the spirit of the original democratic vision," I say.

"Yes," the ghost agreed. "And there are grassroots movements across the country trying to do this. But there's much more. You must abolish corporate personhood, a devilish idea if ever there was one."

"You mean the view, emanating from the 1886 Santa Clara Supreme Court decision, that affirmed the corporation as a 'person' or 'citizen' protected under the Constitution. This decision led corporations to gain rights of speech, privacy, and other rights originally reserved for flesh and blood humans, not corporations."

Are Corporations Persons?

Chief Justice John Roberts's Supreme Court seems to think so. But the Constitution never mentions corporations or offers them protections. Jefferson, who feared corporate tyranny, would turn over in his grave if he knew his precious Bill of Rights protected corporations.

"This is crucially important," the ghost said. "In the 2010 case, *United Citizens*, the Supreme Court ruled, as most Americans now know, that it is unconstitutional to put any limits on the amount of money that corporations could pay for political ads on issues or to support candidates. That horrific decision was based on the doctrine of personhood because the Court equates the right to give money with speech and thus views regulation of political donations by corporations as a violation of their First Amendment personhood rights."

I agreed with the ghost on this one. "The Constitution never mentions the word corporation. The Founders never meant to protect them using the rights of real people because they recognized it could destroy the democratic experiment. Americans are waking up to this—especially with the shock of *United Citizens*. About 80 percent of the public rejected the Court's decision."

"Yes, and grassroots movements are rising to abolish corporate personhood. This struggle will help to define the future of American democracy. But there's one other change we need to mention—because it's rarely discussed—in the great transition struggle to recapture the original idea of corporations as of, by, and for the public."

"What is that?" I asked.

"Many big companies probably should be dismantled," the ghost said. "This is becoming clear with the debate about the huge Wall Street banks after the crisis. But some will remain, and the only way to ensure that they act in the public interest is to have the public take ownership of them."

"Are you talking about nationalization?" I asked. "You know the United States will not support that."

Nobel Laureate Joseph Stiglitz on Nationalization of Wall Street

"It is very clear that the banks have failed. American citizens have become majority owners in a very large number of the major banks. But they have no control. Any system where there is a separation of ownership and control is a disaster ... nationalization is the only answer."

"Don't be so sure," the ghost said. "Do you remember during the crisis, when the government was bailing out Goldman Sachs, J. P. Morgan, AIG, and the other huge Wall Street financial institutions? People suddenly realized that this was a de facto form of nationalization. The United States actually became a major and controlling shareholder in huge financial firms such as AIG—and in the case of the auto companies, such as GM, actually took over the company completely."

"And major economists such as Joseph Stiglitz and Paul Krugman talked openly about the need to nationalize banks and other big companies," I remembered. "But that was during an extreme crisis."

"Don't be fooled," the ghost said. "Crises will keep coming, and Americans will increasingly realize they live in 'Bailout Nation.' And the crises as well as global competition will require that not only the big banks but Big Oil and Big Coal, just as in most other countries, will be nationalized, and operated as public utilities."

"It will take some new very deep crises," I said.

"Perhaps," the ghost said. "But these are inevitable and already apparent."

Localism: Community and Local Living Economies in the United States

"You know," I tell the ghost, "that even many on the US Left will see your alternatives as futile fantasies. They all depend on taking over the federal government through electoral politics. But many of the most lively and visionary activists don't see hope there. They see it in their own communities and their own lives."

"Ahhh," the ghost responded. "Yes, you're talking about the so-called localists, who believe that change begins and ultimately ends at home, in their own communities and their own lives."

"It's a refreshing approach," I say. "Because localists are walking their talk. There's a personal authenticity that ultimately may appeal to millions of Americans and create more change than any frontal assault on Washington. And thousands of local communities creating local farmer markets and bicycle paths and local credit unions may end up changing the world more than the federal government or global agreements ever will."

"You're making a mistake," the ghost said. "Local communities cannot, by themselves, change problems that are systemic. This will take national and global movements. Ultimately, ordinary people must take democracy seriously and take control of their own governments at every level."

> **What Localists Believe You Should Do**
>
> David Korten, a leading localist thinker, writes, "The first step in making a personal contribution to creating the new economy is to declare your independence from Wall Street by joining the voluntary simplicity movement and cutting back on unnecessary consumption. Beyond that, shop at local independent stores where possible and purchase locally made goods when available. Make the same choices as to where you work and invest...."

> **Marx on Localist Limits**
>
> "They endeavor, by small experiments, necessarily doomed to failure, and by the force of example, to pave the way for the new Social Gospel."

"But localist ideas have inspired a massive movement of people all around America," I said. "They want out of the global economy and no part of super-capitalism. They want to build a new world from the ground up in their own lives and communities. Locally owned businesses; town hall democracy; regional economies; alliances among hundreds of thousands of self-governing communities."

"It's a noble and revolutionary aspiration," the ghost acknowledged. "But it has the flaws of the utopian socialism I denounced in my own day. Nonetheless, I've been watching your localists with great interest. They carry a vigor and revolutionary spirit nowhere else to be found on the Left—and many have a more global and political activist vision than the localists of my day. Many act on multiple levels with their slogan, 'Think Global, Act Local.'"

"The localists are active in communities all over the country, from Portland, Oregon, to Portsmouth, New Hampshire," I say. "Many are even small business entrepreneurs, strong believers in markets at the local level but essential and novel players in the war against global super-capitalism."

Business Alliance for Local Living Economies

The Business Alliance for Local Living Economies (BALLE) proclaims, "We're proving that these businesses are accountable to stakeholders and the environment. We're helping these businesses flourish in their local economies. And we're leveraging the power of local networks to build a web of economies that are community-based, green, and fair—local living economies."

"The local entrepreneurs are a fascinating localist group. They hate the Walmarts and other super-capitalist corporations who are destroying their businesses and communities. There are hundreds of small business people involved with the Business Alliance for Local Living Economies (BALLE), and they prove there can be transformative business people. BALLE is North America's fastest growing network of socially responsible businesses, comprising over 80 community networks in 30 US states and Canadian provinces, representing over 22,000 independent business members across the United States and Canada. You can't make a social revolution without businesspeople. They want to remake the economy from the ground up, believing that only a local economy can be self-governing."

"That seems to be the premise of the localists," I say. "Small is beautiful. And include everyone in the community. You won't exploit your neighbor who you know and depend on to watch your kids."

"Let's not romanticize locality. Local communities have often been racist and tyrannical, anything but democratic," the ghost responded. "And historically many small business owners have been anything but progressive—in fact quite the opposite as we discussed."

"So why do you see promise in localism?" I ask.

"I have serious reservations that we've discussed. They must develop as part of a broad national and political movement to transform the capitalist system. But these are people who are already beginning to live the alter-capitalist revolution. Look how they eat. Their farmer markets are a true alternative to corporate agriculture, more democratic and far more ecological. Or how they bank. By putting money in local credit unions, they are showing how to get by without surrendering everything to Wall Street. Or how they work—in small self-managed co-ops in Portland and Seattle. Or how they buy. By shopping at local businesses, they are showing we don't need Walmart and other big box stores. Or how they get around, on bikes or just plain walking. It seems pedestrian, if you pardon the pun, but it's an embryo of a true alternative way of life. And by taking over local city councils, they can actually legislate their vision in a way impossible for now at the national and global levels."

"No doubt," I agree, "that localism is a truly subversive idea in the age of globalization and global warming. And the ability to live the revolution right on your front porch and in your city hall, with your neighbors, gives everyone hope. But you seem the last ghost who would counsel giving up on national and global change. After all, super-capitalism concentrates power in Wall Street and DC. If you don't pull the change levers there, the larger society will keep moving with the super-capitalist train."

"Yes," the ghost says, "but the best lo-calists see all that. They also realize that revolutionaries who don't live and dance their own revolution burn out and never inspire others."

Dancing at the Revolution

Famed Marxist-anarchist, Emma Goldman, said, "If I can't dance, I don't want to be part of your revolution."

"You don't really believe in change until you live it," I say. "And only the localists are living proof right now that TINA is a lie."

"Yes, but there's more," the ghost says. "In the age of the Internet, local actions are never just local. Alter-capitalist local successes go viral at lightning speed. Localists in the United States are building alliances with like-minded community activists in Europe, Latin America, Africa, and Asia, sharing pictures and ideas on Facebook and email. And they are meeting up with them at the Social Forums and building alliances for common action against Walmart, Wall Street, and free trade treaties."

"So localism is not really just local."

"It's a global movement," the ghost said, "and you see a lot of local activists showing up at national protests in DC and at the anti-globalization rallies around the world."

"But we have a progressive movement fragmented into thousands of vibrant activists making local change, but unable to unite and create the larger changes we need on Wall Street and DC and at the World Trade Organization."

"That's the ultimate challenge for the localists," the ghost agreed. "They need to be self-conscious glocalists. The global activists need the localists to succeed, and the localists need the globalists. Localists know that local farming markets cannot solve global warming since that requires a global treaty capping and taxing carbon. But the global treaty is just so much paper if the localists are not leading the way with their local green businesses and farmer markets. There will be no revolutionary garden if it's not planted together by the two groups."

27

Will the World Be Ruled by Money or Human Rights?

Only a few months after the Battle of Seattle, huge legions of workers, students, environmentalists, and other protesters are massing on the streets of Washington. Their targets are the International Monetary Fund and the World Bank, the sister institutions of the World Trade Organization. The concerns are not US jobs, sweatshops, and sovereignty but the well-being of 3 billion people in the world who lack enough food or access to basic sanitation. The outcome of the ten-day siege of Washington will help determine the future of globalization and whether the world will be ruled by money or human rights.

The IMF and World Bank provide credit and aid to poor nations through structural adjustment programs—SAPs—designed to correct trade imbalances, pay down debt, and promote transparency and modernization.

SAPs, which some critics dub the "cold bath," require open markets, privatization, deregulation, reduced wages and social programs, and currency devaluation. Such strategies free up funds to repay massive debts to Western banks and governments and increase exports over imports, but they erode the living standards of millions of desperately poor people, triggering bread riots from Caracas to Jakarta.

Two key factors explain why the IMF and the World Bank have helped escalate inequality and poverty in Africa and Latin America. First, the terms of SAPs are dictated by Washington and Western lenders. Harvard economist Jeffery Sachs calls the IMF a "neocolonial" government permanently ensconced inside the governments of scores of Third World nations.

Second, despite encouraging humanitarian rhetoric about targeting poverty, IMF policy is crafted on corporate rather than human terms. Debt repayment still bleeds money from rickety schools without textbooks in Uganda and unstocked health clinics in Port-au-Prince. Market liberalization comes at the expense of domestic industry throughout the Third World, and freer capital flows overwhelm African and Latin governments' ability to create jobs and food security.

This represents a perversion of the 1944 Bretton Woods Agreement that created the IMF and World Bank. The architects of Bretton Woods—the economist John Maynard Keynes and FDR's aide Harry Dexter White—championed a world of freer but still highly regulated trade to help governments pursue full employment and social development. The protesters in Washington are the true inheritors of Keynes and White when they support a globalization based on labor rights and social democracy.

The WTO and the IMF have severed the original Bretton Woods connection between expanded trade and human rights. More open markets and fiscal discipline are liberating, as Keynes wrote, only when linked to global regulation of capital flows that protects public investment and national social welfare policy.

Current liberalization policies sabotage the socially protective state—in the United States and in Europe as well as in the developing world—which explains why the IMF and World Bank are losing credibility globally.

The Seattle and Washington protests signal an unpredictable new popular movement that is anticorporate, proglobalist, and unites workers in rich and poor nations. Communicating by Internet, it seeks new global institutions and rules of corporate conduct anchored in a higher morality than money.

The IMF and the World Bank are technically UN agencies; their successor institutions must embrace and enforce the 1948 UN Declaration on Human Rights and the International Labor Organization's Conventions on labor rights. When these have teeth and new terms of trade help erode debt and redistribute resources to poor nations, a new global consensus will support freer trade and global investment.

But until the world economy is governed in the spirit of Keynes and White and the UN founders, every major trade meeting will be under siege, and corporations will correctly fear that their global investments are threatened.

Thomas Jefferson refused to sign on to the US Constitution until it was anchored in a Bill of Rights. Only when the new global constitutional order now being shaped by the WTO, the IMF, and global financial markets links worldwide property protection to human rights will globalization gain the consent of the world's people.

SECTION C
Activism and What You Can Do

28

What You Can Do Now

After listening to and being persuaded by many of the ideas I present here, people often bring me down to earth with a simple comment. Yes, I think you're right, and I want to do something. But what is it that I can do? Here, in a nutshell, is what I answer.

1. Practice Self-Awareness: Reflect deeply and often about your own place in the corporate world. How do you participate in it? How does the corporate world shape your life and values—and those of your family? Do your corporate roles as worker, manager, consumer, or shareholder make you a better person? Is corporate morality your morality? How does the corporation benefit you and how does it oppress or control you? From your place in the corporate world, how do you benefit or hurt others?

2. Educate Yourself and Others: Join a group to read and talk about the corporation and your lives. The nineteenth-century populists met in each other's kitchens to read about and discuss their problems, while sponsoring traveling lecturers to speak in their communities. Form your own group from your workplace, church, or community. Let this be both a consciousness-raising group about your own experiences as employee, consumer, or shareholder, and an educational group for reading and analyzing corporate power, economic democracy, and the corporate high road.

3. Just Say No: Many communities are organizing to prevent corporations from taking over their schools, hospitals, or social services. Think of the battles to save community hospitals from giant for-profit chains such as Columbia HCA. Consider the fact that corporations addicted to short-term profits may be providing the curricula for your kids at school or determining what drugs or treatment your doctor can provide. Join community efforts—and you will surely find them in your town or city—to keep corporations and the market mentality out of spheres in your life where they don't belong.

4. Buy Smart: Use your power as a consumer wisely. Buy union-labor or "no sweat" clothes, but make sure the labels mean what they say: no sweatshops. Boycott corporations that abuse workers or the environment. Students at Duke, Brown, and other universities have persuaded their schools not to buy products—from caps to sweatshirts—from vendors who do not sign codes of ethical conduct. Get your city or state to use their own massive consumer power by passing selective purchasing laws, such as the Massachusetts Burma law that imposes a 10 percent penalty on any vendor to the state doing business in the outrageous dictatorship of Burma today. Twenty-nine cities have joined Massachusetts, and Vermont may soon add its name.

5. Create Good Money: If you are an investor—small or large—think of where your money is going and how you can invest it to enhance your values and citizenship as well as your wallet. Invest in socially conscious companies and you may want to examine socially responsible investment funds such as Franklin Research or Development in Boston or a small company called Good Money—which puts out an informative guide you can find on the Web. Pressure your church, union, or pension fund to use a socially conscious approach in their own investment decisions.

6. Get Your Company on the High Road: You and your company should join Business for Social Responsibility, headquartered in Washington, DC, or other business groups committed to high road practice. You can get lots of practical ideas from them about what to do, and they will benefit from your views about how to move the corporate responsibility movement beyond its current limits toward positive populism. Think of one practical business initiative your company could take that would truly improve the lives of your fellow workers or the community and fight for it.

7. Support Economic Alternatives: Support worker-owned businesses, community-owned enterprises, small, locally owned businesses, governmental and nongovernmental enterprises, and nonprofits—all part of the growing alternatives to corporate America. Tell people about them. Work for them. Lobby for government tax breaks for them. Corporations survive only by accepting vast corporate welfare—the alternatives need public support too.

8. Unite: UNITE is a coalition of labor unions in the needle trade industry seeking to end sweatshops. Support it with time or money as a symbol of your endorsement of a labor movement that fights for social justice rather than just more money for its members. Think about the kind of union you could support in your workplace—which may be quite different from a traditional union—and get involved in efforts to organize such positive unions or other worker organizations. Pay attention to the AFL-CIO under its new leadership, read their new publications, and if you like what they're saying, send them money and support them in their new organizing efforts among part-timers (as at UPS), low-paid service workers, office workers, and even professionals such as doctors and middle managers.

9. Be a "Civil Society" Activist: Think of one corporation that is making your community a less civil place to live. Join others who are seeking to "civilize" it, close it down, or get it out of your community. Almost every major corporation—from Microsoft to Wal-Mart—has been confronted by nationwide coalitions of community groups seeking to preserve their own civility and autonomy. Join their efforts.

10. Vote Populist: Believe it or not, there are politicians in both the Democratic and Republican parties who are voicing populist concerns—about downsizing, economic insecurity, big money in politics, inequality, corporate mergers and monopolies, and corporate welfare. Throw your voice and vote behind those with the most forceful and positive message. Look also at the small new parties—such as the New Party or the Greens—which are speaking more directly about corporate power and economic democracy. Try your hand at writing a positive populist platform and send it to your local newspaper or Senators and Representatives.

11. Join a Populist Organization: Join one of the many consumer groups, unions, churches, or new explicitly populist groups—such as the Alliance for Democracy, Friends of the Earth, Public Citizen, and United for a Fair Economy. Find out about these organizations on the World Wide Web, get their literature, call them, and join them on the issues they are fighting for— from campaign finance reform to new corporate charters to a fair tax code.

12. Own Your Own Job: Thousands of corporations are offering forms of worker ownership through Employee Stock Ownership Plans (ESOPs) and retirement options. Make sure your corporation is one of them and fight to make sure the ownership is truly meaningful—giving a voice and a vote, not just a dividend payment. Write for more information to the Center on Employee Ownership in Oakland, California, a fount of useful information for businesses and workers interested in worker ownership.

13. Support Women at Work: Think of the millions of young women all over the world forced to work in degrading conditions within the corporate controlled export zones of the Third World. They make the clothes you wear and assemble the stereos you listen to. Think also of the working women here at home, including thousands thrown off welfare—who suffer most in the new world of temp and part-time labor. If you are already a feminist, make sure your favorite women's organization has not forgotten these working women. Rethink your own feminist values in the light of your understanding of the corporation, and make sure you are not just thinking about middle-class women. Help develop and support—with your money and time—a populist feminism.

14. Join the Race to the Top: Think about the global race to the bottom and the proposals advanced here to create a race to the top. Join forces with the hundreds of grassroots groups—you can find them on the Web—which are fighting the MAI, promoting inclusion of labor and environmental standards in NAFTA and the WTO, and demanding that corporations and nations respect human rights and democracy over profits. Choose one campaign—for example, the struggle against MAI—and join with others who are trying to get their city councils to pass a resolution against MAI as undermining local, state, and federal sovereignty.

15. Stand Up for Your Rights: Corporations are taking away your rights and constitutionalizing new ones of their own. These may be as simple as your right to go to the bathroom at work or to keep your e-mail private. Or as complex as the corporations' new right to give billions of dollars to political candidates as a form of First Amendment free speech. Stand up for your rights in the workplace and the community. Write to your local newspapers about how you feel about corporations reading workers' e-mail or using the Bill of Rights to defend their corruption of politics with big money. Send the positive message that corporations that empower workers and vest them with rights will be more productive as well as more democratic.

16. Join the Campaign for a Living Wage: Communities all over the nation are fighting for "liveable wages" enforced by their city governments. Populist activists in this campaign are outraged that millions of Americans work forty hours or more and remain poor. In Baltimore, Minneapolis, and other cities, the city council has passed an ordinance requiring that any employers doing business with the city pay a minimum wage adequate to pull a family out of poverty. Get your city on board.

17. Bust the Trusts: Even *Business Week* is asking its readership whether it's time to dismantle the Microsoft monopoly. When banks get as big as the near-trillion-dollar Citicorp-Travelers merger, even conservatives get scared. Many long-distance companies are assailing the local phone companies' monopoly. Join one of the many consumer and populist groups—led most visibly by Ralph Nader—that are leading a new campaign to recharter and potentially dismantle the huge transnational corporate monopolies that now sit astride the world.

18. Take Democracy Seriously: You are lucky to live in a country that embraces the value of democracy. If your right to vote were taken away in your community, you would be frightened. But your right to vote at work is no less important to your well-being, so you have to become a champion of economic democracy. Demand your stakeholder right to vote in the workplace through any means possible: ownership, unionization, professional association, team representation. Talk about it frequently and seriously enough that others will listen. As corporate power expands to control much of government itself, your constitutional right to vote outside the workplace becomes increasingly meaningless as well. You will have to fight to reclaim a meaningful vote in a political system where both parties speak the language of business. This means supporting social movements, political candidates, and populist parties who speak openly about the dangers of corporate sovereignty, and who propose concrete plans for making democracy real, both in the corporation and in the nation at large.

29

From Bowling Alone to Bowling Green

On the first day of my classes, I often warn my students that they might need some industrial-strength Prozac by the end of the semester. That is because social topics can be truly depressing. We sociologists show that today's problems are big and frightening and are wired into our social systems. It is not easy to find solutions or to see how one person can do anything about them.

This seems true in spades about global warming. A pessimist could easily conclude that we are creating our own specieswide holocaust, gassing ourselves to a collective death with carbon emissions. She could look at her own child or grandchild or great-grandchild and conclude that the whole family tree is cooked. An optimist can, of course, come to a different conclusion: that because humans created this crisis, we still can solve it. Most climate scientists are telling us that time has not yet run out. But they are also warning us that the window for action is closing rapidly.

This leaves each of us with an overwhelming responsibility to make global warming a gut truth and devote as much time as we can to solving it. This is the biggest moral obligation humans can have: saving our precious human species as well as many other species with whom we share this beautiful planet. If that sounds too idealistic or softheaded, it is also the most hardheaded, self-interested thing we can do: act to ensure our own survival and that of our children.

But it is one thing to say this, quite another to get off the couch and try to make a real difference. This book has offered many reasons that people might choose to remain couch potatoes and slouch toward an overheated future of collective disruption, despair, and death. Even though Americans and many others in the world have become worried about global warming, it is not yet on the front burner. We have turned pale green, but we will have to act bright green if we are going to survive. On some days, this moves me back toward Prozac. But on other days, I see that green awareness has grown faster than I ever imagined possible—and that there are so many people and movements and leaders who are beginning to take creative, contagious action.

The situation reminds me of the film *Pleasantville,* where everyone is living in a 1950s world of living death, without any color in their conformist, doomed universe (filmed in grainy black and white). But a few people, including a time traveler from the future, rise up against this dead world and start to break the lifeless, authoritarian rules. They begin to see and paint colors—orange and red and, yes, green—and then they themselves begin to turn from pale white to the vibrant flesh color of truly living beings. All of Pleasantville eventually blossoms into radiant color.

So we need to reenact our own real version of Pleasantville, the world of grim and compliant global warming, and break its tight, deadly hold on us. In this chapter, I look at a few people who have begun to struggle against their own pale green—and against the paleness of our whole society. They are not necessarily leaders or heroes, just ordinary people, some of whom have done extraordinary things. My hope is that seeing some of their failures and obstacles will make us feel less guilty about our own weaknesses or couch potato inclinations. More importantly, some of their ideas and successes may inspire us to believe that we can make a difference. They may help us think about what we can to do to help stop global warming and propel us off the couch.

In the service of truth in advertising, I want to say something first about myself. People rightfully want to know whether authors and teachers walk their talk. A lot of us do not. I see myself as a mixed case, not a couch potato but not a hero-activist or a great charismatic leader. I am one of many in my generation struggling to balance the demands of a busy career and personal life with my values and my desire to make a better world.

I am a child of the 1960s and 1970s, part of the generation that actively rebelled against the literal Pleasantville of the 1950s. This makes me a classic baby boomer. I was a young activist who landed in jails protesting segregation in the South and agitating against the Vietnam War at huge Pentagon rallies. Some of my brother and sister protesters ended up dropping out of conventional careers and becoming full-time activists. My route was somewhat different. Even as I was registering black voters in Mississippi summers, I was eager to get on with school and my intellectual career. I lived in tension between the demands of my personal ambitions and of my activist politics.

My dissertation adviser, sociologist Richard Flacks, wrote a book that captured this tension. Flacks distinguishes between "making a life" and "making history." Making a life is focusing on the hard challenges of creating a personal life and a career that work. Making history is working to change society, as full-time activists do. Flacks concludes that most of us will always be focused on the challenges of personal life, but he remains optimistic. Great change can come when just a small minority decides to make history.

My own path was to try bringing the two life tracks together. I did not want to give up either my career or my political commitments. But although the tension was real, and it still creates a tug of war inside of me, there were ways to do both together. As an academic, I had a lot of freedom to teach about political subjects and encourage my students to believe in their capacity to change the world. I could write about the big social justice questions that were central to my academic discipline and to my activism. I could use my standing and resources in the university to help community activists wage their social justice campaigns. As I became more aware of the urgency of the global warming issue, I integrated it into my teaching and writing, helped my university think about how to build sustainability into the whole curriculum as well as the physical operation of the university, ran workshops on climate change with community groups and managers, did media shows on global warming and social justice, and worked with community, national, and global activists to push the Obama administration and global social movements to stop climate change and heal our planet.

A big life lesson for me has been that I cannot ignore my own psychological needs or force myself to give up my career ambitions. Although I still wrestle with this issue, I have largely accepted that my personal needs and career aspirations are going to drive much of my action. What gives me some peace has been my ability to harness a huge amount of my career energy into teaching, writing, and engaging in actions that advance my social justice aims. This is no perfect solution—I wish I could give up self-interest and focus only on the larger good. I have evolved a little more in that direction but not enough to satisfy my conscience.

Is my imperfect solution relevant for others? Academics have unusual freedom to meld work and politics. But if others share some of my dilemma, they can integrate political education and activism into nearly any profession or job. A journalist can make sure to deliver the news about green products, policies, debates, and movements. A lawyer can work in the growing field of environmental law and justice and represent environmental activists who need legal help or companies seeking to go green. An architect, carpenter, electrician, mechanical engineer, or plumber can help design or build the greenhouses, offices, cars, mass transit, and power grids needed to lower our carbon footprint. Each of these workers makes money and a career by making green social change.

The green revolution is an open door for almost everybody to blend personal and political lives. After all, going green is partly a matter of personal lifestyle. A person can recycle, insulate the house, install solar panels, buy a hybrid car, and make other lifestyle changes, all both personal money-saving lifestyle choices and a micro form of green political activism. I have made small personal steps of this kind and want to make more. I recently went to a local community meeting about how to shed 5,000 pounds a year of carbon emission in my daily life at home. I am now part of a neighborhood "eco-team" working together to keep ourselves on a "carbon diet." I have also started going to a committee of my local city council exploring how the schools, heating and water systems, and overall carbon footprint of my town can be reduced. Seeing my neighbors come out in large numbers to meetings like this has been a source of hope. I have made new friends while learning about reducing my own carbon footprint.

Do personal lifestyle changes really make a difference? The truth is they will not by themselves stop global warming, which can be solved only by the big system changes I have described. But they have symbolic and strategic value that should not be minimized. When a person recycles, remembers to turn off the lights when leaving a room, unplugs a cell charger when not in use, or insulates the house, she is becoming more personally committed to the larger green struggle. I find that my own growing awareness about these little daily decisions increases my commitment to do more in my community and more with green political activists in national struggles. Lifestyle changes also have effects on the people around me. I can inspire others to think about living greener, too. This green "social contagion" is a major benefit of personal lifestyle changes.

The biggest lesson of my own story is that political action—or making history—can enrich our personal lives. Flacks emphasizes the tension between making a life and making history, but his historical analysis shows that a big reason people become and stay activists is because doing so is personally rewarding. That has certainly been true for me. One of my great personal and professional pleasures is writing. It is a meditation for me and concentrates my mind and spirit, distracting me from personal anxieties while also giving me the simple joy of crafting artful sentences. Much of my writing has been about politics and social justice and is one form of activism, thus allowing me to indulge myself personally, deal with my psychological needs, and make my very small contribution to history.

There are many other ways besides writing books to indulge a passion for writing or other creative expression while moving the green revolution forward. A person can blog for green websites or write letters to the editor or op-eds about local and national green issues. I have a friend Ken who loves to write and formed a one-person writing company. He educates young people and companies on how to think, write, and communicate about the green issues (mostly about water use) that are his professional specialty. He also writes his own personal column on the environment in his local community newspaper.

Many of the most interesting people I have encountered—and some of my good friends—are people I meet in activist circles. We all have a hunger for community, and activists have often satisfied that very human yearning through their social movements. Historians write about the "romance" of communism during the Great Depression because so many activists fell in love with other activists, some marrying and creating "red diaper" babies.

Left activists lived together in cooperative apartments, sent their kids to the same summer camps, came together around folk music and political poetry, and built long-term friendships and community that nonactivists often lacked. More recently, activists in the New Right have found a similar sense of community in Evangelical churches and politics. The Obama "permanent campaign" and groups such as Moveon.org have virtually revolutionized politics in this spirit, with heavy reliance on the Internet. They have used MySpace, Facebook, and meet-ups in kitchens and dining rooms to ignite the chemistry of personal relationships that builds political movements. Politics becomes intertwined with helping an increasingly disconnected population connect, make friends, and build a personal community.

My own life experience supports this so strongly that I feel truly sorry for the majority that never gets politically involved. For me, politics has always been a route out of America's Pleasantville and a road into excitement, adventure, new ideas, fascinating people, and strong communities and friends. The fight for a better world has made my personal life so much more interesting and "connected" that I can make a case for political engagement on purely personal or selfish grounds. I think the personal payoff of green politics is especially big; it can connect a person with good people, welcoming local community groups, lifestyle adventures, new ideas, and life-saving national and global political movements.

Peter Crawley: A Businessman Who Stopped a Dam and Turned Green

I turn now to my friend Peter, because he inspires me and may inspire others. He is in his late forties and originally hails from Plymouth, Massachusetts. He has worked in his own family's small real estate business and is now married and raising a young son. He is not an academic, he is not famous, and he is not a self-identified political activist. But I have watched him evolve in his own green life adventure and seen him turn people on—really move them off the couch—to start their own green adventures. There is something about him that makes others want to make a difference and believe in their own ability to do it. I wish I could bottle Peter and clone him because it might be one of the surest ways to ensure the success of the green revolution.

I became most impressed with what Peter has to teach us when I watched him lead a workshop session with mainstream managers who did not think of themselves as political activists. Peter's workshop was about getting involved in one's own local community as a form of green activism. He made it very personal. He told a story about his own decision to get involved in a battle with a local real estate developer who dammed up a river to build a condo complex. The project would make the developer a lot of money but damage the ecosystems of the marshlands nearby and the fish migrations in the river.

This was happening in the town in which Peter had grown up, and although he had moved to a nearby town, his parents still lived there. It was not an easy decision for Peter to get involved. He had recently started his own business and was raising his young son. He had also begun to take some classes to prepare for his new career. Money was tight, and he did not have a lot of free time. He would likely choose to make a life rather than to make history.

But Peter decided to get involved. Some of his friends from the community invited him to conversations about the dam problem. His parents had moved to a place on the river itself and told him about their own concerns. He began meeting with a few of the community folks. Because he knew the town and the main players so well—the concerned people living on the river, members of the town government, and various people in the local real estate business, including his own father and the developer who had dammed the river—he became a logical person to try starting negotiations among the various groups to find a solution.

The negotiating was not fast or easy, but Peter eventually helped build a set of community partnerships and activists who succeeded in getting the dam removed. People trusted him because he is a reconciler without an ax to grind and with the good of the community clearly at heart. He is honest, open, and driven by strong values. Peter was good at working across differences to find points of agreement, while also learning how to rally people and use the regulatory system when necessary to be effective in confrontations with the developer and votes at public committee meetings. Peter was becoming one of America's thousands of green community activists—whose focus, as I show shortly, would expand to state and then regional, national, and global issues.

Peter told his story in a way that riveted the workshop participants— probably because of his quiet authenticity and unpretentiousness. The participants talked a lot about that authenticity, his heartfelt community values, and how he made the idea of activism seem personally relevant and even exciting to them for the first time. Peter converted some couch potatoes that day into people who would no longer ridicule protesters and would begin to think about stepping up.

What the participants wanted to know was what made Peter decide to get and stay involved, given his time and money constraints. It was the same thing I wanted to know, because I am constantly dealing with competing demands on my own time—and I always want to know what moves people to choose activism. Peter thought it was not any one factor but had to do with his very personal ties to the place and the people, as well as his core values. He had grown up in this community and played as a boy near the river. He had spent his boyhood years in Plymouth on the ocean and in the bay where the river flowed out; he loved the outdoors, water, wind, and sun. The folks living near the proposed dam were his friends or his family. Maybe the most important thing was that his parents had lived much of their lives in the town and were upset about the dam project; they could look out their window in their current house and see the river. Peter's father, as a real estate developer and longtime resident, felt a stake in the fate of the community—and that had helped shape Peter's own strong feelings about the local environment. Peter said that his feelings for his elderly parents played a big role in tipping him to do something.

To me, this reveals the strong connection between personal life and political action. A lot of invisible emotional and personal threads tugged Peter toward his community activism. He would not have decided to spend so much time if he did not have such a strong identification with his family, friends in the community, and the river. His activism was a way of defending his personal life and community. It also was a clear expression of his deepest values.

When Peter talks about his growing political identity as an environmental activist, anyone listening will soon be deep in conversation with him about culture, community, and values. He is a progressive, but his cultural approach to politics reminds me of Evangelical conservatives who come to politics driven by their own brand of morality and spirituality. Peter's community-oriented, value-driven approach tells us that green politics may become quite different from much traditional liberalism and leftism and may motivate a new breed of activists who are disconnected and often alienated from traditional progressive politics. A closer look at Peter's values suggests that the green movement may begin to activate millions of liberal people who are turned off by the conflictual, angry style of Left-leaning movements and who are looking for something more "positive." The green movement may also attract surprising numbers of value-driven and community-oriented conservatives.

Peter is a homespun philosopher. Raised in a traditional Catholic family, he grew up with a strong religious feeling. In college, however, he took classes in Eastern philosophy that appealed to him as his Catholic faith waned and led him to begin a Buddhist meditation practice. He backpacked several times around Asia—Cambodia, Laos, Thailand, and rural China—and was drawn spiritually to traditional Chinese culture and its worldview. He liked the culture's emphasis on harmony with community and nature. The Chinese view of morality and community, balance and harmony, seemed very appealing.

Peter eventually married a Chinese woman, whom he had met in the United States. Peter moved deeper into a life bridging Western and Eastern values of family, community, and compassion. I find him one of the more harmonious people I know and one who naturally thinks about the good of the community and the environment. Finding balance seems at the center of Peter's life adventure—and as he gets more deeply into green politics, it seems natural to me that he would be focused on lightening his own carbon footprint while helping his community and society live in harmony with nature.

Peter revealed to me, however, that he had not always had these values. He had grown up as a conventional American guy interested in business and socializing. He described himself as competitive, aggressive, and wanting to make a lot of money. After working in his family business, he had gone to work for John Hancock Insurance and some other big financial service companies. He made some money, kept partying, and was getting into a high-consumption lifestyle.

But his introduction to Eastern philosophy in college and his repeated backpacking excursions in poor areas in Asia began to shift his thinking about life. He noticed in rural Asia that people lived more simply, with a respect for the land they farmed and the community they belonged to. They lived more in tune with nature in a way that probably resonated with his own boyhood love of the outdoors. Peter felt that even though these people enjoyed none of the pleasures of the Western consumer lifestyle, many of them seemed to be living on the land and in their communities in peace. Their lifestyle was simple, even grindingly poor, and he did not romanticize it. He was keenly aware of the disregard for nature and human rights displayed by modern Asian business and government. But through his rural travels and readings in Eastern philosophy, he developed a vision of life based on not doing violence to the land, community, and environment that one operated in and loved. This would become a tenet of his green philosophy and politics.

He saw a materially poor life in many communities in Asia, but one lived simply and "from the heart," illustrating a moral philosophy that he had read about in Buddhism and that was becoming more attractive to him as he found himself falling away from his consumerist lifestyle. His childhood religiosity was evolving into a new personal ethics of simplicity and compassion. All of this began to create big changes in Peter, even as he continued to work in business.

His drive for money lost its appeal, and he began to question his lifestyle and US consumerism itself, which contrasted so deeply with the simplicity and respect for nature he had found in Asian villages. He increasingly felt that American big houses and cars were unnecessary and artificial, even a type of violence against the natural world. This personal change in thinking was converging with the growth of the US environmental movement and a Western culture increasingly concerned about climate change and sustainability. Peter found himself getting interested in green thinking and community action, one of the reasons behind his decision to get involved in the dam project. That decision was a reflection of the new green direction his life would take, anchored in the community values of his boyhood and family and bolstered now by his new Eastern moral interests and the new Western green culture.

At midcareer, Peter is now in an educational program to retool and work in the field of environmental science and management. He has gotten more involved with other community social justice projects. Peter's personal green adventure symbolizes to me a green turn in American lifestyles and politics that integrates personal life and politics. It spans traditional ideological divisions and also melds local and global issues.

Peter's political activism has been mainly at the community level—something hardly new but perhaps more central to green politics than to other progressive politics, because building local economies is so inherently essential to stopping climate change. He is also becoming interested in the national and global politics of global warming, a natural extension of his concern for the preservation of his local community. He feels that the local and the global are intimately connected but that global activism must start with personal values and always be anchored in one's own life and community. Otherwise, it risks becoming as impersonal and disconnected as the corporate system it is trying to transform.

His green politics is an expression of his Eastern values but is also very American in its community spirit. Peter gives me optimism that all kinds of Americans, whether liberal or conservative, may become green activists. Watching Peter and the workshop participants makes me hopeful that millions of people who have never been politically active will join Peter, himself not an activist until now, and turn bright green in their own fight against Pleasantville. The emerging green majority may find green politics a new just-right type of activism.

The biggest lesson I take from Peter is that making heartfelt connections to people and nature—especially family and friends and newcomers on the shared common ground in a community—is one of the biggest incentives to become an activist today, especially a green activist. The community spirit that Alexis de Tocqueville described as so defining of Americans is what pulled Peter—along with his changing value system, his love of nature, and his desire for a "life of the heart"—off his couch and into activism on the dam project. The connections he deepened with family and old and new friends—and with nature—were some of the biggest personal rewards. Preserving the river and local environment was a way of saving his own community and expressing his core values. Peter has found a way to make a life and make history at the same time through his green activism.

Making friends and building community are increasingly important for the millions of Americans whom political scientist Robert Putnam describes as isolated and "bowling alone." Peter's example suggests that green politics may be fueled by a new search and respect for community. Rather than bowling alone, Peter is "bowling green," his way of finding and preserving common ground with other people and our imperiled natural world.

Bill McKibben: A Writer and His Students Step It Up

The last person I want to write about is Bill McKibben. He is an influential environmental writer and activist whose book *The End of Nature* helped inspire the climate change movement. I do not know McKibben personally, and I do not know enough about him to offer a good biographical snapshot. But I want to turn briefly to his "Step It Up" campaign, a 2007 project that began with McKibben and a few of his students. It evolved in a few months into one of the largest and most intriguing national campaigns to stop global warming. Step It Up shows how a few people without money or prior political experience can make a huge impact.

An intriguing fact about McKibben, which he confesses in the book he coauthored with his students, is that he had had almost no prior experience in political activism. He was a writer and a public figure, but he was a political novice and knew almost nothing about activism. Many environmentalists are like this and have never been that comfortable with either Left or Right politics. In this sense, they are like Peter and may take new ideological directions that break the mold of familiar liberal/conservative divisions. They may also, as McKibben and his students did, invent new kinds of political strategies that work well for the millions of other Americans who have been turned off by politics and have never been activists.

McKibben and his students wrote a book about Step It Up, with the specific goal of showing how one person can make a difference. They proved that political amateurs without experience, money, or high-powered connections can actually create quickly a local and national climate change initiative that grabs headlines across the country. Step It Up was a campaign for a day of action in more than 1,400 local communities to put pressure on Congress to cut carbon emissions by 80 percent by 2050. The day of action was April 14, 2007.

The idea started with McKibben's own personal frustration that time was running out to solve global warming. Not having been an activist, he decided he should do something, anything, that he thought might focus people's attention on climate change. He figured he would walk across Vermont to the steps of the city hall in Burlington, where he would sit until he was arrested. But then he learned that the police would be perfectly happy to let him sit there as long as he wanted.

McKibben shared his story with a small group of students, who began to meet regularly in a "Sunday evening club" to figure out a better strategy. Most of the students were no more politically experienced than McKibben, but they shared his passion and urgency about global warming. They decided to create the Step It Up campaign as a way to capture media attention and put pressure on nearly every congressperson by organizing coordinated local events in the 1,400 local communities. They hoped this would trigger new action and begin a newly focused national movement to stop global warming.

Knowing so little about movements, they decided the best thing was to "just move." In a few weeks, they organized a short walk in Vermont that drew a lot of support and was a lot of fun. The number of people who joined in—and the coverage—convinced them they should think bigger. In a few months, on April 14, they would get the whole country moving—or at least so they dreamed.

After the huge success on April 14 that they never really expected, they decided that even though they had obviously not stopped climate change, or created a true national movement to sustain the struggle, they had done far more than they expected. Their plan had spread across the country. Local organizers they had never heard of joined in from towns and cities from Alaska to Florida. Community activists very much like my friend Peter had decided that it made sense to Step It Up together. Each local community group designed its own typically very creative, colorful, and charismatic event and created a national mosaic described in thousands of newspaper stories around the country. Moreover, important figures in Congress had taken note and publicly endorsed the project, including Steny Hoyer, one of the Democratic leaders in the House of Representatives. Hoyer signed on when one of the local Step It Up groups in his own town organized an April 14 canoe ride up a brook to his backyard, giving the powerful congressman a local taste of their global warming passion.

The McKibben group in Middlebury decided to interview many of the local organizers to see why and how they had pulled off these community actions. The group figured this might help an emerging global warming movement devise strategies to grow fast and to refrain from constantly having to reinvent the activist wheel. What group members wrote will look naïve and obvious to some veteran activists, but the truth is that their naïveté may have been an asset, forcing them to create a different kind of politics for a new era, part of the reinvention of movements discussed in the last chapter.

***

Their experience punctuates many of the ideas of movement renewal I have already described and adds some hopeful conclusions. I take from their success, first and foremost, that a small number of ordinary people working together with hardly any money can quickly pull off dramatic climate change actions that affect the nation. That should give hope to every individual or small group that it can make a difference.

Second, I see evidence here of a new generational politics. The McKibben core of Sunday night activists and the majority of the Step It Up local organizers around the country were young. Their visions, goals, strategies, tactics, and general way of being activists were new. This reminds me of the shock of the new youth politics of the 1960s, but this new generation's approach is unique.

Third, this new generational politics—and the green issue itself—seems to be breeding a new movement philosophy called the "Noah Principles." It focuses on partnerships and flexible positive solutions and is driven as much by hope and love as by anger or dogma. Overall, this Noah style is less divisive, less ideological, more collaborative, and more harmonious than the movements of the sixties.

I regard all these factors as improvements on my generation's movement style, but this new style is not a perfect model and is still evolving. Solving global warming means confronting huge corporations and entrenched political elites that will fight against green regime change with everything they have. The new movement must be mobilized to overcome this resistance. It must know how to confront as well as collaborate.

The green movement is also more localized and decentralized and loosely networked than the sixties movements were. And the environmentalists who have chronicled the new movements, such as Paul Hawken, see this localization as the natural outcome of the issue itself. Global warming is such a huge and urgent global crisis that there is no time to create a single party or a single ideological doctrine. We need millions operating now on their own steam, using the Internet to network, to ensure that as many can get involved now, locally, in every corner of the world with their own approach. Saving the splendid diversity on the planet requires a splendid diversity of movements.

One of McKibben group's own conclusions is that the Internet and electronic networking are key to this new generational politics. This is the first generation that has grown up on the Web and has made online communities and friends. This Web savvy logically translates into a politics that can use the Internet for global movement networking in a way that no prior generation could.

I see the localized, decentralized, and electronically networked style of organization to be another major advance of the young green movement. But, again, it has some of its own problems. One is that localized and decentralized movements sometimes have trouble networking with enough clout to create systemic change in Washington and the other global centers of power. We will not solve global warming without a strategy for overcoming the centralized power of fossil fuel capitalism—which is going to require some centralization of power in the green movement.

The local will have to be integrated with a global political vision and strategy. This global challenge to global capitalism and its fossil fuel foundation must deal with power as well as love. The new politics cannot ignore the fact that capitalist realities are extremely resilient and entrenched in national and global institutions and treaties. Localist politics must have a serious, hardheaded vision of how to confront and change corporate power beyond the local level. It must be prepared to do real regime change and transform the US and global capitalist order.

In 2009, McKibben and his colleagues took the Step It Up model to the global level. He called for October 24, 2009, as an "international day of climate action" focused on the Copenhagen meetings. Using much the same approach as the Step It Up campaign, this new movement will be a crucial test of the efficacy of the emerging movement's Internet savvy and sophistication, with McKibben using his organization's websites 350.org and 350.org/oct24 as home base. Given that the Copenhagen meetings are the most important meetings ever held on global climate change, the world's future hangs in the balance. Success at Copenhagen will require the kind of grassroots mobilization that McKibben is trying to catalyze, and the early efforts, at this writing, seem to parallel the successful community spirit and innovative use of technology that led to the Step It Up campaign's earlier achievements. Nonetheless, mobilizing now on a global scale, with so much at stake, will require a far greater engagement and collaboration with the vast and diverse movements that Paul Hawken describes in *Blessed Unrest*. And this means linking innovative climate change movements like McKibben's with all-out participation by global labor and peace movements, which must be collectively focused on the common goal at Copenhagen of saving the planet.

All of these goals will also require a special new relation between the movements and the president, as well as with leaders in other countries. Neither the movements nor the president and other world leaders can succeed without each other. Only the president has the moral authority and the constitutional emergency powers to create the systemic changes we need in the United States. But only the movements will offer the push and the pull that will move him to live up to those constitutional responsibilities. The same is true on the world stage, where the demands of movements must collectively focus on all the world's leaders. Copenhagen will be a crucial test, where the rubber meets the road. Leaders may well fail to achieve the radical greenhouse gas global caps and carbon tax agreements we need. Global movements will have to redouble their efforts—not just for and at Copenhagen but for years afterward—partly by linking local communities in nations across the world as part of a new "glocalist" movement.

The new green movement—full of the creativity and exuberance of youth—has yet to prove that it is up to the huge challenge it faces. But the green movement is growing faster than any movement I have seen. It gives me hope that we have a chance to solve global warming and in the process remake our economy and renew our community and harmony with one another and the earth.

Notes

Chapter 1

1. David DeGraw, "The Critical Unraveling of US Society," *Public Record,* November 19, 2009, p. 1, posted on http://pubrecord.org/commentary/6084/critical-unraveling-society/.

2. David Brooks, "The Materialist Fallacy," *New York Times,* February 14, 2012, posted on www.nytimes.com/2012/02/14/opinion/brooks-the-materialist-fallacy.html.

3. Robert Reich, *Beyond Outrage* (New York: Vintage, 2013).

4. Arianna Huffington, *Third World America* (New York: Broadway, 2011).

5. The film is based on a book by Joel Bakan, *The Corporation* (New York: Free Press, 2005).

6. Bakan, *The Corporation,* pp. 56, 72–73.

7. Lance's Lexicon, posted on www.dailymail.co.uk/sport/othersports/article-2264346/Lance-Armstrong-interview-10-important-quotes.html#ixzz2TOU9lciH.

8. Ibid.

9. Ibid.

10. See the documentation in my book *The Wilding of America* for a more elaborate discussion. Charles Derber, *The Wilding of America,* 5th ed. (New York: Worth Publishers, 2009).

11. Ibid.

12. Bakan, *The Corporation.*

13. For a more elaborate discussion, see Derber, *The Wilding of America.*

14. "Obama War Powers under 2001 Law 'Astoundingly Disturbing,' Senators Say," *Huffington Post,* May 17, 2013, posted on www.huffingtonpost.com/2013/05/16/war-powers-obama-administration_n_3288420.html.

15. Jared Diamond, *Collapse* (New York: Penguin, 2011).

16. American Psychiatric Association, *Diagnostic and Statistical Manual of Mental Disorders,* 4th ed. (Washington, DC: American Psychiatric Association, 2000).

17. Ibid.

18. Martha Stout, *The Sociopath Next Door* (New York: Three Rivers Press, 2006).

19. Robert D. Hare, *Without Conscience* (New York: Guilford Press, 1999).

20. Charles Dickens, *A Christmas Carol* (New York: Dover Publications, 1991).

21. See a good selection of Marx's work in Robert C. Tucker, *The Marx-Engels Reader* (New York: Norton, 1972).

22. Karl Marx and Friedrich Engels, *The Communist Manifesto,* in ibid., p. 337.

23. Ibid., p. 345.

24. For a good selection of Weber's works, see H. H. Gerth and C. Wright Mills, *From Max Weber* (New York: Oxford University Press, 1958).

25. Max Weber, *The Protestant Ethic and the Spirit of Capitalism,* cited online at www.goodreads.com/author/quotes/42041.Max_Weber.

26. Emile Durkheim, *Suicide* (New York: Free Press, 1997).

27. Alexis de Tocqueville, *Democracy in America*, book 1, chapter 2. Cited in Steven Lukes, *Emile Durkheim* (New York: Penguin, 1973), p. 197.

28. Ibid., p. 198.

29. Durkheim, *Suicide.* Cited in ibid.

30. See Emile Durkheim, *The Division of Labor in Society* (New York: Free Press, 1997).

31. Erich Fromm, *Escape from Freedom* (New York: Holt, 1994).

32. Herbert Marcuse, *One-Dimensional Man* (Boston: Beacon Press, 1968). See also *Eros and Civilization,* 2nd ed. (New York: Routledge, 1987).

33. Karl Marx, *Capital,* volume 1, chapter 1, in Tucker, *The Marx-Engels Reader.*

34. Herbert Marcuse, quote posted on www.goodreads.com/author/quotes/49930 .Herbert_Marcuse.

35. Paul Baran and Paul Sweezy, *Monopoly Capital* (New York: Monthly Reader Paperbacks, 1966).

36. Ibid., p. 281.

37. Harry Braverman, *Labor and Monopoly Capital* (New York: Monthly Review Press, 1974).

38. Ibid., pp. 105–106.

39. Ibid., p. 108.

40. See Immanuel Wallerstein, *The Essential Wallerstein* (New York: New Press, 2000).

41. Ibid.

42. C. Wright Mills, *The Power Elite* (New York: Oxford University Press, 1956).

43. Ibid., p. 347.

44. C. Wright Mills, *The Sociological Imagination* (New York: Oxford University Press, 1957).

45. George Orwell, *1984* (New York: Signet, 1950).

46. George Orwell, *Animal Farm* (New York: Plume, 1983).

47. See especially Orwell's *1984.*

48. Ibid., pp. 61–62.

49. Ibid.

50. John Kenneth Galbraith, *The Affluent Society* (New York: Mariner, 1998).

51. John Kenneth Galbraith, *American Capitalism* (New York: Transaction Publishers, 1993).

52. John Kenneth Galbraith, *The New Industrial State* (Princeton, NJ: Princeton University Press, 2007).

53. John Kenneth Galbraith, *The Age of Uncertainty* (Boston: Houghton Mifflin, 1977). Cited on www.basicincome.com/basic_capital.htm.

54. Paul Krugman, "The One Percent's Solution," *New York Times,* April 25, 2013, posted on www.nytimes.com/2013/04/26/opinion/krugman-the-one-percents-solution.html?_r=0.

55. See Paul Krugman, *End This Depression Now* (New York: Norton, 2012).

56. Krugman, "The One Percent's Solution."

57. Ralph Nader, *Unsafe at Any Speed* (New York: Grossman, 1972).

58. Ralph Nader, *The Ralph Nader Reader* (San Francisco: Seven Stories Press, 2000).

59. Nader quoted from 2008 Green Presidential Debate moderated by Cindy Sheehan, January 13, 2008, posted on www.ontheissues.org/Celeb/Ralph_Nader_Corporations.htm.

60. Ralph Nader, *Cutting Corporate Welfare* (San Francisco: Seven Stories Press, 2000).

61. Noam Chomsky, *American Power and the New Mandarins*, 2nd ed. (New York: New Press, 2002).

62. Noam Chomsky, *Understanding Power* (New York: New Press, 2002).

63. Noam Chomsky and Edward Herman, *Manufacturing Consent* (New York: Pantheon, 2002).

64. Noam Chomsky and Edward Herman, *The Real Terror Network* (Boston: South End Press, 1999).

65. Chomsky, quoted on www.imdb.com/title/tt0338357/quotes?item=qt0535468.

66. Howard Zinn, *You Can't Be Neutral on a Moving Train* (Boston: Beacon Press, 2002).

67. Howard Zinn, *A People's History of the United States* (New York: Harper Perennial, 2005).

68. Howard Zinn, quote posted on www.goodreads.com/author/quotes/1899.Howard_Zinn.

69. Greg Ruggiero, "Occupying with Noam Chomsky," the Blog, www.huffingtonpost.com/greg-ruggiero/noam-chomsky-occupy_b_1464658.html.

70. Ibid.

71. Howard Zinn, quote posted on www.goodreads.com/author/quotes/1899.Howard_Zinn.

Chapter 4

1. This paragraph on marketing guns to youth draws on Mike McIntire, "Selling a New Generation on Guns," *New York Times*, January 27, 2013, p. 1.

Chapter 15

1. Rachel Maddow, *Drift: The Unmooring of American Military Power* (New York: Crown, 2012).

2. Michael Moore, *Bowling for Columbine*, quote cited in "Synopsis for Bowling for Columbine," posted online at www.imdb.com/title/tt0310793/synopsis.

3. Richard Nixon, quote from an interview with David Frost, posted online on "BrainyQuote," www.brainyquote.com/quotes/quotes/r/richardmn128949.html.

4. Russ Thurman, *Shooting Magazine*, July 2012, posted online at www.shootingindustry.com/u-s-firearms-industry-today-2012/.

5. Martin Luther King Jr., "Beyond Vietnam," April 4, 1967, posted online at http://brainz.org/martin-luther-king-speech-beyond-vietnam/.

Credits

The readings included in this volume have been used with permission from the following sources. They appear in condensed form, and all footnotes, endnotes, and references have been omitted.

Chapter 2: *The Wilding of America: Money, Mayhem, and the New American Dream* (New York: Worth Publishers, 2011), pp. 1–21.

Chapter 3: *The Pursuit of Attention: Power and Ego in Everyday Life* (New York: Oxford, 2000), pp. 18–31.

Chapter 5: *Marx's Ghost: Midnight Conversations on Changing the World* (Boulder, CO: Paradigm Publishers, 2011), pp. 52–67.

Chapter 6: *The Surplus American: How the 1% Is Making Us Redundant* (Boulder, CO: Paradigm Publishers, 2012), pp. 3–26.

Chapter 7: *Corporation Nation: How Corporations Are Taking Over Our Lives—and What We Can Do about It* (New York: St. Martin's Press, 1998), pp. 11–28. Reprinted by permission from St. Martin's Press. All rights reserved.

Chapter 8: *Regime Change Begins at Home: Freeing America from Corporate Rule* (San Francisco: Berrett-Koehler Publishers, 2004), pp. 23–56. www.bkconnection.com.

Chapter 9: "Romney's '47 Percent' Blunder Reveals the Hidden Heart of His Agenda," with Yale Magrass, Truthout.org, October 9, 2012. Reprinted with permission.

Chapter 10: *People Before Profit: The New Globalization in an Age of Terror, Big Money, and Economic Crisis* (New York: St. Martin's Press, 2002), pp. 35–58. Reprinted by permission from St. Martin's Press. All rights reserved.

Chapter 11: "Kochamamie Democracy," *Tikkun Magazine*, October 23, 2012. www.tikkun.org.

Chapter 12: *Morality Wars: How Empires, the Born-Again, and the Politically Correct Do Evil in the Name of Good*, with Yale R. Magrass (Boulder, CO: Paradigm Publishers, 2008), pp. 35–62.

Chapter 13: "The 'Wright Problem,'" with Yale Magrass, *New York Times*, May 1, 2008.

Chapter 14: "What Does It Mean to Call McCain a 'War Hero' Candidate?" with Yale Magrass, *Christian Science Monitor*, April 14, 2008. www.csmonitor.com.

Chapter 16: *Greed to Green: Solving Climate Change and Remaking the Economy* (Boulder, CO: Paradigm Publishers, 2010), pp. 105–115.

Chapter 18: "Consumerism and Its Discontents," *Truthout*, May 27, 2013. Reprinted with permission.

Chapter 19: *Hidden Power: What You Need to Know to Save Our Democracy* (San Francisco: Berrett-Koehler Publishers, 2005), pp. 150–180. www.bkconnection.com.

Chapter 20: "History's Magic Mirror: America's Economic Crisis and the Weimar Republic of Pre-Nazi Germany," with Yale Magrass, *Truthout*, November 1, 2012. Reprinted with permission.

Chapter 21: *The New Feminized Majority: How Democrats Can Change America with Women's Values*, with Katherine Adam (Boulder, CO: Paradigm Publishers, 2008), pp. 60–75.

Chapter 22: "Capitalism: Big Surprises in Recent Polls," *Common Dreams*, May 18, 2010.

Chapter 23: "The New America Is Not about Identity Politics," *Truthout*, December 31, 2012. Reprinted with permission.

Chapter 25: *People before Profit: The New Globalization in an Age of Terror, Big Money, and Economic Crisis* (New York: St. Martin's Press, 2002), pp. 127–142. Reprinted by permission from St. Martin's Press. All rights reserved.

Chapter 26: *Marx's Ghost: Midnight Conversations on Changing the World* (Boulder, CO: Paradigm Publishers, 2011), pp. 154–166.

Chapter 27: "Will the World Be Ruled by Money or Human Rights?" *Boston Globe*, April 15, 2000.

Chapter 28: *Corporation Nation: How Corporations Are Taking Over Our Lives—and What We Can Do about It* (New York: St. Martin's Press, 1998), pp. 333–339. Reprinted by permission from St. Martin's Press. All rights reserved.

Chapter 29: *Greed to Green: Solving Climate Change and Remaking the Economy* (Boulder, CO: Paradigm Publishers, 2010), pp. 217–230.

CPSIA information can be obtained
at www.ICGtesting.com
Printed in the USA
FFHW011245191219
57136973-62695FF